At the Heart of Work and Family

Families in Focus Series

At the Heart of Work and Family

Engaging the Ideas of Arlie Hochschild

Edited by

ANITA ILTA GAREY
KAREN V. HANSEN

FOREWORD BY BARBARA EHRENREICH

RUTGERS UNIVERSITY PRESS
NEW BRUNSWICK, NEW JERSEY, AND LONDON

Library of Congress Cataloging-in-Publication Data

At the heart of work and family : engaging the ideas of Arlie Hochschild / edited by Anita Ilta Garey, Karen V. Hansen.

p. cm.— (Families in focus)

Includes bibliographical references and index.

ISBN 978-0-8135-4955-2 (hardcover : alk. paper) — ISBN 978-0-8135-4956-9 (pbk. : alk. paper)

1. Work and family. 2. Hochschild, Arlie Russell, 1940—Criticism and interpretation. I. Garey, Anita Ilta, 1947– II. Hansen, Karen V.

HD4904.25.A8 2011

650.1—dc22

2010021012

A British Cataloging-in-Publication record for this book is available from the British Library.

Visit our Web site: http://rutgerspress.rutgers.edu

Manufactured in the United States of America

To Arlie Russell Hochschild,

who, by word and example,
encourages so many to sing
their own song

Contents

PART II
Work/Family Feeling Rules for Managing the Heart

PART III
Emotional Geography of Invisible Work

PART IV
Commodifying Intimate Life

Foreword

American sociology, pre-Hochschild, was a pretty arid undertaking. I turned to it again and again in the sixties and seventies—for insights into subjects ranging from class inequality, gender relations, and the nature of the professions, to the behavior of crowds—only to be numbed by colorless categorizations and abstractions such as "roles" and "institutions." It is as if a band of academics had gone off to explore this thing called "society" and returned to report that there were no *people* in it.

Arlie Russell Hochschild did not single-handedly revive the dying enterprise of sociology. As this volume ably testifies, she has been extraordinarily successful at recruiting colleagues and co-conspirators—not only the graduate students she has so conscientiously nurtured but also untold numbers of other scholars who have worked with her or passed through her research center on the Berkeley campus. And she would be the first to give credit to those imaginative exceptions among mid-twentieth century sociologists—C. Wright Mills and Erving Goffman—whose work originally attracted her to a field that was otherwise distinctly uninviting, especially to young women.

The simplest way to sum up her contribution is to say that Arlie put the *people* back in sociology. Where other sociologists had seen "institutions" such as marriage, she saw kitchen table negotiations over who folded the laundry or took out the garbage. While others saw a gendered division of labor, she saw the strain behind the flight attendant's smile, the loneliness of the immigrant domestic worker, the frustration and claustrophobia driving the female white-collar worker. Arlie once told me that she felt most "truly alive" when she was interviewing people, and I can imagine her sitting with one of her informants, her face skewed with that singular Arlie combination of empathy and concentration, beginning to assemble, with the endless patience of a miniaturist, some huge new insight that would shake us all.

And she's gotten our attention again and again—not only because she humanizes what might have been sociological abstractions, but also because she has had the talent and facility to *name* them in ways that anyone could understand: the "time bind," the "second shift," the "work of emotion management," and the "heart transplant" required of paid childcare workers. It's commonplace to observe that Arlie is a popular writer as well as a scholar, and is as likely to be found in magazine columns and newspaper op-eds as in academic journals. What always takes my breath away is her ability to condense sweeping sociological phenomena into the unforgettable phrase that works its way into the entire culture. This is sociology on a mission—crafted and packaged to change the very society that it studies.

It sounds a little overly gendered: A feminist sociologist brings the subject of individual emotions into sociology. Isn't that the role of women, to be aware of emotions, to try to "manage" them in themselves and others? So let me emphasize that—besides the obvious fact that many male scholars have accompanied Arlie into the "sociology of the emotions"—she has helped restore some of the grand sweep and moral passion of those foundational thinkers, Marx and Durkheim. If no subject is too "small" and quotidian for Arlie, neither is any too grand or sweeping. Again and again, her work takes us back to the questions that launched the social sciences in the first place: What does the market economy do to human relationships and our personal sense of selfhood? In what ways does it free us from traditional constraints—or leave us isolated and hollowed out?

But no young scholar or other truth-seeker should be intimidated by the fact that Arlie is one of the great, even iconic, social thinkers of our time. Yes, her work is informed by dazzling intellect and deep moral passion, but I know her well enough to know that, whatever she's done and accomplished, for whatever reasons, she's also done it because it was *fun*. This is the most personal secret I have to reveal about Arlie: she likes to play.

Give Arlie an idea or a question and she goes after it like a dolphin engaging some colorful and unexpected object in the water. She sniffs, she prods, she pokes around on all sides of it, and she searches far behind it. She toys with it obsessively and cannot let it go—unless, of course, there's someone around to toss this delightful object back and forth with. This fascinating collection should be read as a challenge to take up the Hochschildian project—and have a good time doing it!

Barbara Ehrenreich

Editors' Acknowledgments

Many people assisted us in bringing this project to fruition. We thank Annette Lareau, who invited us in 2006 to co-organize with her a one-day conference that would present papers highlighting the work and ideas of Arlie Russell Hochschild. The conference, "The Importance of Being Conceptual: Exploring the Sociological Contributions of Arlie Russell Hochschild," which was held during the 2007 Eastern Sociology Society meetings in Philadelphia, provided the rich soil from which the seed for this book grew. A few of the chapters in this book began as papers from that conference. We also thank the Eastern Sociological Society for their support of that event. At an early point in the process, we greatly benefited from Margaret Andersen's astute advice about publishing details and catchy titles—thank you, Maggie. Our introduction to this book benefited immeasurably from careful readings and insightful comments from a number of readers. Specifically, we thank our incomparable colleagues: Mignon Duffy, Margaret K. Nelson, Debra Osnowitz, and Nicholas Townsend, as well as the anonymous outside reviewers. A team of Brandeis University graduate and undergraduate students enthusiastically stepped up to read sections of the book and comment on potential cover art: Clare Hammonds, Yoon-Jin Kim, Vanessa Lopes Munoz, and Desiree Murphy. We are grateful to the dean of arts and sciences at Brandeis, Adam Jaffe, for generously helping to finance the permission fees essential to reprinting some of the articles in the volume, and to Judy Hanley, senior administrator in the sociology department, for her unfailing support and good humor. As anyone who has created an edited collection knows, the formatting of disparate pieces into a unified whole is a necessary but time-consuming job that requires skill and attention to detail; it is an additional gift if the person enjoys reading the material. Vanessa Lopes Munoz is the ideal editorial assistant in all these ways, and we sincerely thank her for her work on this book. Rutgers University Press has been enthusiastic about this book from its inception. We appreciate the insights of Adi Hovav, our acquisitions editor, and the full-throttled support from Marlie Wasserman, our editor who saw us through to publication. We are delighted that *At the Heart of Work and Family* is the first book in Rutgers' new series Families in Focus. We thank our series coeditors, Naomi Gerstel, Rosanna Hertz, and Margaret Nelson, for their wholehearted support of this project.

Acknowledgments are not complete until they mention and thank the folks at home—the "family" of "work and family." Our families create the foundation and context that has shaped our ability to work on this book while practicing our vision of kinship. Anita Garey thanks Nicholas Townsend, Sasha Friedman, TyAnn Garey, Margot Garey, Hannah Lawrence, and Shaaron Garey for their unqualified support—and for the joy they bring to her. Karen Hansen thanks Andrew Bundy, Evan Hansen-Bundy, Benjy Hansen-Bundy, and Eva Hansen for always being there with abundant bear hugs, love, and laughter. Finally, Anita and Karen are thankful for their twenty-five years of friendship and collaboration.

Guide to Topics

CAREERS

Hertz, "'Why Can't I Have What I Want?': Timing Employment, Marriage, and Motherhood"

Hochschild, "Inside the Clockwork of Male Careers"

Ortiz, "Wives Who Play by the Rules: Working on Emotions in the Sport Marriage"

Schulz, "Framing Couple Time and Togetherness among American and Norwegian Professional Couples"

CAREWORK

DeVault, "The Family Work of Parenting in Public"

Erickson, "Emotional Carework, Gender, and the Division of Household Labor"

Hansen, "The Asking Rules of Reciprocity"

Lan, "Remaking Family through Subcontracting Care: Elder Care in Taiwanese and Hong Kong Immigrant Families"

Pugh, "Consumption as Care and Belonging: Economies of Dignity in Children's Daily Lives"

Rivas, "Invisible Care and the Illusion of Independence"

Thorne, "The Crisis of Care"

CHILDHOOD/CHILDREN

Berhau, Lareau, and Press, "Where Families and Children's Activities Meet: Gender, MESHing Work, and Family Myths"

Pugh, "Consumption as Care and Belonging: Economies of Dignity in Children's Daily Lives"

CLASS DIFFERENCES

COMMODIFICATION

DIVISION OF HOUSEHOLD LABOR

EMOTION WORK

FEELING RULES

GENDER

GLOBALIZATION AND CAREWORK

KINSHIP NETWORKS

Nelson, "Love and Gratitude: Single Mothers Talk about Men's Contributions to the Second Shift"

Thorne, "The Crisis of Care"

MARRIAGE

Hertz, "'Why Can't I Have What I Want?': Timing Employment, Marriage, and Motherhood"

Ortiz, "Wives Who Play by the Rules: Working on Emotions in the Sport Marriage"

Schulz, "Framing Couple Time and Togetherness among American and Norwegian Professional Couples"

Thai, "Homeland Visits: Transnational Magnified Moments among Low-Wage Immigrant Men"

MEN AND MASCULINITY

Hochschild, "Inside the Clockwork of Male Careers"

Nelson, "Love and Gratitude: Single Mothers Talk about Men's Contributions to the Second Shift"

Ortiz, "Wives Who Play by the Rules: Working on Emotions in the Sport Marriage"

Schulz, "Framing Couple Time and Togetherness among American and Norwegian Professional Couples"

Thai, "Homeland Visits: Transnational Magnified Moments among Low-Wage Immigrant Men"

MOTHERHOOD

Garey, "Maternally Yours: The Emotion Work of 'Maternal Visibility'"

Hertz, "'Why Can't I Have What I Want?': Timing Employment, Marriage, and Motherhood"

Hochschild, "Childbirth at the Global Crossroads"

Nelson, "Love and Gratitude: Single Mothers Talk about Men's Contributions to the Second Shift"

PARENTHOOD/PARENTING

Berhau, Lareau, and Press, "Where Families and Children's Activities Meet: Gender, MESHing Work, and Family Myths"

DeVault, "The Family Work of Parenting in Public"

Garey, "Maternally Yours: The Emotion Work of 'Maternal Visibility'"

Hertz, "'Why Can't I Have What I Want?': Timing Employment, Marriage, and Motherhood"

Schor, "The Viacom Generation: The Consumer Child and the Corporate Parent"

Thorne, "The Crisis of Care"

RACE/ETHNICITY

DaCosta, "Interracial Intimacy on the Commodity Frontier"

Hochschild, "Childbirth at the Crossroads"

Lan, "Remaking Family through Subcontracting Care: Elder Care in Taiwanese and Hong Kong Immigrant Families"

Ortiz, "Wives Who Play by the Rules: Working on Emotions in the Sport Marriage"

Schulz, "Framing Couple Time and Togetherness among American and Norwegian Professional Couples"

Thorne, "The Crisis of Care"

SECOND SHIFT (SEE "DIVISION OF HOUSEHOLD LABOR")

WORK AND FAMILY THEORIES

Garey, "Maternally Yours: The Emotion Work of 'Maternal Visibility'"

Garey and Hansen, "Introduction: An Eye on Emotion in the Study of Families and Work"

Hansen, "The Asking Rules of Reciprocity"

Hochschild, "Afterword"

Hochschild, "Childbirth at the Global Crossroads"

Kibria, "The Globalization-Family Nexus: Families as Mediating Structures of Globalization"

WORKPLACE STRUCTURE

Hochschild, "Inside the Clockwork of Male Careers"

Schulz, "Framing Couple Time and Togetherness among American and Norwegian Professional Couples"

Smith, "Shift Work in Multiple Time Zones: Some Implications of Contingent and Nonstandard Employment for Family Life"

At the Heart of Work and Family

Introduction

AN EYE ON EMOTION IN THE STUDY OF FAMILIES AND WORK

Anita Ilta Garey and Karen V. Hansen

> *"Well," said Mrs. Zuckerman, "it seems to me you're a little off. It seems to me we have no ordinary spider."*

In E. B. White's classic children's story, *Charlotte's Web*, Charlotte, a spider, spends all night spinning a web with the words "some pig" in the center. Charlotte hopes her web will save the life of her friend Wilbur, a pig whom farmer Zuckerman plans to butcher. Charlotte's plan works, and in the morning when the farmer sees the magnificent web, he is amazed and runs to tell his wife: "We've received a sign, Edith—a mysterious sign. A miracle has happened on this farm. . . . There can be no mistake about it. A miracle has happened and a sign has occurred here on earth, right on our farm, and we have no ordinary pig" (White 1952, 80). To which Mrs. Zuckerman, a woman who recognizes the labor *and the laborer* behind the "miracle," replies, "It seems to me we have no ordinary *spider*." Edith Zuckerman's keen observation is one that is shared by many work-family scholars who point out, and thus "make visible," the activities, experiences, and dynamics that are often obscured by a taken-for-granted perspective that ignores *how*, *where*, or *by whom* things are made.

For more than three decades, Arlie Russell Hochschild has been a sociological Mrs. Zuckerman, pointing out social facts that had gone unnoticed because they were rendered invisible by taken-for-granted perspectives. Hochschild also shares Charlotte's talents for addressing conundrums with erudition and creativity. Her concepts and analyses have shaped the way an entire generation of scholars understands work and family. The chapters in *At the Heart of Work and Family* bring together work by authors who use Hochschild's concepts as they explore work and family issues. These selections not only make visible the effort involved in what people do, but they also encompass a "sociology of emotion" perspective. The sociology of emotion focuses attention on how people manage their feelings in order to negotiate tensions that arise within and between the linked spheres of work and family.

Research and writing is best thought of as a conversation between scholars. Each new contribution to the field must address that which came before while providing new insights and moving the conversation forward. Inevitably, the rich scholarship on work and family is the product of many sociologists, historians, family studies scholars, anthropologists, social psychologists, and economists. However, regardless of where one enters the conversation, it is necessary to engage Hochschild's work and the concepts and theories she developed in order to participate fully in the scholarly conversation on families and work. Hochschild's place in sociological theory in general is well established (Adams and Sydie 2001; Farganis 2007; Stones 1998).[1] Her theoretical contributions reach far beyond sociology. Her books and articles have been translated into many languages, and her work is cited prolifically by scholars and practitioners in a wide range of fields, including business, economics, psychology, family studies, gender studies, political science, and anthropology (Jacobs 2007). In the area of work and family, Hochschild's theories and concepts permeate the field, and her books, *The Managed Heart* (1983), *The Second Shift* (1989), and *The Time Bind* (1997), have become standard required reading in college courses.

The most recent of these books was published in the 1990s, and students in our classes often ask, "Haven't things changed?" or "Are these concepts still useful?" In other words, they wonder if the situations described and the concepts proposed at an earlier time still apply to the contemporary world.[2] Their questions were anticipated fifty years earlier by the sociologist Herbert Blumer, who noted that concepts, even when arrived at by close empirical observation, must be continually linked to the "world of experience" (Blumer 1969, 168). Blumer wrote that concepts develop and gain precision "as observation becomes grounded in fuller experience and in new perspectives" (183). The chapters in *At the Heart of Work and Family* apply Hochschild's concepts to the twenty-first-century environment and ask whether and how, as descriptions of ongoing social processes, these concepts continue to be useful to the examination of social settings and structural dynamics.

Making Work Visible: History, Structure, and Meaning

Although "work, employment, and careers" as well as "families, marriage, and parenting" were both established fields of study prior to the 1970s, it was the wave of scholarship combining the two as a single topic that transformed the terms in which work and family were studied (Jacobs 2007). In the years since, the sociology of "work and family" has become a major field of study.

In the early 1970s feminist historians and sociologists began making women's productive labor visible (Easton 1976; Hartmann 1981, 1983 [1976]). Although women had always been laborers and producers within a family economy, they also became wage laborers with the advent of industrialization. Women continued to bring resources into the household in both urban and rural environments (Osterud 1991). Despite their multiple and essential contributions, women were generally erased from the narratives about work (productive labor) in the United States until the resurgence of feminist inquiry and its demands for an inclusive perspective.

Women's labor force contributions had been obscured by the way history was written with an emphasis on economic and public social structures (Kessler-Harris 1982; Laslett 1973; Reiter 1975; Rosaldo and Lamphere 1974; Rowbotham 1973; Tilly and Scott 1978; Zaretsky 1986). The private world of home and family was treated as separate and peripheral to "real" history until feminist scholars revealed the multiple connections and the many ways that the home was also a work site. Women performed reproductive labor, including cleaning, rearing children, and feeding the family. That labor maintained workers and produced future workers engaged in wage labor, in effect making capitalist production possible. Some scholars took this analysis to its logical conclusion and argued that women should be paid wages for housework (Dalla Costa 1972). In the tradition of Mrs. Zuckerman, they revealed the invisible work that produces home and family.

Sociologist Arlene Kaplan Daniels makes the case that "the concept of work should include all the work in the private world of the home, the volunteer work in the public sphere, and the emotion work in both public and private worlds. All these activities involve real work—only it is work that is sometimes difficult to fit into a commonsense perspective that focuses only on remuneration for effort" (Daniels 1987, 412–413).[3] The framing and recognition of unpaid work in all spheres of life as "work" has been critical to understanding both employment and family life.[4]

An early example of the way in which a focus on invisible work illuminated the field is Hanna Papanek's (1973) concept of "the two-person career," by which she meant the unacknowledged and typically unseen participation of wives in their husbands' professional careers and elite occupations.[5] Once identified and described, such participation, often considered essential to the husband's position, could be seen in the careers of corporate executives (Kanter 1977, 110–113), politicians and government officials (Whip 1982), religious leaders (Schwartz 2006), and sports professionals (Ortiz, this volume), among others. Interestingly, although she did not name the concept as Papanek did, Hochschild identified the same phenomenon in an early article examining the duties of the diplomat's wife. She noted that being an ambassador's wife was a profession in itself (Hochschild 1969).[6]

Seeing the work women did in the two-person career as both *labor* they were contributing and *an expected part of their husbands' jobs* challenged ideas about the gendered division of labor and the interdependence of the marketplace, public life, and the household. No longer could they be viewed as unconnected, autonomous domains.

From Macro to Micro

We have described "invisible work" and "the two-person career" as examples of concepts that reveal work/family dynamics. Sociological concepts such as these provide a means to move from a description of what exists to an analysis of what supports and systematically perpetuates particular patterns. A large part of the scholarship on work and family examines the maintenance and reproduction of work-family patterns by examining three sets of institutions: (1) the structure of the workplace (for example, hours, schedules, flexibility, family-friendly options, motherhood penalties, and discrimination based on parental status); (2) the household division of labor (for example, the number of hours of housework, parenting, time-use and multitasking, the gendered division of family work, and caregiving demands); and (3) work/family public policies (for example, government policies and laws such as the Family and Medical Leave Act). Attending to these elements of social structure provides one way to examine the maintenance and reproduction of work/family patterns. For example, if a couple wants to share equally in parenting and the division of household labor, their ability to do so is shaped by the gendered structure of the workplace, the wage gap in men's and women's earnings, the way in which health care in the United States is tied to full-time employment, and the cultural norms to which mothers and fathers are held accountable. Understanding how macro-level cultural, political, economic, and sex-gender systems shape daily life deepens our understanding of work and family dynamics.

Structural approaches thus map out the general landscape in which people live their everyday lives: the mountains, the valleys, the course of rivers, and the borders between land and sea. But they do not take us into the heart of people's journeys through that landscape. The birds'-eye view provided by a map does not show us what the world looks like to those on the ground making the journey. Is the river a refreshing place to rest or a barrier blocking the way forward? The answer is both situational and subjective, and people's actions depend in part on the meaning the river has for them. The same thing is true in sociological analysis. The meaning of what might appear to be a constant entity is context dependent and thus varies. To take a sociological example, the relationship between money and power is not the same in every situation. Although we might expect that a woman's share of the housework would be reduced when she earns more than her husband does, empirical studies have found that women who earn more than their husbands tend to do a *larger* share of the housework than women whose husbands earn more than they do (Gerstel and Sarkisian 2006, 244; Hochschild 1989; Tichenor 2005). However, this seeming paradox is resolved when considered in terms of the symbolic meanings of breadwinning to masculinity, homemaking as "women's work," and the assignment of the second-shift in heterosexual marriages. The extra work that these women do to compensate for the power that is typically attached to money affirms both their own and their spouses' gender identity and eases tensions in the marriage (Hochschild 1989; Tichenor 2005).

Structural approaches alone, therefore, cannot fully explain work/family dynamics. Both macro-level structures and micro-level experiences must be examined in order to make sense of the social world. The micro-level study of work and family as it is lived and experienced requires examining not only interpersonal interaction, but also the meanings that shape and constitute those interactions (Blumer 1969). Work/family scholars have examined the meanings that people give to their work, jobs, and careers; their roles as family members; the division of housework and caregiving; their performance as mothers and fathers; and the ways in which household work is divided. The investigation of the micro-level should not, however, be restricted to what people think (the cognitive level).

The work presented in this collection takes the position that what people think is inextricably bound up with how they feel. Therefore, to explore meaning is to examine not only what people *think* about some object (person, place, or thing), action, or situation, but also how people *feel* about the object, action, or situation. More than that, it involves peeling back layers of meaning to explore not only how people feel, but also how they think they *should* feel, and what they think others think they should feel. Beyond that, exploring meaning is to examine what people do about the disjuncture or "pinch" (Hochschild 1983) between what they feel and what they think they should feel. These layers of meanings and feelings and their connections to what people do, or think they should do, are the subject matter of the "sociology of emotion." How these layers of meanings and feelings affect work and intimate life is the focus of *At the Heart of Work and Family.*

A Sociology of Emotion Approach to Work and Intimate Life

The sociology of emotion focuses on what people feel, how they make sense of their feelings, how their feelings affect their actions, how they manage their feelings, and how they display the appropriate feelings in given situations (Hochschild 1975b). Other approaches, such as the psychological or biological study of emotions, focus on the individual or the physiological rather than on cultural norms and the social construction of emotion. A *sociological* approach to the study of emotion looks beneath the surface appearance of emotion to focus on the way emotions are culturally constructed and shaped by social norms (Hochschild 1979). Hochschild's essay on "The Sociology of Feeling and

Emotion" (1975b) and her subsequent article on "Emotion Work, Feeling Rules, and Social Structure" (1979) marked the emergence of the sociology of emotion as a distinct area of sociology, which, like the sociology of work and family, has developed over the past four decades (Turner and Stets 2005).

People manage their emotions in order to act appropriately in social situations, to display interest or sympathy, or to control anger or disappointment. In her groundbreaking study, *The Managed Heart*, Hochschild (1983) brought the sociology of emotion to the study of paid work. In this study of flight attendants, Hochschild distinguished between the kind of emotion management we all do in our personal daily interactions (emotion work) and the kind that is done as part of job expectations (emotional labor). Emotional labor, she argued, is a particular kind of emotion management: "emotional labor is sold for a wage and therefore has exchange value" (Hochschild 1983, 7n). This construction of emotional labor brilliantly expands a Marxist materialist critique of capitalism to include the invisible labor of producing emotional states for the market. In other words, just as a husband's career requires the work of his corporate wife, the flight attendant's job *requires* the management of her emotions.

Applied to the study of work and family, the sociology of emotion goes beyond the tension between the structure of work and the obligations of family life to focus on how people *feel* about these tensions. The thread running through all of Arlie Hochschild's work, both in the area of working families and more broadly, is her attention to emotion. She has said, "Whatever problem I'm trying to figure out, I keep a close eye on people's emotions." Indeed, this "eye on emotion" is at the core of Hochschild's contributions to our understandings of work and family. In contrast to studies that frame the work/family problematic solely in terms of economic forces, bargaining power, and financial necessity, research that incorporates a sociology of emotion explores the meanings we give to our work, our families, and the interaction between the two. In doing so, it reveals how these meanings are imbued with power by our emotions.

In *The Second Shift*, for example, Hochschild (1989) examined the lives of dual-earner couples to illuminate what was happening beneath the surface of sped-up lives and competing demands brought about by women's increasing participation in the formal labor force, married couples' permanent need for two incomes, the expectations of equality in marriage, and inflexible and outmoded workplace structures. Focusing on how men and women *felt* about their family life and, specifically, about the division of household labor and child care within their families, Hochschild went to the heart of work and family. She discovered that satisfaction with the division of labor, and with the marriage itself, was related more to each spouse's feelings about gender ("gender ideologies"), appreciation ("the economy of gratitude"), and fairness (doing "the second shift") than to any objective measurement of hours spent or tasks performed. Importantly, the degree of alignment between a husband's and a wife's gender ideologies and the balance in their economy of gratitude predicted the well-being and perceived happiness in a marriage over and above anything else. *The Second Shift* shed light on what could not be explained by looking solely at occupation, income, class, ethnicity, or personality, and it demonstrated the necessity of using a sociology of emotion perspective in the study of dual earners and the household division of labor.

Feelings, however, do not operate independently of structure. If, for example, some work/family structural tensions are relieved, then feelings and even feeling rules might shift, although not necessarily in predictable ways. Since most of the recommendations aimed at relieving work/family stressors have focused on structural changes and called for family-friendly workplace and governmental policies (Heymann 2000; Wisensale 2001), the question arises: How might feeling rules and emotion work operate if structures were more conducive to the meshing of work and family? The United States lags far behind other industrialized countries in policies that would assist families, such as paid parental leave, high quality childcare programs, and reduced work schedules (Gornick and Meyers 2005), and most workplaces in the United States do not offer much, if anything, in the way of such benefits. Hochschild explored this conundrum in *The Time Bind* by studying workers at a Fortune 500 company that had actually been applauded for its European-like family-friendly policies. She began by looking at the ways in which families made use of such policies and soon discovered that, with the exception of the flextime benefit, very few workers took advantage of company programs that would allow them to spend more time at home with their families. On the contrary, rather than using options such as part-time schedules, job-sharing, or paternal leave, employees were increasing the number of hours they worked each week, with full-time employees working an average of forty-seven hours a week (Hochschild 1997, 26–27).

Hochschild made sense of this seeming paradox by explaining that the emotional context of home and work was shifting. The workplace was becoming a site of emotionally positive experiences and the home, more often than not, had become a site of negative and depleting emotional experiences. For some groups of workers, the workplace met their needs for self-esteem, friendship, meaningful social interaction, and even comfort in the form of a quiet moment at one's desk with a cup of coffee. But home life, contrary to its idealized version of a "haven in a heartless world" (Lasch 1977), was stressful because at home parents faced competing demands and too little time. Initially, and particularly among some feminists, there was a perplexed and sometimes negative reaction to *The Time Bind* and to Hochschild's argument. The criticism of Hochschild's analysis seemed to be based on concerns that her findings lent support to the accusation that dual-earner parents, and particularly *working mothers*, were neglecting home and children. What *The Time Bind* actually did was point to the tension, what Hochschild might refer to as "the pinch," between working parents' values about family life and their actual experiences at work and at home. On the one hand, working parents found perks and benefits at the family-friendly workplace; on the other hand, the demands and daily crises at home made them feel depleted and overwhelmed.

Hochschild was not, however, pointing the finger at individual-level factors. Instead, she was sounding a clarion call for attention to the increased stresses in the home by making visible profound changes in the social fabric of work and family. In a recent study of Army reservists deployed to Iraq, for example, sociologists Michael Musheno and Susan Ross cite Hochschild when they note that many reservists talked about being deployed as "a relief from home life." They "commonly revealed that deployments simplify life by physically removing them from the complexity and burdens of their civilian home lives" (2008, 103). Rather than viewing these insights as unpleasant truths or obstructions to change, we encourage work/family scholars to use them as opportunities to further our understanding of what is to be done. Hochschild's approach to "'work' and 'family' not as distinct sets of activities people do but as enmeshed yet competing emotional cultures" (Hochschild 1997, xx) enables her to explain what might otherwise have remained invisible.

Engaging with Hochschild

In this introduction we have focused on Arlie Hochschild's theoretical contributions to a sociology of emotion approach to the study of work and family. Hochschild's approach, however, is not only disseminated through her written work but also, significantly, through her teaching and mentoring. We, the editors, are fortunate to have been exposed to Hochschildian sociology in myriad ways. In graduate school we read her books and articles and felt the world of sociology open up to us; we attended Hochschild's graduate seminars with students who have since become well-known sociologists in their own right and exchanged ideas with her and with each other; individually, we sat in Hochschild's office on the campus of the University of California, Berkeley, as so many others have done before and since, and sipped a welcoming cup of tea while we earnestly discussed our dissertation research and received the benefits of her creative energy and generous mentoring. As we each began our postgraduate careers in academia, we assigned Hochschild's work in our classes and came to know even better its power and generativity and, for that reason, continue to use it in our teaching. Some years later we again had the opportunity to spend some extended time learning from and engaging with Hochschild when we each spent a year as senior research fellows at the Center for Working Families (CWF).[7] Codirected by Arlie Hochschild and Barrie Thorne, the CWF brought together a dynamic group of work-family scholars. At weekly seminars, and over midday coffee or evening potluck dinners, we discussed our ideas and respective research projects in an atmosphere that fostered innovative and committed scholarship—with an eye on emotion.

Over the years, we have continued to engage with Hochschild in a mutual exchange of ideas that has become a lifelong conversation. This book is a way of sharing that engagement with a larger audience and extending it in multiple directions. The essays were selected because they use, adapt, or further Hochschild's ideas. Some of the contributors were students of Hochschild, some are her colleagues, and some know her only through her work; but all of us have been challenged to grapple with the agenda she has set for sociology.

Organization of the Book

The readings in *At the Heart of Work and Family* are grouped into five parts, each organized around a Hochschildian concept that has become central to the study of work and family. In part one, "Family Time Binds," the readings articulate some of the major tensions around the time-binds faced by employed parents. We begin with an early and classic article by Hochschild, "Inside the Clockwork of Male Careers," in which she makes visible the hidden assumptions that underlie the timetable of careers and the trajectory of families. The other essays in part one examine the kind of time binds that families experience when they try to balance family time with shift work and contingent employment (Smith, chap. 2), absorb the time-consuming arranging, scheduling, and chauffeuring for their children to attend extracurricular activities (Berhau, Lareau, and Press, chap. 3), or divide the labor of emotional caregiving (Erickson, chap. 4). Rosanna Hertz (chap. 5) examines a different kind of time bind in her study of women who want to be mothers but whose life course trajectory has not resulted in the expected prior step of marriage.

Part two, "Work/Family Feeling Rules for Managing the Heart," focuses on the way in which the tensions highlighted in part one are negotiated by the management of feelings. Feeling rules are the patterned expectations of what people are supposed to feel, or not feel, in particular situations. Not surprisingly, the same activities in different cultures are likely to result in culturally specific ways of negotiating work/family time binds. As illustrated in Jeremy Schulz's essay (chap. 6), American women view their partners' long hours of work as necessary and even virtuous, while Norwegian women refuse to rationalize men's overinvestment in careers and jobs because it deprives them of family and couple time. Feeling rules are also connected to particular roles. Margaret K. Nelson's essay (chap. 7), for example, examines this phenomenon by looking at the rules guiding single mothers' feelings of gratitude toward the men in their lives. For these women, the nature of the relationship—a casual date, an ongoing relationship, a cohabiting partner—is a determining factor in whether the man's activities, such as cooking dinner or playing with the children, are tasks that are considered to be an expected component of his role or are considered a "gift" for which the woman should feel grateful. Feeling rules can help to guide us over rough spots by specifying what emotions we are expected to display so that interactions are smooth and not troublesome. Karen V. Hansen's essay (chap. 8), for example, explores the feeling rules that guide understandings about reciprocity in asking for help with child care. Although feeling rules often work to smooth the way in social interactions, they can also create tensions and stress when there is an ongoing rift between what a person *does feel* and what that person thinks he or she *should feel*, as the essay on the emotion management required of the wives of professional athletes so poignantly illustrates (Ortiz, chap. 9). And stress itself is an emotion for which there are feeling rules. When is it appropriate to feel stress? What kinds of things should we feel stressed about? Marianne Cooper's essay (chap. 10) explores the way in which feeling rules about economic anxiety are also situational and depend on cultural specificity and social location.

The readings in part three, "The Emotional Geography of Invisible Work," examine how people negotiate time binds and feeling rules in the ways they present themselves to others. By highlighting some aspects of their activities and deemphasizing others, by noticing some things and ignoring others, they collude to see activities as either "work" or "not work." However, as the readings in part three so clearly illustrate, the salient issue is not the activity itself but *who* is performing that activity. Children, for example, are generally portrayed as consumers rather than as workers or producers within their families. To treat children as having agency and to make visible the work children actually do has important implications for the study of work and family (Thorne, chap. 11). The invisibility of some kinds of work is not only attached to *who* is performing the activity, but also to the *context* in which the activity is being performed. The work of parenthood includes instructing, guiding, socializing, and disciplining one's children, which is sometimes acknowledged as work. But when parenting is performed in public, for example, it may require additional emotion work to create the desired presentation—such as a happy family—to a public audience (DeVault, chap. 12). The relevance of both identity and context to the perceived need to make certain work invisible is illustrated in numerous ways. Working mothers, for example, downplay their employment activities and identities and highlight their maternal identity when presenting themselves as good mothers in the context of their children's lives (Garey, chap. 13).[8] And personal attendants employed to care for disabled people find that part of their work as paid caregivers is to render themselves invisible so that the work they do does not hinder the care-receiver's presentation of self as independent (Rivas, chap. 14).

The readings in part four, "Commodifying Intimate Life," examine how people try to use market solutions to negotiate work/family time binds. The attempt to outsource work that is associated with the social roles of particular family members is not, however, simply a matter of delegating the task. The tasks of "caregiving," for example, are tied to feeling rules about who cares for whom, what constitutes care, and how care is provided. Is it possible to retain the emotional connection to taking care of someone while commodifying and relinquishing the hands-on task of caregiving to a commercial care provider? What are the implications of subcontracting care that has previously been done within the family, such as elder care (Lan, chap. 15), or integrating children into community (Pugh, chap. 17). These essays engage what Hochschild refers to as "the commodity frontier" (2003, 35–36) as they examine whether the strategy of paying someone outside the family ultimately changes the very nature of the carework being performed. And, if it does, are these changes necessarily negative? Juliet Schor (chap. 16) raises concerns about whether corporations are replacing parents in shaping the lives of children, and Kimberly DaCosta (chap. 18) reflects on the multifaceted character of the commodity frontier as she examines the market's use of images depicting multiracial people and interracial families and relationships.

The readings in part five situate the study of work and family in the context of globalization. These readings endeavor, as did Barbara Ehrenreich and Arlie Hochschild in their book *Global Woman*, to "make the invisible visible again" by focusing on the global linkages that organize the work/family lives of people in every part of the world (2002, 12). Each essay in this section addresses a different facet of these linkages. Nazli Kibria (chap. 19) argues that we need to incorporate a dynamic view of the family into our understanding of international economic and cultural connections in order to see that families not only are affected by global forces, but also shape and affect the processes of globalization. In his study of family formation across international boundaries, Hung Cam Thai (chap. 20) examines the connections between First World wages and Third World markets by exploring the transnational search for marriage partners and masculine identity by immigrant Vietnamese men.

We close this section with a recent essay by Arlie Hochschild, who further deepens and extends her concept of the "global care chain." Hochschild originally defined the global care chain as the "series of personal links between people across the globe based on the paid or unpaid work of caring" (Hochschild 2001, 131)—the intricate linkages between paid care work by immigrant workers who must leave their own children to the care of yet someone else. In "Childbirth at the Global Crossroads" (chap. 21), Hochschild illustrates how even pregnancy and childbirth can be commodified and globalized through global care chains. "The worlds of rich and poor," she reminds us, "are invisibly bound through chains of care" (chap. 21).

In this collection, scholars address the complex weave of families and work by examining micro-level interactions within a larger structural context and amidst global linkages. *At the Heart of Work and Family* brings together essays based on empirical research by scholars who engage Hochschild's influential concepts.

NOTES

1. Hochschild is one of the forty theorists included in *Sociological Theory* (Adams and Sydie 2001), which covers the topic from the nineteenth century, beginning with Saint-Simon and Comte, continuing with Marx, Weber, and Durkheim, and ending with the twentieth century and Foucault. Hochschild is the only one of the forty-two whose theoretical work has centered on the work-family nexus. In *Key Sociological Thinkers*, Rob Stones (1998) features essays on seven classical theorists, seven mid-century theorists,

and seven contemporary theorists: Hochschild, Habermas, Bourdieu, Chodorow, Foucault, Hall, and Giddens. And, along with Marx, Durkheim, Weber, Simmel, DuBois, Mead, Goffman, C. Wright Mills, Habermas, and Foucault, Hochschild is one of thirty-two people included in James Farganis's (2007) recent collection of writings by the major theorists in sociology.

2. With the speedup of daily life and the immediate access to events and places via the Internet and related technologies, the length of time it takes for something to become dated has shrunk.

3. For a more detailed discussion of Arlene Kaplan Daniels's attention to invisible work, see Marjorie DeVault's essay "Becoming a Feminist Scholar; A Second-Generation Story" (1999, 11–13).

4. The flourishing subfield of carework and careworkers, which focuses on the unpaid and paid, often invisible, labor of caring for others in both familial and employment settings, is an offshoot of research on invisible work (Abel and Nelson 1990; Duffy 2011).

5. Originally referred to by Papanek as the "two-person single career."

6. "The Role of the Ambassador's Wife: An Exploratory Study" appeared in *Journal of Marriage and the Family* in 1969 and was Hochschild's first professional publication, written when she was still a graduate student. It provides a fascinating view of ideas and perspectives that foreshadow her groundbreaking work on the sociology of emotion. As an aside to those who know her work well, even the "pinch" appears in this early piece: "among diplomatic couples, the wife, although she may in many ways enjoy her role, is more likely to feel the 'pinch' [between personality and role]" (87).

7. The Center for Working Families was an Alfred P. Sloan–funded center for the study of work and family, located at the University of California, Berkeley, from 1998–2002.

8. Although not a satisfactory term (cf. Garey 1999), the term "working mothers" is generally used to refer to employed women with children.

REFERENCES

Abel, Emily K., and Margaret K. Nelson. 1990. *Circles of Care: Work and Identity in Women's Lives.* Albany: State University of New York Press.

Adams, Bert N., and R. A. Sydie. 2001. *Sociological Theory.* Newbury Park, CA: Pine Forge Press.

Blumer, Herbert. 1969. *Symbolic Interactionism: Perspective and Method.* Englewood Cliffs, NJ: Prentice-Hall.

Dalla Costa, Mariarosa. 1972. *The Power of Women and the Subversion of the Community.* Bristol, UK: Falling Wall Press.

Daniels, Arlene Kaplan. 1987. "Invisible Work." *Social Problems* 34:403–415.

DeVault, Marjorie L. 1999. "Ethnicity and Expertise: Racial-Ethnic Knowledge in Sociological Research." In *Liberating Method: Feminism and Social Research,* edited by Marjorie L. DeVault, 84–103. Philadelphia: Temple University Press.

Duffy, Mignon. 2011. *Making Care Count: A Century of Gender, Race, and Paid Care Work.* New Brunswick, NJ: Rutgers University Press.

Easton, Barbara. 1976. "Industrialization and Femininity: A Case Study of Nineteenth Century New England." *Social Problems* 23:289–401.

Ehrenreich, Barbara, and Arlie Russell Hochschild. 2002. *Global Woman: Nannies, Maids, and Sex Workers in the New Economy.* New York: Metropolitan Books.

Farganis, James, ed. 2007. *Readings in Social Theory: The Classic Tradition to Post-Modernism.* 5th ed. New York: McGraw-Hill.

Garey, Anita Ilta. 1999. *Weaving Work and Motherhood.* Philadelphia: Temple University Press.

Gerstel, Naomi, and Natalia Sarkisian. 2006. "Sociological Perspectives on Families and Work: The Import of Gender, Class, and Race." In *The Work and Family*

Handbook: Multi-disciplinary Perspectives and Approaches, edited by Marcie Pitt-Catsouphes, Ellen Ernst Kossek, and Stephen Sweet, 237–265. Mahwak, NJ: Lawrence Erlbaum Associates.

Gornick, Janet C., and Marcia K. Meyers. 2005. *Families that Work: Policies for Reconciling Parenthood and Employment.* New York: Russell Sage Foundation.

Hartmann, Heidi I. 1981. "The Family as the Locus of Gender, Class, and Political Struggle: The Example of Housework." *Signs* 6:366–394.

———. 1983 [1976]. "Capitalism, Patriarchy, and Job Segregation by Sex." In *The Signs Reader: Women, Gender, and Scholarship*, edited by Emily K. Abel and Elizabeth Abel, 193–225 . Chicago: University of Chicago Press.

Heymann, Jody. 2000. *The Widening Gap: Why America's Working Families Are in Jeopardy—and What Can Be Done about It.* New York: Basic Books.

Hochschild, Arlie Russell. 1969. "The Role of the Ambassador's Wife: An Exploratory Study." *Journal of Marriage and the Family* 31:73–87.

———. 1975a. "Inside the Clockwork of Male Careers." In *Women and the Power to Change*, edited by Florence Howe, 47–80. New York: McGraw Hill.

———. 1975b. "The Sociology of Feeling and Emotion: Selected Possibilities." In *Another Voice*, edited by Marcia Millman and Rosabeth Kanter, 280–307. Garden City, NY: Anchor.

———. 1979. "Emotion Work, Feeling Rules, and Social Structure." *American Journal of Sociology* 85:551–575.

———. 1983. *The Managed Heart: Commercialization of Human Feeling.* Berkeley: University of California Press.

———, with Anne Machung. 1989. *The Second Shift: Working Parents and the Revolution at Home.* New York: Viking.

———. 1997. *The Time Bind: When Work Becomes Home and Home Becomes Work.* New York: Henry Holt.

———. 2001. "Global Care Chains and Emotional Surplus Value." In *On the Edge: Globalization and the New Millennium*, edited by Anthony Giddens and Will Hutton, 130–146. London: Sage Publications.

———. 2003. *The Commercialization of Intimate Life: Notes from Home and Work.* Berkeley: University of California Press.

Jacobs, Jerry, moderator. 2007. Conference on "The Importance of Being Conceptual: Exploring the Sociological Contributions of Arlie Russell Hochschild." Philadelphia, March 16.

Kanter, Rosabeth Moss. 1977. *Men and Women of the Corporation.* New York: Basic Books.

Kessler-Harris, Alice. 1982. *Out to Work: A History of Wage-Earning Women in the United States.* New York: Oxford University Press.

Lasch, Christopher. 1977. *Haven in a Heartless World.* New York: Basic Books.

Laslett, Barbara. 1973. "The Family as a Public and Private Institution: An Historical Perspective." *Journal of Marriage and the Family* 35:480–492.

Musheno, Michael, and Susan M. Ross. 2008. *Deployed: How Reservists Bear the Burden of Iraq.* Ann Arbor: University of Michigan Press.

Osterud, Nancy Grey. 1991. *Bonds of Community: The Lives of Farm Women in Nineteenth-Century New York.* Ithaca, NY: Cornell University Press.

Papanek, Hanna. 1973. "Men, Women, and Work: Reflections on the Two-Person Career." *American Journal of Sociology* 78:852–872.

Reiter, Rayna R., ed. 1975. *Toward an Anthropology of Women.* New York: Monthly Review Press.

Rosaldo, Michelle Zimbalist, and Louise Lamphere. 1974. "Woman, Culture, and Society: A Theoretical Overview." In *Woman, Culture, and Society*, edited by Michelle Zimbalist Rosaldo and Louise Lamphere, 17–42. Stanford, CA: Stanford University Press.

Rowbotham, Sheila. 1973. *Hidden from History: 300 Years of Women's Oppression and the Fight Against* It. New York: Vintage Books.

Schwartz, Shuly Rubin. 2006. *The Rabbi's Wife: The Rebbetzin in American Jewish Life.* New York: New York University Press.

Stones, Rob, ed. 1998. *Key Sociological Thinkers.* New York: New York University Press.

Tichenor, Veronica. 2005. *Earning More and Getting Less: Why Successful Wives Can't Buy Equality.* New Brunswick, NJ: Rutgers University Press.

Tilly, Louise A., and Joan W. Scott. 1978. *Women, Work, and Family.* New York: Holt, Rinehart and Winston.

Turner, Jonathan H., and Jan E. Stets. 2005. *The Sociology of Emotions.* Cambridge, UK: Cambridge University Press.

Whip, Rosemary. 1982. "The Parliamentary Wife: Participant in the Two-Person Single Career." *Australian Journal of Political Science* 17:38–44.

White, E. B. 1952. *Charlotte's Web.* New York: Harper & Brothers.

Wisensale, Steven K. 2001. *Family Leave Policy: The Political Economy of Work and Family in America.* Armonk, NY: M. E. Sharp.

Zaretsky, Eli. 1986. *Capitalism, the Family and Personal Life.* New York: Perennial Library.

PART I

Family Time Binds

CHAPTER 1

Inside the Clockwork of Male Careers

Arlie Russell Hochschild

An offhand remark made to me years ago has haunted me more and more ever since. I was talking at lunch with an acquaintance, and the talk turned, as it often does among women academicians just before it's time to part, to "How do you manage a full teaching schedule and family?" and "How do you feel about being a woman in a world of men?" My acquaintance held a marginal position as one of two women in a department of fifty-five, a situation so common that I don't fear for her anonymity here. She said in passing, "My husband took our son to the university swimming pool the other day. He got so embarrassed being the only man with all those faculty wives and their kids." When the talk turned to her work, she said, "I was in a department meeting yesterday, and, you know, I always feel self-conscious. It's not that people aren't friendly. It's just that I feel I don't fit in." She felt "uneasy" in a world of men, he "embarrassed" in a world of women. It is not only the double world of swimming pools and department meetings that has haunted me, but also his embarrassment, her unease.

This conversation recurred to me when I met with the Committee on the Status of Women, a newly formed senate committee on the Berkeley campus. We met in the Men's Faculty Club, a row of male scholars framed on the dark walls, the waitresses bringing in coffee and taking out dishes. The talk was about discrimination and about the Affirmative Action Plan, a reluctant, ambiguous document that, to quote from its own elephant-foot language, "recognizes the desirability of removing obstacles to the flow of ability into appropriate occupational roles."

The well-meaning biologist on the committee was apologizing for his department, the engineer reminding us that they were "looking very hard" for a woman and a black, and another reminding us that things were getting better all the time. But I remember feeling what many of us probably sensed but didn't say: that an enormously complex problem—one world of swimming pools, children, women, another of men in departments and committee meetings—was being delicately sliced into the tiny tidbits a giant bureaucracy could digest. I wondered if anything in that affirmative action plan, and others like it across the country, would begin to merge these double worlds. Such plans ignore the fact that existing academic career patterns subcontract work to the family work that women perform. Without changing the structure of his career, and its imperial relation to the family, it will be impossible for married women to move up in careers and for men to move into the family.

I have heard two standard explanations for the classic pattern of underrepresentation of women at higher university levels, but I doubt that either gets to the bottom of the matter. One explanation is that the university discriminates against women. If only tomorrow it could halt discrimination and become an impartial meritocracy, there would be many more academic women. The second explanation is that women are trained early to avoid success and authority, and, lacking good role models as well, they "cool themselves out."

A third explanation rings more true to me: namely, that the classic profile of the academic career is cut to the image of the traditional man with his traditional wife. To ask why more women are not full professors, or "full" anything else in the upper reaches of the economy, we have to ask first what it means to be a male full professor—socially, morally, and humanly—and what kind of system makes them into what they become.

The academic career is founded on some peculiar assumptions about the relation between doing work and competing with others, competing with others and getting credit for work, getting credit and building a reputation, building a reputation and doing it while you're young, doing it while you're young and hoarding scarce time, hoarding scarce time and minimizing family life, minimizing family life and leaving it to your wife—the chain of experiences that seems to anchor the traditional academic career. Even if the meritocracy worked perfectly, even if women did not cool themselves out, I suspect there would remain, in a system that defines careers this way, only a handful of women at the top.

If Machiavelli had turned his pen, as so many modern satirists have, to how a provincial might come to the university and become a full professor, he might have the following advice: enter graduate school with the same mentality with which you think you will emerge from graduate school. Be confident, ambitious, and well aimed. Don't waste time. Get a good research topic early and find an important but kindly and nonprejudicial benefactor from whom you actually learn something. Most important, put your all into those crucial years after you get your doctorate—in your twenties and thirties—putting nothing else first then. Take your best job offer and go there no matter what your family or social situation. Publish your first book with a well-known publisher and cross the land to a slightly better position, if it comes up. Extend your now-ambitious self broadly and deeply into research, committee work, and editorships to make your name in your late twenties and at the latest early thirties. If somewhere along the way teaching becomes the psychic equivalent of volunteer work, don't let it bother you. You are now a full professor and can guide other young fledglings along that course.

Discrimination

When I entered Berkeley as a graduate student in 1962, I sat with some fifty other incoming students that first week in a methodology course. One of the two sociology professors on the podium before us said, "We say this to every incoming class and we'll say it to you. Look to your left and look to your right. Two out of three of you will drop out before you are through, probably in the first two years." We looked blankly right and left, and quick nervous laughter jumped out and back from the class. I wonder now, a decade later, what each of us was thinking at that moment. I remember only that I didn't hear a word during the rest of the hour, wondering whether it would be the fellow on my left, the one on my right, or me. A fifth of my incoming class was female, and in the three years that followed, indeed, three-quarters of the women (and half of the men) did drop out. But a good many neither dropped out nor moved on, but stayed trapped between the M.A. and the orals, or the orals and the dissertation, fighting the private devil of a writing block, or even relaxing within that ambiguous passage, like those permanent "temporary buildings" standing on the Berkeley campus since World War II.

Much of the discrimination argument rests on how broadly we define discrimination or on how trained the eye is for seeing it. Women have acclimatized themselves to discrimination, expect it, get it, and try to move around it. It is hard to say, since I continually re-remember those early years through different prisms, whether I experienced any discrimination myself. I don't think so. I considered quitting graduate school to the extent of interviewing at the end of my first miserable year for several jobs in New York that did not pan out. Beyond that, my uncertainty expressed itself in virtually every paper I wrote for the first two years. I can hardly read the papers now since it appears that for about a year and a half I never changed the typewriter ribbon. That uncertainty centered, I imagine, on a number of issues, but one of them was probably the relation between the career I might get into and the family I might have. I say "probably" because I didn't see it clearly that way, for I saw nothing very clearly then.

Women Cooling Themselves Out

The second explanation for the attrition of women in academe touches private inequality more directly: women sooner or later cool themselves out by a form of "autodiscrimination." Here inequality is conceived not as the mark of a chairperson's pen, but as the consequence of a whole constellation of disadvantages.

Some things are simply discouraging: the invisibility of women among the teachers and writers of the books one reads or among the faces framed on the walls of the faculty club; the paucity of women at the informal gathering over beers after the seminar. In addition, there is the low standing of the "female" specialties—like sociology of the family and education—which some early feminists like me scrupulously avoided for that stupid reason. The real thing to study, of course, was political sociology and general theory: those were virtually all male classes, from which one could emerge with a "command" of the important literature.

Women are discouraged by competition and by the need to be, despite their training, unambivalent about ambition. Ambition is no static or given thing, like having blue eyes. It is more like sexuality: variable, subject to influence, attached to past loves, deprivations, rivalries, and many events long erased from memory. Some people would be ambitious anywhere, but competitive situations tend to drive ambition underground in women. Despite supportive mentors, for many women there still remains something intangibly frightening about a competitive environment, competitive seminar talk, even about argumentative writing. While feminists have challenged the fear of competition both by competing successfully and by refusing to compete—and while some male dropouts crossing over the other way advise against competing, the issue is hardly settled for most women. For those who cannot imagine themselves inside a competitive environment, the question becomes: How much is something wrong with me and how much is something wrong with my situation?

Models of People and Places

It is often said that a good female "role model" can make up for the pervasive discouragement women find in academe. By role model I mean simply a person whom a student feels she wants to be like or could become. It is someone she may magically incorporate into herself, someone who, intentionally or not, throws her a psychic lifeline. A role model is thus highly personal and idiosyncratic, although she may fit a pattern. I am aware of being part of an invisible parade of models. Even as I seek a model myself, I might be one to students who are, in turn, models to others. Various parades of role models crisscross in the university, each going back in psychological time.

There is a second sense in which we can talk of models—models of situations that allow a woman to be who she gradually gets to want to be. Among the inspiring leaders of this parade are also some sad examples of women whose creativity has cramped itself into modest addenda, replications of old research, or reformations of some man's theory—research, in sum, that will not "hurt anyone's feelings." The other human pinch is remaining single among couples, having one's sexual life an item of amused curiosity. For still others, it is the harried life of trying to work and raise a family; it's the premature aging around the eyes, the third drink at night, the tired resignation when she opens the door to a sparkling freshman who wants to know "all about how social science can cure the world of war and poverty." There are other kinds of models, too.

Women respond not simply to a psychological lifeline in the parade, but also to the social ecology of survival. If we are to talk about good models we must talk about the context that produces them. To ignore this is to risk running into the problems I did when I accepted my first appointment as the first woman sociologist in a small department at the University of California, Santa Cruz. Some very strange things happened to me, but I am not sure that anything happened to the department or university. Sprinkled thinly as women were across departments there, we created a new minority status where none had existed before, models of token women. The first week there, I began receiving Xeroxed newspaper clippings and magazine articles praising the women's movement or detailing how bad the "woman situation" was in medicine or describing Danish women dentists. These clippings that began to swell my files were invariably attached to a friendly forwarding note: "Thought you'd be interested" or "Just saw this and thought of you." I stopped an older colleague in the hall to thank him for an article he had given me and inquired what he had thought of it. He hadn't read it himself. I began to realize that I was becoming my colleagues' friendly totem, a representation of feminism. "I'm all with you people" began to seem more like "You be it for us." But for every paper I read on the philosophy of Charlotte Gilman, the history of the garment union, the dual career family, or women and art, I wondered if I shouldn't poke a copy into the mailboxes of my clipping-sending friends. I had wound myself into a feminist cocoon and left the tree standing serenely as it was. No, it takes more than this kind of "model."

The Clockwork of the Career System

It is not easy to clip and press what I am talking about inside the square boundaries of an "administrative problem." The context has to do with the very clockwork of a career system that seems to eliminate women not so much through malevolent disobedience to good rules, but through making up rules to suit half the population in the first place. For all the turmoil of the sixties, those rules have not changed a bit. The year 1962 was an interesting one to come to Berkeley, and 1972 a depressing one. The free speech movement in 1964, and the black power and women's liberation movements following it, seem framed now by the fifties and Eisenhower on one side and the seventies, Nixon, and Ford on the other.

Age discrimination is not some separate extra unfairness thoughtlessly tacked on to universities; it follows inevitably from the bottommost assumptions about university careers. If jobs are scarce and promising reputations important, who wants a fifty-year-old mother of three with a dissertation almost completed? Since age is the measure of achievement, competition often takes the form of working long hours and working harder than the next person. This definition of work does not refer to teaching, committee work, office hours, phone conversations with students, editing students' work, but refers more narrowly to one's own work. Time becomes a scarce resource that one hoards greedily, and time becomes the thing one talks about when one is wasting it. If "doing one's work" is a labor of love, love itself comes to have an economic and honorific base.

The Social Psychology of Career Talk

It is often said that women do not speak up in class as much as men do, and I have noticed it, too, occasionally even in my graduate seminar on the sociology of sex roles. The reason, I suspect, is that they are aware that they have not yet perfected the proper style. (It is often older women, not yet aware of the stylistic requirements, who speak up.) Some say also that women are ignored in conversation because they are sex objects; I think, rather, that they are defined as conversational cheerleaders to the verbal tournament.

Even writing about career talk in cynical language, I find that, bizarrely enough, I don't *feel* cynical, even while I think that way; and I have tried to consider why. I think it is because I know, in a distant corner of my mind, that the very impersonality that competition creates provides the role of the "humanizer" that I so enjoy filling. I know that only in a hierarchy built on fear (it's called "respect," but that is an emotional alloy with a large part of fear in it) is there a role for those who reduce it. Only in a conservative student body is there a role for the "house radical." Only in a department with no women are you considered "really something" to be the first. A bad system ironically produces a market, on its underside, for the "good guys." I know this, but somehow it does not stop me from loving to teach. For it is from this soft spot, in the underbelly of the whale, that a counteroffensive can begin against women's second socialization to career talk and all that goes with it.

Situation and Consciousness

It is for a minority of academic women with children that the contradictions exist in their full glory. My own solution may be uncommon but not the general contours of my dilemma. When I first decided to have a child at the age of thirty-one, my thoughts turned to the practical arrangements whereby I could continue to teach, something that means a great deal to me. Several arrangements were possible, but my experiment was a preindustrial one—to introduce the family back into the university, to take the baby with me for office hours on the fourth floor of Barrows Hall. From two to eight months, he was, for the most part, the perfect guest. I made him a little cardboard box with blankets where he napped (which he did most of the time), and I brought along an infant seat from which he kept an eye on key chains, colored notebooks, earrings, and glasses. Sometimes waiting students took him out into the hall and passed him around. He became a conversation piece with shy students, and some returned to see him rather than me. I put up a fictitious name on the appointment list every four hours and fed him alone or while on the telephone.

The baby's presence proved to be a Rorschach test, for people reacted very differently. Older men, undergraduate women, and a few younger men seemed to like him and the idea of his being there. In the next office there was a distinguished professor of seventy-four; it was our joke that he would stop by when he heard the baby crying and say, shaking his head, "Beating the baby again, eh?" Publishers and book salesmen in trim suits and exquisite sideburns were generally shocked. Graduate student women would often inquire about him tentatively, and a few feminists were put off, perhaps because babies are out of fashion these days, perhaps because his presence seemed "unprofessional."

One incident brought into focus my identity and the university's bizarre power to maintain relationships in the face of change. It happened about a year ago. A male graduate student had come early for his appointment. The baby had slept longer than usual and got hungry later than I had scheduled by Barrows Hall time. I invited the student in. He introduced himself with extreme deference, and I responded with slightly more formality than I otherwise might. He had the onerous task of explaining to me that he was a clever student, a trustworthy and obedient student, but that academic fields were not organized as he wanted to study them; and of asking me, without knowing what I thought, whether he could study Marx under the rubric of the sociology of work.

In the course of this lengthy explanation, the baby began to cry. I gave him a pacifier and continued to listen all the more intently. The student went on. The baby spat out the pacifier and began to wail. Finally, trying to be casual, I began to feed him. He wailed now the strongest, most rebellious I had ever heard from this small armful of person.

The student uncrossed one leg and crossed the other and held a polite smile, coughing a bit as he waited for this little crisis to pass. I excused myself and got up to walk back and forth with the baby to calm him down. "I've never done this before. It's just an experiment," I remember saying.

"I have two children of my own," he replied. "Only they're not in Berkeley. We're divorced and I miss them a lot." We exchanged a human glance of mutual support, talked of our families more, and soon the baby calmed down.

A month later when John had signed up for a second appointment, he entered the office, sat down formally. "As we were discussing last time, Professor Hochschild. . . ." Nothing further was said about the prior occasion, but more astonishing to me, nothing had changed. I was still Professor Hochschild and he was still John. Something about power lived on regardless.

In retrospect, I felt a little like one of the characters in *Dr. Dolittle and the Pirates*, the pushme-pullyu, a horse with two heads that see and say different things. The pushme head was relieved that motherhood had not reduced me as a professional. But the pullyu wondered what the pervasive power differences were doing there in the first place. And why weren't children in offices occasionally part of the "normal" scene?

At the same time I also felt envious of the smooth choicelessness of my male colleagues who did not bring their children to Barrows Hall. I sometimes feel this keenly when I meet a male colleague jogging on the track (it's a popular academic sport because it takes little time) and then meet his wife taking their child to the YMCA kinder-gym program. I feel it too when I see wives drive up to the building in the evening, in the station wagon, elbow on the window, two children in the back, waiting for a man briskly walking down the steps, briefcase in hand. It seems a particularly pleasant moment in the day for them. It reminds me of those Friday evenings, always a great treat, when my older brother and I would pack into the back of our old Hudson, and my mother with a picnic basket would drive up from the suburbs to Washington, D.C., at five o'clock to meet my father walking briskly down the steps of the State Department, briefcase in hand. We picnicked at the Tidal Basin near the Jefferson Memorial, my parents sharing their day, and in that end-of-the-week mood, we came home.

Whenever I see similar scenes, something inside rips in half, for I am neither and both the brisk-stepping carrier of a briefcase and the mother with a packed picnic lunch. The university is designed for such men, and their homes for such women. It looks easier for them, and part of me envies them for it. Beneath the envy lies a sense of my competitive disadvantage vis-à-vis the men to whom I am compared and to whom I compare myself. Also beneath it, I am aware of the bizarreness of my experiment with the infant box, and paradoxically aware too that I am envious of a life I would not really like to live.

Conclusion

To talk as I have about the evils of the system as they affect a handful of academic women is a little like talking about the problems of the suburb while there are people trapped in the ghetto. But there are problems both with trying to find a meaningful career and with having one on the system's terms. The two problems are more than distantly related. Both finding an academic job and remaining humane once you have had one for a while are problems that lead ultimately to assumptions about the families that lie behind careers. At present, women are either slowly eliminated from academic life or forced imperceptibly to acquire the moral and psychic disabilities from which male academics have had to suffer.

The very first step is to reconsider what parts in the cultural recipe of our first socialization to nurturance and caring are worth salvaging in ourselves, and the second step is to consider how to extend and institutionalize them in our place of work. The second way of creating social justice less often speaks up for itself: it is to democratize and reward that cooperative, caretaking, morally concerned, not-always-lived-up-to womanly virtue of the past. We need that in careers among our professors of either sex. My utopian university is not a Tolstoyan peasant family, but neither is it vita talking to vita. It requires a move in the balance between competition and cooperation, doing well and doing good, taking time to teach a child to swim and taking time to vote in a department meeting. When we have made that change, surely it will show in book prefaces and office talk.

A Postscript through a 1991 Prism

As I reflect on this piece written in 1973, I'm struck by what has changed—the increasing numbers of women in sociology and their impact; but also by what has not changed—the clockwork of male careers.

When I was a graduate student, there was no sociology of gender, not much work on women in the subfields where one might have looked: the sociology of change, sociology of the family, sociology of occupations. In 1962 little had been written that was explicitly about women. Between 1873 and 1960 fewer than 1 percent of all books in the *Subject Guide to Books in Print* were expressly on the subject of women. During that time only sixteen history doctoral theses concerned women, one of them, "Recent Popes on Women's Position in Society," written by a man. Today we have an independent subfield and, indeed, an industry. The task is to pick the pearls from the hundreds of articles that appear each year.

If we look at the history since 1960, I think it looks like this: a women's movement arose within sociology too, and it changed who came into sociology and to some extent it changed the talked-about ideas in it. Looking back at the culture at large, certain aspects of the women's movement entered the mainstream of American life through a process aptly described by David Riesman as "resistance through incorporation" (1993 [1964]). American culture incorporated what of feminism fit with capitalism and individualism and it marginalized the rest. The culture incorporated the idea that a woman has a right to a job and to equal pay. But it resisted a real change in the structure of work and in the social character of men. This social change "sandwich" is causing serious strains in American family life.

To understand the women's movement, I now feel we must understand the ideals of the movement itself (equality and the humanizing of a society we would be equal in), the cultural soil in which the ideas are received (individualist and capitalist culture), and the array of interest groups poised to see what they want in the new situation (business seeing a cheap skilled labor pool, men seeking a way out of commitments to children). At the time, we were "seeing" through our ideals and not really understanding the messy way social movements work. We had some growing to do.

The Convergence of Personal and Professional: The Berkeley Sociology Department's Women's Caucus

In 1968 I was an instructor in the department with a master's degree three years behind me. A series of women had come into my office in the fall of that year, each talking casually about dropping out of graduate school. When one highly able student, Alice Abarbinal, said she planned to drop out, I remember dropping what I was doing. "Why would Alice drop out?" I knew why *X* or *Y* might drop out, but Alice? She was doing so well. She seemed so at ease. It was one of those grains of sand that made me question the universe. A week later, after talking with friends, I invited women graduate students to my apartment on Virginia Street. Besides Alice—who did eventually drop out to become a psychotherapist—those who came included Judy Gavin, Dair Gillespie, Sue Greenwald, Suellen Huntington, Carol Joffe, Ann Lefler, Anita Micossi, Margaret (later Rivka) Polotnick, Marijean Suelzle, and Ann Swidler. The late Gertrude Jaeger, then a lecturer in the department, came to that first meeting, escorted to the door and later retrieved, amid much hilarity, by her husband, Philip Selznick.

That evening, we sat in a circle on the living room floor, drank coffee and beer, ate a lot of potato chips, and felt a certain excitement. I remember asking whether there was some problem we shared as women that was causing us to become discouraged. One by one we went around the circle: "No." "No." "No." One woman said, "No, I have an incomplete, but I had a hard time defining my topic." Another said, "I have been blocked too, but I have a difficult professor, nothing to do with his being a man." Someone else said, "I'm just not sure about this discipline—it's me." No one hinted that there might be a link between these hesitations, dropping out, and being a woman. I remember turning to a friend and confiding, "Never mind, we tried." But after adjourning the meeting, a curious thing happened: no one left. Two hours later, graduate students were huddled in animated groups, buzzing about professors, courses, housing, boyfriends. An invisible barrier had disappeared.

Apart from Gertrude Jaeger, no professors in our department were women. Yet a fifth of the graduate students were women, hoping one day to become professors. How was this to happen? That was the question our meeting allowed us to unbury. After that first meeting, we met periodically for several years. We were at our best in questioning the basic concepts in sociology, and in trying to picture what sociology would look like if women's experiences counted as much as men's. What are "social status" and "social mobility," concepts so central to our discipline? How do you measure a woman's status—by her husband's occupation (as it was done in the sixties) or by her own occupation? And if she's a homemaker, how do we appraise her status? Do we measure her occupational mobility by comparing her occupation with her father's? With her mother's? Or again, what are the stages of moral development? Are these the same for women and for men? Are nonverbal gestures understood through the same framework of meaning for men as for women? In those years there was some talk about race, ethnicity, and sexual choice, but these were topics whose centrality was yet to be fully understood.

In 1969 I was invited to edit an issue of *TransAction* magazine on the role of women, and various members of the caucus submitted articles. Anita Micossi wrote an article on women's liberation as a religious conversion. I suppose for some of us the movement had elements of that, but if so we converted to a very talky intellectual religion—Unitarianism, say—where the main point was to reinterpret the scriptures. Meanwhile, over the next few years we learned of similar small groups springing up in English, in history, in anthropology departments. There is now a sex and gender section of the American Sociological Association with over a thousand members. Lucy Sells's dissertation data showed that the number of graduate women who dropped out of the sociology department decreased after the formation of our caucus.

If there had not been a social movement such as came along in the sixties, we would not have had that first meeting of the caucus, and probably would not have developed that intellectual world as deeply as we did. I think those questions are partly behind my book *The Managed Heart* (1983), and behind my essay "The Sociology of Emotion and Feeling: Selected Possibilities," in Marsha Millman and Rosabeth Kanter's 1975 edited collection, *Another Voice.* The idea of taking the world of emotions and feelings seriously went along with taking women's experience and public perceptions of that experience seriously. From there it was a small step to propose making the study of emotions more central to sociology. I think others drew inspiration from this collective consciousness in a similar way.

I have been deeply influenced by the writings of Erving Goffman, by his focus on the have-nots of dignity and by the poetry in his viewpoint. At the same time, the scrappy, politicking Hobbesian world in which characters such as Preedy (in *Presentation of Self in Everyday Life,* 1959) strut around almost seemed to describe a male world from the point of view of a highly sensitive and pained critic. But I began to think that such a vantage point left some things out. My direct contact with Goffman came after he had left Berkeley. He was teaching in the late sixties when I was a student, but it was his habit to brusquely shoo out auditors. Discouraged by his manner, I left along with the others. But I went home and carefully read everything he wrote. When he came back to the University of California, Berkeley, after accepting a position at the University of Pennsylvania, he visited a faculty study group that I had joined. (This was after I had my Ph.D., had taught at the University of California, Santa Cruz, and returned to Berkeley as an assistant professor.) It was through this group that I got to know him. Once or twice I sent him articles, and he called me with wonderfully trenchant comments and warm human support. To me it was God himself calling. Years later, when he was sick with cancer, I called several times to see how he was doing, and humorously he turned the question around, "So how are your emotions?" After he died, his widow called to tell me that a paper of mine on "emotion work" was on his desk. That still means a lot.

So I had a foot in two worlds as I was working on *The Managed Heart.* If I had been only in the Goffman world or only in the world of the Berkeley Women's Caucus, the *Managed Heart* might never have been born. *The Second Shift* (1989) and, in some way, everything I have written since, is an extension of *The Managed Heart.*

During my graduate student years, my personal adviser and thesis adviser, Neil Smelser, responded to my struggling papers with insightful clarity and human care. He had more students than any other professor in the sixties, many different in approach and topic from him, but he nurtured us all. I found in him a pillar of support, for which I am extremely grateful to this day.

Current Concerns about Women and the Workplace (Postscript 1994)

The number of women doing industrial work worldwide has doubled since 1950. But they have done such work without the services they need, without changes in ideas about what was previously "men's work," and without altered ideas about a proper workday. So the price of women's entrance into the labor force has often been high: hurried childhoods, a scarcity of personal leisure, new emotional uncertainties. Given this new reality, the question is: How can we unstall a "stalled revolution"?

In addressing this question, I've begun to question what we mean by family, what we mean by work, and how we might create a healthy balance between the two. What gender strategies do women pursue to arrive at a balance? What emotional geography lies beneath these strategies and what emotional consequences follow from them?

Let me end my essay with a reflection about women of color. When I hear my graduate students struggling to de-center gender theories woven around white suburban homes, questioning the universality of Nancy Chodorow's theory of gender personality, or asking where black women are in Rosabeth Kanter's theory of corporate life, I am seized by a sense of déjà vu. In the sixties at our meetings on Virginia Street we were ferreting out the androcentrism in functionalism and Marxism. Now my graduate students are helping ferret out the ethnocentrism in feminist theory, itself derived through just such lines of questioning. Maybe that's what it's all about. Each generation cuts its intellectual teeth on the best social theory of the day, exploring every detail to see just how far it reaches when you ask whose experience it speaks to.

The clockwork of male careers has proved easier to join than to change. More women, including women of color, have careers. But careers themselves still fit into the same giant clock. The struggle to balance work and family is one we will have to continue into the next century.

But the challenge to this clockwork, and to the basic ideas and interests that sustain it, has inspired good ideas. I used to imagine that the sociologist got a brilliant idea sitting alone in the library, like the lone scientist concocting a potion in the garage. But behind any great idea, of course, is a great climate of opinion. It is the very culture of challenge that may well produce the enduring ideas of the future.

ACKNOWLEDGMENTS

Reprinted from *Gender and the Academic Experience: Berkeley Women Sociologists*, edited by Kathryn P. Meadow Orlans and Ruth A. Wallace, by permission of the University of Nebraska Press.

REFERENCES

Goffman, Erving. 1959. *Presentation of Self in Everyday Life.* New York: Anchor/Doubleday.

Hochschild, Arlie R. 1983. *The Managed Heart: Commercialization of Human Feeling.* Berkeley: University of California Press.

Hochschild, Arlie R., with Anne Machung. 1989. *The Second Shift: Working Parents and the Revolution at Home.* New York: Viking.

Millman, Marcia, and Rosabeth Kanter, eds. 1975. *Another Voice: Feminist Perspectives on Social Life and Social Science.* Garden City, NY: Anchor Press/Doubleday.

Perkins, Al. 1968. *Dr. Dolittle and the Pirates.* New York: Random House.

Riesman, David. 1993 [1964]. *Abundance for What?* New Brunswick, NJ: Transaction Publishers.

CHAPTER 2

Shift Work in Multiple Time Zones

SOME IMPLICATIONS OF CONTINGENT AND NONSTANDARD EMPLOYMENT FOR FAMILY LIFE

Vicki Smith

People who hold one permanent, five-day, forty-hour-a-week job (Monday through Friday, eight to five) are in the minority in the United States. Only about 30 percent of employed Americans regularly work this standard schedule (Presser 2003, 15). If not on standard schedules, when are we working and how are our jobs organized? The Bureau of Labor Statistics classifies fourteen million of us as having "alternative work arrangements." These independent contractors, and on-call, temporary help agency, and contract company workers find common ground in the fact that they lack secure employment or predictable hours of work.

Approximately 5 percent of the total U.S. workforce holds more than one job. Two-fifths of all employed Americans punch a time block on evening, graveyard, or weekend shifts, or shifts that rotate. Like those with alternative work arrangements, these nonstandard workers might work full or part time, but they have secure employment and irregular (although not necessarily unpredictable) work schedules. Finally, another group in the broadly defined nonstandard workforce—over thirty-two million part-timers—share with shift and weekend workers the luxury of (relatively) secure employment contracts and fixed schedules, but uniformly work less than thirty-five hours a week, even if they would prefer more.[1]

Contingent, nonstandard, and part-time work are important and widespread in the alternative employment landscape today.[2] And as one can imagine from reading this brief description of the many ways in which jobs can be organized, the study of how alternative employment affects family life does not produce a black-and-white, one-dimensional story. While these figures tell us something about our first shift—the work shift for which we earn a wage—they don't reveal how nonstandard work affects our second and third, unpaid shifts. Arlie Hochschild's claim about the tripartite division of labor on which families depend—the first shift of the paid job; the second shift of unpaid housework; and the frustrating and little-appreciated third shift of "noticing, understanding, and coping with the emotional consequences of the compressed second shift" (1997, 215)—takes on new hues in the context of alternative employment. Experiences of these arrangements vary considerably depending on a jobholder's class, gender, and race or ethnicity, as well as on her or his marital status, occupation, education, training, and skills. One thing holds constant, however: in its various forms and across different classes, nonstandard and other forms of employment uniquely shape the quantity and quality of time we experience with our families.

A few common scenarios illustrate the range of experiences that fall within this broad category and help us debunk some popular stereotypes. Take temporary employment, for example. We often associate temporary employment with the freedom to choose flexible work schedules: people can selectively seek temp jobs on the days, the hours, and the months of the year that they wish. Many assume that even though temporary workers lack a secure or regular employment contract, the benefits of continual change, new opportunities, choice, and flexibility outweigh the disadvantage of insecurity. But the realities of temporary work are more diverse and often fall short of these idealized depictions.

The number of temporary workers employed as assemblers, warehouse, or clerical employees has exploded over the past three decades as corporations struggled to cut the size and cost of their permanent labor forces. These working-class temps typically earn low wages, work within strict hours set by employers, and toil under the close supervision of supervisors and managers. If they decline an assignment from their temporary placement agency, they risk being passed over by the agency the next time a job comes available. Between these constraints on time, choice, independence, and wages, these working-class temps lack the material resources and temporal richness that could enable them to enjoy the fruits of flexibility. Many prefer permanent work but can't find it, meaning that they work as temps involuntarily and that they belong to what the Census Bureau calls the underemployed. Their employment options are limited and temporary positions are often the only ones they can find (Smith and Neuwirth 2008).

Independent professional contractors, on the other hand—highly skilled temporary workers such as computer programmers and engineers—often work in their own home offices or on the site of a "good" employer, enjoy considerable autonomy, and earn handsome wages. Many are prosperous enough to be able to set up separate computer labs in their own homes. These contractors often have considerable leeway to dictate the terms of work—when they work, for whom they work, and for how much—whether to employers who hire them directly or with agencies who find contract jobs for them. And the majority of independent contractors prefer to work on these temporary but more privileged terms (Barley and Kunda 2004; Meiksins and Whalley 2002; Osnowitz 2005). Although we shouldn't overstate the degree of this "free agent's" flexibility and freedom, it is indisputably larger than that of the working-class temp.

Let's sharpen the picture of temporary employment even more by profiling yet a third case of a low-wage temporary worker. Today we find this case less often than we would have in mid-twentieth century; nevertheless, another well-known member of the temporary workforce of the twenty-first century is the married woman with children. This woman chooses temporary employment because it allows her to adjust her paid job to her child care and other family responsibilities; specifically, it enables her to easily enter and exit the labor force. Often, she is married to a full-time wage earner who is the primary source of financial support (Marler, Tolbert, and Milkovich 2003). This temp's safety net—access to a living wage—allows her to take temporary sales, clerical, or assembly jobs at select times. She lacks the financial and professional advantages of professional contractors but she also lacks the deep anxiety and frustration of the full-time, involuntary temporary worker, stuck in the underemployed class.

Examining the working-class temp, the free agent contractor, the mom-as-temp—all common today—sheds light on how temporary jobs, broadly defined, offer different degrees of compensation, choice, opportunity, flexibility, and autonomy. Moreover, it suggests that these differently configured employment relationships create varied capacities for stress-free and surplus family time.

The nonstandard, part-time job introduces more shades of grey into a discussion of the effects of contingent work on family life. In today's service economy part-time workers—according to some definitions, the largest segment of the contingent workforce—have regular, ongoing employment but reduced hours: typically between twenty and thirty-five hours per week.[3] Most jobs in the part-time sector are characterized by low wages, low skill levels, and little discretion. Nonetheless, whether flipping hamburgers in a fast-food establishment, bathing and dressing the elderly in a nursing home, or working cash registers in big-box retail stores—common occupational activities for part-time workers—many part-timers prefer more work hours. This group of the underemployed faces an additional handicap: employed for fewer hours to begin with, their bosses often send them home early if business is slow (Newman 1999; Talwar 2002), making it hard for job holders to stabilize and rely on their income. Working shorter hours for employers who structure jobs on a part-time basis in order to hold down labor costs, part timers might hold multiple jobs, day and night, in order that they and their families might survive (Presser 2003).

Yet high-end part-timers would tell us a different story. Creative professionals who negotiate for reduced hours in a full-time career position also fall into the part-time category. While their managers and coworkers pressure them to maintain the forty-hour-plus work schedules typical of the male career model, these "temporal pioneers and rebels," as Peter Meiksins and Peter Whalley (2002) call them, struggle to push back the temporal boundary in the map of family life. Not only do they possess the professional value, status, and know-how to successfully negotiate down the number of hours they work, earning but a portion of their professional salary, they may be capable of holding their own financially with one job (see Kropf 2001 for discussion of part-time professionals). In the more likely event that she or he is married to another professional, this part-timer has access to an impressively high income (Blair-Loy 2003, chap. 2).

We need to consider one more wrinkle in time before we can fully explore the implications of contingent work for family life: when do all these workers work? In the 24/7 economy, many people work night and weekend shifts. In 2004 about one-fifth of wage and salary workers in the United States regularly worked a shift that was all or partially outside a conventional day shift (evening shifts between two o'clock in the afternoon and midnight; night shifts between nine o'clock in the evening and eight o'clock in the morning; and rotating shifts where the hours regularly changed), while about 16 percent of workers worked at least one weekend day (McMenamin 2007, tables 5 and 10).

Nonstandard work schedules have proliferated for a variety of reasons in the United States. Americans increasingly expect to be able to purchase goods and services at any time of the day, night, or week, thus employers hire considerable numbers of service workers to staff the always-open stores, restaurants, and entertainment venues that provide them. Indeed, poorly paid service workers comprise the vast majority of nonstandard workers (Presser 2003, 20–25). Technological changes now make it possible for workers to conduct financial transactions in global markets at all times as well as making it possible for large numbers of workers to work on an on-call 24/7 basis (Moen and Roehling 2005; Presser 2003, 3–6).

People accept nonstandard employment for many reasons. Workers might be inclined to work on a nonstandard schedule because it allows them to structure their paid work around family responsibilities, as Anita Garey's (1999) research on night-shift nurses well illustrates. In order to maximize household income a worker might hold down a permanent part-time job sometime during the night while working a regular day job—a pattern of labor market participation that labor economists call moonlighting. In households with two working parents, one may work day shifts and the other night shifts so that one parent is always present to care for children. And many people simply can't find jobs organized on a regular schedule. Moonlighters and other multiple job holders have become increasingly common in the United States in recent years, mostly due to the need for additional household income.

The reader might conclude from these observations that contingent, nonstandard, and other forms of alternative employment polarize Americans into an advantaged class and a disadvantaged class. Confirming this, Jerry Jacobs and Kathleen Gerson (2004) identify a major dividing line in the U.S. workforce, between the overworked and the underworked, the people who would like to work more hours and those who would like to reduce the number of hours of their jobs. In itself, this reflects a poignant class divide: people who prefer more hours often desperately need the added income, while those who would like to cut back (and can) tend to be professionals who are cushioned by many forms of financial, familial, and emotional resources. And, indeed, the current employment system of nonstandard and contingent work is built on such cross-class inequality.

Consider further two statistics. Low-income families with children are most likely to have members who work nonstandard hours and weekends, and nonmarried women with children are more likely than married women with children to work on irregular, nonstandard terms (Presser 2003, 65–69). In other words, those who are already disadvantaged by class position and marital status are further disadvantaged by the terms of their employment, typically low-wage, irregular jobs that are the only jobs they can obtain.

Consider also how these employment relations stratify people into those who can benefit from new consumption and labor markets and those whose labor sustains these markets. For example, living in a 24/7 economy may seem to many people to be evidence of progress in our busy, overly scheduled society, but low-wage parents on nonstandardized schedules have good reason to view the round-the-clock business world with greater cynicism. The latter gain the dubious privilege of having an abundance of low-wage jobs to choose from at night and on weekends, while well-paid professional contractors gain the luxury of being able to purchase the products and services sold by night-shift and weekend workers any time they wish. While people with limited experience, training, and education must leave their families to take night jobs as convenience store workers—an occupation that poses one of the highest risks of being fatally assaulted while working—highly educated and well-paid professionals and their families can secede to gated communities, protected by another set of vulnerable, part-time minimum-wage workers: security guards whose ranks have proliferated in the last few decades (see Reich 1991, chap. 23).[4]

However, while contingent and nonstandard work opens up class-specific tensions and calculations about work and family (Who can find a job? How many hours of work can he or she find? Who can be home when? Who will care for the children and who will do the housework? Who decides who does what?), and widens the gap between the privileged and the less privileged, it also introduces within-class family contradictions and tensions as well.

When Home and Work Merge

As generations of feminist scholars have showed, the demarcation between family and work, public and private has never been clean-cut in the modern era.

Aside from the fact that ever since the emergence of the wage-labor market in the 1800s working- and middle-class men and women have carried out paid work in the home, we know that many types of unpaid household/family activities constitute work as well (DeVault 1991; Luxton 1980). Feminist scholars find that family members, with women leading the way, are unpaid careworkers, tending to the needs of children, the elderly, the disabled, and the sick (Hansen 2005; Meyer 2000). Even our intimate personal relations with children and partners can feel like hard, challenging work (Hochschild 1989, 1997).

Despite these long-standing continuities, the boundaries between paid work and home life have visibly shifted and blurred in distinct ways over the past several decades. For many middle-class people, the "work" portion increasingly colonizes the "home" portion of the "home-work continuum" (Nippert-Eng 1995). Today, we don't always have a choice about the degree to which we import home into work because new technologies greatly diminish our capacity to hold firm the boundary between the two. Increasing numbers of workers, from a variety of occupational and professional backgrounds, use (and feel they must use) computers, the Internet, cell phones, fax machines, personal digital assistants, and wireless access to talk, text message, and e-mail in order to stay abreast of their normal workloads from virtually any location at any time (Fraser 2001). Bureau of Labor Statistics data show, in fact, that 15 percent of employed Americans do job-related work at home at least once a week as part of their primary job (U.S. Census Bureau 2008, table 588).

As Noelle Chesley, Phyllis Moen, and Richard Shore (2003) point out, technological innovations create an ability to connect in new ways, making the boundaries between work and family more "permeable" (220). Yet technology can disconnect family members as well. According to some researchers, the penetration of technology into the family has created new metaphors for family roles. When adults who spend inordinate amounts of time working from their home computers neglect their partners and children, they can turn them into "computer widows/widowers" and "computer orphans" (Watt and White 1999, 1).

Contingent work arrangements in particular push the boundaries of work even further into homes because the site of home literally becomes the site of work. In the idealized depiction of the life of the well-paid contractor, a professional parent oversees the household from his or her home office, dealing with the daily rhythms and demands of family life if needed. (The moonlighting, multiple-job-holding parent, on the other hand, simply may be invisible to his or her children during their prime waking hours.) In reality, when work sites, job tasks, and income-earning strategies intermingle with family life, these contingent workers face myriad challenges. Contractors who accept jobs of limited duration and must complete them in their home offices are not exempt from deadlines and expectations for quality work. Indeed, being able to do so is the sine qua non of their professional success. But guaranteeing that we can control the time we need to complete a job, that our time will be uninterrupted by noise, emotions, conflicts, crises, and other routine aspects of family life—all are near impossible in the chaos of family life, as countless mothers and fathers have discovered when they attempt to combine paid work at home with childrearing and household management. (The comic strip *Pajama Diaries* humorously portrays the ongoing travails of a mother who attempts to do her freelance graphic-arts work while at home with her children. Even though she pays a baby sitter to watch the kids while she's working at her computer, she must contend with endless distractions and demands from the latter.)

While contractors may have the "freedom" and the "flexibility" to work during the quiet, uninterrupted nighttime hours when children sleep, these hours rarely coincide with adults' peak alertness and productivity. It is hard to guarantee an employer that you will finish a contracted job and a high-quality product under these circumstances. For this reason, professional contractors interviewed by Osnowitz (2005, 91) reported that, in contrast to the idealized depiction of work life blending with family life, they monitored the boundaries between their paid contract work and the unpaid domestic activities by tuning out the demands of housework and family members.

Contractors must be attentive to protecting their work space from family life but they also must protect family life from the potentially unsettling influence of paid work. Patricia Roehling, Phyllis Moen, and Rosemary Batt (2003) study dual-earner couples and find strong evidence of the work spillover—the "transfer of mood, affect, and behavior between work and home" (91) that characterizes dual-career couples' daily lives. Stress, tension, and frustration spill from the public world of paid work to the private world of home and family. When work and family are coterminous; when the psychic, not to mention the physical space between home and work is minimal; when the site of home becomes a work site—work-generated moods, affect, and behaviors threaten to flood family lives, not simply spill over into them.

Neither are families with workers at home protected from the speed-ups and work intensification that we associate with workers in the corporate world. Well-paid, home-based contractors have been known to double up their work loads, accepting and simultaneously working on multiple jobs in case they don't have a contract job forthcoming. Work intensification allows them to accumulate what Stephen Barley and Gideon Kunda call a "cash reserve" (2004, 230) in preparation for dry periods. Workers "income shift" like this, according to economists, to average their revenue across the year, stashing away money for those inevitable periods of unemployment. But the innocuous-sounding act of income shifting combined with work intensification can obscure a shifting of time away from family and household activities.

There are other indicators of the colonization of home by work life. In addition to using homes as full-time workplaces, contingent employment relationships also increase the likelihood that temporary workers—working-class temps and well-paid middle-class contractors alike—use more space and time in their homes for another type of labor market activity, albeit one that we seldom count as such: the premarket work of the personal job search. Nearly all people who want to find a job undertake a job search, so what is unique about job seekers in the contingent labor market? Both working-class temps and high-level contract workers must spend greater amounts of time in labor market preparation activities and searching for work. It inheres in the nature of the positions: because the jobs and contracts they obtain are time delimited, these contingent workers experience more instances of job loss and more job searches. They enter and leave the job market more frequently.

In their home workshops, whether in bedrooms transformed into private "offices" or in collective family living spaces, job seekers read self-help books directed at their particular plight, surf the Internet to research different companies, blog with other members of their occupational or employment communities (and the community of the unemployed; see http://www.assup.org, Associated Support Services for Unemployed People), network with people via e-mail and telephone, use computers to continually update cover letters and résumés, and fax these materials to employers or send them as electronic attachments. The labor process of the job search requires time and space; it succeeds with rationalized search techniques, skilled use of cutting-edge technologies and informational resources, high levels of self-organization, cultural competency in interactions, and continual emotion management to produce oneself as the optimistic and confident job candidate (Ehrenreich 2005; Smith 2001, chap. 5; Smith, Flynn, and Isler 2006).

Many contract workers clock in their labor market preparation activities over the regular time that they do contract work. Barley and Kunda (2004), for example, found that high-end contractors—even when working on a full-time assignment that they enjoyed and paid them well, whether they worked in their homes or in corporate offices—continually strategized about the future. They worried about what assignments might next come their way, whether their skills might become obsolete, whether they were sufficiently cultivating networks with people who could assist them when an assignment ended—in other words, even when employed, these affluent workers were unable to relax or take their futures for granted. For this reason, they spent a fair amount of time sharpening their skills, attending state-of-the-art classes and workshops, and attending professional association meetings in their fields. According to Barley and Kunda, "developing human capital became an ongoing activity that shaped contractors' lives. Not only did they spend significant amounts of uncompensated time maintaining, extending, and enhancing their expertise, but many also altered the contours of their living space and their leisure activities to optimize their ability to learn" (2004, 263).

Continual learning, the buzz word of high-tech contracting and the source of a competitive edge for these professionals, "became a central life activity that blurred the boundary between work and everyday life" (Barley and Kunda 2004, 263). Aside from turning part of their homes into a workshop, contingency shaped the amount of leisure time that contractors reserved for family life. Contrary to popular stereotypes that working on a temporary, contract basis gives people greater flexibility to use their time the way they want or to take time off between assignments, Barley's and Kunda's "itinerant experts" were reluctant to devote "downtime" to their families. Rather than heading out for a family vacation, contractors used their downtime to learn new skills and engage in networking activities. These career entrepreneurs calculated the costs of labor market inactivity and banked for the future by building and maintaining the up-to-date expertise they needed to find the next job. Downtime did not equal more or better leisure/family time; contractors converted downtime to career-building time.

People who work at home, who lack secure employment contracts or ongoing jobs, face a level of unpredictability and uncertainty unknown to other home-based workers who have permanent employment contracts, such as telecommuters. The social relations of the household, which carry their own emotions, stresses, irritations, and frustrations, are at odds with the rhythms and demands of the insecure, contingent work world. Required to carve out a zone inside the messiness of household life, where they can work as though they are in a "real" workplace, pressured to complete projects by a deadline, and continually worrying and strategizing about the next job, home contract workers operate in separate but proximate universes with other family members.

These unsettled arrangements require new calculations and negotiations of the household workday, first, second, and third shifts combined. Nonstandard work, for example, can leave parents with no option but to pass each other in the day or night, handing over management of the second shift and its household tasks to their partner as one returns from first-shift work and the other leaves for it. Temporary employment can inequitably burden one parent who is waiting to hear about a job assignment with primary responsibility for the unpaid second shift, but then turn the household division of labor, not to mention careful negotiations between adults, upside down when a temp job comes through. This unpredictable and rapid change in paid work assignments leaves the question of who is responsible for child and household care open to continued dispute, negotiations, and arduous emotion work.

Contingent workers stressed out by the insecurity they face day and in day out may resist taking responsibility for second-shift housework and the third-shift management of family relations that, Hochschild found in her study of AMERCO in the 1990s, strains adults' patience, affection, and humor. Adults in her study who worked full-time during normal business hours often outsourced second-shift household tasks, paying others for housecleaning or child care. But few parents have the option to completely avoid responsibility for the discomforting, parent-specific third shift of family hecticness and children's emotions. For the parent who works a graveyard shift, the open-ended and sometime unmanageable third shift is akin to their mandatory overtime shift.

Multiple Time Zones of Postindustrial Families

Mixing together contingent or nonstandard work conditions with families produces many empirical and analytical shades of grey. Nearly every form of nonstandard work generates pressing and contradictory dialectics: choice yet constraint; flexibility yet uncertainty; temporal and occupational opportunities yet household/familial compromises; and changing gender relations yet work and employment conditions that reinforce the traditional household division of labor. Historically, the micropolitics of second- and third-shift management have probably never been so complex and fraught with contradictions.

Who can resist noting how the patterns associated with contingent work collide with another, countervailing trend of the twenty-first century: children's speeded-up and loaded-on activities, whether school, extracurricular, or employment. We live in a culture of stressed, hurried, and overscheduled children, recognized in the expert literature on parenting, in the popular media, and in scholarly research (including Lareau, DeVault, and others in this volume). Working-class kids often hold low-wage jobs after school and on weekends. Middle- and upper-middle class kids have become career entrepreneurs themselves. In addition to the unprecedented numbers of hours they spend on homework, they instrumentally pursue the extracurricular activities that will make them more marketable to competitive colleges. While homes have become workshops for many adults who engage in pre–labor market (the job search) and labor market (paid employment) activities, homes have become pit stops for kids, the place where they sleep, eat (sometimes), and meet up with parents to hitch rides to activities–and if kids drive, they don't even require chauffeuring.

For those who care about family and work, the change from preindustrial and even industrial household activities and family texture over time is remarkable. E. P. Thompson, distinguished historian of the transition from preindustrial to industrial society in Britain, characterized the home economy of the preindustrial household as a family connected temporally, emotionally, and productively. To be sure, preindustrial lives were hard, according to Thompson. Girls baked, brewed, cleaned, and executed other chores. All children tended to fields and farms regardless of season. Despite all this, Thompson "supposed a graduated introduction to work, with some relation to the child's capacities and age, interspersed with running messages, blackberrying, fuel-gathering, or play. Above all, the work was within the family economy and under parental care" (Thompson 1966, 334).

Today, children are more likely to be electronically blackberrying, detached from households for major portions of the day, and pursuing activities that have little connection to their families. These scheduling incongruities expand the number and the quality of individual time zones operating within contemporary families, making them extraordinarily different, not only from Thompson's romanticized preindustrial family economy, but even from families two or three decades ago. All employment restricts the amount and quality of time we spend in our households; nonstandard employment, however, has a unique power to make the family a site of several, nonsynchronized, even if loving time zones for its members. Contingent work arrangements do not simply reconfigure the hours of work and the terms of the employment relationship; they produce a profound experiential spectrum across and within families.

NOTES

1. These data come from two sources: Presser (2003), U.S. Census Bureau (2008, tables 590, 591, 594), and the U.S. Bureau of Labor Statistics (2005).

2. I don't include flextime or flex scheduling in my characterization of nonstandard or alternative work. These terms refer to an employer-sponsored policy that allows employees to structure the beginning and ending hours of their paid jobs in a way that allows them to accommodate their paid work to their family work. For example, using flextime, a parent might arrive at work at 7 A.M. and leave at 3 P.M., in time to pick up children from school (in contrast to conventional schedules, where workers arrive at 8 or 9 A.M. and leave at 5 P.M.). Flextime is usually offered to people with secure permanent jobs (in contrast to temporary/ contract work), who consistently work the same hours and usually Monday through Friday. Approximately 30 percent of all wage and salary workers work on this type of flexible schedule (McMenamin 2007, table 3).

3. Researchers use different parameters to define contingent and alternative work. Some researchers include part-time employment while others don't. If we include part-time employment, the size of the contingent workforce is estimated to be about one-third of total employment. Anna Polivka (1989), who has worked extensively with U.S. Bureau of Labor Statistics (BLS) data on this topic, emphasizes that an important component of contingent work is the degree of job insecurity and that most part-time jobs should not be counted as contingent because they are secure, ongoing positions. Contingent jobs, in her definition, lack an explicit or implicit contract for ongoing employment. Polivka also emphasizes that the hours of contingent work are extremely unpredictable—again, a contrast with many part-time workers who have reduced but predictable hours. The BLS differentiates between contingent workers ("persons who do not expect their jobs to last or who reported that their jobs are temporary") and workers in alternative arrangements (independent contractors, on-call workers, temporary agency workers, and workers provided by contract companies, with independent contractors being the largest and workers from contract companies being the smallest), stating that the two groups overlap to some degree but that a contingent job is not necessarily an alternative arrangement (U.S. Bureau of Labor Statistics 2005, 1). This makes it somewhat confusing to provide a definitive estimate for the size of the contingent and alternative workforce. Nevertheless, the narrowly defined BLS estimate of the size of the contingent workforce at 2–4 percent of the entire workforce gives us a working sense of its parameters.

4. After protective service and law enforcement occupations such as police officer and security guard, the occupations where you would most likely die by an assault or violent act include retail sales cashiers and their front-line supervisors (U.S. Bureau of Labor Statistics 2006).

REFERENCES

Barley, Stephen, and Gideon Kunda. 2004. *Gurus, Hired Guns, and Warm Bodies: Itinerant Experts in a Knowledge Economy.* Princeton, NJ: Princeton University Press.

Blair-Loy, Mary. 2003. *Competing Devotions: Career and Family among Women Executives.* Cambridge, MA: Harvard University Press.

Chesley, Noelle, Phyllis Moen, and Richard Shore. 2003. "The New Technology Climate." In *It's About Time: Couples and Careers*, edited by Phyllis Moen, 220–241. Ithaca, NY: Cornell University/ILR Press.

DeVault, Marjorie. 1991. *Feeding the Family: The Social Organization of Caring as Gendered Work*. Chicago: University of Chicago Press.

Ehrenreich, Barbara. 2005. *Bait and Switch: The (Futile) Pursuit of the American Dream*. New York: Metropolitan Books, Henry Holt and Co.

Fraser, Jill Andresky. 2001. *White-Collar Sweatshop: The Deterioration of Work and Its Rewards in Corporate America*. New York: W. W. Norton.

Garey, Anita Ilta. 1999. *Weaving Work and Motherhood*. Philadelphia: Temple University Press.

Hansen, Karen. 2005. *Not-So-Nuclear Families: Class, Gender, and Networks of Care*. New Brunswick, NJ: Rutgers University Press.

Hochschild, Arlie Russell, with Anne Machung. 1989. *The Second Shift*. New York: Avon.

———. 1997. *The Time Bind: When Work Becomes Home and Home Becomes Work*. New York: Henry Holt and Co.

Jacobs, Jerry, and Kathleen Gerson. 2004. *The Time Divide: Work, Family, and Gender Inequality*. Cambridge, MA: Harvard University Press.

Kropf, Marcia Brumit. 2001. "Part-Time Work Arrangements and the Corporation: A Dynamic Interaction." In *Working Families: The Transformation of the American Home*. edited by Rosanna Hertz and Nancy Marshall, 152–167. Berkeley: University of California Press.

Luxton, Meg. 1980. *More than a Labour of Love: Three Generations of Women's Work in the Home*. Toronto: Women's Press.

Marler, Janet, Pamela Tolbert, and George Milkovich. 2003. "Alternate Work Arrangements." In *It's About Time: Couples and Careers*, edited by Phyllis Moen, 242–258. Ithaca, NY: Cornell University/ILR Press.

McMenamin, Terence. 2007. "A Time to Work: Recent Trends in Shiftwork and Flexible Schedules." *Monthly Labor Review Online* 130:3–15.

Meiksins, Peter, and Peter Whalley. 2002. *Putting Work in Its Place: A Quiet Revolution*. Ithaca, NY: Cornell University/ILR Press.

Meyer, Madonna, ed. 2000. *Care Work: Gender, Labor, and the Welfare State*. New York: Routledge.

Moen, Phyllis, ed. 2003. *It's About Time: Couples and Careers*. Ithaca, NY: Cornell University/ILR Press.

Moen, Phyllis, and Patricia Roehling. 2005. *The Career Mystique: Cracks in the American Dream*. Lanham, MD: Rowman and Littlefield.

Newman, Katherine. 1999. *No Shame in My Game: The Working Poor in the Inner City*. New York: Russell Sage Foundation.

Nippert-Eng, Christena. 1995. *Home and Work: Negotiating Boundaries through Everyday Life*. Chicago: University of Chicago Press.

Osnowitz, Debra. 2005. "Managing Time in Domestic Space: Home-Based Contractors and Domestic Work." *Gender & Society* 19:83–103.

Polivka, Anne. 1989. "On the Definition of 'Contingent Work.'" *Monthly Labor Review* 112:9–15.

Presser, Harriet. 2003. *Working in a 24/7 Economy: Challenges for American Families*. New York: Russell Sage Foundation.

Reich, Robert. 1991. *The Work of Nations: Preparing Ourselves for 21st Century Capitalism*. New York: Vintage Books.

Roehling, Patricia, Phyllis Moen, and Rosemary Batt. 2003. "Spillover." In *It's About Time: Couples and Careers*, edited by Phyllis Moen, 101–121. Ithaca, NY: Cornell University/ILR Press.

Smith, Vicki. 2001. *Crossing the Great Divide: Worker Risk and Opportunity in the New Economy*. Ithaca, NY: Cornell University/ILR Press.

Smith, Vicki, Heather Flynn, and Jonathan Isler. 2006. "Finding Jobs and Building Careers: Reproducing Inequality in State-Sponsored Job Search Organizations." *Worker Participation: Practices and Possibilities.* Special Issue of *Research in the Sociology of Work.* 16:375–402. Amsterdam: Elsevier/JAI Press.

Smith, Vicki, and Esther B. Neuwirth. 2008. *The Good Temp.* Ithaca, NY: Cornell University/ILR Press.

U.S. Bureau of Labor Statistics. 2005. "Contingent and Alternative Employment Arrangements, February 2005." http://www.bls.gov/news.release/pdf/conemp.pdf.

———. 2006. Table A-6. http://www.bls.gov/iif/oschwc/cfoil/cftb0218.pdf.

U.S. Census Bureau. 2008. Statistical Abstracts of the U.S. http://www.census.gov/compendia/statab.

Talwar, Jennifer Parker. 2002. *Fast Food, Fast Track: Immigrants, Big Business, and the American Dream.* Boulder, CO: Westview Press.

Thompson, E. P. 1966. *The Making of the English Working Class.* New York: Vintage.

Watt, David, and James White. 1999. "Computers and Family Life: A Family Development Perspective." *Journal of Comparative Family Studies* 30:1–15.

CHAPTER 3

Where Families and Children's Activities Meet

GENDER, MESHING WORK, AND FAMILY MYTHS

Patricia Berhau, Annette Lareau, and Julie E. Press

A recent study suggests that among families of college-educated parents with two children, the children are spending approximately twenty-five hours per month in organized activities. Time diary data from a nationally representative study estimated that a child of a mother with a college degree spends approximately three hours and twenty minutes each week attending organized activities (Lareau and Weininger 2008). As with other aspects of child rearing, significant numbers of hours are likely to be devoted to managing children's leisure activities—a substantial burden, especially for those in the labor force. Hence, having children participate in such programs generates a variety of parental "activity management" labor.

Yet, a systematic analysis of activity management is generally absent from the sociological literature on family labor and work-family conflict. This is unfortunate since the labor is an important feature of family life, particularly for middle-class families. Much of the literature has focused on labor such as preparing family meals or helping children get ready for bed, but parents' actions related to their children's organized leisure activities move far beyond the walls of the home.[1] Activity management involves the coordination of family life with institutional deadlines that have limited flexibility and substantial variability in demands over short periods of time. These demands are not simply additive; they increase geometrically.[2] In this chapter we focus on the parental work involved in maintaining children's participation in extracurricular activities such as scouts, church activities, music, art, and dance instruction, and various formally organized sporting activities (for example, soccer, football league, and basketball programs). In the first part of the chapter, we discuss the contours of the work itself. We describe four main areas of activity management labor: Mental, Emotional, Social networking and pHysical labor (MESH). Although the categories are interwoven and there is some overlap involved, we identify distinct characteristics for each aspect of activity management.

In the second part of the chapter, we turn to the question of how MESH labor is divided between parents in our study and how parents make sense of those gendered divisions. Arlie Hochschild's use of the concept "family myths"[3] (1989) helped us to understand how couples were able to ignore the seemingly obvious gendered nature of the division of children's activity management. Hochschild argues that couples and families often collaborate in the creation of "versions of reality that obscure a core truth in order to manage a family tension" (Hochschild 1989, 19). Among the families in our study, explanations of "who did what" in the management of children's activities were based on two prevalent family myths: the myth of equal involvement and the myth of a skills-based division of labor.

Research Methods

This chapter draws on data collected for a larger study of the rhythm of children's lives outside of school (Lareau 2003), but focuses on an important issue not elaborated there. Data were gathered on the families of eighty-eight children between the ages of eight and ten. Thirty-two of the children and their families lived in a medium-sized midwestern city ("Lawrence"); the remainder (n = fifty-six) lived in the metropolitan area surrounding a large East Coast city. Observations were conducted in third-grade classrooms, and the participating families were drawn from these schools. Approximately one-half of these families were white and one-half black; one family was interracial.[4] All of the couples were heterosexual. The sample was deliberately constructed to include middle-class (n = thirty-six), working-class (n = twenty-four), and poor families (n = twenty-eight); class was defined using a combined measure of education and occupational position.[5] Much of these data were collected during extensive interviews with the children's mothers and, when present, fathers (or guardians).[6] Observations were also conducted during children's organized activities that required parent labor, such as soccer activities, basketball programs, and baseball games as well as PTA meetings, school fairs, and book sales.[7]

In addition to the interviews, observational data were gathered between 1994 and 1996 on a subset of twelve children and their families, selected to represent all combinations of class, (child's) gender, and race included in the larger sample. This highly intensive phase of the study entailed daily visits by a multiracial team of researchers with the participating families.[8] Middle-class children were much more likely to participate in organized activities than were children from working-class and poor families (Lareau 2003). Hence, the patterns that we describe in this chapter are more common in middle-class families in our sample than in the other families we studied. Still, some working-class children took part in organized activities. Regardless of class, mothers were more likely than fathers to carry out the labor connected to children's involvement in organized activities.

MESH: A Typology of Activity Management Labor

The use of these categories helps to highlight the extensive nature of activity-management demands by delineating the types of skills parents utilize in facilitating their child's participation. Activity management involves MESHing the preferences of the families with the inflexible constraints of institutions. In addition, the labor is fragmented. This fragmentation, which appears impossible to avoid, has a significant impact on the daily lives of mothers. It also makes it difficult to outsource the work to others, including fathers.

Mental Labor of Coordination

At its heart, the work parents do to facilitate their child(ren)'s participation in organized activities is a mental game. Even before an activity begins, before forms are filled out, and before the children are chaperoned, someone must mentally calculate the impact of the child's involvement on family members' schedules. Indeed, time constraints associated with clashes between the schedule of an activity and that of parents (or other caregivers) and siblings was a key factor that gave parents pause when it came to enrolling children in activities. Parents had to consider their own schedules with work and other commitments, as well as competing interests and obligations of both the child in question and his or her siblings. When soccer season begins before basketball season ends, parents have to figure out a strategy to manage the clash. Saturday morning scouts may work out fine in the family's schedule, except on those weeks when gymnastics meets are held.

One family's experience helps to illustrate the point. The Nicholses are a white, middle-class family with two parents and two children. Here, Ms. Nichols details the contours of a typical summer evening:

> Yesterday, Lisa started swimming at 5:30. . . . David's [softball] game was 5:45 and so we took two cars. [My husband] Harry took his mother, and I dropped Lisa off at the swimming pool and talked to her new coach and asked if we could come in and observe and took David and got him settled so he could start his game. They were delayed starting. Harry and his mother came. We waited. We then left together and observed Lisa for about thirty-five or forty minutes; went back to the game and watched David a little more. Then I went to the pool [the practice ended at 7 P.M. that day], brought Lisa home, and went back to the game. Dana fixed herself leftovers out of the refrigerator.

The Nicholses' evening involved twelve car trips with multiple drop-offs and pick-ups. Each child and adult needed to know what role he or she would be playing in the schedule and when. Someone—in this case, Ms. Nichols—had to do the crucial work of mapping out a strategy ahead of time and then supervising and monitoring implementation.

Complicating the mental planning and coordinating in which parents must engage is the ever-changing nature of children's activity schedules. In addition to year-round shifts in the school calendar (for example, varied dismissal times, days off, vacation weeks, summer vacation), children's activity commitments commonly change several times during the course of each year. While some activities follow the school calendar (for example, scouts), most have shorter seasons. Sports leagues, for example, generally run no more than ten or twelve weeks. Even shorter in duration are the multitude of summertime sports and activity camps in which children can enroll. Each new registration brings with it a host of parental responsibilities, including the task of mentally coordinating the demands of the new activity with others still present. Moreover, parents must react when activities are canceled due to inclement weather or other unpredictable events. This happened for five games during one rain-soaked soccer season in Lawrence. Special events are also common in children's activities, whereby recitals and tournaments take place at times outside of the regularly scheduled activity.

In addition to calculating issues of transportation and the family calendar, the mental work of activity management is one of equipment acquisition and maintenance. Routinely, parents need to figure out where to obtain the necessary items, purchase them (in some instances, mentally calculating this into their family budget), and then maintain them. Uniforms need to be regularly laundered to be ready in time for the next game. Special shoes or instrument accessories need to be located as family members run out the door. In some households, parents even devise systems to help their children find such items when needed. The systems seemed to meet with varying degrees of success, both in terms of the parents' skills in setting them up and the children's willingness or ability to comply.

Indeed, some parents demonstrated considerable talent and attention in keeping on top of their family's activities, particularly with regards to their children. Ms. Stanton, a married African American mother of one, was one such parent. In order to keep on top of the various requirements associated with her daughter's schedule, she maintained a filing system for all of "Hope's paperwork," as well as an up-to-date calendar of events. "This is Hope's box [*pointing*] That's [my husband's and my] basket. I take care of the bills, and this is the calendar, and most of the stuff on the calendar is Hope. Like last week, 5:30 in the evening dance, Tuesday talent show, she had a talent show after school, and then she had scouts and she had to bring a two liter bottle. Wednesday she had dance. Thursday she was supposed to have her fan club, but that was canceled." Upon learning about any schedule changes or additions or equipment requirements (for example, supplies needed for special art projects), Ms. Stanton would write them on the calendar. In addition, she kept a box for any additional paperwork, such as permission slips or notices for school and activity-related events. Asked how often she thinks about the logistics of her daughter's activity schedule, Ms. Stanton described it as "constant."

Physical Labor in Meeting Institutional Demands

In addition to mental labor, parents must use physical labor in managing children's activities. In order to have a child's baseball uniform ready in time for a game requires that someone think ahead about when it needs to go into the washing machine in order to be dry by the time it is needed. That part of the job is mental. The part of actually putting a load of laundry in the machine and getting the clothes washed and dried is the physical aspect of the task. Thus, filling out forms, writing checks, standing in registration lines, being at events, taking a child to the doctor for a required physical, getting to the store to purchase equipment, baking for the bake sale—these are the physical tasks of activity management. Here we consider parents' coordination efforts from the seemingly more mundane perspective of actually getting the jobs done.

The time and effort necessary to execute the physical aspects of the tasks varied greatly. For example, registering a child for an activity might take no more effort than sitting down at one's dining table, filling out the form, writing the check, finding an envelope and a stamp, and walking to one's own mailbox to leave the stuffed envelope for the mail carrier to pick up. Other times, parents needed to be at a certain place at a certain time for registration. Several working-class parents, in particular, spoke of difficulties accomplishing these administrative tasks at the appointed time slot. For highly desirable activities, such as a low-cost summer recreational program, it could mean an overnight campout. Even with technological advances such as the Internet, children's activities are often run by small organizations assigning places on a first-come, first-served basis.

The most obvious type of physical labor that parents as activity managers engaged in was chauffeur. Particularly among the middle-class families we studied, dropping off and picking up children was an integral part of family life. Like most families with children in the United States, the families in our study generally had more than one child. In these households, the complications involved in meeting the demands imposed by the children's activities increased geometrically with each additional child. Such families commonly had at least one night per week that was deemed "crazy." Parents repeatedly got into and out of their cars, executing many pick-ups and drop-offs. For some families, such as the white middle-class Wallaces, the driving demands were intense. The Wallaces had three children, aged fourteen, ten, and eight. Ms. Wallace described herself as "spend[ing] a lot of time in the car." Ms. Wallace sighed, "because the three kids have gone in three different directions." "Sometimes," she admitted, "I think that's a little much."

Emotional Labor

The labor involved in managing children's activities was emotional, as well as mental and physical. Managing emotions—those of others as well as oneself—is part and parcel of the work.[9] Blending cheerleading and coercion, parents reminded youngsters to practice their musical instruments, urged them to get dressed quickly to avoid being late for sports practice, encouraged their efforts on the field, consoled them when their teams lost, and praised them for jobs well done. They responded to their children's requests for support, for example, by sitting in on the end of music lessons or watching a child practice a difficult maneuver.

At times, parents' work in this regard was quite subtle. Cheers of, "That's it!" and, "You can do it!" were interspersed with conversations between parents on the sidelines. High stakes performances, in particular, revealed the ways in which parents were emotionally invested—on behalf of their child—in the experience. For example, one father in the study visibly winced each time his son hit a wrong note at the end-of-the-year piano recital. He looked pained. Parents also "kicked" themselves when they felt that they had "screwed up" an aspect of a child's schedule. One middle-class mother, for example, was distraught about how she and her husband had mismanaged things for her son. They had taken the children to see their grandmothers in another state for a number of summers, and her son was unable to participate in softball. When, at the end of third grade, he began softball for the first time, he was "behind" the skill level of the other children. Since her son typically excelled in sports, it was upsetting for him—and her—that he was publicly struggling with fundamental skills.

Parents also sometimes held conflicting philosophies about children's activities. Parents disagreed, for example, on the need to emphasize the competitive versus recreational dimensions of sports. Some coaches insisted on rotating each player to each position, even if they were in a playoff, while other coaches preferred to play their most talented players. These conflicts created bad feelings; in some instances the conflicts led children not to be invited to other children's birthday parties. As one mother said, "You hate to see that happen, but it is just too uncomfortable" (See also Grasmuck 2005).

In terms of the parent-child relationship, the emotional work for parents as activity managers frequently centered on cajoling. It was not uncommon for children to resist going to a practice or event that they later appeared to thoroughly enjoy. Other times, children seemed to change their minds about participation midstream, and parents were left in a quandary as to how to handle their child's resistance. Should they require that they continue because they are "part of a team" or cut their losses and simplify their schedule? In one white working-class family, football participation became a point of contention. "Sometimes when it was hot out when they first started the practices ... He just didn't want to go because of the heat and he didn't want to do all them laps, running around at the field because it's a long run. He just didn't want to do it." As a result, he quit after about three weeks. The parents required him to call his coach, his father drove him to turn in the equipment, and the parents got a refund on half of their money. The next night the coach called and "wanted him back, so he decided he would go back." His mother had a talk with him. "I just told him that if he wanted to re-sign up I would sign him up, but I don't want to hear nothing about [him saying], 'I'm not going to practice. I'm not going to practice.' You've got to go to practice. It's a very important part of it. So we made him go to practice. Some nights he [still] didn't want to go, and I said, 'Jimmy, you've got to go.'"

Social Networking

Since children were constantly aging, their interests developing, and the availability of activities shifting, parents were often required to update obsolete information about available programs, instructor and program reputations, seasonal schedules, and registration deadlines. Information gathering was a central component of parents' coordination efforts. They drew, in particular, on the resources of other parents. One father, whose wife had unexpectedly died from an illness, felt at sea as he managed his son's karate lessons. Mr. Tyson, an African American lawyer, had an uneasy feeling that his son was not progressing in karate as quickly as he should. He worried it might be linked to racial discrimination. But he felt that he did not have enough information to assess the situation, including about the skill levels of the other children and how the karate teacher reacted to parents' complaints. He felt his wife would have been "on top of it."

Many mothers, indeed, continuously participated in and cultivated their social networks with other mothers. Whether at activity events or on the telephone in between, mothers befriended each other at least partly in search of information, car pools, and, to some extent, friends for their children. In one household, the importance of social networking became all the more apparent as a result of what seemed to be the mother's lack of talent in that regard. Mr. Victor, an African American middle-class father, complained about his wife's shyness as central to her reluctance in getting too involved in church activities. He resented that he had to be the "icebreaker" for his wife, who did not work outside the home. "My wife is not a very outgoing person. . . . She just does not go out of her way to get involved very much. She's the type that if you come and get her and say, 'Let's go,' then she will go with you and be happy, but she doesn't go looking for that type of social involvement. . . . I think, personally, that if she goes [to church] and I'm not there, she's uncomfortable." Mr. Victor understood that in order to take advantage fully of the church experience, particularly the social experiences that went on outside of the service, his wife had to be willing to interact in a much more concerted, sociable way with other members of their church. Showing up was not enough.

Indeed, as with many types of "invisible labor" social networking did not appear remarkable to the parents we spoke to and observed—that is, until it went undone. Only then did parents seem to notice its value. One mother did, during the course of our interview, come to realize how much help she had from a friend when she first moved to her area. "I did have one friend who told me about [the town]. I just thought of that. She told me about teachers and which teachers to request and told me, you know, I came to the Fourth of July party before we moved, she told me 'get her involved in dance.' She signed her up for Brownies, to get her into the social life. So, I forgot about that." The fact that the mother "forgot about that" highlights the hidden nature of the labor. It is perhaps particular to the work women do in caring for their families that we tend to dismiss the value of actions that might be simultaneously viewed and experienced as leisure and as work (DeVault 1991). Indeed, the friendships and acquaintances parents developed and maintained in the course of managing their children's activities were highly rewarding to many of the parents in the study. But they were also crucial to being successful at this "job." It was a primary way in which parents got information and could call in favors, as when needing another parent to give his or her child a ride home. Parents engaged in social networking as part of activity management, and these "weak ties" could yield valuable information (Granovetter 1985). Yet developing and cultivating them was work.

Defining Features: Institutional Constraints and Fragmentation

MESH work has a significant impact on family life, and there are key features of activity management that set it apart from other aspects of childcare and paid labor, including deadlines, institutional constraints, and fragmentation. For one, as alluded to above, the deadlines associated with children's activities are generally quite strict. There are deadlines for registrations, which may or may not require competitive punctuality on the part of parents. Once children are enrolled, there are ongoing deadlines for drop-offs and pick-ups. Parents in the study spoke of feeling at times enormous pressure to get children to activities on time. One white working-class mother described her efforts to juggle her own schoolwork, her daughter's swimming lessons, childcare arrangements, and dinner:

> There was a time when she was taking swimming lessons twice a week. And it was really tight for me . . . It was so tight . . . I would get back from school, pick her up, and rush back over to swimming lessons. I [would get caught] in traffic coming back from school and would be thinking that she would be late for swimming. I had just a few minutes to rush in and grab her. She never seemed ready to go. Get her coat on and get everything ready—"Do you have your bathing suit on?" "No, I don't have it on." . . . Then we'd get there and then I'd have to rush home and make dinner. . . . I didn't like that rushing around. . . . It used to kind of drive me crazy.

Indeed, minutes count when families are trying to get children to and fro at the appointed hour. To be fifteen minutes late for a forty-five-minute lesson, for example, means missing one-third of the lesson. Perhaps more important, parents have to be on time to pick up their children from activities. Parents were considered to be extremely late when arriving only six or eight minutes after an event was scheduled to end. At such times, adults could be found walking around, quizzing children about their transportation arrangements.

In our study, most families dealing with these institutional deadlines had more than one school-aged child. As we saw earlier with both the Nichols and Wallace families, multiple children in multiple activities can turn what would appear to be simple tasks (for example, deciding whether to enroll a child in the chess club or driving a child to swimming) into complex decisions and maneuvers.

Dropping off or picking up a child at an activity is not necessarily a taxing or time-consuming endeavor, but because it must be done at a specific time, parents engaging in this work frequently have their afternoons and evenings broken up into small fragments. Parents, particularly mothers, have to decide if it is worth coming home or rushing off to the grocery store while their child is at a practice session, or whether they should stay and bring along a folder of bills to pay, or chat with the other parents. It is not quite enough time to really accomplish anything. And, of course, there is the issue of entertaining siblings during the interim. Ms. Nichols, a white middle-class mother explained, "Well, a lot of the times you are just sitting and waiting, because you don't want to go all the way home and have to come back twenty minutes later. So, sometimes there are two hours there, and maybe I'll get as much as an onion chopped and ready to sauté, and then I have to leave again, and maybe I'll get to actually come back and sauté the onion." Ms. Nichols found this situation unnerving. As she explained, she "aimed" her frustration at her husband, all but demanding that he pick up the children from activities after she had dropped them off. But this was not always possible, and, like other parents in the study, her time was broken up into small bits in which it was difficult to accomplish much of anything. It is perhaps for this reason more than any other that parents' efforts in this regard are often difficult to put one's finger on. Since they take place in small segments spread throughout a given day, week, or month, they do not appear to add up to much worth noting. Those doing the work are often at a loss to explain "where the day went." And yet, the effect on the content and character of the everyday life of those doing the work (and, indeed, others affected by it) is considerable.

In sum, the components of MESH work may, on their own, not sound particularly complex or even time consuming. But the characteristics of this work are such that it is central to the template around which family life takes place. And, unlike other aspects of housework and childcare, the fact that much MESH work takes place at the time and place of an outside institution's choosing lends a rigidity to it that is not generally found in those other forms of family work. Although a number of scholars have pointed to the deadline character of household chores (Hochschild 1989), few households run on such a tight clock as children's organizations do, where having dinner or doing laundry six or eight minutes late would be considered to be extremely late.

Family Myths and the Gendered Division of Activity Management

Although it is widely recognized that there is a gender division of household labor in chores, the popular media portray fathers as playing a more central role with regard to children's activities than in other areas of family life. Research on fathers does show a historical increase in the amount of time fathers spend in child care, but mothers continue to spend more time than do fathers (Bianchi, Robinson, and Milkie 2006). Although there is evidence in our study of fathers who heavily directed children's activity, overall we do not find evidence of fathers taking a leadership role in doing MESH labor in our small nonrandom study. Fathers' participation in this work was limited both in kind and scope. Men "helped out" and "pitched in" to accomplish tasks that played out as being primarily, if not exclusively, women's responsibilities. In those instances where family members acknowledged mothers' primary responsibility for MESHing work, respondents referred to a variety of nongender factors to explain this imbalance in family labor. We use Arlie Hochshild's notion of "family myths" (1989) to explain how parents negotiate the disjuncture between the sense of men's greater participation and the "facts on the ground."

Myth of Equal Involvement

In many of the families in the study, fathers stressed how involved they were in their children's lives. For example, fathers contrasted themselves to their own fathers and reported that they took a much more active role than they had (Townsend 2002). Many fathers attended or even coached children's sports activities. Mothers also reported that some of their husbands "totally" handled certain children's activities. Thus, in many (but not all) families, parents emphasized the active role that fathers played in children's organized activities.

However, both in interviews and during field observations, mothers and fathers demonstrated that it was mothers who overwhelmingly handled activity management. Just as trash removal and mowing the lawn remain tasks by and large performed by men, we found that the management and facilitation of children's participation in organized activities was largely, if not exclusively, "women's work."

In middle-class families, fathers' absence from decision making around children's activities was unmistakable.[10] In responding to interview questions, mothers virtually always used "I" (or, more rarely, "we") as they explained how a child came to be involved (or not) in a given activity (for example, "I signed him up for piano" or "last summer I didn't sign him up"). Fathers did not use such wording. Their accounts of their son's or daughter's participation were peppered with references to the actions of their spouses (for example, "she had him in . . ." or "she couldn't get her into . . ."). As one father put it, "She starts the kids out young with their activities." On occasions when fathers mentioned they had played a role in initiating an activity for a child, we asked follow-up questions. Inevitably, as the excerpt below from an interview with Mr. Murry, an African American college graduate (working as a UPS driver) reveals, when we probed for details, the "we" became a "she":

> INTERVIEWER: How did [your son] get involved in [karate, bowling, and soccer]?
>
> FATHER: We signed him up for it, and if he didn't like it, we wouldn't have continued it.
>
> INTERVIEWER: Who signed him up?
>
> FATHER: Umm, his mother. [*Father and interviewer laugh*]

Indeed, fathers demonstrated their peripheral role to these processes through their lack of knowledge about their children's schedules and other details of their lives. While mothers had such information at their fingertips, most fathers we talked to spoke in far more general terms, often referring to what "probably" happened. Fathers who were more specific often contradicted themselves. For example, Mr. Wolman, a white middle-class father of two was asked about the scheduling of his daughter's Brownie meetings:

> MR. WOLMAN: [They ran] about an hour. 4:00 to 5:00 or 4:00 to 5:30.
>
> INTERVIEWER: So, she gets out of school at . . .
>
> MR. WOLMAN: Okay. Let me take that back. She gets out of school about 3:00 or 3:30 and there can't be a half hour of dead time in between. They must take up with the Brownie meetings right after school, within a few minutes.

Similarly, when asked about how it happened that their child got registered for activities, fathers tended to have little information to offer. Mr. Clayton, a college graduate working in sales, had difficulty answering questions about his son's tennis lessons:

> INTERVIEWER: And how did he get involved in [tennis camp]?
>
> MR. CLAYTON: I don't know how, originally. I think someone told my wife something about a tennis camp. Um, and he had always . . . I don't know. I don't even remember when tennis first became an interest. I just know that one day I remember hearing them talk about tennis, so, uh, my wife looked into, or, somebody was talking to her about a tennis camp and "voilà!" [*both laugh*], that's how it happened.

As Mr. Clayton's notion suggests, it is as if by magic that children's participation takes place.

When speaking about the details of fathers' participation, both mothers and fathers described the majority of fathers' efforts in terms of "helping out" or "pitching in" as per a mother's instruction. One middle-class father spoke for many when he explained his family's pattern this way, "[My wife's] more of a promoter of a lot of these activities. I give my blessing to it and will do whatever I can to help facilitate it. She is the one who seeks these things out."

Indeed, many fathers spoke of being "happy to help." But doing so seemed to take place only at their wife's behest. For example, Ms. Marshall had a demanding full-time job; her husband's work was less challenging. Mr. Marshall stood by, ready to help "if she asks me." As he said in reference to gymnastics: "If she asks me to pick 'em up at four o'clock then I'll be more than happy to." In none of the couples in the study were dads in charge.[11]

In this way, the work fathers did with respect to children's activities was far more mechanical in nature than that of mothers. They carried out tasks assigned to them by their wives. Hence, fathers' MESH responsibilities were physical rather than mental, social, or emotional in nature. Mothers seemed to do virtually all of the mental work of coordinating family members' schedules. Social networking was certainly engaged in by some fathers, but for the most part, fathers were disengaged from these circles. With respect to emotional support, as in other arenas, children appeared to rely primarily on mothers rather than fathers.

Of course, some fathers did coach teams and even held leadership roles in sports leagues. While individuals varied in their approach, coaching and the like could involve considerable time commitment. Duties included organizing (and attending) games and practices, informing parents about rainouts and rescheduled events, as well as handling sometimes controversial issues about the role of competition in children's lives.

But, unlike the mothers who coached teams and led scout troops, the fathers in these positions relied upon their spouses to provide crucial behind-the-scenes assistance. Consider, for instance, the many hidden duties of Ms. McNamara, a middle-class white mother whose husband was president of the soccer league and coached a team. "In previous seasons I've been in charge of uniform pass-out and collection, which has probably taken about fifty hours a season. There have been seasons where it's been tons and tons and tons of hours." Ms. McNamara also spoke of answering the phone "dozens of times," printing out the weekly refreshment schedules, answering many questions from parents during games, and helping out at the end-of-season tournament. A similar pattern of wives assisting their husbands took place in other families. Like the support provided by wives of managers and executives (Kanter 1977; Ostrander 1984), wives whose husbands were in leadership positions related to their children's activities supported their spouses in numerous visible and invisible ways. The husbands showed no reciprocal sense of obligation to help their wives.

Myth of a Skills-Based Division of Labor

When asked about the active roles mothers played in MESHing work, neither mothers nor fathers gave explanations that were connected to gender or to their gendered parental role. Instead, their answers were based on mutual understandings about whether the division of labor was connected *not* to gender but rather to the individual temperament, personality, skills, or unique characteristics of the mothers. For example, each woman was described as better suited to handling children's activities, not because she belonged to the group "women" or "mothers," but because the tasks involved were seen as being more in keeping with her individual temperament. One father whose wife had died two years earlier spoke about his wife as being "the type" who stayed abreast of children's progress with an activity. "That was just more of her personality. She was, uh, much more outgoing in that venue than I was." Mothers were seen as the ones who had the wherewithal to keep up with the numerous details associated with children's participation ("she's more energetic") or were deemed "more sociable" in keeping an ear to the neighborhood grapevine. Similarly, women often described themselves and men often spoke of their wives as being "organized" or liking "to stay active" as reasons why the mother in the family was involved in heavy commitments to their children's organizations. In one household, the father explained his wife's involvement with music recitals by noting that "she's very musical," although he played an instrument and listened to music frequently and could certainly be considered "very musical" himself. In another family the husband suggested that his wife's greater participation had to do with the fact that "she's a very dominant person."

Relatedly, mothers' greater participation in children's activities was often explained in terms of the greater importance that they placed on them. Mothers, for example, spoke of simply being more committed than their husbands to the idea of organized activities as beneficial to children. Ms. Caldis worked forty hours a week as a nurse while her husband, who called himself "Mr. Mom," worked part time at home. Yet she did the activity management. She attributed it to her priorities: "I guess [he] doesn't see that activities are as important as I do. He probably would just let them pretty much direct themselves and do whatever they wanted to. . . . Pretty much I guess that what we've decided, since I think they're important, I pretty much do it. And then we just compromise. . . . So, because I see it as a priority more than he does, I probably do it more." Fathers and mothers also explained that fathers had less suitable time available to help children. In part, the reasons for this were the same ones that Hochschild (1989) noted in her study of dual-earner couples in the 1980s—fathers were more likely than mothers to spend time on their own leisure activities. For some fathers, their leisure activities monopolized their available out-of-the-office time. For example, in one white middle-class family, Ms. Wallace explained that her husband's frequent golf outings made him unavailable to share much of the family labor. "My husband is a golfer . . . he plays in a lot of tournaments and in the fall there are several weekends that he is away. . . . on Saturdays he's usually busy. And Sundays and Wednesdays. He plays a lot. So, when he's available, he is willing to help . . . but I would say in the last two months, he's only been available 25 percent of the time."

In the black middle-class Milton family, the mother (who worked full time) managed all the details associated with the two children's activities. Mr. Milton had only one responsibility in this area. Moreover, what assured his regular availability to help was the task's timing, which conveniently corresponded to his own leisure activity. "She generally does all that kind of stuff. Only thing I do is take [the older son] to wrestling on Saturday. And that's mainly because I drop him off at the wrestling; I go to the gym and exercise, then pick him up and bring him back home. So I don't need to stay with him."

Summary

Despite visible images of fathers on the soccer field on a Saturday morning as well as a general societal sense that the gendered division of household labor has broken down in the area of children's activities, we found little evidence in our small nonrandom study to support this position.[12] This is not to say that fathers had no role. Indeed, particularly for sporting activities, fathers coached and could be found picking up and dropping off children and observing on the sidelines. Nevertheless, as one adds up all of children's organized activities through a calendar year, it is clear that fathers almost always had supporting roles in these productions; moms had the lead.

Final Thoughts

For decades now, the increased participation of women—particularly those with young children—in the paid workforce has been a central area of inquiry in sociology of the family. We have seen how this change has had ramifications for family life, especially with regards to the division of household labor. Fathers' household hours have increased, but a significant gender gap remains. Women have, to some extent, adjusted by lowering their standards and simply allowing certain tasks to go undone or to remain undone for longer periods (Bianchi 2000; Bianchi, Robinson, and Milkie 2006).

While helpful in understanding household dynamics and the power of gender in contemporary society, these studies have, for the most part, accepted assumptions about the nature of household tasks themselves. Although rooted in acknowledgment of changes to family life (greater participation of women in the paid workforce), most studies of housework and child rearing have defined household labor in ways that reflect outdated conceptions of child rearing (Mintz 2004). Particularly in middle-class families, the tasks associated with raising children in twenty-first century America involve the management of many organized activities.[13]

Thus, at the same time that more women with school-aged children have come to participate in the paid labor force, the contours of childhood in America have changed. With increased participation in organized activities, the work of raising children has altered dramatically. Scholars have missed this.

In this chapter, we have examined the nature of the work parents do in facilitating their children's participation in organized activities. In addition, we have highlighted the importance of gender to the accomplishment of these tasks. While the definition of a good childhood may be different in 2010 than it was in 1970 (more organized activities, less child-directed play), among couples with children it is primarily a mother's job to see to it that children have that good childhood.

The work of managing children's activities has largely eluded sociological research on the family. The labor we term "MESH" is so fragmented and taken for granted that it is largely invisible to the participants themselves. In interviews, mothers' and fathers' preliminary self-reports of the labor involved were often partial and incomplete. Only extensive probing in in-depth interviews and observations in the home altered our understanding of the processes. The "now you see it, now you don't" aspect of MESH labor makes it difficult for participants to describe and researchers to capture.

A family activity that takes the equivalent of a full-time job for one month is, we suggest, worthy of consideration in scholarship on families. But the MESHing of family life is largely invisible to sociological researchers. Studies of activity management are necessary to better understand the gendered division of labor within families and the way that division of labor affects work/family life.

NOTES

1. The literature on the gender division of labor is voluminous. For classic work, see Hochschild (1979, 1989, 1997). On the difficulty of creating egalitarian relationships, see Deutsch (1999). On fathers' view of their contributions to the home, see Townsend (2002) and Marsiglio (1995). On the invisible labor of coordination, see DeVault (1991), Griffith and Smith (2004), and Walzer (1996). On the symbolic claims mothers make in juggling full-time labor-force participation and motherhood, see Garey (1999). On the impact of social desirability in survey research, see Press and Townsley (1998). On historical changes in motherhood, see Hays (1996). Also see the other chapters in this volume.

2. Parents, particularly women, multitask and do many activities simultaneously (for example, supervise homework during meal preparation and laundry completion). But the activities that parents do in promoting children's lives are not captured by a better measure of multitasking, since the tasks are different than other household tasks.

3. Hochschild notes that she is "indebted" to Antonio J. Ferreira, "Psychosis and Family Myth," *American Journal of Psychotherapy* 21 (1967): 186–225, for the term "family myth" (Hochschild 1989, 280n3).

4. As in many studies, there is a confounding of race, class, and family structure. The middle-class families were disproportionately two-parent households, while the poor families were overwhelmingly single-parent households.

5. Middle-class children are those whose households have at least one parent who has a college degree and is employed in a position with a significant amount of occupational autonomy, usually in a professional or managerial position. Working-class children are those whose households have at least one parent employed in a position with limited occupational autonomy, usually in a skilled or semiskilled position. Parents' educational level may be high school dropout or high school graduate, or may include some college courses, often at a community college. This category includes lower-level white-collar workers. Poor children are those whose households have parents on public assistance and do not have steady participation in the labor force. Most of these parents are high school dropouts or high school graduates.

6. Our sample included stepparents, boyfriends, grandmothers, and guardians caring for children, as well as biological parents. For brevity, in the text we use the term "parent" to refer to the person primarily responsible for caring for the child and the one with whom the child lived. Usually, but not always, this was the biological parent. Mothers and fathers were interviewed at separate times; where possible, noncustodial fathers (or grandparents) who played an important role in their children's lives were interviewed as well. The second author (a middle-age white woman) and a small group of white and African American assistants conducted a total of 137 interviews. Each interview lasted approximately two hours and followed a specific format that included ample opportunity for respondents to provide open-ended answers.

7. As other research has shown, boys and girls often (but not always) were enrolled in different activities. The role of gender in shaping children's experiences is beyond the scope of this chapter. For the classic piece, see Thorne (1992). See also Hofferth and Sandberg (2001) and Sandberg and Hofferth (2001). For a debate about the importance of social class on children's activities, see Lareau and Weininger (2008), Hofferth (2008), Hughes (2008), and Mahoney and Eccles (2008).

8. Although both parents and children registered their awareness of being observed, family members appeared to relax and routines resumed over the course of regular, repeated visits. As the families became accustomed to the presence of the researchers, behaviors that initially had been absent (for example, swearing, squabbling) began to emerge. For a fuller and more detailed description of the methods used in this research, see Lareau (2003).

9. Here, we use the term "emotional labor" to parallel in linguistic construction the other "labors" that MESH comprises, but we are aware that our use in this context is different than Hochschild's definition and use of "emotional labor" (Hochschild 1983). What we are describing as the emotional labor component of MESH is the management of emotions (what Hochschild refers to as "emotion work") in the negotiation of family life and children's activities. Erickson (this volume) refers to this kind of emotion work in the service of caring for others as "emotional carework."

10. Lareau has written about how her interviews with fathers yielded limited information, since, for the most part, the fathers had only general and incomplete information about their children's organized activities (2000).

11. We had two single fathers in the study, both of whom were widowers. Both had also hired older women to help with the child care and homework. In these families, the fathers enrolled children in activities, but, as noted earlier, they also felt that they were not always up to the task, particularly the social networking and mental coordination.

12. In a time-diary analysis of a nationally representative sample of children's organized activities, Lareau and Weininger (2008) found that the number of hours that children participated were sensitive to mothers' hours of labor force participation; as mothers' hours increased, time spent in organized activities decreased. Children's hours in organized activities were not, however, sensitive to fathers' hours in the labor force.

13. Of course, changes to the everyday lives of American children are partly related to increased participation of women in the workforce. The point here, however, is to understand the ramifications of those changes, rather than tease out the root causes.

REFERENCES

Bernard, Jessie. 1991. "The Good-Provider Role: Its Rise and Fall." In *The Family Experience*, edited by Mark Hutter, 467–485. New York: Macmillan.

Bianchi, Suzanne M. 2000. "Maternal Employment and Time with Children: Dramatic Change or Surprising Continuity?" *Demography* 37:401–414.

Bianchi, Suzanne M., John P. Robinson, and Melissa A. Milkie. 2006. *Changing Rhythms of American Family Life*. New York: Russell Sage.

Deutsch, Francine M. 1999. *Halving It All: How Equally Shared Parenting Works*. Cambridge, MA: Harvard University Press.

DeVault, Marjorie. 1991. *Feeding the Family: The Social Organization of Caring as Gendered Work*. Chicago: University of Chicago Press.

Garey, Anita I. 1999. *Weaving Work and Motherhood*. Philadelphia: Temple University Press.

Granovetter, Mark. 1985. "Economic Action and Social Structure: The Problem of Embeddedness." *American Journal of Sociology* 91:481–510.

Griffith, Alison and Dorothy E. Smith. 2004. *Mothering for Schooling*. New York: Routledge.

Grasmuck, Sherri. 2005. *Protecting Home: Class, Race, and Masculinity in Boys' Baseball*. New Brunswick, NJ: Rutgers University Press.

Hays, Sharon. 1996. *The Cultural Contradictions of Motherhood*. New Haven, CT: Yale University Press.

Hochschild, Arlie R. 1979. "Emotion Work, Feeling Rules, and Social Structure." *American Journal of Sociology* 85(3): 551–575.

———. 1983. *The Managed Heart: Commercialization of Human Feeling*. Berkeley: University of California Press.

———, with Anne Machung. 1989. *The Second Shift: Working Parents and the Revolution at Home*. New York: Viking.

———. 1997. *The Time Bind: When Work Becomes Home and Home Becomes Work*. New York: Metropolitan Books.

Hofferth, Sandra. 2008. "Linking Social Class to Concerted Cultivation, Natural Growth and School Readiness." In *Disparities in School Readiness: How Do Families Contribute to Successful and Unsuccessful Transitions into School?* edited by Alan Booth and Ann C. Crouter, 199–206. New York: Lawrence Erlbaum Associates.

Hofferth, Sandra L., and John F. Sandberg. 2001. "Changes in American Children's Time, 1981–1997." In *Children at the Millennium: Where Have We Come From, Where are We Going? Advances in Life Course Research Series*, ed. Sandra Hofferth and Tim Owens, 193–229. New York: Elsevier.

Hughes, Diane. 2008. "Cultural versus Social Class Contexts for Extra-Curricular Activity Participation." In *Disparities in School Readiness: How Do Families Contribute to Successful and Unsuccessful Transitions into School?* edited by Alan Booth and Ann C. Crouter, 189–198. New York: Lawrence Erlbaum Associates.

Kanter, Rosabeth Moss. 1977. *Men and Women of the Corporation*. New York: Basic Books.

Lareau, Annette. 2000. "My Wife Can Tell Me Who I Know: Methodological and Conceptual Problems in Studying Fathers." *Qualitative Sociology* 23(4): 407–433.

———. 2003. *Unequal Childhoods: Class, Race, and Family Life*. Berkeley: University of California Press.

Lareau, Annette, and Elliot B. Weininger. 2008. "Time, Work, and Family Life: Reconceptualizing Gendered Time Patterns through the Case of Children's Organized Activities." *Sociological Forum* 23(3): 419–454.

Mahoney, Joseph L., and Jacquelynne S. Eccles. 2008. "Organized Activities for Children from Low- and Middle-Income Families." In *Disparities in School Readiness: How Do Families Contribute to Successful and Unsuccessful Transitions into School?* edited by Alan Booth and Ann C. Crouter, 207–222. New York: Lawrence Erlbaum Associates.

Marsiglio, William, ed. 1995. *Fatherhood: Contemporary Theory, Research, and Social Policy.* Thousand Oaks, CA: Sage.

Mintz, Steven. 2004. *Huck's Raft: A History of American Childhood.* Cambridge, MA: Belknap Press of Harvard University Press.

Orange, Robert M., Francille Firebaugh, and Ramona K. Z. Heck. 2003. "Managing Households." In *It's About Time: Couples and Careers,* edited by Phyllis Moen, 153–167. Ithaca, NY: Cornell University Press.

Ostrander, Susan A. 1984. *Women of the Upper Class.* Philadelphia: Temple University Press.

Press, Julie E., and Eleanor Townsley. 1998. "Wives' and Husbands' Housework Reporting: Gender, Class, and Social Desirability." *Gender & Society* 12:188–218.

Sandberg, John F., and Sandra L. Hofferth. 2001. "Changes in Children's Time with Parents: United States, 1981–1997." *Demography* 38:423–436.

Steir, Haya, and Marta Tienda. 1993. "Are Men Marginal to the Family? Insights from Chicago's Inner City." In *Men, Work, and Family,* edited by Jane Hood, 23–44. Thousand Oaks, CA: Sage Publications.

Thorne, Barrie. 1992. *Gender Play: Girls and Boys in School.* New Brunswick, NJ: Rutgers University Press.

Townsend, Nicholas. 2002. *The Package Deal: Marriage, Work, and Fatherhood in Men's Lives* Philadelphia: Temple University Press.

Walzer, Susan. 1996. "Thinking About the Baby: Gender and Divisions of Infant Care." *Social Problems* 43:219–234.

CHAPTER 4

Emotional Carework, Gender, and the Division of Household Labor

Rebecca J. Erickson

Emotional connection and support have been considered essential, if not *the* essential, characteristics of marriage and family life since at least the mid-twentieth century. Although the functionalist theory that produced the idea that women are primarily responsible for these expressive/emotional tasks while men are expected to perform instrumental/breadwinner ones has been broadly criticized, family scholars continue to confront the legacy of inequality signified by this initial description (Osmond and Thorne 1993). For example, this legacy remains evident in the well-established finding that women, even when they are employed full time, perform the bulk of routine housework and child care (Coltrane 2000; Fuwa 2004; Lincoln 2008; Shelton and John 1996).

Researchers attempting to explain this persistent gendered effect have suggested that these patterns of household labor allocation are related to how men and women construct culturally appropriate gender identities (Berk 1985; Ferree 1990). This gender constructionist approach has drawn attention to the symbolic importance of family work (for example, the routine activities that feed, clothe, shelter, and care for both children and adults) and how people do gender, as well as to the potential for variation in the gendered meanings associated with doing each type of household task (Coltrane 2000, 1209; DeVault 1991; Garey 1999; Twiggs, McQuillan, and Ferree 1999; West and Zimmerman 1987). To date, however, this line of research has yet to fully examine how the emotional carework components of family work may advance social scientific understanding of the relationship between gender and the division of household labor.

This study extends the analysis of gender and household labor by specifically examining the performance of emotional carework—that is, activities that are concerned with the enhancement of others' emotional well-being and with the provision of emotional support (Erickson 1993).[1] These activities require time, effort, and skill. They reflect "the warm and caring aspects of the construction and maintenance of interpersonal relations ... what Arlie Hochschild (1979) calls the positive aspects of 'emotion work'" (Daniels 1987, 409). Building on Erickson (1993), I show that expanding the traditional definition of family work (for example, housework and child care) to include emotional carework provides a unique avenue of support for the view that the division of household labor varies according to culturally based constructions of gender rather than on the basis of biological sex.

The Case for "Emotion Work"

George Levenger's (1964) initial argument for including emotional behavior in studies of marriage was grounded in the social psychology of groups (Parsons and Bales 1955; Thibaut and Kelley 1959). From the standpoint of marital partners, emotional behaviors were different from more instrumental family tasks such as cooking and cleaning because they could not be delegated to persons outside the group. Levenger's (1964) research provided evidence for the importance of emotional expressivity by showing that it was more strongly related to marital satisfaction than the performance of instrumental tasks.

Few other researchers examined emotional behavior as a requisite task performed by marital partners. Instead, its performance, along with that of housework and child care, came to be seen as a natural expression of women's love for their husbands and children. As the women's movement gained momentum in the late 1960s and early 1970s, however, assumptions about women's roles began to break down and their marital and familial behaviors began to be reconceptualized and analyzed as work.

In her classic essay on "invisible work," Arlene Daniels (1987) explained that applying the concept of work only to those activities for which people are paid renders much of women's activities invisible. Although Anne Oakley (1974) and others had made this case for housework and child care over a decade earlier, Daniels was among the first to make such a claim for the performance of emotion work in the family. Daniels argued that because the work people perform provides a clue to their status in society, it constitutes a central pathway to identity. She further illustrated how the recognition of an activity as work tends to infuse it with a certain level of "moral force and dignity" (Daniels 1987, 404). In that women perform more family work than men, failing to characterize these activities as work serves to invalidate women's essential contributions to social and community life and, in this way, contributes to the reproduction of gender inequality.

Today, Daniels's (1987) argument has largely been accepted when applied to housework and child care activities. It has been more difficult, however, to see comforting, encouraging, and facilitating interaction as characterizing a work role. Such difficulty may be because these activities are closely associated with women's natural or feminine tendencies and with culturally based assumptions about love and intimate family relations (DeVault 1991; Erickson 1993; Thompson and Walker 1989). Women themselves often discount the time and effort involved in caring work not only because it is expected to be a spontaneous expression of love, but also because the illusion of effortlessness is part of doing the work well (Garey, this volume; Hochschild 1983).

That husbands and wives may have to work at caring and intimacy contradicts what many may wish to believe about love and marriage. Offering encouragement, showing appreciation, listening closely to what someone has to say, and expressing empathy with another person's feelings (even when they are not shared)—day after day, year after year—represents emotional carework of the highest order.

Given Western assumptions about the close relationship between gender and emotion, examining the performance of emotional carework as a distinct type of family work task may yield new insights into how the construction of masculine and feminine conceptions of self are connected to the reproduction of a gendered division of household labor (Lutz 1988).[2] Because women are held accountable for the performance of emotional carework in ways that men are not, explicit recognition of this work also may prove helpful for developing a more complete understanding of how people construct conceptions of themselves as men and women.

Predicting the Division of Family Work

Over the years, family scholars have adopted different theoretical approaches to predicting the division of family work. One approach has been to suggest that a combination of relative individual resources, time constraints, and gender ideology could account for much of the variation in who performs domestic labor. Although each of these factors has been shown to account for some of this variation, being female has remained the primary predictor of family work performance (Coltrane 2000; Shelton and John 1996). Another, more recent, approach has sought to understand the gendered meanings associated with performing particular family work tasks. Referred to here as gender construction theory, this second perspective suggests that spouses actively construct the allocation of family work tasks in ways that affirm and reproduce their gendered conceptions of self (Ferree 1991; Twiggs, McQuillan, and Ferree 1999).

Relative Resources

The relative resource model proposes that marital partners negotiate the division of household labor using the basic principles of economic exchange. According to this perspective, the spouse who brings more resources to the marital relationship will be able to use these resources to "buy out" of the performance of household labor. In this case, the other spouse, being more dependent, will end up doing—or at least being responsible for—more of this family work. This is considered a gender neutral theory in that the "buy out" should work similarly for men and women (Brines 1994). In sum, the relative resources theory suggests that the greater one's economic dependence, the more family work one will perform (for example, housework, child care, and emotion work).

Time Constraints

The time constraints approach theorizes that people who spend more time in paid work have less time available to perform household labor (Artis and Pavalko 2003; Coverman 1985). Again, this theory is gender neutral in that both husbands and wives are expected to perform family work to the extent that other demands on their time allow them to do so. The time constraints approach suggests that the more hours one spends in paid employment, the less family work one will perform.

Gender Ideology

Emerging out of socialization theories, the model of gender ideology predicts an inverse or negative relationship between traditional attitudes and an egalitarian division of family work (Blair and Lichter 1991; Kamo 1988). The perspective assumes that a more traditional ideology reinforces a division of labor in the home in which women perform more of the work traditionally associated with being female (for example, housework, child care, and emotion work). Although this relationship has tended to hold more strongly for men than for women (Presser 1994; Shelton and John 1996), studies have generally provided support for the expectation that holding a traditional ideology will be associated with wives performing more family work. The gender ideology perspective would therefore suggest that the more traditional one's gender ideology, the more housework and child care wives will perform. I also expect that the more traditional men's gender ideology, the *less* emotional carework they will perform, and that the more traditional women's gender ideology, the *more* emotional carework they will perform.

Gender Construction Theory

Women continue to perform the bulk of routine housework and child care, and to feel more responsible than men for this work regardless of income, time constraints, or ideology (Braun et al. 2008; Lincoln 2008; Shelton and John 1996; Spain and Bianchi 1996). Attempting to account for this empirical fact, feminist scholars have suggested that the rise in women's paid employment has not led to a similar increase in men's domestic labor because the nature and meaning of women's involvement in family work is different from men's (DeVault 1991;

Hochschild 1989; Thompson and Walker 1989). This theory suggests that the models described earlier do not adequately account for variations in the division of household labor because they fail to consider the gendered meanings husbands and wives derive from the performance of family work.

Researchers using gender construction theory propose that the gendered allocation of household labor persists because it signals the extent to which husbands and wives have constructed gender appropriately. As long as women are held (and hold themselves) accountable for family work in ways that men are (and do) not, the performance of this work will remain more central to how women construct a gendered sense of self, and, in so doing, their behavior will continue to reflect such (self-) expectations (Sanchez and Thomson 1997). Because femininity continues to be conceptualized in ways that emphasize care, concern, and connection to others, one also expects that women would be more likely than men to define family work as reflecting such expressivity and to behave in ways that are consistent with such meanings (DeVault 1991; Mederer 1993; Spence 1984). In this situation, performing family work is less likely to be experienced as an alienating burden than as an expression of what it means to be a real wife and/or mother (Berk 1985; DeVault 1991; Hochschild 1989).

The study reported in this chapter contributes to the body of research on the meanings associated with family work by shifting attention from gendered tasks to gendered selves. For example, to what extent might one's construction of self as masculine or feminine be associated with the performance of particular types of family work? Such a question builds on the idea that the same behavior (or task performance) takes on different meanings depending on the implications it holds for a person's self-conception. We can assume that individuals who construct their gendered selves in more feminine terms are more likely to attribute positive meanings (for example, concern, loving care, nurturance) to family work tasks that traditionally have been performed by women. As a result, we would expect these individuals to perform such tasks more frequently. This positive relationship between characteristics associated with femininity and the performance of traditionally female tasks should hold even when controlling for the effect of biological sex. One final question of interest concerns whether men's and women's construction of gender will affect their performance of housework, child care, and emotional carework in similar ways.

To summarize, gender construction theory provides a theoretical basis for examining the extent to which gender is associated with the performance of family work. For example, we can hypothesize that the more feminine characteristics men and women apply to themselves, the more household labor they will perform. Support for gender construction theory requires that the performance of family work be related to these gendered constructions more strongly than to relative resources, time constraints, gender ideology, and biological sex. To test these ideas, I first use the total sample and control for the effect of biological sex. Then, I explore the results for men and women separately.

I expect that constructing gender in masculine terms will be negatively related to the performance of family work, regardless of one's biological sex. In contrast, constructing gender in feminine terms will be positively related to the performance of family work.

In addition to the theoretically motivated relationships noted above, several other variables are typically entered into the statistical models as controls. These variables include age, education, number of children, and presence of preschool children.[3]

Method

Data and Sample

The data presented here are part of a larger study designed to investigate the relationships among work, family, and health among a community-based sample of dual-earner, married parents.[4] The data for this study were collected during the spring of 1996 and consist of responses to a mailed questionnaire. The final sample consisted of the 335 married parents who were employed full time and for whom complete data were available. It should be noted that the responses were obtained from men and women who were not married to one another. Women comprised 67 percent ($n = 225$) of the final sample. And 93 percent of the sample was white. The age of the respondents ranged from twenty-three to sixty-eight years, with a mean of thirty-nine years. The respondents' educational levels ranged from having some high school experience to having a graduate degree, with most having completed some college coursework. Respondents' marriages ranged in length from less than one year to thirty-one years, with a median of fourteen years, and they also reported having approximately two children under the age of eighteen. Among those who had children under eighteen living with them at home, 35 percent of the respondents had at least one preschool child and 78 percent reported having at least one school-age child. Compared to the county from which it was drawn, this sample tends to underrepresent black men and overrepresent those with more than a high school education. As a result, caution should be used in generalizing the results to the population of employed, married parents as a whole.

Measures

Dependent Variables. The measures of housework and child care assessed the relative amount that each task was performed by respondents and their spouses. Wives' housework assessed the relative amount that husbands and wives performed five routine household tasks: grocery shopping, cooking meals, doing dishes, doing the laundry, and cleaning the bathroom. Child care referred to activities specifically involving children. This scale included the following nine items: keeping track of children's activities, taking children to appointments, attending children's performances/games, driving children to activities, chaperoning children's activities, playing with the children, disciplining children, supervising the children's homework, and reading to or with the children. Consistent with Rebecca Erickson's work (1993), a respondent's emotional care work was measured using a summated scale of eight items measuring the amount of emotional carework performed by the respondent. Respondents were asked to indicate how often in the last six months they engaged in each of the following behaviors: initiated talking things over, listened closely to their spouse's innermost thoughts and feelings, recognized the importance of their spouse's feelings even if they did not share them, offered encouragement, respected the spouse's point of view, did favors for the spouse without being asked, let the spouse know they were appreciated, listened closely to what the spouse wanted to say about his or her day (1 = never, 3 = sometimes, 5 = very often).

Independent Variables

Relative Resources. Relative resource theory proposes that the spouse who brings relatively more resources (for example, income) to the relationship will perform less family work. A score of zero indicates that the spouses contributed equally to the family's income. Negative scores indicate the economic dependence of the spouse on the respondent. By contrast, the more positive a score, the more economically dependent the respondent is on the spouse.

Availability. The time constraints model suggests that the division of family work depends on the amount of time each spouse is available to do the work. Among dual-earner couples, availability is measured as the amount of time husbands and wives spend in paid employment. Respondent's labor force hours and spouse's labor force hours measured the number of hours per week each spent in the paid labor force.

Gender Ideology. The gender ideology explanation posits that spouses will view the performance of family work differently depending upon their attitudes about gendered family roles (i.e., gendered ideologies). Those holding a more traditional gender ideology are more likely to view family work as being appropriately performed by women. Traditional gender ideology was measured by asking respondents to indicate the extent of their agreement with the following statements: A wife's wages should only be supplementary to the main wages earned by the husband; spouses should share the responsibility of earning a living for the household (reverse coded); when there are small children in the home, it is better that the mother not work outside the home; ideally, it is better if the man works to support the household and for the woman to take care of the home; and, even though a wife may work outside the home, the husband should still focus most of his attention on earning a living.

Gender Construction. The construction of gender was measured using the instrumental-masculine and expressive-feminine subscales of the Personal Attributes Questionnaire (Spence and Helmreich 1978). These scales assess gender construction in terms of the respondent's self-perceived possession of personality traits that are stereotypically believed to differentiate between women and men but that are considered socially desirable in both (Spence 1984). For example, two items included in the masculine-instrumental scale were (1) not at all independent—very independent and (2) very passive—very active. Two of the items used in the feminine-expressive scale were (1) not at all emotional—very emotional and (2) not aware of others' feelings—very aware of others' feelings. In each case, items were coded so that higher scores reflected greater masculinity-instrumentality or femininity-expressivity, respectively.

Predicting the Performance of Family Work

In the discussion of results, I focus only on those related to the performance of emotional carework. I encourage readers to see Erickson (2005) for further details.

Table 4.1 presents the results of regression analyses used to predict the performance of emotional carework for the total sample and separately for men and women. The analysis thus accounts for the effects of both biological sex and the construction of gender in masculine and feminine terms. In the analyses predicting housework and child care (not shown here), biological sex was the primary correlate of performing these types of family work, even when the effects of relative resources, time constraints, and gender ideology were included (see Erickson 2005). These results support the view that biological sex is the most important determinant of family work when that work is measured as housework and child care (Shelton and John 1996).

The findings for emotional carework are quite different. In contrast to housework and child care, the first column of results in table 4.1 illustrates that the performance of emotional carework is significantly influenced by respondents' construction of gender rather than by their biological sex. Those who see themselves in more feminine-expressive terms are significantly more likely to perform emotional carework ($\beta = .356, p \leq .001$). Somewhat surprisingly, seeing oneself in masculine terms is also positively related to emotional carework performance ($\beta = .132, p \leq .01$). In addition, respondents who espouse a more traditional gender ideology are less likely to perform emotional carework ($\beta = -.107, p \leq .01$).

The results of the analysis presented in the first column of table 4.1 do not provide support for the relative resources model or the time constraints model. Moreover, no statistically significant support was found for the gender ideology model. Because the predictions about the effects of gender ideology on emotional carework depend on the biological sex of the respondent, the negative relationship between ideology and emotion work in the population should not

TABLE 4.1

PREDICTING THE PERFORMANCE OF EMOTIONAL CAREWORK FOR THE TOTAL SAMPLE AND BY GENDER

	Total sample (n = 335)			*Men (n = 110)*			*Women (n = 225)*		
Independent variables	*B*	*SE B*	*BETA*	*B*	*SE B*	*BETA*	*B*	*SE B*	*BETA*
Female	.128	.673	.013	—	—	—	—	—	—
Respondent's age	.055	.046	.075	.107	.083	.136	.039	.055	.055
Respondent's education	−.257	.175	−.077	−.248	.366	−.064	−.418	.200	−.139*
Number of children	−.137	.257	−.028	.480	.603	.078	−.361	.275	−.083
Presence of preschool children	.589	.575	.062	1.134	1.121	.110	.324	.673	.037
Economic dependency	.422	1.057	.033	.676	2.394	.038	−.097	1.210	−.006
Respondent's hours of employment	−.022	.027	−.055	.016	.065	.022	−.036	.030	−.093
Spouse's hours of employment	.024	.023	.068	−.003	.050	−.008	.040	.026	1.098
Traditional gender ideology	−.166	.083	−.107*	−.366	.177	−.205*	−.068	.094	−.048
Masculine-instrumental	.128	.052	.132*	−.057	.091	−.059	.273	.065	.285***
Feminine-expressive	.372	.060	.356***	.454	.116	.399***	.274	.072	.254***
Constant		18.72			19.31			19.01	
Adjusted R^2		.20			.16			.19	
F		8.53***			3.00**			6.24***	

Note: B = unstandardized regression coefficient; SE B = standard error of the unstandardized regression coefficient; Beta = standardized regression coefficient
* = $p \leq .05$
** = $p \leq .01$
*** = $p \leq .001$

be interpreted as a test of these hypotheses. Such a test requires the use of separate analyses for men and women. These results are discussed later and are presented in the second and third columns of table 4.1.

In analyses not shown here, gender construction theory was not supported in regard to housework or child care. However, the theory did receive support in regard to the performance of emotional carework. The expectation that seeing oneself in feminine-expressive terms—regardless of one's biological sex—would be positively related to the performance of emotional carework received strong support in that being female had no statistically significant effect on emotional carework (see table 4.1, column 1). Further, there is a positive relationship between defining oneself in feminine-expressive terms and the performance of emotional carework, and this was more than 2.5 times stronger than any other relationship in the model. In contrast, the results were opposite than expected in regard to masculinity-instrumentality in that this gender construction was also positively related to the performance of emotional carework (see table 4.1, column 1).

When the analyses were repeated for men and women separately, the results show that men who construct their gender identity in more feminine terms are more likely to perform emotional carework (table 4.1, column 2). In contrast, men who espouse a more traditional gender ideology tend to perform less emotional carework ($\beta = -.205$, $p \leq .01$). This last result supports my expectation that the more traditional men's gender ideology, the less emotional carework they perform. However, the hypothesized relationship between *women's* gender ideology and emotional carework did not receive support (for example, the regression coefficient was not significant; see table 4.1, column 3).

Among women, scoring high on the masculinity scale or high on the femininity scale are both positively related to the performance of emotional carework. These results indicate that women who see themselves in more feminine-expressive terms tend to perform more emotional carework than those who score lower on the feminine-expressive scale ($\beta = .254$, $p \leq .001$). Interestingly, women who apply masculine-instrumental traits to themselves also perform more emotional carework than those who score lower on this scale ($\beta = .285$, $p \leq .001$). This latter finding suggests that the meaning of the activities that comprise emotional carework performance may indeed be different for men and women.

Discussion

The results suggest that including emotional carework in studies of household labor provides new insights into the gendered meaning and allocation of family work tasks. In so doing, this research lends support to the view that husbands and wives perform family work in ways that facilitate culturally appropriate constructions of gender. The finding that emotional carework was more closely associated with the construction of gender than were housework and child care provides evidence that emotional carework matters to our efforts to discern how gender influences the meaning and division of family work.

To be sure, this study represents merely an initial step in developing a more complete understanding of the relationship between gender and emotional carework. Nonetheless, consider the findings that constructing gender in feminine terms led to more emotional carework among men, whereas among women more emotional carework was performed by those who considered themselves to be quite feminine *and* by those who considered themselves to be quite masculine. In that the masculinity scale reflects agentive, self-assertive, and instrumental traits (Spence 1984), the results for women suggest that the performance of emotional carework represented a form of instrumental action, not merely an expression of their "kindness toward others." For a woman who constructed her sense of self in these masculine or instrumental terms, providing emotional support to her husband was an integral part of her family work role. In contrast, men construed their performance of emotion work as merely part of their interpersonal relationship with their wives, not as part of how they constructed themselves in agentive terms.

The tendency to conceptualize emotional carework as work suggests that women recognize that they are held accountable for the performance of this work in ways that men are not. This is consistent with Susan Shaw's (1988) observation that men are more likely than women to characterize household labor as leisure rather than work. In sum, these results provide a new avenue of support for gender construction theory and illustrate how reconceptualizing family work to include emotional carework can inform our understanding of the complex relationship between "doing gender" and "doing family" (Thompson and Walker 1989). In contrast, the results for the total sample provide no support for the relative resources and time constraints models, and quite marginal support for the gender ideology approach. Consistent with most research in this area, biological sex had the strongest effect on the allocation of housework and child care.

Conclusion

The time and energy required to provide emotional support to others must be viewed as an important aspect of the work that takes place in families. These behaviors have commonly been overlooked because they tend to be seen only as reflections of interpersonal intimacy or love. Such a view parallels the once conventional approach to housework and child care that existed prior to those tasks being reconceptualized as part of a work role rather than natural characteristics associated with being female. Continued neglect of emotional carework within the family work literature risks perpetuating the view that being an emotional caretaker is something women are rather than something women do. By continuing to overlook the part that emotional carework plays in the creation and maintenance of marriages and families, researchers are unlikely to achieve full appreciation of the subtle ways in which cultural conceptions of woman, wife, and mother, along with man, husband, and father, are reproduced.

ACKNOWLEDGMENTS

An earlier version of this chapter appeared in *Journal of Marriage and Family* 67 (May 2005):337–351 published by John Wiley & Sons Ltd.

NOTES

1. This chapter is based on a 1995–1996 study that was intended "to bring emotion work back to the center of family work scholarship" (Erickson 2005, 347). Since then, as the chapters in this volume attest, much has been done to continue the study of emotion work in the context of work/family life. The important contribution of the present chapter is in the way it brings attention to and analyzes the importance of studying emotional carework in the context of the household division of labor [*editors' note*].
2. The conceptualization and analysis of emotional carework in this chapter builds upon the path-breaking work of Hochschild (1980, 1989) and Berk (1985) through an explicit testing of hypotheses that are theoretically consistent with their work and that are specifically targeting the efforts that it takes to make others feel cared for and valued.
3. See Erickson (2005) for the empirical reasons for including these in the models that were tested.
4. For more information on data collection and measures used, see Erickson (2005).

REFERENCES

Artis, Julie E., and Eliza K. Pavalko. 2003. "Explaining the Decline in Women's Household Labor: Individual Change and Cohort Differences." *Journal of Marriage and Family* 65:746–761.

Berk, Sarah F. 1985. *The Gender Factory: The Apportionment of Work in American Households.* New York: Plenum Press.

Blair, Sampson L., and Daniel T. Lichter. 1991. "Measuring the Division of Household Labor." *Journal of Family Issues* 12:91–115.

Braun, Michael, Noah Lewin-Epstein, Haya Stier, and Miriam K. Baumgärtner. 2008. "Perceived Equity in the Gendered Division of Household Labor." *Journal of Marriage and Family* 70:1145–1156.

Brines, Julie. 1994. "Economic Dependency, Gender, and the Division of Labor at Home." *American Journal of Sociology* 100:652–688.

Coltrane, Scott. 2000. "Research on Household Labor: Modeling and Measuring the Social Embeddedness of Routine Family Work." *Journal of Marriage and Family* 62:1208–1233.

Coverman, Shelley. 1985. "Explaining Husbands' Participation in Domestic Labor." *Sociological Quarterly* 26:81–97.

Daniels, Arlene K. 1987. "Invisible Work." *Social Problems* 34:403–415.

Devault, Marjorie L. 1991. *Feeding the Family: The Social Organization of Caring as Gendered Work.* Chicago: University of Chicago Press.

Erickson, Rebecca J. 1993. "Reconceptualizing Family Work: The Effect of Emotion Work on Perceptions of Marital Quality." *Journal of Marriage and Family* 55:888–900.

———. 2005. "Why Emotion Work Matters: Sex, Gender, and the Division of Household Labor." *Journal of Marriage and Family* 67:337–351.

Ferree, Myra M. 1990. "Beyond Separate Spheres: Feminism and Family Research." *Journal of Marriage and Family* 52:866–884.

———. 1991. "The Gender Division of Labor in Two-Earner Marriages." *Journal of Family Issues* 12:158–180.

Fuwa, Makiko. 2004. "Macro-level Gender Inequality and the Division of Household Labor in 22 Countries." *American Sociological Review* 69:751–767.

Garey, Anita Ilta. 1999. *Weaving Work and Motherhood.* Philadelphia: Temple University Press.

Hochschild, Arlie R. 1979. "Emotion Work, Feeling Rules, and Social Structure." *American Journal of Sociology* 85:551–575.

———. 1983. *The Managed Heart: Commercialization of Human Feeling.* Berkeley: University of California Press.

———, with Anne Machung. 1989. *The Second Shift: Working Parents and the Revolution at Home.* New York: Viking.

Kamo, Yoshinori. 1988. "Determinants of Household Division of Labor: Resources, Power, and Ideology." *Journal of Family Issues* 9:177–200.

Levenger, George. 1964. "Task and Social Behavior in Marriage." *Sociometry* 27:433–448.

Lincoln, Anne E. 2008. "Gender, Productivity, and the Marital Wage Premium." *Journal of Marriage and Family* 70:98–125.

Lutz, Catherine A. 1988. *Unnatural Emotions: Everyday Sentiments on a Micronesian Atoll and Their Challenge to Western Theory.* Chicago: University of Chicago Press.

Mederer, Helen J. 1993. "Division of Labor in Two-Earner Homes: Task Accomplishment versus Household Management as Critical Variables in Perceptions about Family Work." *Journal of Marriage and Family* 55:133–145.

Oakley, Anne. 1974. *The Sociology of Housework.* New York: Random House.

Osmond, Marie W., and Barrie Thorne. 1993. "Feminist Theories: The Social Construction of Gender in Families and Society." In *Sourcebook of Family Theories and Methods: A Contextual Approach,* edited by Pauline G. Boss, William. J. Doherty, Ralph LaRossa, Walter R. Schumm, and Suzanne K. Steinmetz, 591–623. New York: Plenum Press.

Parsons, Talcott, and Robert F. Bales. 1955. *Family, Socialization and Interaction Process.* Glencoe, IL: Free Press.

Presser, Harriet B. 1994. "Employment Schedules among Dual-Earner Spouses and the Division of Household Labor by Gender." *American Sociological Review* 59:348–364.

Sanchez, Laura, and Elizabeth Thomson. 1997. "Becoming Mothers and Fathers: Parenthood, Gender, and the Division of Labor." *Gender & Society* 11:747–772.

Shaw, Susan M. 1988. "Gender Differences in the Definition and Perception of Household Labor." *Family Relations* 37:333–337.

Shelton, Beth A., and Daphne John. 1996. "The Division of Household Labor." *Annual Review of Sociology* 22:299–322.

Spain, Daphne, and Suzanne Bianchi. 1996. *Balancing Act: Motherhood, Marriage, and Employment among American Women.* New York: Russell Sage Foundation.

Spence, Janet T. 1984. "Gender Identity and Its Implications for the Concepts of Masculinity and Femininity." *Nebraska Symposium on Motivation* 32:59–95.

Spence, Janet T., and Robert L. Helmreich. 1978. *Masculinity and Femininity: Their Psychological Dimensions, Correlates, and Antecedents.* Austin: University of Texas Press.

Thibaut, John W., and Harold H. Kelley. 1959. *The Social Psychology of Groups.* New York: Wiley.

Thompson, Linda, and Alexis J. Walker. 1989. "Gender in Families: Women and Men in Marriage, Work, and Parenthood." *Journal of Marriage and Family* 51:845–871.

Twiggs, Joan E., Julia McQuillan, and Myra M. Ferree. 1999. "Meaning and Measurement: Reconceptualizing Measures of the Division of Household Labor." *Journal of Marriage and Family* 61:712–724.

West, Candace, and Don H. Zimmerman. 1987. "Doing Gender." *Gender & Society* 1:125–151.

CHAPTER 5

"Why Can't I Have What I Want?"

TIMING EMPLOYMENT, MARRIAGE, AND MOTHERHOOD

Rosanna Hertz

Stuck. Virtually every woman I interviewed expressed the feeling. Something conspired to disrupt the trajectory of love to marriage to children. Joy McFadden pointed the finger at her demanding job and a shortage of candidates in the marriage market.[1] She declared herself unwilling to settle for compromises: a marriage arrived at to serve other ends. Claudia D'Angelo acknowledged her tug-of-war between independence and intimacy and the difficulties it caused her in her relationships with men. She worried about marriage transforming her independence into narrowed opportunities, as it had for her mother. And when she did become involved with a man, he didn't share her desire for children.

In some instances, being stuck meant being mired hip deep in a bog of commitments and bereft of energy or time to search for alternatives. For the vast majority of women I interviewed, however, being stuck was a dynamic thing, like Claudia's tug-of-war. It might appear to outsiders as motionlessness, passivity, or even resignation. But, listening to women such as Claudia and Joy, I clearly got the sense that although it may have been enervating, it was rarely passive.

What are the opposing forces that keep women stuck? Middle-class women, I found, are caught between a battered but resilient ideology of marriage-then-motherhood and the experience of independence and self-fulfillment in a workplace that poses fewer barriers to women than previously. In the late 1970s, when at least half the women I interviewed reached the age of majority, women stopped sporting engagement rings at college graduation and started brandishing their degrees, which galvanized them as agents of change. As they took to heart the expectation for equality in the workplace, middle-class women no longer had to strike a risky bargain with men to achieve economic stability in their adult lives. Marriage receded in importance as women had other options and a greater range of opportunities for defining themselves in the world. While women did not stop seeking marriage, their expectations for the institution were transformed as the need for a man for economic security and social stability fell away, leaving only the idealized image of marriage for love.[2] Unlike generations of middle-class women before them who believed their fate was either marriage and motherhood or spinsterhood and career, these women always expected they would have it all.

While some scholars suggested that it would be difficult to have children and continue to be employed simultaneously, and some early second-wave feminists argued that family obligations to nurture children would make competing equally with male peers difficult, neither scholars nor activists urged women to give up children entirely. Academics, by contrast, argued that it was possible to have it all, but maybe it would be easier to have baby and career sequentially; marriage and heterosexuality were taken for granted.

This chapter is based on an in-depth audiotaped interview study I conducted between 1995 and 2004 with sixty-five single mothers who were over the age of twenty when they had their first child and were economically self-sufficient at the time of the interview. Women were eligible for inclusion in the sample if they were unmarried and not living with either the father of their child or a romantic partner at the time of birth or adoption *and* at the time of the first interview.[3]

Joy and Claudia represent the two-thirds of women in this study who are middle class. These women grew up imagining white picket fences and perfect children. They worked hard in school with the goal of going to college, even though they did not necessarily anticipate lifelong careers. Everyone assumed they would settle down and raise a family. In their families, men would be the providers. However, when they graduated from college in the mid to late 1970s, Joy and Claudia found themselves in a time of enormous flux.[4] As young women in their early twenties, they were in the midst of a rapid expansion of employment opportunities and an influential women's liberation movement. Most parents, even conservative ones, encouraged their daughters to be "whatever they wanted to be." Family and marriage were put on hold as exciting job opportunities arose and young women started to bring home a paycheck. Joy and Claudia liked making decisions about how to spend the money they earned, and they reveled in the many different ways they could shape their lives as self-sufficient women. The irony, they discovered, was that although they had been raised to follow in the footsteps of their mothers, they were actually imitating their fathers.

By contrast, women with working-class origins usually came from dual-earner families. Working-class moms rarely left the labor force except when their children were babies, and even then some were employed. Even though their parents may have only completed high school, these daughters were likely to have some college education. Unlike the middle-class pattern in which mothers stayed home and raised their families until the youngest child was entering high school, working-class daughters watched their mothers bring home a paycheck, even if the hours they worked made it appear that they were waiting at home for the school bus (Garey 1999).

For example, when Abby Pratt-Evans was growing up, her dad, upon returning home from his construction job, would sit in the living room watching TV, his reward for a long day. Her mom, on the other hand, rushed back from her nursing shift to prepare dinner while Abby and her preteen sister peppered her with questions about carpool arrangements, weekend plans with friends, and math homework. Dinner was always on the table on time, but as Abby grew older she noted that her mom also had worked all day. Abby loved her mother but never could stand how her mother allowed her father to sit and not help every night. Women who came from working-class backgrounds were simultaneously proud of their mothers' employment achievements and sad that it was their mothers who were doubly burdened with keeping family life together. These women worried that unless they redefined marriage, their husband's employment would slowly overshadow their own and they would become their mothers. Women in this study were too committed to pursuing their employment and independence to let that happen. The surge of importance employment took on for the women in this study is not without context. Second-wave feminism, emerging in the 1960s and 1970s, emphasized the struggle for equal opportunity. Focusing on the transformation of social structures, including law, education, and employment, second-wave feminism sought to change and expand all aspects of women's and men's lives (Rosen 2001). A few of the oldest women in this study, who had been the first to achieve in the workplace, spoke of a strong attachment to feminism. Mostly, however, these women were free riders, reaping the benefits of feminist activism without feeling part of the movement themselves. They attended college and established their careers in a time of economic expansion when equality was already mandated.

Although higher education and workplace norms have changed to reflect new legislation, the social revolution initiated by women's entry into the economy seems to have stalled at the threshold of the home (Hochschild 1989). Husbands have continued serving as main providers and wives as primary caretakers, even if breadwinning is an increasingly shared endeavor. We once assumed, perhaps naively, that when women became a permanent part of the paid labor force, their husbands would begin to share equally in housework and child care (Hertz 1986). As we now know from over three decades of research on work and family among two-income couples, the division of labor between spouses is not equally shared. Further, the clash between work and family life has become an increasing concern as academics expose the ways American families experience a shortage of time (see also Schor 1991; Hochschild 1989, 1997; Moen 2003; Jacobs and Gerson 2004; Milkie et al. 2004).

The majority of the women I interviewed described themselves as having been strongly committed to work prior to motherhood. They have occupations as diverse as lawyers, managers, consultants, waitresses, and aerobics instructors. Many work in the service sector in feminized occupations (such as nurses, secretaries, social workers, and elementary schoolteachers). Others work in major corporate, university, and nonprofit settings as managers, professors, and lawyers. A smaller group is self-employed, including small-business owners, writers, Web designers, and contract workers for corporations and hospitals. Annette Barker, a senior manager with a local high-tech firm, described with pride her rapid rise in the company's ranks in the early to mid-1980s after completing her MBA:

> I was working for a company that I had been with for six years, that I had grown up with, that I had gone from being an entry-level programmer to a senior programmer, a project leader and a manager, a director. My career developed there and my identity was my work. I kept getting promoted and with each promotion I continued my pace. I reached a pretty lofty position.

Likewise, Abby, who has master's degrees in both educational administration and educational psychology, threw herself into her work as an elementary schoolteacher, winning awards for her innovative style. Abby dreamed of moving up the ladder, too:

> I teach gifted and talented children and I love working with young children, particularly troubled kids. I put in extra time developing a new curriculum. I was always working on making myself as a teacher more child-friendly . . . Still . . . I wanted to move up. So I went back to get certified to be a principal.

Both Annette and Abby received great personal satisfaction from their workplace accomplishments, but, like Leigh, a journalist groomed for the national stage, they marveled at how they had gotten so ensnared in the rush to status that they lost track of their plans for motherhood. Leigh Newell explained:

> It was an era where we were constantly reading about the first woman lawyer to do this, the first woman to *senior* VP at that. And there was very little discussion about motherhood. Now, when I got into my late thirties and began looking back even then and thinking, "Why didn't I do some of these things? Why didn't I think more about having children?" Then of course you get into that thinking, "Well, was the message right?" But motherhood just wasn't on my radar screen. It just wasn't.

The belief that it takes a partner to have a child was a cultural mandate that even these successful women were unable to ignore. Most busied themselves with work, hoping the right partner would materialize and start the sequence. As a result of women's diminishing economic need for marriage, they were more fully able to invest in the romanticized vision of the institution, in which the magic of love overshadows more practical considerations.

Claudia, who shared similar experiences with many of the other women in this study, talked about how she couldn't fathom moving out of her college dorm to follow a boyfriend who had entered graduate school. In her words, "the relationship had potential but the timing was off." Timing, I was told repeatedly, was critical to forming intimate and lasting relationships. Timing was not simply a matter of finding the right person. Both people had to be ready to commit, and not just to a relationship but also to a future that included marriage and children. Lily Baker, age thirty-nine and with a one-year-old conceived through anonymous donor insemination, described succinctly what for her turned out to be nearly two decades of bad timing and weak commitments:

> The way I look at it in a nutshell is that in my twenties, I wasn't ready. In my thirties I was. I dated three men in my thirties. The first one wasn't ready to get married; I would have married him, wise or unwise. The second one I would have married, but he said, "You're the most wonderful woman I've ever dated, but I'm not in love with you." And the third one I definitely expected to marry. I was like, "Oh, I'm glad the other two didn't work because this is the One for me." And he wasn't ready.

Like Claudia, Lily felt she had time on her side. She was convinced that a much better prospect was just around the corner.

This is not to say that these women, heterosexual or lesbian, lacked in relationships. The overwhelming majority described long-lasting and, in many instances, very fulfilling commitments. But in every instance, whether the relationship was simply romantic or included cohabitation, marriage, or partnership, circumstances conspired to stop things short of the full package—commitment with children. Women, whether heterosexual or lesbian, wanted ideally to parent with partners. Men's ambivalence about commitment loomed large in women's accounts, and a man's waffling often derailed plans for moving forward. Over coffee, Nadine Margolis gave me the last story of the man she had dated.

> I looked at his drawings for this house he was building. And I said to myself, "This man does not want to have children." And that night I asked him about it, and he said that he did not want to have children. And I said, "Yes, I did want children." We parted quietly from that night. I could just tell from the way the drawing was done; there was no place for a child to get next to a parent. This was definitely not someone who wanted children, or who had thought about it.

Nadine abandoned a secure, richly drawn future plan for a life together and stepped out alone into unmapped territory. Similar to other women in this study her relationship ended when she raised her wish for children. She was not willing to settle for a life without children; he could not commit to her vision of a family life.

Nicole Shiff, forty-five years old with two adopted young teens, claimed that after twenty-plus years of continual dating she could tell in the first fifteen minutes of a date if there was even a slim chance that there would be a second date. She explained how incompatible she was with a man who responded through a dating service shortly after her long-term relationship ended.

> I went out with a guy who pulled out a list as I was reading the menu and said, "I have questions." I said, "Okay." I thought he was joking. And he said, "When you go shopping and you come home, what do you do?" I said, "I [put] the groceries away, get a cold drink, put my feet up, and say, 'Thank God that's over.'" I said, "What do you do?" He said, "Well, I line up all the peas." And I'm listening to this and I'm thinking, "This is a joke." So then he goes, "Where do you squeeze the tube of toothpaste?" I said, "Wherever my hand lands. I don't give it a lot of thought." And he said, "Oh, no, I always squeeze from the bottom to the top front." Now I started to figure out that he was serious. This was not joking. I said, "You know, we're not compatible. Why don't we just have a nice dinner and we won't see each other again." And he said, "Okay."

These two accounts point to frustration with a lack of eligible partners. The men Nadine met could not commit to a relationship that included future children. By contrast, Nicole's date knew exactly what he wanted, and she was not it.

Frequently, some women succumbed to moments of self-blame for not finding a marriage partner. The pressure to find suitable partners is not limited to straight women; gay women in this study also felt a sense of failure to find someone with whom they could both spend their life and have a child. At some level, self-doubt and self-criticism insinuated themselves into every woman's story: "Is there something wrong with me? Am I to blame? Did I refuse to compromise? Am I naive?"

The women I interviewed looked toward marriage and found themselves depressed by the dwindling odds of finding love that would lead to children. As they believed marriage to be slipping further and further out of their reach, motherhood, on the other hand, moved closer, drawn in by their desire for children. As Claudia put it, women were "running two races and losing at both." Faced with the decision to choose one or the other in order to win, women found themselves making a difficult life decision. While social norms dictated throwing the baby out with the bathwater—that is, discarding motherhood because marriage seemed unattainable—women salvaged the baby. Women shed the burden of marriage, determined to win the race to motherhood alone.

In earlier generations, this sense of being stuck most likely would have resulted in spinsterhood—in becoming the "favorite aunt," to use Joy's words. Both Joy and Claudia believed that marriage and children would happen naturally and effortlessly. Joy was caught up in enormous professional demands that limited her social life. Claudia framed her story around ambivalent relationships, even though she also had a demanding career as a clinical psychologist. Neither woman rejected marriage as a social institution; indeed, both honored it by exhausting virtually every route to marriage before electing to have a child as a single mom. Similarly, the lesbian women in this study embraced the idea of a stable partnership with the same fervor as the straight women; they, too, clung tenaciously to the ideal of motherhood even when the possibility of having a partner was remote.

Stymied in their efforts to give and get commitment, many women have abandoned the belief that marriage is an essential part of the family equation. The women in this study set marriage aside, fully realizing that as they aged motherhood could slip out of their grasp. These particular women refused to be driven to the altar by their desire for children. Reserving marriage only for love, they no longer reserved motherhood for marriage. Lori-Ann Stuart, a forty-one-year-old lesbian with a four-year-old son described how her plans to parent with her partner of three years fell apart when her partner left her: "So when we were involved, we always said, "Yeah, we'll have kids together." She left. She fell in love with someone else and left conveniently right around the time when we had had said, "OK, this is when we're going to start finding a donor, etc." After we broke up, for a couple of years I couldn't deal with the whole idea of having a kid. I just couldn't separate that we were going to have a kid together to what was I going to do now? I couldn't see myself parenting without a partner." Entering the dating market again, Lori-Ann decided that her own biological clock overrode finding a partner. She called back the close friend whom she had approached to become a known donor when she was partnered.

To become a single mother is not an inherently selfish act, because what drives parenthood is neither wholly altruistic nor completely self-absorbed. These women's decisions to become mothers reflect the broader mandates of American culture that tie motherhood to womanhood, parenthood to adulthood. Their decision is akin to that made by their partnered heterosexual peers, although it is not sheltered by social norms. Parenthood in the context of single mothers is regarded with needling suspicion by much of the rest of society, as it is a threat of the unthinkable—families without dads, the ultimate displacement.[5] No longer constrained by social pressures in the same ways as before, women are still stuck by the fear that two parents (even same-sex parents) are inherently better than one. However, at some point motherhood becomes a more compelling force than fear. As Susan Jaffe, forty-eight with a nine-year-old, described it:

> Time was running out and I began to start wrestling with the idea that I might not meet someone in time. And so I knew that by this time I really had a *strong* desire to have a child. And it didn't abate. It got increasingly larger. I knew that I would be really unhappy if I didn't have a child. I'd made a decision that

> come hell or high water, I was gonna have a child. But I hadn't decided how, even though my first choice was not to be a single parent. My first choice was to have a partner.

Many women suddenly and overwhelmingly become hungry for the motherhood they have put on the back burner up until this point.[6] As their desire for a child overtakes them, other considerations such as work, success, and the search for a suitable partner pale. Single motherhood can be the solution to the dilemma for these women.

However, the decision to go it alone is not made overnight. Joy elected an anonymous donor after deciding against the possibility of complications that might occur with a known donor. Claudia delayed applying for adoption until her age nearly disqualified her. The paths to single motherhood are diverse and involve complex decisions about timing, insemination or adoption, and racial, ethnic, religious, and ideological considerations (Hertz 2006).

ACKNOWLEDGMENTS

Reprinted from *Single by Chance, Mothers by Choice: How Women Are Choosing Parenthood without Marriage and Creating the New American Family* (New York: Oxford University Press, 2006), by permission of Oxford University Press, Inc.

NOTES

1. All women quoted in the text are identified by pseudonym, and I have changed certain details for some women to protect their identity, such as sex of child, exact occupation, and community of residence.

2. Marriage once joined families in economic and political alliances. Often love occurred outside of marriage. Love as the basis for marriage is a modern invention and far from universal. Coontz (2005) argues that it is love as the basis for marriage that has made this institution fragile. The expectations for marriage as personal fulfillment were very low throughout history; love was a threat to a properly ordered marriage.

3. While the majority of women in this study are white, 46 percent of the families are either transracial or minority. The majority of women are heterosexual; eleven are lesbian or bisexual single mothers. The majority of women had children between the ages of two and seven, though a quarter had children over eight at the time of the first interview. At the time of the first interview, 65 percent of the women (forty-two) held at least one advanced degree beyond a bachelor's, 22 percent (fourteen) held an associate's or bachelor's degree, and the remaining 14 percent of the women (nine) had completed at least high school, often with some college.

4. These are the older group in this study. A younger group graduated in the 1980s, and they followed on the path established by their older sisters.

5. David Blankenhorn (1995), founder and president of the Institute for American Values, blames women for the phenomenon of fathers becoming increasingly superfluous to family life. He urges Americans to value fatherhood once again.

6. What motivates women (or anyone for that matter) to have children is a complex question. I use this idea of "mother hunger" because it was frequently brought up in my interviews as an internal explanation for the desire for children, but I remind the reader that this group of women, those that pursued motherhood and succeeded in having children, are predisposed to this explanation. Other women decide not to pursue motherhood, but these women are not in this sample. A comparison would be necessary to answer the question of where baby hunger comes from.

REFERENCES

Blankenhorn, David. 1995. *Fatherless America: Confronting Our Most Urgent Social Problem.* New York: Basic Books.

Coontz, Stephanie. 2005. *Marriage: A History.* New York: Viking.

Garey, Anita Ilta. 1999. *Weaving Work and Motherhood.* Philadelphia: Temple University Press.

Gerson, Kathleen. 1998. "Gender and the Future of the Family: Implications for the Post-industrial Workplace." In *Challenges for Work and Family,* edited by Dana Vannoy and Paula Dubeck, 11–21. New York: Aldine de Gruyter.

Hertz, Rosanna. 1986. *More Equal than Others: Women and Men in Dual-Career Marriages.* Berkeley: University of California Press.

———. 2006. *Single by Chance, Mothers by Choice: How Women Are Choosing Parenthood without Marriage and Creating the New American Family.* New York: Oxford University Press.

Hochschild, Arlie, with Anne Machung. 1989. *The Second Shift.* New York: Viking.

———. 1997. *The Time Bind: When Work Becomes Home and Home Becomes Work.* New York: Henry Holt and Co.

Jacobs, Jerry A., and Kathleen Gerson. 2004. *The Time Divide.* Cambridge, MA: Harvard University Press.

Moen, Phyllis, ed. 2003. *It's About Time: Couples and Careers.* Ithaca, NY: Cornell University Press.

Milkie, Melissa, Marybeth Mattingly, Kei Nomaguchi, Suzanne M. Bianchi, and John P. Robinson. 2004. "The Time Squeeze: Parental Statuses and Feelings About Time with Children. *Journal of Marriage and Family* 66 (3): 739–761.

Rosen, Ruth. 2001. *The World Split Open: How the Modern Women's Movement Changed America.* New York: Penguin Books.

Schor, Juliet. 1991. *The Overworked American.* New York: Basic Books.

PART II

Work/Family Feeling Rules for Managing the Heart

CHAPTER 6

Framing Couple Time and Togetherness among American and Norwegian Professional Couples

Jeremy Schulz

In *The Second Shift* (Hochschild 1989), we meet several couples in which the two partners find themselves at odds over the man's allocation of attention and emotional energy between his work and the relationship. In one of those couples, Seth Stein voluntarily withdraws from his romantic life so that he can give all of himself to his job as an attorney. This shift of time and energy away from the relationship distresses his wife, Jessica. Eventually, she settles for a temporally and emotionally "downsized" relationship (Hochschild 1989). Stung by his retreat from family life, Jessica eventually puts herself at an emotional remove from their family life as well. But Seth is willing to pay the high cost his workaholism exacts at home, even though he has two children to raise. Despite this emotional and physical disengagement, Seth is untroubled by guilt and does not agonize over his emotional and physical unavailability.

Whether by choice or necessity, many professional men behave as Seth does, carving out sixty-hour workweeks and traveling out of town on a moment's notice. This is especially true for many of the men who work in demanding and remunerative professional jobs such as consulting, law, and finance. Lavishing their time and energies on work, many of the men who work in these "extreme jobs" let their job claim the lion's share of their time, energy, and attention (Hewlett et al. 2007).[1] As a consequence, these men give most of themselves to their work and little of themselves to their significant others. These men can end up depriving their partners of companionship and intimacy, aspects of romantic unions that many women cherish (Gerstel and Gross 1984).

Like Jessica, the women partners of professional men can easily find themselves sharing their lives with an absent partner who cannot or will not spare the time and energy needed for a healthy and fulfilling relationship. However, many women in this situation find themselves weighing this deprivation against the economic and social benefits they derive from a relationship with a successful professional man. For the woman who puts a high price on her partner's occupational achievement and earnings, it may be worth it to support him in his efforts to secure status and money through occupational achievement and the work hours that often go hand and hand with it. A less than ideal level of emotional and temporal investment on the part of a boyfriend or husband married to his job may be an acceptable price to pay for such women.

The tug-of-war between work and intimate relationships is one that can be seen through a variety of lenses by both women and men. Both parties must ascribe meaning, or "frame," the situation according to the norms and expectations relating to work and romantic companionship they find most resonant and compelling (Goffman 1959, 1974; Hochschild 2003). Framing rules also determine whether particular emotional responses are appropriate or inappropriate, given the situation at hand (Hochschild 2003). This chapter explores these acts of framing in contrasting cultural settings. It poses the question of how the men and women in heterosexual couples assess the man's career, his engagement with work, and his diversion of time and energy toward work and away from the relationship.

The frames individuals bring to these themes are not only the product of their own life circumstances; they also reflect the institutional and cultural landscapes of the societies in which they live and work. Individuals' judgments about work absorption and downsized relationships betray the presumptions about working life and couplehood that resonate most strongly in their society. The contrast between the frames favored by individuals socialized in different societies is best studied through a cross-national comparison. In this cross-national comparative study, I look at the ways in which men and women from two different countries interpret the man's commitment to his job, the demands of high-powered careers, and the importance of couple time and companionship in the life of the couple. By counterposing the framing work that occurs within quasi-matched groups of American and Norwegian couples,[2] this chapter pinpoints differences in the ways that upper-middle class American and Norwegian men and women grapple with the man's allocation of time and energy between his work and the relationship.

This cross-national comparison can reveal much about how men and women socialized in different societies differ in their approaches to both working life and intimate relationships. In terms of work culture, research has shown that American professionals have a strong attachment to occupational achievement and career success, often measured by money income. Occupational achievement has long stood at the center of the American upper-middle class life project focused on upward mobility (Lamont 1992; Bellah et al. 1985).

The upper-middle class Norwegians, living and working in a more egalitarian and less career-oriented society, experience less pressure to put occupational achievement at the center of their lives (Frønes and Brusdal 2000). As citizens of a prototypical Scandinavian social democratic state, Norwegians can count on a very generous state for myriad social services and supports, including a guaranteed year-long paid maternity/paternity leave, paid disability leave, and publicly funded daycare facilities. Moreover, there is a stark contrast between American and Norwegian policies on work hours. The Norwegian government's strictly enforced work hours regulations mandate a basic thirty-seven-and-a-half-hour workweek for state employees and employees of large private enterprises, with a maximum ten hours of overtime per week (Torp and Barth 2001). In order for nonmanagerial workers to exceed these hours, firms must obtain special dispensation and must often pay extra wages. As a consequence, the modal Norwegian worker works far fewer hours than the modal American worker, clocking almost 400 fewer work hours per year than her American counterpart (OECD 2004). Further, while only 5 percent of employed Norwegians routinely worked more than forty-eight hours per week between 2000 and 2005, 19 percent of American workers exceeded this threshold during this same span (ILO and Routledge 2007, 46–51).

The more "tender" Norwegian culture does not encourage the all-consuming dedication to work often embraced in the more performance-oriented "masculinist" work-life culture of the United States (Birkelund and Sandnes 2003; Hoftstede 1998). Cross-national studies lend support to the idea that Norwegians find the "live to work" ethic less appealing than citizens of most other countries; of all the nations in Europe, it was in Norway that the fewest people judged a successful career as a necessary ingredient of the "good life, and that the highest proportion of the population judged annual vacations an indispensable element of the good life (see Mykkeltvedt 2005). Such cultural differences also have consequences for the ways in which Americans and Norwegians approach romantic life. As Norwegian anthropologists have noted, partnered Norwegians of both genders tend to observe characteristically Scandinavian ideals concerning parity, equality, and reciprocity in their romantic relationships (Gullestad 1992; Lien, Lidén, and Vike 2001). These cultural differences between the United States and Norway make these two societies well suited to a cross-cultural comparison.

The Study and the Respondents

I conducted twenty-four qualitative interviews with six American and six Norwegian heterosexual couples in which both the men and women were between twenty-eight and thirty-eight years of age. All the American couples reside in the San Francisco Bay Area, a California metropolitan area known for its large population of high-earning professionals and high cost of living (Florida 2005). The Norwegian couples all reside in Oslo, the country's largest urban center. Like San Francisco, Oslo has a comparatively high proportion of professionals in its population and has a high cost of living in relation to other urban areas within the country.

Through a painstaking selection process, I assembled two groups of couples anchored by male partners who are "quasi-matched" with respect to their occupational and sociodemographic profiles (Crompton and Birkelund 2000). Half of the focal male respondents in each country were selected from MBA alumni lists kept by one of each country's most prominent business schools. The other half were either recruited through a specific employer, a particular global consultancy, or through referrals from other respondents. Both sets of men are of similar age, have undergone a similar education, and have traveled along very similar occupational paths, pursuing "big-time" professional success in competitive fields such as management consulting and banking (Orrange 2007). In each couple, the male partner works as a successful corporate professional in a demanding business services field. All twelve relationships were long-term committed partnerships, having endured for at least two years, whether the couples were married or cohabitating. Four couples in each country had not yet had children; the others had either one or two children under the age of five.

Two of the Norwegian men and four of the American men held extreme jobs that required in excess of sixty work hours a week.[3] Whereas four of the six Americans traveled out of town on a weekly or biweekly basis, none of the Norwegians traveled out of town more than twice a month. While the men in the two groups hold a narrow slice of jobs, and match up quite well in terms of their occupational and socioeconomic profiles, their female partners, who all work full time, hold a wider variety of positions. The American women included a dentist, a schoolteacher, and a marketing manager, while the Norwegian women included a store manager and an administrative assistant. All of the Norwegian women and all but one of the American women held full-time jobs. On average, the Norwegian women worked slightly less than their American peers, but both groups of women averaged around forty-five hours per week.

The American Women: "Absence Is a Fact of Life"

Legitimizing and normalizing framings predominated in the American women's commentaries on their partners' work commitments, the consequences of these commitments for the relationships, and their own adaptations to their partners' work-related unavailability. Doing without long stretches of couple time was a burden that some of the American women found hard to bear. While they did not wish for a temporally downsized relationship and a romantic life without much couple time, they viewed these drawbacks as a price well worth paying (Hochschild 1997). Their partners' unavailability was interpreted as an inevitable by-product of a demanding business career in which they had a large

TABLE 6.1

AMERICAN AND NORWEGIAN COUPLES' WORK HOURS

Couple	*His typical work hours (per week)*	*Her typical work hours (per week)*	*Typical gap (hours)*	*Number of children*	*His occupation*	*Her occupation*
AMERICAN COUPLES						
Carl and Kathy	60+	60+	0	0	Investment banking	Corporate accounting
Allen and Wilma	50	50	5	0	Corporate marketing	Elementary schoolteacher
Chris and Alyssa	60+	40	20	1	Management consultant	Dentist in private practice
Stan and Sara	60+	45	15	0	Management consultant	Retail executive
Victor and Nancy	60+	45	17	1	Management consultant	Marketing manager
Nick and Cara	65+	43	22	0	Management consultant	Corporate strategy consultant for retail firm
NORWEGIAN COUPLES						
Tobias and Elsa	45	45	0	0	Investment manager for bank	Investment manager for bank
Dag and Christina	45+	45	3	2	Independent entrepreneur	HR manager for engineering firm
Jørgen and Anita	50+	45	5	2	Management consultant	Marketing manager for retail firm
Matthias and Annette	55+	45	13	0	Management consultant	Public legal advisor
Gunnar and Hilde	65+	40	25	0	Principal in own business services firm	Manager of retail store
Stein and Vigdis	65	50	15	0	Management consultant	Administrative assistant for executive

stake. Many of the American women also cast their partners' working life as a legitimately all-consuming domain that had rightful claims on a large share of their partners' time, energy, and attention.

For the American women who enjoyed substantially more leisure time than their spouses, the man's success in his high-flying business career was an objective that necessarily involved long hours and frequent travel. Nancy, a corporate manager married to Victor, a management consultant, "understood" the imperative to put in many late nights at the office. She wanted to see Victor, a person she described as "driven," succeed in his high-powered management consulting job. He had "always wanted the job," she explained, so she "owed it to him" to support his efforts in the career department. And she knew well that management consulting was the kind of extreme profession where one has to "prove oneself" by putting in the "time and the sweat equity." Revisiting the period before their child, Nancy remembered that she managed to keep herself occupied during the evenings while her husband Victor toiled at the office. She explained, "I could go hang out with friends, and my parents live a few minutes away; I would exercise or read, go to bed early, I don't even know, but time flies, I could watch TV, I wasn't twiddling my thumbs. . . . I'm pretty good . . . I mean I'm fine with being on my own . . . and finding things to do." His evening absences did not constitute a "big issue" for her.

The ability to amuse oneself was also a point of pride for Cara, the younger partner of Nick, a management consultant at a high-powered firm. Because of Nick's frequent travel out of town, Cara was accustomed to very long and frequent periods of separation, some of them over five weeks. As she had worked herself in the same firm, Cara knew the lifestyle of the management consultant well. She realized she knew that she could not "realistically" expect to see Nick much during the week. But this unavailability was not a "big deal." After all, she declared, his absences during the week made her more "productive" and left her time to hang out with her friends and family.

Other American women also devalued leisure time companionship as a dispensable aspect of the relationship far less important than their partners' career success and job-related contentment. For Wilma, a successful corporate attorney married to Allen, an entrepreneur who often worked deep into the night, her husband's career success trumped her desire for leisure-time companionship. The priority for her was that her husband would do "whatever it took" to succeed in his work, even if this meant filling his evenings and weekends with work instead of spending the time with her. "If I could have my wish . . . of course I would wish that he would be home at seven o'clock if I'm home at seven o'clock, but I wouldn't say that I'm terribly unhappy about it . . . I s'pose that you would find people who would wish their partner were around at any point in time . . . for me I don't want to be married to somebody who has a job that they're not into." Wilma cared much more about Allen's willingness to work long hours than his ability to provide companionship.

Just as the American women normalized their partners' demanding jobs and their work devotion and tried to minimize the importance of couple time in their relationship, they framed their own acquiescence to this lack of togetherness as a justifiable and even rational response to the situation. This reflexive framing was particularly apparent in the commentary of Sara, a voluble woman in her early thirties with her own demanding career in the fashion world. Sara came closer than any of the other American women to acknowledging the problematic character of her partner's working life. During the entire lifetime of the relationship, from dating through marriage, her husband, Stan, had traveled extensively on out-of-town assignments. As a result, they had rarely spent more than two consecutive days together at a time. She remembered the early stages of the relationship when she barely saw him one day out of every week, and she was not even certain whether he was keeping "another family" in the Texas city where he spent the Monday through Thursday portion of the week.

Despite these weekly disappearing acts, Sara was very "patient" with Stan's absences in the beginning of the relationship. However, as the relationship progressed, she found it increasingly difficult to resign herself to occupying "second" place behind his career. Now that they were a married couple sharing a residence and planning a joint future, Stan's absences had become increasingly vexatious. She wondered whether they would ever be in a position to have children or even a dog on account of Stan's working hours and travel schedule. She dreaded her future as a "bosses' wife widowed by the company." But she had not pushed him to change jobs. She rationalized her own hesitancy to force the issue, explaining: "I'm not gonna push him [to get a more relaxed job at Sedate Corp.]. I don't know. I'm not going to ask for ridiculous things. I'm not an *irrational* person." From her perspective, by accommodating his work absorption she was not only adapting to an immutable reality, but also validating her own character as a rational person.

For the women, their partners' career aspirations, however disruptive to their relationship, deserved their deference. And yet, in their framings of both their partners' working life and their relationships, they all enlisted frames that rendered greedy jobs and downsized intimate relationships both normal and legitimate. Such was not the case with their Norwegian counterparts.

The Norwegian Women: "Why Can't We Be Together More Often?"

In the commentaries of the Norwegian women, such legitimizing and normalizing frames were nowhere to be found. Even though the Norwegian women's partners did not work as many hours or travel as much as their American counterparts, the Norwegian women assailed even relatively mild forms of work absorption and work overcommitment as unwarranted and detrimental to their quality of life. Whereas the American women characterized their partners' live-to-work approach as necessary and even virtuous, the Norwegian women refused to rationalize what they framed as an overcommitment to job and career. They expected to see their partners during the week, as well as the weekends. There was no good reason, they asserted, that their partners had to regularly work longer than "normal" hours and sacrifice their legitimate needs for frequent companionship. It was only because their partners had fallen under the sway of an illegitimately greedy institution, in their framing, that the men gave up so much of their private lives for work and shortchanged their relationship.

Annette could not understand what possessed her partner, Matthias, a management consultant, when he allowed his client work to spill over into their evenings and weekends. In her view, there was no reason why he should make himself available to clients in the evenings when he should be spending time with her and their friends. Given that he was already working over ten hours a day at the office, she declared, he "could well afford to avoid working after the official workday was over." As she explained, "He won't let go of the endless work which the workday consists of, if you know what I mean by that. He always thinks a little bit about work and takes the laptop computer home when he arrives and works for a half hour or so. And I don't like this. I think that when there is free time, which is my time in a way, then he shouldn't use it for work. If he works an hour per evening, it sets limits for what we can do together later on." Annette felt duty-bound to call him on this downright "stupid" habit. It was not fair that he sometimes worked during what was "her time."

Like Annette, Hilde did not think that her partner's job warranted so much of his time, energy, and attention. She excoriated her longtime partner, Gunnar, for his habit of fielding phone calls from clients during the evenings and weekends and his routine of disappearing for an hour or two into his home office in the evenings in the middle of a TV show or a conversation. She did not think that he should be "trading away" so much of his free time just to ensure that his numerous clients were happy all the time. In direct contrast to the American women who rationalized their partners' absences, Hilde refused to justify the parallel life she led in her spare time. She bemoaned the fact that "our [private] lives are independent of each other," charging that "this arrangement doesn't always work out so well." If Gunnar had worked less during evenings and weekends, she argued, then "we could have escaped to the mountains, attended cultural events, seen friends together, or gone to various restaurants and cafés around Oslo." Like Annette, she found it galling and distressing when Gunnar vanished into his home office in the evenings, claiming that he should be working since they weren't doing "anything special" together. In her eyes, it was unreasonable of him to neglect her legitimate desire for evening companionship. "He has to remember that he doesn't live alone. He must remind himself that there is another person who also would like to spend time with him, and who in a way needs some social and physical contact with him, who needs predictability in daily life, especially during the weekends." Instead of minimizing or suppressing her own claims on her partner's time and attention, as the American women do, Hilde framed her desire for companionship as entirely legitimate.[4]

The three Norwegian women who enjoyed a "reasonable" amount of companionship expressed gratitude for the couple time they had at their disposal. According to Anita, whose husband Jørgen had chosen to work for a Scandinavian management consultancy that did not require sixty-hour workweeks, a matching work schedule served as one of the primary foundations for a well-functioning partnership and a healthy family life. Anita was glad that her husband got to work "reasonable" hours and had no trouble "setting aside" enough time to spend with her and their two children. It was important for her that he return home before six o'clock in the evening and eat dinner with the family most nights of the week. It would be "inappropriate," she declared, if she got to see him for only an hour every night.

Whereas the American women framed their partners' twelve-hour workdays and frequent out-of-town travel as a "fact of life" to which they had to adapt, the Norwegian women perceived these hours as unreasonable infringements on their partners' private lives and, by extension, their own private lives. They could not bring themselves to represent the emotionally and temporally downsized relationships as entirely legitimate. This was especially true in regard to the weekday evenings. In the eyes of the Norwegian women, these blocks of time were meant for couple-oriented activities rather than work.

The American Men: "She Should Get Used to It" and "She's Getting a Lot Out of It"

The American men echoed their partners in carrying out framing work designed to normalize and legitimize their immersion in their working lives and their inattentiveness to their partners' desire for companionship and couple time. Like the American women, they represented their greedy working lives and robust work ethics as facts of life to which their partners had to adapt. Nick, the management consultant who rarely saw his partner, Cara, for more than a weekend at a time, complained that Cara had made "unwarranted" requests for him to reduce his work hours. He was particularly taken aback by these requests because she had worked in the same firm herself. It should have been obvious to her, he argued, that his success as a consultant was contingent on his ability to travel and work long hours without her interference. After a few "discussions," he had gotten her to realize that he was not about to "fuck up the work for the next day" by leaving the office before he had completed his work. A weekend-based relationship, he felt, "should be enough for her." Victor, another consultant, manifested the same kind of intransigence over his work hours. Explaining the "facts of life" to his wife with respect to his work responsibilities as a management consultant, he made it clear that he could not simply cut down his hours because "this [effort] is what the job calls for and this is what it takes to do the job."

The American men also expended a great deal of effort rationalizing their partners' acceptance of their work absorption and frequent absences. Imputing a pragmatic framing to their partners, these men explained that the women were invested in their careers, both for altruistic and selfish reasons. As a result, they claimed, the women wisely overlooked the deficiencies of their temporally downsized relationships and focused on the many advantages of a relationship the men likened to an exchange or deal.

These legitimizing frames concerned the women's purported interest in seeing their partners excel in their demanding, long-hours occupations, as well as the futility of trying to alter the men's relationships with their work. Stan, the management consultant who worked eighty-hour weeks and characterized himself as a "burner," knew that his partner, Sara, was uneasy with his work absorption and his open-ended commitment of time and energy to his work and career. In his view, however, Sara was a "pragmatic person" who had married him knowing full well that he would never relinquish his devotional attachment to work and career. Well acquainted with this facet of his personality, she had "come to terms" with her role as the "best other thing" in his life: "[In the beginning of our relationship] she quickly understood that, okay, I'm just that way. [Working really hard] is something I have to do. So, what she was thinking was, 'I'm not going to make him choose between me and the job. I'm just going to try my best to be the other thing in his life.'" Moreover, in Stan's eyes, Sara had a stake in his own high-flying business career. His rise in the business world gave them a level of financial security and affluence that "she enjoyed every bit as much" as he did. For Sara, he indicated, the scarcity of companionship was a relatively small price to pay in view of these tangible benefits.

For the American men, it was only "sensible" for their partners to swallow their discontent with the men's work hours and job commitment. One of the clearest examples of this normalizing framing surfaced in the comments of Carl, an American investment banker married to an accountant. His perspective was that Kathy, his wife, wanted to see him succeed in his remunerative line of work, both for his sake and for her own sake. Moreover, she knew "what she was getting into" when she married him several years into this demanding banking career.

In the case of Victor, a management consultant with a baby, it was the bargaining frame that took center stage in his commentary. In Victor's eyes, his wife was willing to trade companionship during the week for a higher standard of living for them and their child. She had a stake in his career and knew what the family "stood to lose" if he gave up his lucrative but demanding management consultant position. Characterizing his wife, Nancy, as a woman primarily concerned with the economic well-being of the family unit, he spoke of the economic exigencies they faced as a couple with a young child to support and the importance of a large paycheck: "We're at a point where she's great, she definitely understands the lifestyle and, you know, getting a good salary is very important to the family. Now she realizes that if I take a more relaxed job I'll be taking a 30 percent pay cut. So, even if I can get home by sixty-thirty in the evening, we'll have less money. Now she's like, 'hah, maybe it's worth it for him to stay.'"

Chris, another American management consultant, framed his partner's interest in his career as a matter of her own desire for "more flexibility" in her life. By allowing him to work "whenever" the occasion demanded, he pointed out, his wife put herself in an economic position where she could afford to work less herself. Her acceptance of the "deal" between them was thus a matter of simple self-interest, as well as a recognition of his own devotional approach to work. As he put it: "My wife wanted to only work four or three days in a row, so part of the deal was, 'Okay, my husband will have the high-powered job, he'll get paid a lot and he'll have to work when he'll have to work. And I'll get to live a more flexible life that I want.'" Like the other American men, Chris rationalized his partner's accommodating stance toward his own work absorption, underscoring her pragmatism as well as her own self-interest.

The Norwegian Men: "I Should Be Spending More Time with Her"

In the narratives of the Norwegian men, the topics of work, career, and companionship were framed in dramatically different terms. Unlike their American counterparts, they upheld the legitimacy of their partners' complaints about their work habits and their pleas for more couple time. None of the Norwegian men defended the "weekend-only" relationship that figured prominently as a benchmark in the narratives of the American men, particularly those who had worked in management consulting. None of the Norwegian men attempted to legitimate their pursuit of big-time career success as an enterprise that merited their partners' full commitment and support. Further, the three Norwegian men who did work relatively long hours made little effort to rationalize these long hours as a fact of life to which the women should adapt.

Even when they worked in demanding jobs, the Norwegian men expressed a sensitivity to their partners' desire for companionship and couple time. Matthias, a Norwegian management consultant, found his long work hours "frustrating" because they did not allow him enough time with his partner. He appreciated her desire for more companionship in the relationship and respected her "legitimate" wish to feel "prioritized" and to "feel more important than my work." Stein, another management consultant, felt that his job, which required him to work until nine or ten in the evening, "robbed" his girlfriend of the daily couple time that she had every right to want: "I am living with a girl and she is sitting at home waiting for me a lot because she is finished at 4:00 P.M., so that takes a lot of energy from both of us and I do not feel like I can satisfy her on that dimension." His inability to provide sufficient companionship bothered him.[5]

Even Gunnar, perhaps the most work-centered of all the Norwegian men I interviewed, granted the legitimacy of Hilde's complaints about his very long working hours and his constant absorption in his work. He believed that she had "every right" to complain about his attentiveness to his clients and his neglect of her own companionship needs.

For those Norwegian men who had chosen to work at the most demanding jobs, there was an intense concern over the potential harm that their work schedules could inflict on the relationship. The fragility of relationships weakened by the man's unavailability was a common theme in the narratives of the Norwegian men. Stein, for example, worried that he was endangering his relationship because he could not afford to spend any time with his partner during weekday evenings. Matthias indicated that one of his consultant friends was having trouble in his relationship because of his job. His friend's work absorption and long hours had put his relationship under tremendous strain and the relationship "hung by a thread." Unlike the American men, several of the Norwegian men had struck "deals" concerning their work hours and travel patterns with their partners ensuring that they could enjoy several hours of couple time most workdays. Jørgen, for example, had made an agreement with his wife early on in the relationship never to work more than fifty hours per week on a regular basis and to come home by 5:30 in the evening unless there was a crisis at work. This agreement, he recounted, served as the "basis" of their relationship. After all, denying his wife the chance to see him for at least "an hour per day" simply wasn't "fair."

From these interviews we can see that the Norwegian men avoided the normalizing and legitimizing frames enlisted by their American counterparts. None of the Norwegian men sought to explain why their partners were right to overlook their work absorption and let them focus on building high-flying careers in demanding fields. Despite their own high-flying business careers, these men did not frame working life as a legitimately greedy institution or their career success as an overriding imperative trumping their partners' desire for companionship. Instead, they framed their partners' expectations about companionship and togetherness as deserving their consideration. Those men who had trouble fulfilling these expectations expressed considerable guilt over what appeared to them, upon reflection, as an unwarranted level of work absorption.

Conclusion

As evidenced by the contrasting framings used by both men and women in the two countries, work absorption, frequent absences, and downsized intimate relationships meant quite different things to the American men and women as compared with their Norwegian counterparts. Despite everything that the American and Norwegian couples shared in terms of their life circumstances, they attributed quite different meanings to a mode of life where work consumed the bulk of the men's time, energy, and attention. When comparing the frames employed by the two groups of couples, what immediately stands out is the way in which, in each national case, the men's and women's interlocking framings of oversized work commitments complemented each other.

Both the American men and the American women shared the same understanding of work as legitimately demanding in terms of the man's time, energy, and attention. According to the tacit contract between the American men and women, the man's work and career took precedence over the woman's need for companionship. Among the Americans, both women and men framed the man's career as a legitimately greedy enterprise deserving a large amount of time and energy. At the same time, they viewed the couple's joint leisure time as more of a luxury than a necessity. The American men consistently defended work's virtual monopoly over their time and energy while downplaying the effects of their work absorption on their relationship. In making sense of this situation from their partners' perspective, the men repeatedly underscored their partners' interest in seeing them succeed in the lucrative corporate world. The same legitimizing framing of work as an intrinsically greedy institution also predominated among the American women. The American women underlined the legitimacy of their partners' extreme investment in his work and career, justifying the amount of time and energy the men expended in pursuit of this success as necessary while minimizing the drawbacks of their partners' long hours and frequent absences and shrugging off the lack of companionship as an acceptable price to pay.

The tacit contract that bound together the Norwegian men and women did not give the same precedence to the man's desire for career success versus the woman's need for companionship. Both the Norwegian men and the Norwegian women upheld the common presumption that certain parts of the day and week should be off-limits to work. When the Norwegian men did work long hours or travel frequently, they conceded that their partners were being cheated of time and companionship to which the women were entitled. With a vigor unmatched by their American counterparts, the Norwegian women defended their right to couple time in the evenings and weekends, defining their partners' evenings and weekends as their own time. For them, something was very wrong with the relationship and with their partners' priorities if the parameters of their companionship became defined by the man's work absorption.

In conclusion, the responses of women and men to the near-monopoly of work on the man's time and energy are necessarily framed against the backdrop of culturally specific expectations about work and couplehood. Whatever tensions the couple experiences between the man's work absorption and the woman's desire for companionship, these tensions reflect not only the structure of the work-family situation, but also the cultural frameworks employed to make sense of this situation. Both women and men rely on these cultural frameworks in interpreting the man's investment in his work and the relationship.

By showing how these frameworks vary across two different nations and societies, this chapter calls attention to their role in the shaping of the work/family nexus.

NOTES

1. Hewlett defines an "extreme" job as one in which the person must work under considerable pressure to meet demanding deadlines. Most extreme jobs require over sixty hours of work on a regular basis, as well as extensive and frequent travel. However, the extreme jobs to which Hewlett refers also pay much higher salaries than typical jobs and are concentrated in the lucrative business services and technology sectors. See Hewlett et al. (2007) for a more extensive discussion.

2. This study relies on the method of the controlled comparison, a kind of multisite case study in which groups of "matched" respondents are contrasted with one another. Such research designs have been used to great effect to identify individual-level differences attributable to national-societal context (Crompton and Birkelund 2000; Maxwell 1996; Lamont 1992).

3. Half of the six Norwegian men did work substantially fewer hours than their American counterparts, a disparity that makes the gap in frames all the more striking. Of the three Norwegian men who worked substantially over fifty hours per week, two men (Stein and Matthias) worked for international firms that did not observe the Norwegian work hours law (*Arbeidsmiljøloven*) particularly closely. The Norwegian firms, by contrast, took care to observe the work-hours restrictions mandated by the Norwegian Work Environment Act [*Arbeidsmiljøloven*]. This law defines "normal working hours" as no more than forty hours per seven-day period. This ceiling may be raised to forty-eight hours during a seven-day period, but only if both the employer and employee consent in writing to this arrangement. Overtime work beyond this limit is only legal in cases where the employer specifies an "exceptional and time-limited need for it." Overtime work hours are also capped at ten hours per week, and any overtime hours must be compensated at a higher than normal rate. Gunnar, the Norwegian man who worked the longest hours, worked as a principal at his own firm, so he was entirely exempt from these regulations.

4. Unlike her American peers, Hilde had not shied away from confrontation with Gunnar over his work habits and work absorption. She had gotten the message across to him that it was "not particularly wise" of him to cut their evening conversations and meals short in order to resume his work. She was confident that the message had gotten across to him thanks to her frankness on the subject.

5. Stein took this grievance to heart quite quickly and gave up his demanding consulting job for a more relaxed position at a large Norwegian company. He was happy that his new job gave him more time for his family and enabled him to honor his wife's desire for more companionship.

REFERENCES

Bellah, Robert, Richard Madsen, William M. Sullivan, Ann Swidler, and Steven M. Tipton. 1985. *Habits of the Heart: Individualism and Commitment in American Life.* Berkeley: University of California Press.

Birkelund, Gunn Elisabeth, and Toril Sandnes. 2003. "Paradoxes of Welfare States and Equal Opportunities: Gender and Managerial Power in Norway and the USA." In *Comparative Social Research Vol. 21: Comparative Studies of Culture and Power*, ed. Fredrik Engelstad, 203–242. Amsterdam: Elsevier.

Crompton, Rosemary, and Gunn Elisabeth Birkelund. 2000. "Employment and Caring for British and Norwegian Bankers." *Work, Employment, and Society* 14:331–351.

Florida, Richard. 2005. *Cities and the Creative Class.* New York: Routledge.

Frønes, Ivar, and Ragnhild Brusdal. 2000. *På sporet av den nye tid: Kulturelle varsler for en nær fremtid.* Bergen, Norway: Fagbokforlaget.

Gerstel, Namoi, and Harriet Gross. 1984. *Commuter Marriage.* New York: Guilford Press.

Goffman, Erving. 1959. *The Presentation of Self in Everyday Life.* Garden City, NY: Doubleday.

———. 1974. *Frame Analysis: An Essay on the Organization of Everyday Experience.* New York: Harper and Row.

Gullestad, Marianne. 1992. *The Art of Social Relations: Essays on Culture, Social Action, and Everyday Life in Modern Norway.* Oslo: Scandinavian University Press.

Hewlett, Cynthia, Carolyn Buck Luce, Sandra Southwell, and Linda Bernstein. 2007. "Seduction and Risk: The Emergence of Extreme Jobs." New York: Center for Work-Life Policy.

Hochschild, Arlie Russell, with Anne Machung. 1989. *The Second Shift: Working Parents and the Revolution at Home.* New York: Viking.

———. 1997. *The Time Bind: When Work Becomes Home and Home Becomes Work.* New York: Metropolitan Books.

———. 2003. *The Commercialization of Intimate Life: Notes From Home and Work.* Berkeley: University of California Press.

Hofstede, Geert. 1998. *Masculinity and Femininity: The Taboo Dimensions of National Cultures.* Thousand Oaks, CA: Sage Publications.

Lamont, Michele. 1992. *Money, Morals, and Manners: The Culture of the American and French Upper Middle Classes.* Chicago: University of Chicago Press.

Lien, Marianne, Hilde Lidén, and Halvard Vike. 2001. *Likhetens Paradokser: Antropologiske undersøkelser i det moderne Norge.* Oslo, Norway: Universitetsforlaget.

Maxwell, Joseph. 1996. *Qualitative Research Design: An Interactive Approach.* Thousand Oaks, CA: Sage Publications.

Moen, Phyllis, and Patricia Roehling. 2005. *The Career Mystique: Cracks in the American Dream.* Lanham, MD: Rowman and Littlefield.

Mykkeltvedt, Alette Gilhus. 2005. "Nordmenn vil nyte, europeere vil yte." Oslo: Norsk samfunnsvitenskapelige datatjeneste.

OECD. (2004). "Employment Outlook." Paris.

Orrange, Robert M. 2007. *Work, Family, and Leisure: Uncertainty in a Risk Society.* Lanham, MD: Rowman and Littlefield.

Torp, Hege, and Erling Barth. 2001. "Actual and Preferred Working Time: Regulations, Incentives and the Debate on Working Time in Norway." Oslo: Institute for Social Research.

Williams, Robin, Jr. 1964. *American Society: A Sociological Interpretation.* New York: Knopf.

CHAPTER 7

Love and Gratitude

SINGLE MOTHERS TALK ABOUT MEN'S CONTRIBUTIONS TO THE SECOND SHIFT

Margaret K. Nelson

In a classic piece reconsidering material taken from *The Second Shift*, Arlie Russell Hochschild (2003, 116) analyzes the economies of gratitude that emerge within the marital relationship. In doing so she traces gratitude to three sources: to current ideas about honor that derive from a *moral* frame of reference (when we ask, "How lucky am I compared to what the cultural code leads me to expect?");[1] to ideas about current realities that derive from a *pragmatic* frame of reference (when we ask, "How lucky am I compared to what is available to me?"); and to precedents that derive from a *historical* frame of reference (when we ask, "How lucky am I compared to people of my kind in the past?"). Following in a long tradition of anthropology and sociology (e.g., Mauss 1954), Hochschild reminds us that a gift is not a gift is not a gift, but rather it is a "profoundly social affair" whose evaluation depends on the particular social frames of reference applied to it.

Over the past ten years or so, as I have thought about a variety of different issues having to do with the livelihood strategies of single mothers, I have been particularly intrigued by notions similar to these—notions surrounding gift-giving (and gift-receiving), gratitude, and reciprocity. The lives of single mothers are almost invariably characterized by enormous constraint; they thus seem to be an especially appropriate setting in which to see how individuals balance their very real needs for help (of all kinds) from others with attempts to maintain a culturally appropriate response to the world.[2] Moreover, many single mothers are in transition—leaving one relationship with a partner and looking for a new relationship with another. Although some single mothers might prefer to remain single (or find another woman as their partner), recent research suggests that "a majority of unmarried women, including disadvantaged single and cohabiting mothers, value marriage as a personal goal" (Lichter, Batson, and Brown 2004, 2). Single motherhood thus is an appropriate site in which to veer off from the direction Hochschild took of exploring different economies of exchange within the marital relationship over time to that of investigating how a broader trajectory of (romantic) relationships shapes the construction of gifts.

In this chapter, then, I'm going to put on new shoes to retread some ground I've walked before (Nelson 2004) in order to locate issues of relationships of single mothers with the men in their lives within the framework of gifts, gratitude, and exchange. At the broadest level, I ask this question: In what contexts and in what kind of exchanges is gratitude toward men evoked? More specifically, I ask: How does the frame of reference applied to men's actions shift as a relationship passes through different stages? Ideally, to answer these questions I would have longitudinal data, following individual women through the various stages of their relationships with men. Instead, I consider the comments that a number of different women each make at one point in time about men with whom they have been—or are currently—involved. Some women compare and contrast several different men in their lives; some focus only on a current or former partner. In analyzing the trajectory of relationships I piece together these different accounts of women's attitudes—toward the men with whom they lived (however briefly) prior to spending some time as a single mother, toward men they are dating, and toward men with whom they are cohabiting. At the end of the chapter, I speculate on what might happen in the future if they marry these men. Throughout the discussion I focus (albeit not exclusively) on issues of child care and housework.

A note about gratitude. Gratitude has many synonyms: gratefulness, appreciation, thankfulness, thanks, acknowledgment, recognition, obligation, beholdenness, giving thanks, and thanksgiving. Its antonyms include ingratitude, ungratefulness, thanklessness, and unthankfulness. Somewhere between the two—or perhaps off to the side—lies a stance that we could call "taking for granted." That is, the absence of "gratitude" might not always mean that one is "ungrateful," but rather that one assumes the "gesture" as being appropriate but not creating thankfulness or an attitude of being beholden. As Hochschild (2003, 105) reminds us, "we appreciate many acts and objects that we take for granted. But we feel grateful for what seems to us extra. . . . Gratitude involves warmth, thankfulness, and a desire to return the favor." Thus, "gratitude adds to 'thanks' the feeling of an 'intense positive relationship with another person.'"

Conflicts in relationships arise when the two parties to an exchange have different stances toward an action: what one party believes is a gift is not acknowledged as such by another, is dismissed as a routine gesture and taken for granted, or is even rejected as being inappropriate or insufficient. As we all know from our personal lives—as well as from our scholarly ones—interpersonal exchange is a minefield of competing interpretations and misunderstandings.

In what follows, I explore different stages of the relationships single women have with the men in their lives. I focus on how actions are perceived by only one party—the women I interviewed. I suggest that attitudes toward "gifts" are interdependent with the trajectory of relationships themselves and leave open the possibility of conflict at every stage.

Methods

I draw on data collected in interviews with a snowball sample of approximately seventy single mothers with at least one child under the age of eighteen in the state of Vermont.[3] As is the case elsewhere, Vermont's families headed by women are highly likely to be poor; the women in this study were no exception: their median family income (at $21,782) stood almost precisely at the level of single mothers in the state as a whole ($21,125). In other ways, too, the sample is quite representative of single mothers in Vermont. At the time of the interviews, the women included in this study ranged in age from nineteen to forty-five, with an average age of thirty-five (three years younger than the state average for single mothers). Almost two-thirds of the women had previously been married (although not in all cases to the father of their child or children) as is true of 71 percent of single mothers in Vermont. All are white. Most of the previously married women became single as the result of divorce or separation; two women were widows. Among those who had previously lived with the father of their children (whether married or not), at the time of the interviews the women had been living on their own for an average of slightly over four years. The vast majority of the women were interested in having relationships with men and in cementing these relationships in remarriage or in some other form of stable partnership.[4]

Assessing Men's Gifts at Different Moments in Time

The Men They Leave Behind

If there is a generalization that can be made about how the women talk about the men they left behind (or who left them behind) it is this: gratitude is no part of that talk—unless it is gratitude to the men for having left them or for having allowed them to leave without additional harm. Not surprisingly, given that these relationships "failed," the women's accounts are full of bitterness: whatever economies of exchange had prevailed in these relationships are now viewed as being lopsided and unfair.[5] Among those who made reference to the gender division of labor within the home as at least one of the reasons why the relationship dissolved—and there were many women who did so—the specifics are interesting.[6]

Some women believed they had agreed to a relatively traditional division of labor in which she would care for the children and the home and he would support them, but that even within this arrangement he expected her to do too much of the work at home. A woman I will call Stephanie Miller provides one such case.[7] Although she acknowledges that her ex-husband had not originally wanted this kind of traditional division of labor, she is also angry because he accepted it but then, to her way of thinking at least, left way too much of the domestic work on her plate. "The kind of deal [from his point of view] was that I had to do everything with the kids if I got to be home with the kids. I put them to bed and I got them to school and just managed all of the different details of life with little kids that you have to keep track of. And [I] did all of the housework pretty much, and all of the cooking and cleaning and that was the only way it worked for him."

Other women had different arrangements with their male partners. Most of the women had worked outside the home. In these cases, the women's complaints often center on the fact that even though both partners were responsible for bringing in income, the women were left with what they viewed as being too much of the domestic work. Vanessa Menard provides one example of this stance. Speaking bitterly, she described the problems she perceived in her marriage. "I was doing a whole lot of the work. For example, [I would] pick up our daughter after day care . . . and then I would be the one to buy the groceries on the way home. . . . So then I would get home, make dinner while he was spending time with our daughter, usually just watching the TV, but I'd also get home, and I would know that it was at least two hours since he had gotten home, and there was still dirty dishes in the sink, and the dishwasher needed to be unloaded, or he wasn't inclined to start dinner at all, he was working on his hobbies or something."

Stephanie wanted a "traditional" division of labor, but she wanted it with a modern twist; she resented doing "pretty much" all the housework. Vanessa wanted a more equal division of labor (because she too was earning money outside the home); she resented her husband because he didn't do as much as she did. In retrospect, however, it appears that both women apply similar pragmatic codes: both women believed there must be something "better" out there than what they had, and they found the notion of living on their own to be a preferable alternative. And at that historical moment they believed that they *could* live on their own even if some slight stigma remained attached to being divorced in the rural area in which they lived. Hence, perhaps to their husbands' surprise, each of these women "refused" to feel grateful for what they were getting, and each of these women ultimately walked out of her marriage.

The Men They Date

Single mothers (as Stephanie and Vanessa both became) are deeply involved in a broad range of relationships with men. Depending on the women's evaluation of the "future" of the relationship, I classify them into two "ideal" types.

An Open Exchange in Nonromantic Relationships. Single mothers report having a series of exchange relationships with men in which they openly acknowledge that they are uninterested in pursuing the emotional or romantic side of the relationship but remain "attached" because the arrangement fulfills a real material need in their lives.[8] In these cases, the women may well be searching for someone who will offer more by way of emotional or romantic satisfaction even as they settle, temporarily, for what they have. And the women may have initially thought that these particular men would fill the bill of romance. At the time, however, the women view the men as being insufficient for the long haul.

Melissa Henry, for example, was quite clear that she did not think the relationship with her current boyfriend was going to move into anything more permanent; she said that she wasn't deeply "in love" with him and she insisted that she did not want to get married just for security: "I did it for that reason the first time." Even so, Melissa's boyfriend played a significant role in her life, and she was happy to have him continue to do so, at least for the time being. Most important, he repaired her car for her so that she just had to "pay parts," and when her car went on the blink (a major calamity for this mother of four young sons who lives a good twenty miles from her place of employment), he lent his. Melissa was not explicit about what she gave in return for her boyfriend's assistance with her car, but probing this question in other interviews revealed that sex was often at stake. Joan Meyer explained that she was staying in a relationship that upset her and her children "because of financial needs, because I cannot swing it on my own." She then commented that she had found someone to whom she was more attracted, and so she was looking forward to ending the relationship with her current boyfriend. However, she added that she had decided she would stay in the current relationship "until the end of next week so I can have help finishing paying off my kids' bikes." Joan was explicit about the exchange in which she was participating. On her part, she said, she felt obligated to be sexually available in return for the favors he did. "Every time he does something around here I feel that I owe him at least in sexual [ways]. That is what I perceive." And she described a terrible moment when he had insisted on a sexual response from her: "And an example of that is this last weekend I was really, really sick . . . and he still tried [to have sex], and it was like I had my head in a bucket, and we had a tent full of kids."

As the women describe these relationships, it is quite clear (whether or not they enjoy the sex) that because they are not "in love" they are free to assess these relationships with respect to simple economies of balanced exchange; gratitude thus plays no significant role in their assessment of give and take. The women apply a cultural/moral code that says that you pay your way (with whatever you have at hand); a pragmatic code (I'm glad this is available but there might well be other guys out there with whom I could make a similar kind of exchange; this will do until love comes along); and perhaps even a historical code (I might be lucky insofar as I can use sex as a bargaining chip without being seen as a prostitute, which very well might not have been the case some years ago). Having done so, they find no reason to be especially grateful: the men's contributions—the money they offer to help pay for the kids' bikes, the work they do around the home or with their cars—are welcome and even valued for their intrinsic worth, but they are *not* perceived as being gifts within the context of their perception of the relationship; the "intense positive relationship with another person" is missing. Of course it is quite possible that at an earlier stage in the relationship—when (or if) they thought this *was* the man for them—they might have been more grateful; if they change their minds again, gratitude might re-emerge. But when relationships stand outside of love (and I examine love in a moment), women want to believe that they are paying their own way and that they are not beholden.

As a side note, I might add that it often appears that the men they are dating on these terms are quite probably doing considerably *less* than their husbands (or former partners) did: Melissa's "boyfriend" does not make an economic contribution to her home beyond helping out with car repair; Joan's boyfriend does make an economic contribution, but it is piddling when compared to what her husband contributed when they were still living together. But these boyfriends don't generate bitterness (ingratitude) for not doing more; rather there is simple acceptance of what they do offer and a simple calculation that the women have made ample, and even, returns. In short, the "cultural/moral" code of dating without love (from a single mother's point of view) asks little more than a fair exchange of goods and services. When it becomes too costly—if he demands more than she is willing to give, for example—or when she can find a better deal elsewhere, she might very well move on.

Gratitude and Love. In relationships which, for simplicity's sake, I call "love affairs," the women talk very differently about the men in their lives and about the contributions those men make toward their well-being. In these cases, because they construct the relationship differently, they construct men's gestures of support differently; the two constructions go hand in hand. In this new understanding, rather than being disparaged or taken as part of an even exchange, the women view men's contributions to the household economy as highly appreciated gifts of love.

Valerie Ramsey provides a good example. When asked whether her new boyfriend helped out around the house, she said, "When he's here, he will do the dishes. He helps me clean up, and he mows the lawn. He just started that. And I mean, we're just dating! And he will clean up after I cook. Up at his place, he cooks. He does everything." Similarly, Jessica Walsh, comparing her boyfriend to her ex-husband, said with enthusiasm: "I'm not used to someone helping me. . . . And it's like when he does even the dishes, it's like, wow, I've never had someone do my dishes."

In an earlier discussion of these relationships (Nelson 2004), I offered several explanations for why women in "romantic" relationships might want to view men's gestures as gifts for which they adopt the stance of gratitude rather than an obligation to reciprocate. I suggested that women have pragmatic or utilitarian reasons for this perception: by viewing a gesture as a "gift" (like the flowers of a romantic relationship), a woman can be grateful without the requirement of balanced reciprocity. Indeed, neither Valerie nor Jessica suggested that they became obligated to offer the same kind of help that they received from their boyfriends; as single women with burdensome lives, they had urgent reasons for wanting to avoid this kind of reciprocal obligation. I suggested as well that romance has a special allure for women whose everyday lives are marked by the constant calculations of costs and benefits; relationships that they can remove from the demands of daily life might have particular appeal. Finally, I suggested that these options are available to the women *because* they can use a narrative of love to explain why tit-for-tat reciprocity is not required. This narrative reads something like this: if I'm in love, the sex can't be for exchange; therefore, when he does something nice and helpful for me, it's not part of an exchange; it's a freely given gift for which I am grateful (and it comes over and above—or is an element within—the exchange of love and sex in which we both share equally enjoyably). That is, if the women perceive men's gestures as gifts of love, returning the love is sufficient. In short, although the women have practical reasons for wanting to make a shift from balanced exchange to gratitude for a welcome gift, the shift depends on the application of a new cultural code that relies on "romance" and the sentiment of "love." Thus a woman who said that the man to whom she was married never did enough of the housework or was insufficiently involved with his child, now is "grateful" for a man who does the dishes when he visits or plays with the children when he comes to take her out on a date; a woman who had previously made exchanges with a man for car repair now regards another man's help of the same kind as a welcome indication of love. Because it comes *from* love and emerges from his concern, she might feel grateful, but she does not hold herself responsible for returning the "gift." Gifts of love are at the discretion of the giver. The women believe it is wrong to accept the gifts of love if they cannot return the love. Hence, when they don't love, they do interpret men's gestures as requiring exchange.

In all likelihood it might also be the case that the women are applying a new pragmatic code. Experience with "other" men have taught at least some of these women that there's plenty of fish in the sea to be dated and plenty of fish who can repair their cars. But, perhaps, there may not be quite so many fish who can offer *more* than "security" or routine exchanges—fish who can actually make their heartstrings throb. So they consider themselves "lucky" after assessing the alternatives. And they may also be applying a historical code, through which they feel especially lucky that modern life makes available men willing to cook, mow a lawn, or even do the dishes for his girlfriend and play with her children. (Once again, the men are probably doing less than the ex did, but in these cases "less is more.")

Cohabitation

Eventually, in some of these cases of "love," a couple decides to live together, thus taking the next step toward making the relationship something more permanent. At least in the initial moments of this "in-between state" the man who is cohabiting may be regarded by the woman as something like a guest in her home; in this case he can easily earn gratitude for the things he does around the house. Think about it: When guests do little things, we feel grateful. We might hope that the guest will take off the sheets and dump them in the laundry room, and we are grateful when she does that, but we really don't expect her to wash those sheets and remake the bed for the next guest.

Indeed, one respondent, Jackie Ferland, made it clear that as long as her fiancé was "just" cohabiting with her, in her home, she still regarded him as a guest of sorts and constructed his gestures as "help" for which she was grateful.[9] When asked whether he helped out with routine tasks, she said, "I usually cook; he helps clean and [he helps do the] grocery shopping. I usually do most of it, but he does some of that, too. Yard work we both do. It's my—I own the house, so I usually take care of repairs and things and he helps with the yard work." And she noted that though he had a fine relationship with her children and was "somewhat helpful" with their care, "it's very clear to us both that they're not his kids, so most of the burden for their care, their discipline, their nurturing, everything is my own, on my shoulders." Similarly, Amy Phelps said of her fiancé who had moved in to live with her, "He will [help out with the kids] with transportation. He's really not into—the thing that we find with steps is that he's not into discipline. That really comes from me, and I think that's where it needs to come. But he definitely [helps with] transportation or whatever."

In this "guest" status (which goes one step beyond dating in terms of expectations), it appears that it is still relatively easy for men to be "wonderful." Stephanie (who had done "pretty much" all the housework in her relationship with her ex) describes her new boyfriend's contributions to her home with enormous delight—and gratitude. "A lot of what [he does that] I always expected a father would [do] was to come home and check in if I need any help with anything and then go to play with the kids for awhile [and] give me a little break in the day, too."

In short, there are honeymoon periods of cohabitation (and maybe the only honeymoon a single mother can expect to have); as long as the kids and the house are still *hers*, his gestures of support can be regarded as gifts.[10] That is, cohabitation doesn't immediately or entirely shift the cultural frame of reference. Yet things do have to change: cohabitation is no longer *sheer* romance (there are prosaic realities of life together to manage), even if it is not quite "marriage" either (they may still have separate responsibilities, separate finances). Over time, one might imagine, that more and more of his gestures are taken for granted as she comes to expect more from him. Indeed, the hesitations of both Jackie ("It's my—I own the house so . . .") and Amy ("He's really not into—the thing that we find with steps . . .") suggest that change may be in the wind. Jackie offers home ownership as an explanation for why her fiancé doesn't do more work there, but she doesn't quite want to say that it is just her house and hers alone. Amy offers the soon-to-be stepparent relationship as a reason for her fiancé's lack of involvement in discipline, and thus she cuts herself off from saying that this is a character attribute on his part. Three months later, these two women might not have been editing themselves so closely.

As Relationships Evolve

Unfortunately, because my research was focused on single mothers, with the exception of one woman to whom I'll turn in a moment, I didn't follow the women who were dating or cohabiting into marriage. From other people's research, however, we do know that second marriages are even less stable than first marriages, even though the division of labor (and the distribution of power) may be more egalitarian in these relationships and there may be no more conflict than in first marriages (Coleman, Ganong, and Fine 2000, 1291; Coltrane 2000, 1222; MacDonald and DeMaris 1995).[11]

As I've thought about these data that document the instability of second marriages, I've wondered this: is a man's contribution to the domestic work relevant to this instability and, if so, precisely how and why? Furthermore, when does a man move from being boyfriend who charms the children and their mother, cohabitant who is helpful in limited ways, to stepfather who might not be good enough at discipline and now "merely" plays with the children before dinner? That is, how, when, and why do people decide that the honeymoon is over and that a new standard should be applied? Asking this question is, of course, another way of asking at what point, and for what reasons, gestures of "assistance" in the household cease to be an occasion for gratitude and come to be taken for granted—or maybe even seen as being insufficient contributions to the household dynamics.

Of course, as some of the comments above suggested, the seeds of a taken-for-granted stance or even of dissatisfaction may already be present in a relationship in which the "new" man views the house and kids as hers rather than his. Jackie and Amy could accept that "steps" were different during the transition stage of newly cherished cohabitation and that a fiancé could retain some distance from *her* children. However, the lone married woman in this study, April Yeaton (who had contacted me in response to a notice about my interest in interviewing single mothers), had difficulty coming to terms with her husband's failure to engage fully with her child once he had become that child's stepfather. "The mother part about it is definitely a single mother. I mean, single as part of relationship I'm not, but as far as the motherhood part, I am. There's no . . . you know, if [my son] is sick, I'm the one who takes care of him. You know, there's no sharing."

And when this difficulty, combined with difficulties around his stronger relationship to his own son from his first marriage, almost led to their splitting up the previous summer, April said she was held back from leaving because she had nowhere to go. "I don't know where I would go. I really don't. . . . I just didn't know what I would do. I mean financially. . . . I would try to find something real cheap that had heat and electricity included, and was within walking distance [of my work and my son's school] so I didn't have to have a car. But . . . I really don't want to live that way! I mean I like having a few dollars in my pocket, and I wouldn't if it wasn't for [my husband]." Indeed, now it seemed that she had done precisely what Melissa Henry had hoped to avoid—she had married for security—and she wasn't sure she could manage on her own again. And rather than feeling grateful for what she had, she was in despair over what she didn't have.

Discussion and Conclusion

As noted in the beginning of this chapter, thinking about gratitude is another way of highlighting the fact that the meaning of gifts is always contextual. Not only are flowers themselves a cultural gift, but the flowers that are unexpected (you seemed to be having a tough week, Darling, enjoy the daisies) are quite different from the flowers that arrive in lieu of unfulfilled obligations (I didn't get home on time, but have some lilies) or as apologies for serious misbehavior (I slept with her, but you get a dozen roses). Something the same is quite obviously true of domestic actions like playing with the children before dinner or doing the dishes. As I've shown above, these actions were regarded very differently in different situations: insufficient contributions in first marriages, part of a balanced exchange in unromantic dating or in "failed" love affairs, an amazing gift of love in romantic dating, an expected but still quite nice gift in cohabitation and, quite possibly, insufficient in the next marriage. As the women moved toward marriage, they came to expect considerably more and to appreciate what they received considerably less.

There is a special irony here. In romantic relationships these women had an interest in perceiving gestures of support as "gifts," so that they were "merely" beholden but not bound by the obligations of exchange; once they began to cohabit or actually move on to marriage, they had an acute interest in viewing these gestures quite differently and perhaps even in taking them for granted.

In her essay "Emily" in *The Friend Who Got Away*, Heather Abel (2005, 149), writing about her relationship to her mother, said, "I've changed the rules of our friendship so many times she's dizzy." One wonders whether in heterosexual relationships as well men sometimes, and not quite unreasonably, get similarly dizzy.[12] They might wonder why washing the dishes is now perceived as the least they can do rather than a highly appreciated gesture of love and support, especially since they have less interest in these changes in perception; in fact, these are precisely the changes that they have an interest in resisting.

Don't get me wrong. In saying as much, I'm not letting men off the hook. Of course men *should* know better: they should know that the rules that apply when they are dating will be different from those that apply when they are cohabiting and that these, too, might change again once they have made the formal commitment to be a husband and stepfather. And they should also be able to figure out that some things should *not* change (he should still bring the flowers). But his timing for these shifts might well differ from hers. And, in all likelihood, she might not know herself just when—or even why—she is starting to apply a new standard (enough with being distant, he *is* the child's stepfather; enough with treating the house as if it is mine alone, he *lives* here). That is, these new expectations, new attitudes, might creep up on her as well as on him. And both of them might have special difficulty figuring out the appropriate frame of reference to apply as they enter new stages for which our society does not yet have clear cultural rules: What are the obligations of each party in a cohabitation relationship where the home and the children are hers? What are the obligations of the stepparent relationship, particularly in those cases where the children still have an involved father?[13]

Toward the end of her essay, Hochschild writes that "something fundamentally social bedevils many modern marriages . . . [because] marriage is . . . [a] joining of two—often different, usually shifting—stances towards gender" (2003, 118). True enough. And as I've tried to make clear in this chapter, individual shifts have their own histories associated with multiple relationships and multiple stages within a single relationship. In a world where not only are stances toward gender changing rapidly, but also there is no clear pattern for relationships and where people are forging new types of relationships, it may be hard for all concerned not just to tell when the honeymoon is over—but even when it begins.

NOTES

1. I might note that the notions of "cultural" and "moral" are conflated here. To be sure, this is one way of thinking about these issues, but there is another way of thinking: not all "cultural" frames of reference are necessarily moral, although they do apply a standard that prevails in a given society.

2. At this historic moment, in most circumstances this appropriate response appears to require that one pay one's own way, that one not be dependent but repay the gift; we can well imagine that there would be other places and other times when dependence was regarded less harshly.

3. A fuller discussion of methods can be found in Nelson (2005).

4. Very few of the women indicated that they were interested in relationships with women. Whether those relationships would follow similar trajectories is a question that these data cannot answer.

5. I fully recognize that these accounts are both retrospective and one-sided. I assume little about whether they are accurate descriptions of men's behavior or even accurate accounts of the feelings the women had at the time during which they were attached in some way to the men they are discussing.

6. For a fuller account of why women leave marriages and the degree to which their responses hinge on gender issues, see Kurz (1995).

7. All names are pseudonyms.

8. For a fuller discussion of these kinds of relationships, see Edin and Lein (1997), Edin (2000), Nelson (2004), and Seccombe (1999).

9. I contend that this is somewhat different from the way that "help" is defined in a marriage, where women might perceive that the domestic tasks are *their* responsibility and that

the men are simply "helping" them. In the case of cohabitation, the women accept the fact that the men do not (yet) have full responsibility for the home or the children.

10. It may also be the case that he is actually doing more than married men do. On this point, see Coltrane (2000, 1222).

11. For explanations for why second marriages break up, see Schmiege, Richards and Zvonkovic (2001).

12. Thanks to Anita Garey, I am reminded here of Goode's essay, "Why Men Resist," in which he comments that men who perceived their work outside the home as a "gift . . . to their wives and children" might have been "hurt or angry" at learning that their wives felt otherwise (1982, 140–141).

13. On this issue, see Coontz (1997) and Sarkisian (2006).

REFERENCES

Abel, Heather. 2005. "Emily." In *The Friend Who Got Away: Twenty Women's True Life Tales of Friendships that Blew Up, Burned Out or Faded Away*, edited by Jenny Offill and Elissa Schappell, 135–151. New York: Broadway Books.

Coleman, Marilyn, Lawrence Ganong, and Mark Fine. 2000. "Reinvestigating Remarriage: Another Decade of Progress." *Journal of Marriage and the Family* 62:1288–1307.

Coltrane, Scott. 2000. "Research on Household Labor: Modeling and Measuring the Social Embeddedness of Routine Family Work." *Journal of Marriage and the Family* 62:1208–1233.

Coontz, Stephanie. 1997. *The Way We Really Are: Coming to Terms with America's Changing Families.* New York: Basic Books.

Edin, Kathryn. 2000. "What Do Low-Income Single Mothers Say About Marriage?" *Social Problems* 47:112–133.

Edin, Kathryn, and Laura Lein. 1997. *Making Ends Meet: How Single Mothers Survive Welfare and Low-Wage Work.* New York: Russell Sage Foundation.

Goode, William J. 1982. "Why Men Resist." In *Rethinking Family: Some Feminist Questions*, edited by Barrie Thorne with Marilyn Yalom, 131–150. New York: Longman.

Hochschild, Arlie Russell, with Anne Machung. 1990. *The Second Shift: Working Parents and the Revolution at Home.* New York: Avon Books.

———. 2003. "The Economy of Gratitude." In *The Commercialization of Intimate Life*, edited by Arlie Russell Hochschild, 104–118. Berkeley: University of California Press.

Kurz, Demie. 1995. *For Richer, For Poorer: Mothers Confront Divorce.* New York: Routledge.

Lichter, Daniel T., Christie D. Batson, and J. Brian Brown. 2004. "Welfare Reform and Marriage Promotion: The Marital Expectations and Desires of Single and Cohabiting Mothers." *Social Service Review* 38:2–25.

MacDonald, William L., and Alfred DeMaris. 1995. "Remarriage, Stepchildren, and Marital Conflict: Challenges to the Incomplete Institutionalization Hypothesis." *Journal of Marriage and the Family* 57:387–398.

Mason, Mary Ann, and Jane Mauldon. 1996. "The New Stepfamily Requires a New Public Policy." *Journal of Social Issues* 52:11–27.

Mauss, Marcel. 1954. *The Gift: The Form and Reason of Exchange in Archaic Societies.* Glencoe, IL: Free Press.

Nelson, Margaret K. 2004. "Reciprocity and Romance." *Qualitative Sociology* 27:439–459.

———. 2005. *The Social Economy of Single Motherhood: Raising Children in Rural America.* New York: Routledge.

Sarkisian, Natalia. 2006. "'Doing Family Ambivalence': Nuclear and Extended Families in Single Mothers' Lives." *Journal of Marriage and Family* 68:804–811.

Schmiege, Cynthia J., Leslie N. Richards, and Anisa M. Zvonkovic. 2001. "Remarriage: For Love or Money?" *Journal of Divorce and Remarriage* 36 (1–2): 123–140.

Seccombe, Karen. 1999. *"So You Think I Drive a Cadillac?" Welfare Recipients' Perspectives on the System and Its Reform.* Needham Heights, MA: Allyn and Bacon.

CHAPTER 8

The Asking Rules of Reciprocity

Karen V. Hansen

In this essay I probe the hesitation—that considered pause—before requesting help. The social tensions between obligation, perception, and need reveal the complex ways that people interpret and negotiate reciprocity. The unspoken but observed conventions reveal a disjuncture between what people feel they need and what they think they can acceptably ask. Understanding Arlie Hochschild's concept of "feeling rules" is helpful in understanding the dynamic (1983). She defines feelings rules as those notions that "guide emotion work by establishing the sense of entitlement or obligation that governs emotional exchanges" (1983, 56). Hochschild zeroes in "on the pinch between 'what I do feel' and 'what I should feel'" (57). Following from this insight, asking rules specify the conditions under which a person can ask for help in the context of assessed need and capacity. The self-imposed hesitation that accompanies asking rules makes a person pause and consider the trade-offs.

The networks that I have studied are constructed to help employed parents care for their school-age children (Hansen 2005). Relations within a network of care for children operate via a culturally specific logic of reciprocity, which is premised on trust, obligation, and mutuality. Building on Margaret Nelson's (2000) earlier work, I argue that the features of reciprocity change depending on relational context and economic location. In contrast, I am interested in reciprocity in the context of networks of many people rather than dyadic, romantic relationships. By studying networks in different class locations, I seek to analyze the ways in which social location and kinship mediate reciprocity and people's interpretations of it. When and under what conditions do people decide they can ask for a favor or help with their childrearing? And what cultural values guide them in their decision making?

Within sociology, the concept of reciprocity generally refers to mutual giving and receiving (Hogan, Eggebeen and Clogg 1993; Nelson 2000; Weinberg 1994). However, the nature of reciprocity has been the subject of ongoing debate. Social exchange theory, the dominant approach to networks and reciprocity in sociology, primarily analyzes exchange dynamics from a utilitarian perspective (Blau 1964; Coleman 1988; Homans 1958). The economic model assumes a scarcity of resources and zero sum outcomes (Nelson 1993).

I argue that because the networks I study center on children, reciprocity is more compelling. Not only do children represent the next generation of a kin group, caring for them can be fun and satisfying. A child is a person with whom to have a relationship, as well as someone who needs adult attention and supervision (Ruddick 1998; Thorne 2001). As the symbolic center of these networks, the child can be the invaluable gift that an anchor, the person at the center of the childrearing project, gives back to network members (Hansen 2005; Nelson 2000). And while that gift can include emotional attachment and playfulness, rationality and instrumentalism can also motivate reciprocal relations. Parents construct networks because they need help.

That which is given and taken in reciprocal actions is not self-evident or easily measured. Sociologically, it is not just what people count that is interesting, but *how* they count it. People's perceptions of being a part of a network and the relations with the parent and the child shape their sense of reward and their assessment of the cost of obligation.

Method of Inquiry

My method, which is to approach each network as a case study, is motivated by my desire to analyze particular networks in their entirety and to get a fuller picture, from multiple vantage points, of caring for children and supporting parents. This case study approach enables me to analyze the interactive process of reciprocity. The networks in this study achieve some form of balanced reciprocity that has unfolded in the context of ongoing relationships. By studying connected individuals, it is possible to observe the relational context of a particular act of help and analyze the ripple effects on multiple members of the network. In studying reciprocity in a broader context of community and kin, the process of trading and paying back unfolds, spills over, and incorporates relationships outside of the original exchange. In adult networks structured around the care of children, most exchanges involve at least a triangle in considering obligations, costs of involvement, and payback.

This research is based on a larger study of forty open-ended, qualitative interviews that I conducted in northern California from 1999 to 2000 (Hansen 2005). I began by recruiting four white parents who met several criteria: They (1) had at least one child between the ages of five and twelve; (2) had a partner in rearing their children; and (3) were employed. At the end of my first interview with each anchor, I asked her/him to list those who were involved in caring directly for the child or children (excluding institutional caregivers) and those who provided emotional or practical support and/or advice to the anchor with respect to children. I then interviewed *all* people, the entire "ensemble," as Hertz and Ferguson

(1998) put it, involved in the network. No person refused an interview. The lists generated by anchors included neighbors, siblings, spouses, parents, friends, and babysitters (paid and unpaid). Approximately one-third of those network members were men, and two-thirds were women. The study included one network each from four economic locations: working class, middle class, professional middle class, and upper class.

The first network, the working-class Cranes, part of a four-generation system of care, is based in the San Joaquin Valley of California. Patricia Crane, the anchor and mother of a six-year-old, has worked many jobs, including assembly work in the electronics industry, and most recently at two jobs, one in sanitary maintenance at a truck stop and one as a driver at a car auction. She now lives with her mother, Fran, and her son in a one-bedroom apartment. Patricia's network of care consists of her mother, her brother, her next-door neighbor, Tracy, and the father of her son, to whom she has never been married. As Patricia tells it, Fran has taken care of her son since his birth, and her friend, Tracy, is the only nonfamily member who has ever cared for him.

The second network, the Beckers, is anchored in a solidly middle-class family in a diverse, urban center. The Becker network is wealthy in its people resources and moderate in income. At the center is Dina Becker, a freelance photographer, her husband, Mark Walde, a schoolteacher, and their two children, ages eight and six. Their system for rearing children is built around a split shift strategy and buttressed by considerable kin help. In her network, Dina includes her husband, her mother, her father, her two brothers, and three of her sisters.

The third network, the Duvall-Brennans, is well off financially but stretched extremely thin in terms of people. It is anchored by two full-time attorneys, Maggie Duvall and Jack Brennan. They have two children, one in kindergarten, age six, and a three-and-a-half-year-old in full-time day care. Maggie and Jack are active, intensive co-parents and co-anchors. The caregiving network they enumerate consists of Jack's brother and his co-resident partner, three former neighbors, two friends from Maggie's women's group, and Jack's sister who lives on the East Coast. The network list is substantial (it includes eight people), but the ties are thin and brittle.

The fourth and final network, the Aldriches, is anchored by Sarah Aldrich, who grew up in a family with considerable wealth and works full time as a philanthropist. Sarah is the mother of two children, ages fourteen and eleven. After seventeen years of marriage, Sarah separated from her husband, Alex Brolin, a developer, about a year and a half before I first interviewed her. They have a joint custody arrangement in which the children spend half of their time at each parent's home. The separation makes the logistics of child raising much more complicated, even though Alex lives only two miles away. Sarah's network of care includes her full-time nanny, her mother, her best friend, the mother of her son's best friend, her husband, and a babysitter who has worked for her approximately once a week for ten years.

The Dynamics of Reciprocity

To initiate the process of reciprocal trades, network members assess and interpret their own situation and that of others, and negotiate what is possible given the circumstances. As Alvin Gouldner puts it, "The *norm* of reciprocity holds that people should help those who help them, and therefore, those whom you have helped have an obligation to you. The conclusion is clear: if you want to be helped by others you must help them" (1960, 173; emphasis in original). Network members feel obliged to repay someone who has given them help. One way to recruit someone into helping is to help that person first.

When one accepts a favor or gets involved in an exchange, the expectation of return—the hook of reciprocity—necessarily shapes the interchange. A person is obliged to accept what is given and give something in return. The reciprocity covenant has power above and beyond an individual, even though it is individually negotiated. The language of indebtedness expresses the sense of obligation and the exigency of creating balance in the relationship. Liability hangs over the debtor; the lingering obligation nags at the person until it can be met. What may appear to be a gift has strings attached.

Gouldner makes the critical distinction between normative reciprocity and that which results from status duties. In effect, he emphasizes the difference between a *normative* imperative and a kin obligation. Thus, if a person helps because it is incumbent upon him or her as a kin member, that action can be analytically distinguished from someone doing a favor.

In making this argument, Gouldner ignores two important issues: the social construction of kinship and the fact that kin can also engage in reciprocal relations with one another. He fails to register that status obligations have meaning and impact only if the kinship is socially recognized. As many sociologists and anthropologists have demonstrated, kin obligation does not unfold by virtue of blood ties (Finch and Mason 1993; Schneider 1980), but must be socially recognized in order to "count" as relations. This enterprise is ideologically charged and historically changing (Thorne 1992). When acknowledged and active, kinship is a social status that comes with obligations and expectations for behavior.

Second, kin can and do have reciprocal relations with each other over and above their status duties. While the ideology of kinship privileges the care for children and invokes kin obligation, exchanges unfold among active kin that could not be expected merely out of duty. Reciprocity in the context of rearing children is built on mutuality, trust, and a sense of responsibility that culturally informs kinship. Because the standards are high, some kin are necessarily excluded from meeting these criteria. Moreover, the networks I studied include both kin and non-kin. While reciprocity among active kin may operate differently from that among non-kin over the long run, kin also observe the asking rules of reciprocity.

The Asking Rules

An appropriate request for help has to fit suitably into the proper context of time, place, and circumstance, as judged by the network member asking and the member being asked. He or she necessarily anticipates how another person might interpret the request. Obligation and entitlement centrally influence what network members suppose they can ask for and what the norm of reciprocity will oblige them to repay. The overarching situation and the specific content of the favors both enter into a person's calculation of whether or not to ask, as do the estimated consequences of receiving the help.

Once one is engaged in an ongoing network of care for children, a challenging aspect of negotiating the multiple relationships involves what Nelson calls "the fine art of asking" (2000, 311). Determining when and where to ask, finessing that uncomfortable place between what one needs and what someone else can give, takes practice and judgment. The act of asking acknowledges one's needs and interdependency. Nelson's single mothers felt it was "difficult" to ask for help (2000, 310). As with others in a U.S. culture that celebrates independence, the single mothers hesitated to ask because they wanted to consider themselves self-sufficient. Among other things, they feared that asking for help might stigmatize or compromise them. The asking rules of reciprocity help to overcome this fear, but they also insert a pause when it is socially necessary. The following five asking rules prescribe what people ought to do and proscribe what they ought not do.

Rule One: Ask Only If Your Request Does Not Impose upon Someone

The underlying premise of the first asking rule is that one should not impose. A request triggers a change in action; it prompts someone to do something they would not otherwise do—inconvenient at least and a major sacrifice at most. Consequently, asking "too often" or "too much" constitutes an imposition. However, definitions of "too much," and therefore of what constitutes an imposition, are socially constructed. When Dina Becker thinks, "I've asked my parents too many times in a row," she will call a brother to help her. Similarly self-regulating, attorney Jack Brennan considers whether to ask his brother and his partner to babysit the children: "They're interested in seeing [the kids] and they will babysit occasionally. We don't impose on them because we're not quite sure how much they really enjoy it . . . So they do help out, but we kind of try to modulate it so that it's something we're comfortable with and they're comfortable with."

Caitlin Becker James, sister to Dina Becker, talks about arranging coverage for her children while she travels. She incorporates Dina into her plan, but tries to do so without creating a burdensome arrangement: "We try to work her part of it when she already has kids at home, or at least one, because it doesn't quite seem fair, if she only has a few hours a day, to give her my child during those hours. I might as well give her my child when she already has another child . . . And she'll be doing childcare. And then it helps her, because then they go off and play as opposed to it being a burden."

As with other aspects of constructing networks and negotiating reciprocity, the meaning of "impose" gets interpreted differently in various situations with assorted people. Something that feels easy to one person may be viewed as a burden to another.

Interestingly, while the consideration of imposing modulates requests across class, the word "impose" is not a part of the lexicon of help in the working-class Cranes or the upper-class Aldriches. "Impose" is a word used primarily by the professional middle-class network members. Other network members consistently use the term "burden" in relation to childcare; they recognize that at a bare minimum taking care of a child is a weighty responsibility. But whereas childcare might be work, it is not necessarily intrusive. Even in the context where children are seen as gifts, they simultaneously create more work and feel like an extra load, just as paying the bills and cleaning house do. For Patricia Crane's brother, Ben Crane, childcare becomes a burden only when it infringes upon his freedom—for example, if he already has plans to hang out with his friends. One friend of Sarah Aldrich, Lydia Dunn, exercises her sense of entitlement by calling upon members of her local neighborhood to help her keep an eye on her adolescent sons. She feels no compunction in calling the grocery store in her elite community to see if her son might be outside. By virtue of their place of business in the community, the storekeepers have incurred obligations to their patrons. Lydia is decidedly *not* worried about imposing. Consistent with other research on the upper class (Baltzell 1989, 1991), from her perspective, people owe her. She is unfettered by a sense of guilt that she is asking for something extra. In contrast, in her friendship with Sarah Aldrich, one based on equality and mutuality, she monitors the cumulative impact of her requests.

Imposing has a sharper, more treacherous edge among the professional middle-class network members. If someone is perceived as being overextended, asking that person for a favor amounts to an imposition. Rebecca Hoffman, of the professional middle-class network, talks about her reluctance to call upon attorneys Jack Brennan and Maggie Duvall: "They're working at faraway jobs. They're not working at home, so they feel a little bit more stretched." Ruth Bergman also mentions Jack's and Maggie's commute and their extreme overwork in considering whether she would ask them to do something for her in return for her babysitting. "I want to be respectful of their time; because given not only their two kids, but given where they work, literally their work location, it's pretty difficult." Importantly, by not asking, the Duvall-Brennan network members hedge their network involvement. They limit the number of reciprocal obligations they incur vis-à-vis the Duvall-Brennans, although they are involved in extensive reciprocal negotiations with others in their own network. And, by being too busy, the Duvall-Brennans successfully limit what others ask of them and as a result their network becomes more fragile and their asking practices more cautious.

Rule Two: In Order to Ask a Favor Related to Childcare, You Have to Be Close

The second asking rule builds upon the first by linking imposition to the degree of relationship: The closer you are, the higher the threshold of imposing. The calculation rests on the supposition that caring for children is hard work, people are busy and stressed, and one has to be in a solid relationship before asking.

"Close" can imply degree of kinship, trust, proximity, or emotional connection, or some combination thereof. The imperative of closeness, like that of imposing, is related to philosophies of childrearing. Fundamentally, sharing a childrearing philosophy and establishing trust shape how people initially construct, or stage, their networks of care for children (see Hansen 2005). As Annette Lareau (2003) has so insightfully demonstrated, childrearing approaches vary by class. Is the labor-intensive, highly relational, concerted cultivation of the middle class linked to recognition of the difficulty of caring for children in this particular way? Might that recognition make middle-class network members more hesitant to leave their children with someone, unless the person was close? This would suggest that networks and social relationships constructed around working-class childrearing and the accomplishment of natural growth might take on different dimensions than middle-class networks. If a member is sufficiently close, it is harder to impose upon them; closeness ameliorates imposition.

Not surprisingly, for several people, kin, by definition, pass this threshold. For a few, like Dina Becker, kin symbolize closeness: "Everybody's so stressed that if you were to ask them to fill in in a pinch, it would stress them more. . . . I feel I would have to be so close to them, it'd be like my sister." The middle-class Beckers have an exclusively kin-based network. For them, biological kin are close by definition, although in-laws are not. Socially recognized kinship mediates Dina's concerns about imposing. In effect, she worries that a similar request of friends might jeopardize that relationship; she would find it "risky." Friends can be close, but relationships are more fragile and therefore asking tests the friendship.

Amanda Brennan adheres to this asking rule in recounting a time when her children were little and she was very ill. Her brother, Jack Brennan, was a twenty-year-old who liked children, was good with her children, and came over to help. Amanda talks about his participation as an affirmation of their relationship: "That's how close we were. I could ask him to do it, and he did it." The fact that she could ask him to help her when she was sick was a measure of their closeness in her mind. It was not just his fraternity that entitled her to ask for help, but their strong connection. For the professional middle-class Duvall-Brennans, "close" is defined emotionally, not in terms of kin relations. For them, all of their relationships seem more tentative and delicate.

Rule Three: Ask Only If Your Request Falls within the Hierarchy of Recognized Needs

Having children means that a parent has acute needs, ones that are socially recognized as greater than those of a person who does not have children. This recognition is paired with a parent's sense of entitlement about meeting the needs for shelter and safety of the child. Thus asking rule number three privileges the needs of mothers and fathers.

In assessing the legitimate grounds for asking for help with children, paid employment and marital work also rank high. However, the principle of hierarchy underlying the third asking rule varies by network and gender. In the working-class network, Tracy Johnson recognized Patricia Crane's stress and exhaustion and acted to alleviate it by taking her son for a few days. In contrast, Dina Becker's husband, Mark, of the ever helpful, middle-class Becker clan, does not feel he can ask anyone in the network to babysit while he exercises, which is his main pastime. Although the network members babysit when he works, to him a request to cover time to exercise would be unacceptable. And yet, the Becker network members readily and gladly take care of the children when Mark and Dina go out on a date. This kind of support for pleasure must be understood in the context of what Karla Hackstaff (1999) calls a "culture of divorce," where people recognize the prevalence of divorce and act to thwart it by encouraging and facilitating romance in marriage. Virtually all of the networks had people who supported others in their attempts to go out and spend time nourishing their marital relationships.

Illness within the networks is similarly high in importance and immediacy in the hierarchy. When working-class Patricia Crane's mother was in the hospital, the urgency of attending to her prevailed over all other imperatives. As the network mobilized, every member recognized the importance of making life work for Patricia through this crisis as she cared for her mother and anchored the home front. Interestingly, the focus of support centered on Patricia as much as it did her mother. People within the network recognized that Patricia's mother depends on her for support, so helping Patricia became a way of helping her mother.

Reciprocity acts as a regulator, enforcing norms by determining what counts as a need, what gets supported, and what does not. Mark Walde expresses his reluctance to ask for "extra things": "I'd rather do it myself; I'd rather not bother." Essential things are fine, but "extra things" are not worth it. Without knowing exactly what he would have to give back in the long term in order to balance the trade, he must decide if going for a run is worth the incurred obligation.

Rule Four: Do Not Ask If the Price Seems Too High

In Mark Walde's desire to exercise, the stakes appear low. However, the dynamic points to a fourth asking rule: Do not ask if the price seems too high. The calculation incorporates considerations of the sting of asking as well as the obligation to return the favor and the cost of doing so. Asking implies recognition of reliance on others; it is an admission of interdependence. This asking rule can prevent someone from asking altogether. Dina Becker's mother, Susan Becker, ruminates over the choices she made while a young mother, especially when it came to relying on her mother-in-law, with whom she did not have the best relationship: "My mother-in-law would . . . have come, but I wasn't particularly close to her . . . I had a feeling that if I had gotten ill and she had to come, she would have come, but she would have [*laughs*] blamed me for staying out late or [*laughs*] not putting on a sweater, and getting [sick]. . . . There was a certain judgmentalness. . . . I would have hesitated to call, unless I was on my deathbed."

Paying back may involve more of a sacrifice than a person wants to make. Another example illustrates the calculations about price in a series of trade-offs Byron Russell and Rebecca Hoffman, members of the Duvall-Brennan professional middle-class network, made as they tried joining a babysitting cooperative in their neighborhood. Consistent with the philosophy that led them to share childcare with the Duvall-Brennans when their children were toddlers, the babysitting co-op appealed to their community-oriented childrearing sensibilities. Byron recounts their involvement:

> Because we have other people we could use, especially my mother, it didn't seem worth it to us to have one of us away for the evenings. So it was kind of *a big price to pay*, for having somebody come here another day and then you didn't know the person. . . . It's more stressful when you don't have a relationship, if somebody's essentially a stranger or a bare acquaintance. It's more stressful taking care of their kids and it's more stressful having them take care of yours. So we only did it once. [Emphasis added].

This approach—of using community chits to build a network of helpful acquaintances—is an example of continuing civic engagement around the country (Sirianni and Friedland 2001). However, the overriding issues of familiarity and convenience ended Byron's and Rebecca's desire to make it work, because in the end, the price seemed too high, especially since they have alternative caretaking options available.

The price of obligation varies by class; and the determination of value operates relative to a particular cultural and economic context. Thus Rule Four is deeply influenced by class contingencies and involves assessing the cost in terms of material value as well as time. The urgency of a need enters into the calculation of whether the cost is worth paying and if one can absorb it, given the resources at hand.

Another side of price resides in the obligation to return the favor or the help—the cost of engaging in reciprocity itself. For example, each week upper-class Sarah Aldrich prepares a dinner to take to the family of a friend beset by cancer. While she cooks, her full-time nanny helps her prepare and deliver the meal. It is entirely likely that faced with a comparable situation, professional middle-class Maggie Duvall would be motivated to act similarly. However, for her the cost would be enormous. Most weekdays she arrives home after 6:30 P.M., following a twelve-hour day that includes a two-hour commute as well as a high-pressure work environment. Once she arrives, her two young children require undivided attention if she is going to fulfill her commitment to intensive mothering. While she and her husband co-parent, she does not have extra home support to help her run errands or cook. Therefore, the price extracted for preparing weekly meals for a friend would be exceedingly high, measured in effort, exhaustion, and time taken from a life she can now barely manage.

Rule Five: Do Not Ask If You Know Your Request Will Be Rejected

Fran Crane, grandmother in the working-class network, censored her requests by observing a fifth asking rule: Do not ask if you know your request will be rejected. Fran testified to a lifelong history of rejection by her mother. Despite the endless time and effort Fran expended taking care of her mother, she insisted that she neither expected nor received anything in return: "I wouldn't ask my mother for nothing [*laughs*] . . . She wouldn't do it, to begin with. I've been told 'No' so many times. Why would I want to waste my breath to ask her anymore? [*laughs*]." She accepts caring for her mother as her kin obligation, her duty. And as a kin imperative, she fully intends to honor it. Nonetheless, she sees other aspects of their relationship as bound by normative reciprocity, which demands a return in the long run. Fran's refusal to ask for anything allows her to set limits on what she gives and how much she takes of the emotional flack her mother doles out.

This asking rule speaks to an important convention that most observe but don't articulate. Fran Crane was the only person to state Rule Five explicitly. Most people handle this imperative by excluding those who might reject their request from their networks of care. The difficulty for Fran Crane arises from the fact that she is an essential figure in her mother's care network, although the reverse is not and could not be true (not only because of infirmity, but also because of inclination). While this may occur across class, the kin twist may be more an issue for working-class and middle-class folks who include more kin in their network and for whom kin obligation is more integral to everyday life (Hansen 2005; Roschelle 1997).

Discussion and Conclusion

The asking rules of reciprocity uncover the agreed-upon assumptions about when and under what conditions one can ask for help with school-age children. Examining the facets of the asking rules and their sensitivity to social location provides insight into the social organization of reciprocity in particular and networking in general. It is possible that other asking rules inform networks organized around needs other than childcare and childrearing advice.

Based on the evidence in this research, I would argue not that the rules vary by class location, but that they are invoked differently across class. Despite the fact that networks consist of kin and non-kin, the asking rules apply to everyone. The meaning of kin status varies by social location, and the number of active kin in a network may likewise fluctuate, but the asking rules remain the same. As with class variation, they are utilized and interpreted with sensitivity to the particular relationship and circumstance.

The asking rules sometimes operate in tension with each other. For example, one's understanding of a hierarchy of need may come square up against the situational definition of "impose." People evaluate asking rules in the shifting context of their operational networks of care and in their negotiated assessments of need and capacity.

Networks are not merely the products of deficits, although they spring up in response to a family labor shortage. Nor are they outcomes exclusively of privilege, although without sufficient resources anchors have difficulty constructing and sustaining effective networks. Having a pool of potential members from which to draw, identified via friendship and kinship, creates an essential kind of wealth for parents as they rear children. When individuals asking for help claim kinship, they have a kin advantage because they can invoke kin obligation as well as the reciprocity covenant.

The practice of interdependence exhibited in these networks acts at odds with the ideology that celebrates self-sufficiency and independence in U.S. culture. At the same time, people's ambivalence about it reflects that ideology. Pertinent to the topic at hand, an adult's motivation to ask for help or advice is tempered by beliefs about what one should need and what one can ask for. These negotiated assessments moderate the asking rules of reciprocity, the normative agreements by which people abide when they engage in relationships of give and take.

ACKNOWLEDGMENTS

Reprinted from "The Asking Rules of Reciprocity in Networks of Care for Children," *Quantitative Sociology* 27, no. 4 (2004), with kind permission from Springer Science + Business Media and CCC.

This essay has been greatly enhanced by the careful reading and astute criticisms of Anita Garey, Rosanna Hertz, Nazli Kibria, and Nicholas Townsend. I especially want to thank Peggy Nelson, the most reciprocal of colleagues, who has been ever generous and eager to engage intellectually in our shared curiosity about reciprocity.

REFERENCES

Baltzell, E. Digby. 1989. *Philadelphia Gentlemen: The Making of a National Upper Class.* Philadelphia: University of Pennsylvania Press.

———. 1991. *The Protestant Establishment Revisited.* New Brunswick, NJ: Transaction Publishers.

Blau, Peter. 1964. *Exchange and Power in Social Life.* New York: Wiley.

Coleman, James. 1988. "Social Capital in the Creation of Human Capital." *American Journal of Sociology* 94:S95–S120.

Finch, Janet, and Jennifer Mason. 1993. *Negotiating Family Responsibilities*. New York: Tavistock/Routledge.

Gouldner, Alvin. 1960. "The Norm of Reciprocity: A Preliminary Statement." *American Sociological Review* 25:161–178.

Hackstaff, Karla. 1999. *Marriage in a Culture of Divorce*. Philadelphia: Temple University Press.

Hansen, Karen V. 2005. *Not-So-Nuclear Families: Class, Gender, and Networks of Care*. New Brunswick, NJ: Rutgers University Press.

Hertz, Rosanna, and Faith I. Ferguson. 1998. "Only One Pair of Hands: Ways That Single Mothers Stretch Work and Family Resources." *Community, Work and Family* 1: 13–37.

Hochschild, Arlie Russell. 1983. *The Managed Heart: Commercialization of Human Feeling*. Berkeley: University of California Press.

Hogan, Dennis P., David J. Eggebeen, and Clifford C. Clogg. 1993. "The Structure of Intergenerational Exchanges in American Families." *American Journal of Sociology* 98:1428–1458.

Homans, George. 1958. "Social Behavior as Exchange." *American Journal of Sociology* 63:597–606.

Lareau, Annette. 2003. *Unequal Childhoods: Class, Race, and Family Life*. Berkeley: University of California Press.

Nelson, Julie A. 1993. *Beyond Economic Man: Feminist Theory and Economics*. Chicago, IL: University of Chicago Press.

Nelson, Margaret K. 2000. "Single Mothers and Social Support: The Commitment to, and Retreat from, Reciprocity." *Qualitative Sociology* 23:291–317.

Roschelle, Anne R. 1997. *No More Kin: Exploring Race, Class, and Gender in Family Networks*. Thousand Oaks, CA: Sage.

Ruddick, Sara. 1998. "Care as Labor and Relationship." In *Norms and Values: Essays on the Work of Virginia Held*, edited by J. G. Haber and M. S. Halfon, 3–25. Lanham, MD: Rowman and Littlefield.

Schneider, David. 1980. *American Kinship: A Cultural Account*. Chicago: University of Chicago Press.

Sirianni, Carmen, and Lewis Friedland. 2001. *Civic Innovation in America: Community Empowerment, Public Policy, and the Movement for Civic Renewal*. Berkeley: University of California Press.

Thorne, Barrie. 1992. "Feminism and the Family." In *Rethinking the Family: Some Feminist Questions*, edited by Barrie Thorne with Marilyn Yalom, 3–30. Boston: Northeastern University Press.

———. 2001. "Pick-up Time at Oakdale Elementary School: Work and Family from the Vantage Points of Children." In *Working Families: The Transformation of the American Home*, edited by Rosanna Hertz and Nancy L. Marshall, 354–376. Berkeley: University of California Press.

Weinberg, Davida J. 1994. "Reciprocity Reconsidered: Motivations to Give and Return in the Everyday Exchange of Favors." Ph.D. diss., University of California, Berkeley.

CHAPTER 9

Wives Who Play by the Rules

WORKING ON EMOTIONS IN THE SPORT MARRIAGE

Steven M. Ortiz

You can't show anger in front of Dennis. So now you can't really do anything with that anger. So it's a short fuse. It stays right there at the surface all the time.

—Stacy

Stacy is disillusioned. When she married her husband, Dennis, a major league baseball relief pitcher, she expected him to be just as involved in their marriage as he was in his career. However, she gradually and reluctantly came to acknowledge a growing competition between his career and their marriage. It became quite clear that his career came first—a reality many wives of professional athletes share.

The sport marriage is a type of career-dominated marriage that is firmly embedded in the world of professional sports (Ortiz 2006). In career-dominated marriages, one spouse, usually the husband, performs a high-stress and sometimes high-profile occupational role (e.g., corporate executive, military officer, physician, entertainer, police officer, clergy member, or politician) in a male-dominated occupational world (see Hochschild [1969] on the ambassador's wife). Despite the increasing number of women in the workforce, the growing expectation that women will have their own careers, and the continuing trend of dual-earner/dual-career marriages, the career-dominated marriage continues to flourish in the world of professional sports. Women married to professional athletes learn through marital and emotional socialization to be responsible for the care work in the family, to enact a "wife of" role, and to participate within the marriage in a "two-person career" (Finch 1983; Papanek 1973).

In this chapter, I focus on how women in sport marriages use emotion management as a form of usually invisible marital labor that is an essential part of the career-dominated marriage (Hochschild 1983, 1990).[1] Athletes' wives internalize and normalize an unwritten book of rules for wives of professional athletes that requires them to work on their emotions (Ortiz 1997). In order to convey the "right" emotions, these wives learn what is appropriate to feel in particular situations ("feeling rules") and how to convey that emotion to others ("display rules") (Hochschild 1979, 563–570). They use a variety of strategies in managing their emotions to conform to these guidelines. When what a wife actually feels does not correspond to the specific feeling rule for the occasion, she may put on a more acceptable emotional expression—smiling, for example, because the occasion is meant to be a happy one, even though she may be feeling sad about something else. This is referred to as "surface acting" and differs from "deep acting," in which people try to conform to social expectations by working to change their underlying feelings—trying to feel happy, for instance, rather than simply looking happy (Hochschild 1983, 35–46).

Like other athletes' wives, Stacy believes she must conform to the expectations of her husband, his team organization, and his occupational world. She consciously monitors how she thinks she should feel and how she should or should not display her feelings. Additionally, she learns to subordinate her emotions to those of her husband and others in his occupational world. Emotion management enables wives to conform to or appear to conform to the unwritten rules of the sport marriage, but at the same time it can be detrimental or have costs for these women.

This chapter is based on my long-term ethnographic work with forty-seven wives of professional athletes and one ex-wife (Ortiz 2001a, 2003a, 2005a). I also relied on participant observation, personal documents, and newspaper and magazine articles. In addition, I kept a journal of field notes documenting my reflections, observations, interactions, emotions, and experiences. After three full years of immersion, I spent an additional year conducting intermittent interviews as I gradually, and with great difficulty, exited from the field (Ortiz 2004). These long-term collaborative relationships put me in a rare position to observe closely the wives' personal dilemmas, anxieties, stressors, and crises in their everyday life. I was gradually accepted by several of the wives into their world as a male insider, which was evident when I was able to establish reciprocity by becoming involved in activities such as helping with domestic tasks, running errands with or for the wives, shopping or house-hunting with them, house-sitting, and attending games and team events/functions with them. In addition, they allowed me to lend a sympathetic ear, provide emotional support, and share secrets and gossip. Their frankness surprised me, because these women—whose trust is often violated—are fiercely protective of their privacy and do not easily trust outsiders. Their sincere sharing and fascinating revelations, combined with my observations of them in various private and public situations, helped me to understand the expectations and demands placed on them, the depth of their sacrifices, the value they place on marital and family stability, and the extent to which they manage their emotions.

Constructing Career-Dominated Relationships

Athletes' wives usually lead lives characterized by geographic mobility or instability. They must adjust to their husbands' regular and extended absences from home because of work-related travel. They are in the public eye and must contend with fans, groupies, invasions of privacy, media scrutiny, and other consequences of their husbands' status as celebrities. They are expected to follow the moral codes implied in the public images of their husbands as positive role models. They must learn to accept a status hierarchy among the wives married to the men on their husbands' teams. In addition, these wives must cope with various sources of stress associated with professional sports (Ortiz 2002). As they manage and cope with the occupational spillover into marital and family life, athletes' wives also attempt to fulfill the numerous complex and unspoken expectations inherent in their roles. In so doing, they support and contribute to their husbands' careers in what is often a behind-the-scenes pattern of involvement.

When male professional athletes, who are highly visible entertainers, are in the flow of the game, they come to life; they are "on." Yet this man at work is not always the same man the wife gets at home. Robyn admitted, "I'm jealous of that. I wish he was more energetic, more likable at home." When he is in non-work-related situations, he is no longer completely "on" as an entertainer. In fact, where his marital and family responsibilities are concerned, he tends to be "off." It is not uncommon for a husband to be emotionally distant, aloof, passive, or "recharging his batteries" as he waits for the next game or work-related activity. At the ballpark, arena, or stadium, his wife—like his fans—sees the brilliant man she wants at home. But men in professional sports may have difficulty transitioning to marital and family roles. When they are home, they may withdraw from family life.

These wives want their husbands to be more involved in and emotionally connected to their marriages and families. Interestingly, although these husbands exert significant control in their marriages, they seem reluctant to "take charge" when they are home during the season. They usually do not share family responsibilities or effectively contend with everyday life outside their occupational world. It is the wives who make the travel arrangements, discipline the children, handle the family finances, and supervise repairs and improvements in the home.

Although a wife appears to be in control of the family's domestic life, a power imbalance that favors the husband exists. For these husbands, being in control means making things go their way and having others do what they want, and they seem to expect certain things from their wives. Much of a wife's marital labor is a response to the demands of her husband's career, and her marital compliance is a response to these implicit expectations. The husband's sense of his own importance and the importance of his career and what it can provide for the family can overshadow the work their wives contribute to the marriage and career. Jill explained: "Craig always says, 'We wouldn't have what we have today if it wasn't for football.' Or he'll say, 'How many professional football players are there in the United States?' So he's one of the chosen few. He's special. He's important. He uses that on me."

To compensate for this power imbalance, some wives escalate their level of involvement in family and home management, thereby increasing their husbands' dependence. It is this dependence that may lead some professional athletes to install their wives in the role of mother. In the social construction of his wife as a mother figure—which I call the motherization of the wife—a husband emphasizes motherhood instead of womanhood or personhood in relating to his wife (Ortiz 2006). In the role of mother, she becomes a parent to him and vulnerable to his insistence that she embrace this role in their relationship (Goffman 1961, 106–107). As Tanya recalled, "Once I became the mother hen and I became his caretaker, he couldn't see me any other way but how his mother was. And he treated me like his father treated his mother." Although they find it annoying or irritating, some wives find it easier to accept this maternal role toward their husbands because it can help to avoid conflict and preserve some measure of stability in their hectic seasonal lives. A wife enacts this enabling role and tries to minimize any distractions because she believes it benefits her husband's career and the marriage. Once this pattern becomes embedded in the relationship, however, her deference to her husband and his career can become emotionally draining. As Sharon's story illustrates, accommodating her husband this way can have serious consequences over time.

> We were so codependent and dysfunctional because I was all wrapped up in Walt's life. In other words, I took control. But I was frustrated because the end result was on how much he scored and how much he made. So, in other words, all of my work saw no results. Walt gave everything to me and became the latent adolescent. He never took any responsibility for anything. I did the bills. I did the taxes. I did the investing. I had my babies on my own. I did everything, and with tremendous anger. And the more I did, I literally cut his balls off more and more in my own eyes. And the joke among sports wives is we're so masculine because in our own eyes we've de-balled them. And you have, physically, emotionally, intellectually, and socially, because we've become so controlling. We're just as much at fault as they are for letting it happen because we all buy into this maternal take-care-of-me mentality—"I'm on the road. Cook for me. Screw me. Have my shirts clean for me." And we do that. And so what we literally do is clip their wings, and we're the man-woman at home. It's almost like we don't need them because the paycheck comes in, and they're gone so much. The scary reality is you learn to totally live alone, and he's a guest in his own home!

At some point, most wives tire of their husbands' passivity or their attempts to manipulate them. As Robyn insisted, "I get tired of being mommy." But stepping out of the supportive mother role usually proves difficult.

Doing Emotion Work

In their attempts to follow the unwritten rules of the sport marriage, the wives rely on emotion management strategies in private and public life. Their emotion work includes efforts to avoid "misfeeling" and thus being sanctioned for violating, disregarding, or failing to conform to the appropriate feeling rules in certain situations (Hochschild 1979, 564).

Presenting Her Wife Face

Believing that they have a responsibility to their husbands and that it is in the best interest of the husband's career, many athletes' wives make an effort to convey the "right" public image of the "good" player's wife. Beth confided, "You're only a reflection of who they are," and Robyn stated, "I just have to make sure that I don't act in a way that's going to bring an embarrassment to the ball club." Responding to the public demands of their husbands' occupation and attempting to maintain distance between their real self and the public role of player's wife, the vigilant management of a "wife face" becomes a significant aspect of their "face work" in public life (Goffman 1961, 1967; Ortiz 2005b). Maintaining their poise and avoiding being in "wrong face" or "out of face" frequently involves the use of surface acting strategies (Goffman 1967, 8–9). For example, an athlete's wife is expected to maintain emotional composure and proper decorum during a game. Obeying the rules of game etiquette, she will comply with certain feeling and display rules. Kathleen, for instance, believes that if she is disappointed in her husband's performance, she should not express it. "Doing his job, he has to have such a high self-esteem. You know? I think I'm careful not to chisel away at that. I make him feel good about himself so he can go out there on the [pitcher's] mound and feel good about himself. If he does blow a save, I shouldn't be disappointed."

Wives in sport marriages carefully bury their feelings and avoid displaying disappointment in their husbands' less than stellar performances because it could imply lack of wifely support to those in the team organization, fans, and television cameras. If she is very disappointed, embarrassed, or angry because of something that occurred during or prior to the game, she will suppress those feelings and apply a surface acting strategy by putting on a "happy face" to display her encouragement and support.

In addition, these wives understand that they should avoid expressing spontaneous or extreme emotions such as anger or unrestrained joy, because displaying the "wrong" emotion at the wrong moment may reflect negatively on her, her husband, and other wives. For example, a wife is expected to be excited for her husband when he performs well, but she must not display too much excitement because, as Gwen insisted, "You don't want to draw attention." She is understandably concerned if her husband is seriously injured, but most wives believe that it is not a good idea to express too much fear or distress because they are expected to display a certain amount of strength or stoicism to the public. Similarly, a wife would do best to avoid confronting or irritating spectators who are intoxicated, verbally abusive, or heckling her husband. Instead, she should suppress her anger and use a surface acting strategy to convey that she is not affected by such offensive behavior.

Sharing Moods

During the season, wives are expected to emotionally conform to certain situations, and this can involve "mood sharing," by which wives subordinate their emotions to the husband's or the team's emotions (Ortiz 1997, 233–236). For instance, when Beth and Cliff, a major league baseball player, are alone in the car on the ride home after a game, Cliff is unresponsive and Beth knows that this is because he is emotionally decompressing. By sharing his mood and empathizing with the demands of his emotional labor (Hochschild 1983, 7), she avoids discussing sensitive family matters because she knows he needs time to disengage from the game, and she does not want to upset him. If he is willing, she encourages or allows him to evaluate or vent his feelings about an injury, his performance, his team's performance, or the game in general. She tries to be supportive and is careful not to criticize, admonish, correct, or tease him. Beth won't express her own feelings if they are contradictory to his. She displays only emotions that reflect and share his emotions. In general, an athlete's wife tends to be reluctant to create any problems or upset her husband during the season, and she usually waits until after the season is over to try to discuss her concerns or feelings with him. Stacy explained: "I want to let him play well. Come to think of it, I can't think of many of the wives that I know that would just say what was on their mind if they were upset during the season, and go into a big deal about it."

Although most wives prefer to stay home when their husbands are on the road during the season, others view road trips as opportunities to be more emotionally intimate and to better manage their fears about how their husbands might behave while away from home. When a wife travels on the road with her husband and his team, she soon becomes aware of the feeling and display rules shared by her husband's teammates in different road-trip situations. For example, if the team loses a game, tension and stress permeate the airplane or bus and the mood is usually quiet and somber. Teammates expect the wives to share in displaying disappointment. As Marsha observed, "It's like a death in the family because everybody's in mourning. You *need* to be upset, and you have to *show* that you're upset, at the loss." Stacy addressed the necessity of understanding the appropriate display rules when she confided, "I always wonder how I'm supposed to look because you're supposed to be disappointed, and you're supposed to be quiet." Shelia recalled a time when she violated the rules about mood sharing: "One time I was on a trip with the Bobcats . . . and several wives were on this trip and we had just gotten our brains beat out in Meadowville. And something happened on the bus. It was so funny. And a couple of us were just cracking up, and one of the coaches turned around and said, 'In case you girls didn't notice, we just lost three games in a row.' I was like, 'Oh.' But, I mean, it was still funny. I couldn't help it. I know you're not supposed to do that."

Managing Her Emotions at Home

An athlete's wife is fairly autonomous during the season while her husband is traveling, and this seems to be agreeable to her husband because his attention is on his career. But when he is home during the off-season, a power shift can occur—one that can be to his advantage and intensifies her sense of powerlessness. In this domestic situation, it is not uncommon for a wife to believe that her autonomy is limited or lost because of the ways her husband tries to use power to control her and their family. "When Craig's home, he's usually in control," Jill confided. "He likes to be in control of really everything he does outside of football." Wives attempt to provide a relatively stress-free home life as their husbands' transition from one season to another, and during these times they find it necessary to rely more often on emotion management skills. Jill discovered that emotion management strategies were useful in suppressing her anger, frustration, or resentment when her husband became critical, overbearing, and demanding. She explained: "He said, 'How long is it going to take you to paint the garage? Three weeks?' And I said, 'I don't know how long it's going to take me to paint because I have kids to take care of. I can't be painting the garage and taking care of kids, and cleaning the house, and cooking dinner, and doing laundry.' And he didn't say anything. He thinks that I should just do the whole thing today. I could say to him, 'Then you do it yourself if you want it done that fast.' But then he'd get all mad."

Instead of being honest with Craig about how she feels, Jill suppresses her feelings in order to keep the peace. Knowing he will be home only for a short time, she attempts to act as if everything is fine, perhaps even pretending to be cheerful. However, sustaining surface acting in this manner can be exhausting, problematic, or, in some cases, impossible.

Given her husband's frequent and extended absences from home during the season, a wife initially may be happy to have him home. However, by the time the off-season is over and he leaves for spring training or training camp, she is usually relieved and quite pleased to see him go because his departure may signify the return of her autonomy; in these situations, she may experience a confusing mix of feelings, including guilt and sadness. In any event, departures can be emotionally difficult. Robyn confided:

> We already drive each other nuts when it gets down to like February first. I want him to leave so bad I can hardly stand it. Just get out of here. And then I

> get all stressed out because he's going to leave and I really don't want him to. I want him to just go "click" and be gone. I don't want him piddling around and saying, "Well, I think I'll leave this day or that day." It's the same thing when they leave for a road trip. I hate it. So it stresses me out. So we get into a big fight. I want to go with him and I can't. That's why it stresses me out. So that's my way of dealing with it.

Performing Her Wifely Duty

The wives' awareness of a culture of adultery in their husbands' occupational world and the persistent presence of groupies and other sexually available women intensifies their fear that their husbands might be sexually unfaithful when they are on the road (Ortiz 1997, 1998, 2001b; 2003b). In the motherization process, a husband makes a sharp distinction between his wife, who is home caring for their children, and other women who are "out there" and sexually available. He may not always be comfortable with his wife's sexuality, especially if he cannot control it, or if he has desexualized her. Shelia maintained: "They don't really see their wife as a woman. That's probably one big reason why the guys fool around. These women they see out on the road, they don't have kids dragging along behind them and they're dressed fit to kill every minute. They don't think of their wife in that way." Thus, when a husband returns home from a long road trip during the season and his wife is delighted to see him, she may attempt to initiate a romantic or sexual encounter. If he has motherized her—and based on the degree to which he has—he may become confused or uncomfortable and have difficulty relating to her sexually, perhaps even refusing her advances.

In contrast, lovemaking can also be a "wifely duty." When sexual interactions such as lovemaking become an obligation, they may be less about love and more about sexual compliance—a form of sexual subordination that results in an emotional cost for the wife. The degree to which it costs her depends on how much she believes she should provide emotional support to her husband, how much she suppresses uncomfortable feelings, and how much she is affected by her displays of compliance. It also depends on the extent to which she suppresses her concerns or fears about the possible consequences of her noncompliance. Her fear that her husband will have or is having an affair can lead to emotional sensitivity—even hypersensitivity—about their sexual relationship or the sexual availability of other women (Ortiz 2001b). In Shelia's case, suppressing her fears about her husband, Frank, can be difficult to manage. "Every time he went on a road trip, I'm like, 'Oh, I know he's out with somebody. I know he is.' And then I just thought, 'This is dumb. I'm going to drive myself nuts. Unless he gives you a reason, don't think about it.'"

Despite her best efforts to manage and conceal her anxiety, Tanya's worst fear was realized when she discovered that her husband, Derrick, had extramarital sex with several different women in the first few months of their marriage. In another case, during her pregnancy, Kellita began to suspect that her husband,

Donald, was having an affair. Although he initially denied it when she confronted him, sometime after their son was born she hired a private investigator, who confirmed her suspicions. Eventually, Donald admitted that he was having an affair, and Kellita attempted to manage her confusing, intense, and painful emotions. She struggled over which emotion was appropriate and which feeling rules applied: "Should I feel this anger or should I not? And then you want to justify do I feel this way or not?" Wives like Tanya and Kellita try to cope with an unexpected and entirely unwelcome situation by working on their emotions before and after receiving the bad news of a husband's sexual unfaithfulness.

The fear about her husband's possible sexual infidelity usually prevents a wife from withholding sex. Arisa confided, "God, I wouldn't withhold because there were too many women out there that want to give it [to him] for you." As Beth's story illustrates, he may exploit this fear and seek her compliance by emphasizing the availability of other women on the road and their keen interest in male professional athletes:

> We had just made love the night before, I think, or two days before, and he acted like it's been a month or a year. It just came out of the clear blue sky. Cliff said to me, "I thought I married this woman that really liked sex a lot. I think you're really in a slump right now." And I said to him, "Listen, if we did it every single day you would still think I'm in a slump. I don't know why you're this way, but it's almost like no matter how much you get, it won't be enough." It was not that I think about him cheating. But he alluded to it when he said, "Well, I'm sure there's some girl out there that wants to get it on with me."

When wives of professional athletes engage in sex as a "wifely duty," they do so out of concern for their marriage, out of fear that their husbands will engage in extramarital sex, and out of their desire to avoid conflict. As Sharon admitted, "You feel like a whore after a while. You just lay down for them and that's shitty. I think a lot of professional sports wives feel like that. It's sex on demand."

Escaping from Emotions

Despite their best efforts to do emotion work, wives may experience "emotive dissonance" (Hochschild 1983, 90). This occurs when the separation of feeling and display become difficult to sustain over long periods of time and lead to a wife becoming confused about what she genuinely feels. In addition, failure to comply with feeling and display rules, and failure to appropriately manage emotions in private or public life, can result in being or feeling criticized, ostracized, or stigmatized by the husband or others (Goffman 1963). A common response to this emotive dissonance is for wives to respond to major stressors or sudden disruptive crises by attempting to escape from their emotions. They try to numb themselves emotionally, because "not feeling" seems preferable (see Hochschild 1983, 187–188). Kathleen described this emotion avoidance or evocative denial when she talked about what it was like for her.[2] "I feel like sometimes I just was a machine, and I just blocked out everything so I could keep going. I feel like I stepped out of my body. I opened myself up and I stepped out. And the emotional part, the feelings stayed in a closet, and the robot part, the physical part did the work."

Another story reveals the serious consequences than can occur when a wife feels she can no longer do emotion work or avoid their authentic emotions. In deference to her husband, Matt, Dana did not establish her own career, and her own expressed need to have an identity separate from that of the wife of a professional baseball player was not met. She felt trapped in this enabling role and was tired of it, yet she kept performing the expected roles. She constantly felt unhappy about not meeting her own needs and guilty about not being able to please others. She stated: "I have desires and wants of my own, but they're conflicting because this other part of me feels that I need to serve other people, and to put other people before me. But you know what? I never could figure that out. It's like I never could understand why I did that."

The consequences of trying to manage their emotions can eventually have a profoundly negative effect on their emotional stability, as Dana's story illustrates. On a day much like any other day, she got into her car and drove away from her home. A short time later, she purposely steered her car directly toward a tree. She was emotionally exhausted and experiencing the cumulative effect of deferring to Matt and his baseball career. Although Dana lived to talk about that day, she had decided at that point in her life that there was no way of solving her many problems and she was tired of living. She explained: "You feel abandoned. You feel that you're not good enough. You feel that this is the only thing in life that you can do. I was angry. I was furious. You could not have put one more drop of water in that boiling pan. I mean I was just ready to boil over and that's what I did. And it was like, 'Who's there for me? I'm there for everybody else.'"

Conclusion

Given their commitment to their career-dominated marriages, the wives of professional athletes who participated in this study have learned to normalize their use of emotion management to follow the unwritten rules of the sport marriage. In doing so, these women provide their husbands and their husbands' occupational world with the power and control necessary to take advantage of, exploit, or oppress them. But this in no way implies that they are submissive or weak; they make a choice to enact the roles and perform the marital labor that makes it possible for their husbands to succeed in their careers. Their marital labor and their sense of self are validated by their husbands' occupational success. As they become socialized in their career-dominated marriages, these women become aware of the consequences of breaking the unwritten rules, but they are not completely aware of the personal and marital costs of following them.

When a wife continually tries to manage her fears, suspicions, insecurities, or anxieties, or to avoid emotions in coping with stress, there is an emotional cost, such as emotional exhaustion or burnout. This can, in turn, lead to some form of marital burnout or, as in Dana's case, self-destructive tendencies. Emotion management and emotion avoidance promote patterns of denial that can result in confusion or ambivalence about genuine emotions. Despite her good intentions, her feelings for her husband, and her marital labor, she risks jeopardizing her identity and sacrificing marital satisfaction. By her definition, she has been a "good wife"—but at what cost to her?

At some point, some wives realize that striving for marital and family stability is not enough and that searching for some measure of emotional well-being is equally, if not more, important. Other wives resign themselves—perhaps with a sense of futility—to the obligations of the career-dominated sport marriage.

NOTES

The ethnographic research reported in this chapter was supported in part by grants from the American Sociological Association Minority Fellowship Program and the Department of Sociology, University of California, Berkeley. I am deeply indebted to Arlie Russell Hochschild for her inspiration and for her generous and supportive mentorship. I am also thankful to others for their invaluable insights and suggestions on various sources that form much of the basis for this chapter. I am particularly grateful to Anita Garey and Karen V. Hansen for their thoughtful comments and editorial direction. Finally, I extend my sincere appreciation to the wives for sharing their lives and heartfelt stories with me. Although their names and the names of the husbands, teams, and cities are pseudonyms, their experiences have been preserved.

1. This chapter provides an opportunity to apply the emotion management perspective in developing and expanding ideas I have explored in previous works (e.g., Ortiz 1997, 2002, 2005b, 2006).
2. For a discussion of these ideas see Ortiz (2001b). A special thank you to Arlie Russell Hochschild for suggesting these ideas in past discussions.

REFERENCES

Finch, Janet. 1983. *Married to the Job: Incorporation in Men's Work.* London: Allen and Unwin.

Goffman, Erving. 1961. "Role Distance." In *Encounters: Two Studies in the Sociology of Interaction,* 83–152. Indianapolis: Bobbs-Merrill.

———. 1963. *Stigma: Notes on the Management of Spoiled Identity.* Englewood Cliffs, NJ: Prentice-Hall.

———. 1967. "On Face-Work: An Analysis of Ritual Elements in Social Interaction." In *Interaction Ritual: Essays in Face-to-Face Behavior,* 5–46. Chicago: Aldine.

Hochschild, Arlie Russell. 1969. "The Role of the Ambassador's Wife: An Exploratory Study." *Journal of Marriage and the Family* 31:73–87.

———. 1979. "Emotion Work, Feeling Rules, and Social Structure." *American Journal of Sociology* 85:551–575.

———. 1983. *The Managed Heart: Commercialization of Human Feeling.* Berkeley: University of California Press.

———. 1990. "Ideology and Emotion Management: A Perspective and Path for Future Research." In *Research Agendas in the Sociology of Emotions,* edited by Theodore D. Kemper, 117–142. New York: State University of New York Press.

Ortiz, Steven M. 1997. "Traveling with the Ball Club: A Code of Conduct for Wives Only." *Symbolic Interaction* 20:225–249.

———. 1998. "Strategizing Marital Survival: How Wives of Professional Athletes Cope with Groupies." Paper presented at the annual meeting of the American Sociological Association, San Francisco, CA, August 21–25.

———. 2001a. "How Interviewing Became Therapy for Wives of Professional Athletes: Learning from a Serendipitous Experience." *Qualitative Inquiry* 7:192–220.

———. 2001b. "When Sport Heroes Stumble: Stress and Coping Responses to Extramarital Relationships among Wives of Professional Athletes." Paper presented at the annual meeting of the American Sociological Association, Anaheim, CA, August 18–21.

———. 2002. "Constructing Dependency in Coping with Stressful Occupational Events: At What Cost for Wives of Professional Athletes?" *Sociology of Sport Online* 5, no. 2 (November–December). http://physed.otago.ac.nz/sosol/v5i2/v5i2_2.html.

_____. 2003a. "Muted Masculinity as an Outsider Strategy: Gender Sharing in Ethnographic Work with Wives of Professional Athletes." *Symbolic Interaction* 26:601–611.

———. 2003b. "Managing Public Encounters with Groupies: A Goffmanesque Analysis of Strategic Performances by Wives of Professional Athletes." Paper presented at the annual meeting of the Pacific Sociological Association, Pasadena, CA, April 3–6.

———. 2004. "Leaving the Private World of Wives of Professional Athletes: A Male Sociologist's Reflections." *Journal of Contemporary Ethnography* 33:466–487.

———. 2005a. "The Ethnographic Process of Gender Management: Doing the 'Right' Masculinity with Wives of Professional Athletes." *Qualitative Inquiry* 11:265–290.

_____. 2005b. "The Wife Face as Face Work: Acts of Diplomacy in Public Life by Wives of Professional Athletes." Pater presented at the annual meeting of the Pacific Sociological Association, Portland, OR, April 7–10.

———. 2006. "Using Power: An Exploration of Control Work in the Sport Marriage." *Sociological Perspectives* 49:527–557.

Papanek, Hanna. 1973. "Men, Women, and Work: Reflections on the Two-Person Career." *American Journal of Sociology* 78:852–872.

CHAPTER 10

Emotion Work in the Age of Insecurity

Marianne Cooper

"The 'social' goes far deeper than our current images of self lead us to suppose. Social roles and relations do not simply reflect patterns of thought and action, leaving the realm of emotion and feeling untouched, timeless, and universal. No, there are social patterns to feeling itself. Our task, as sociologists, is to invent both a magnifying glass and a pair of binoculars that permit us to trace the many links between a world that shapes people's feeling and people who can feel."

—Hochschild, "The Sociology of Feeling and Emotion: Selected Possibilities"

Judging by its staying power as one of the most e-mailed news stories of the week, the *New York Times* article "In Silicon Valley, Millionaires Who Don't Feel Rich" clearly struck a chord with many people (Rivlin 2007). Building from the premise that those with millions of dollars should feel rich, the article takes us into the upside down world of some extremely well-off individuals in Silicon Valley who, despite being among the top wealth holders in the country, don't feel totally secure, worry about the rising costs of healthcare and college, and continue to put in long hours at work in the hopes of earning even more money. To make sense of these seemingly irrational feelings, the article notes the high cost of living in the Valley as well as the unusual standard of comparison there, where keeping up with the Joneses can mean not simply owning a house with a pool, but also owning a mansion, a private jet, and a vacation home. In such an environment, one informant observed, "You're nobody here at 10 million dollars."

This article appeared just as I was completing two years of fieldwork in Silicon Valley exploring, through interviews and ethnographic research, how fifty families from across the socioeconomic spectrum think about, experience, and create security.[1] I, too, had discovered an oddity in my research among upper-income families, namely that for them a lot of money in the bank didn't necessarily equate to a strong sense of financial security. On several occasions, informants with large assets, even some with over a million dollars in investments, did not describe themselves as rich and expressed anxiety about their financial situations. Odd findings, however, were not just reserved for the well off in my study. I also had the disquieting experience of having some with much less, even people without any savings at all, tell me they felt things were fine or insist that they could get by with very little, while at the same time many seemed to be preparing themselves, bracing themselves, or getting themselves to be okay with less. In light of this discovery, a second headline could be written to bookend the one about the rich in Silicon Valley. It would read, "In Silicon Valley, Bad Off Workers Who Don't Feel Bad Off" or more accurately, "Bad Off Workers Who Try Not to Feel Bad Off." My curious finding that well-off people tend to anxiously yearn for more and less well-off people tend to convince themselves that they are fine with less are both, I believe, emotional responses at the individual level to profound economic and political changes. I call these emotional responses the upscaling and downscaling of security. The upscaling of security involves the ratcheting up of the expectations and desires for what those at the top need to feel secure. The downscaling of security involves the curtailment of expectations and desires for what those at the middle and below need. This essay examines the emotional landscapes that lie behind these security processes. In doing so, it seeks to explore the implications of changes in inequality and in the nature of risk that have occurred in American life.

The View through the Binoculars

To trace the connections between people's feelings about security and the broader social world that helps shape those feelings, we need to set our sights on the large-scale, macroeconomic story that surrounds my microlevel, phenomenological study of security. When we look out that far, what comes into focus over the past forty years is the drastic rise of both income and wealth inequality in which those at the top have received most of the gains. During the 1980s, the decade that recorded the sharpest rise in inequality, there was a widening of inequality throughout the income distribution. In that decade workers earning the least saw their wages decline by 14.1 percent, workers earning the most saw their wages increase by 8.1 percent, and the wages of workers in the middle were flat (Boushey and Weller 2005).[2] The pattern of increasing inequality that continued during the 1990s and through the turn of the century looked a little different, with inequality growing steadily and continuously between the highest earners and those in the middle and inequality decreasing between earners at the middle and those at the bottom (Autor et al. 2007). Since the 1990s inequality has grown because the incomes of the highest earning Americans have grown faster than the incomes of both the middle class and the poor (Burtless 2007). On balance then, the rate of income growth among households over the past three decades has been extremely uneven. From 1976 to 2005 the income of the poorest households grew by only 6.3 percent, incomes for households in the middle grew by 21 percent (less than 1 percent a year), while the incomes of the top fifth of households grew by 80 percent (Bernstein 2007a). The rise in income inequality sees no signs of abating, as data recently released from the Congressional Budget Office shows that household income inequality grew faster from 2003 to 2005 than over any two-year period going back to 1979 (Bernstein 2007b). Moreover, wealth inequality has grown even more than income inequality. In the beginning of the 1960s, the richest Americans held 125 times more wealth than that of the median wealth holder. By 2004 the wealthiest had 190 times more wealth than the typical household (Mishel, Bernstein, and Allegretto 2006, 251). From 1984 to 2004, the top 20 percent of households received 89 percent of the total growth in wealth, while the bottom 80 percent received just 11 percent (Wolff 2007). This remarkable rise in inequality since the postwar years has led some to argue that the United States has not seen such high levels of inequality since right before the Great Depression (Piketty and Saez 2003).

Though the main macroeconomic story surrounding the families in my study is of income and wealth inequality, another important trend also shaping people's lives is a shift in the management of risk.[3] Over the last few decades in both governmental policy and employment relations there has been a shift away from sharing the risks involved in managing lives, taking care of families, and safeguarding futures and a movement toward more and more self-provisioning.[4] Underlying the increase in the number of risks people must now manage themselves, such as providing their own healthcare or building and managing their own retirement savings, is neoliberal political ideology which holds that people will work harder and make better decisions if they are on their own to defend against the vicissitudes of life. Indeed, neoliberal doctrine looks askance at dependence, arguing that it undermines people's initiative and instead celebrates risk and uncertainty as the source of self-reliance. The logic of this premise is that people should build their own safety net, and that the more enterprising and industrious someone is, the better the safety net they will be able to construct.[5] Packaged as changes that will allow individuals to have more control over their own destiny, the real message that has emerged from declines in employer-sponsored pensions and health benefits, and reductions in the levels of governmental aide for higher education and welfare benefits, is that you are on your own.

The rise in income and wealth inequality and the shift of risk onto individuals and their families are not merely changes in the social facts on the outsides of people's lives. Rather, by looking at the upscaling and downscaling of security we can see the ways in which these outside social facts can shape the insides of people's hearts and minds.

The Upscaling of Security

> We are probably in the top 1 percent of all American households, which probably puts us in the top quarter percent of all worldwide households, right? . . . So I can't complain . . . [but] I still don't feel rich. (Paul Mah, a forty-eight-year-old technology executive)[6]

A million dollars is not what it used to be. This is a key finding from the "The True Value of Wealth," a recent report by the financial services firm Barclay's Wealth (2007) based on their survey of high worth individuals. The report explains that while a million dollars used to be the gold standard for wealth, today's gold standard is now closer to $10 million. This increase is partly due to inflation and a rise in costs associated with a life of luxury, but it is also a result of a change in the criteria people now use to assess their own wealth. It seems that the proliferation of billionaires and multimillionaires has altered, at the top, understandings of what it means to be rich. As a consequence, people who objectively possess substantial wealth don't always subjectively feel wealthy. A wealth expert cited in the report notes that in his work it is a common occurrence to "see affluent individuals, with what we would think of as sizeable assets, who still don't feel that they are truly wealthy because they are comparing themselves with people who are wealthier than they are" (Barclay's Wealth 2007, 7). Other surveys confirm these findings. A survey conducted by Worth-Roper Starch found that the majority of Americans in the top 1 percent of earners do not think of themselves as rich (Barclay's Wealth 2007). Another survey by PNC Advisors, a wealth management firm, found that for their clients to feel financially secure, virtually all of them would need to double their level of net worth or income (PNC Advisors 2005). Those with $10 million or more needed a median of $18.1 million to feel secure; those with $5 million or more felt they needed $10.4 million, and those with $500,000 to $1 million felt they needed $2.4 million.

That the standards for judging wealth appear to be on the move is reflected in the feelings of those like my interviewee, Paul Mah, who doesn't feel rich even though he knows he is among the top 1 percent of wealth holders. We could write off Paul's feelings as simply another example of the hedonic treadmill, that as people's incomes rise, so too do their expectations, thus they are never satisfied with what they have. Yet, hedonic treadmills themselves, those rising expectations, are shaped by the social world that envelope them. They are shaped by the particular form of stratification in which they are embedded. Hence, if the rungs of the class ladder were closer together, it is likely that rising expectations would rise only so high. But in the context of extreme inequity, when vast fortunes begin to dot the horizon, expectations appear to become limitless and we see the existence of upscaled desires.

Undoubtedly, the upscaling of security is linked to sky-high inequality. However, it is also likely linked to the transformation in risk that has occurred in tandem with our new gilded age. According to Milton Pedraza, the chief executive of the Luxury Institute, the reason $10 million signifies wealth today is because that is the "level of wealth where people feel protected from the hazards of the world" (Barclay's Wealth 2007, 7). And this, it seems, is what the goal is at the top, the ability to be impervious to risk, to be immune to the vicissitudes of life, to be completely self-reliant. This ethic is most clearly revealed by the sentiments of Rob Newman, who was only able to feel truly secure once he had become independent of everything else:

> I kind of felt secure with twenty-five million dollars cash in the bank and no mortgages, but even then I didn't feel totally independent. I don't know why, I mean it's hard to spend twenty-five million dollars . . . [at that point] I was spending less than the money was making every year so I guess intellectually I thought, "I'm independently wealthy." And for anybody, particularly somebody with a mathematical mind you'd think, "Well of course, look at the numbers. You're independently [wealthy], you don't have to be concerned." But when you throw in the emotional insecurity about really wanting to be financially secure . . . I'm not sure I felt that until I had thirty or thirty-five million. Sometime after that I started feeling [we were] financially secure and probably our kids would be financially secure, because at that amount of money you are definitely not spending what you're making every year nor will your kids be able to. (Rob Newman, a fifty-two-year-old technology executive)

The inflated notions of security held by those with the most resources in my study led many of them, like Paul Mah and Rob Newman, to be plagued throughout their lives by the sense that they didn't quite have enough. To manage this anxiety, a main form of emotion work this group engaged in was, ironically enough, to think about their concerns, financial and otherwise, incessantly. As opposed to trying to ignore or submerge their fears, it was more common among this group to shine a spotlight on them. Thus, the way they managed their worry was to worry. In doing so, the goal was to distill and quantify the exact nature of the problem in order to come up with potential solutions. Paradoxically, rather than placating their fears, the emotional result of this spotlight approach was to sharply heighten their levels of anxiety. Michael Handley, an upper-income father, illustrates this form of emotion work and its relentless and anxiety-provoking nature when he explained how he deals with his concern that his nest egg might not be enough to pay for his child's education and his own retirement if another influx of cash from stock options does not come his way. Michael said, "I'm consciously aware of where the nest egg is and, okay, if I got to ride this the whole way, how do I manage it? What does that mean? What's the trajectory? What are my options? What's my plan B here? You must have a plan B. It's not enough to say, 'Oh this will work out.' You can't have that kind of confidence [if] you're not always kind of working your angle." To dial down his worry regarding his finances Michael actively manages his assets and creates contingency plans. Yet, ironically, by actively managing his financial concerns he is continually reminded that he is falling short. Accordingly, his worrying provides little solace for him and instead stokes his anxiety.

Through this anxious ratcheting up at the top of what it takes to feel secure and in what it takes to feel rich, we are able to see the internalization, to an extreme degree, of the "ownership society's" commandment for people to build their own safety net and stand on their own two feet. The desire to be invulnerable and to amass such high levels of security reflects, at the level of feeling, an emotional accompaniment among the affluent to the privatization of concern that has taken place in an era of neoliberalism. Though similar sentiments and emotion work among the well-off may predate this specific historical moment, the upscaling I found among the upper-income families in my study nonetheless reveals a matching or squaring of emotions that fits with affluent individuals' current location within the privatization of risk.

The Downscaling of Security

> I've been broke my whole life, and so it's like if I'm broke it doesn't scare me, it doesn't bother me. (Jenny French, a forty-year-old administrative assistant)

Against the backdrop of high inequality and the shift in the management of risk, those with the most resources in my study upscaled their feelings regarding security. In contrast, the tendency among those with fewer resources was to downscale their feelings. This process involved lowering the bar on their requirements for security, resigning themselves to these reduced levels, and suppressing anxiety when it arose. The downscaling of security can be viewed as a kind of emotion work, in which those of more minimal means worked on their feelings, submerging some and bringing forth others, in order to manage their anxiety in the face of difficult or precarious economic circumstances.

As opposed to the ever-expanding notions of security that I found among those at the top in my study, I found more pared-down notions of security among those in my study who had often experienced financial hardships over the course of their lives. As the above quotation from Jenny French indicates, being broke isn't a concern to her. To feel secure Jenny says she doesn't need many material possessions. Instead, she told me that she feels fine "as long as I have a few bucks in my pocket and my car is running." However, when Jenny recounted a difficult economic time in her life when she was burdened by tax debt and was unable to work because of a serious health issue, she expressed a deep unease with her situation. Jenny explained, "[W]e [were] barely living, eating. We couldn't afford anything. We couldn't afford clothing, nothing . . . We were basically just paying our rent and we did have food . . . it was just like bare necessities. And there were times that I would just pray about it." In such trying circumstances, Jenny's anxiety was placated and her sense of security generated by focusing on the basics. More recently, Jenny's economic situation has improved and she has begun to save money, which makes her feel like she's moving ahead. Jenny said, "So I never used to [save money]. It feels better. It feels good because I'm able to buy the kid's clothing a lot more and you know just be able to get out and do things now." Interestingly, despite Jenny's economic advancement, when asked, she retains a more curtailed notion of security in which "all we really need is like food, clothing, and shelter."

There are several ways to analyze Jenny's more streamlined conception of security. On the one hand, it reflects a kind of resiliency and fortitude that has likely emerged from her repeated ability to get by on very little and make it through difficult times. On the other hand, by minimizing her threshold for security she has a ready-made emotional coping mechanism to employ that has helped her in the past and will help her in the future to cushion the psychic impact of any financial blow. Put differently, her ability to scale back her needs provides her with a kind of emotional armor that helps her defend against feeling insecure should difficulties arise. Thus, even as Jenny strives to put her family into a better economic position, and even as she moves forward in accomplishing that goal, she simultaneously protects herself against future bouts of insecurity by holding in reserve a curtailed definition of security. In hard times, she can call upon this pared-down notion to supply her with a sense that things are okay and that she will ride out the storm.

Scaled-back definitions of security provide a way emotionally to weather life's ups and downs. For example, when Laura Delgado's electricity got turned off because she was unable to pay her power bill, she decided electricity was not a necessity. Describing her situation, she said, "I'm trying to make a game out of it with the kids. We use candles at night, like we're camping . . . I told the kids that people have lived without electricity before. It's not a necessity. TV is not a necessity. They already know cable isn't a necessity." For individuals and families in the grips of financial difficulty, downscaling one's view of security supplies a way to continue to feel secure in spite of real financial insecurity.

Although some interviewees like Jenny and Laura more readily embraced bare-bones notions of security, others tried to resign themselves to their reality of having less than they desired. For example, Marshall Crenshaw, who had recently returned to work as a property surveyor after being laid off from his technology project management job, described his financial situation as "living one step ahead of the red line" [*laughs*]. Living without much of a financial cushion made him feel insecure. He said, "It's not a good feeling. We'd like to have a nice buffer to where you don't have to worry about it . . . 'cause we've got kids that are going to be needing to go to college here pretty soon. And I don't know how we're going to manage that. We haven't really done much preparation for that either." I then asked Marshall if he had any concerns about his savings for retirement and he said, "Well, I mean it doesn't look like I'm ever going to be able to retire." In comparison to Michael Handley, the upper-income father who possesses an ever present concern about his financial situation regarding the costs of his son's college education and his own retirement, Marshall possesses a more fatalistic, if realistic, viewpoint. In this case, rather than being disappointed or frustrated, worrying incessantly, or questioning the fairness of the new "you're on your own" retirement system, Marshall seems resigned to the new economy reality that without pensions, large numbers of people will never be able to save enough to retire or fully retire. Such resignation serves to manage down Marshall's own expectations about his future, thus quelling any unhappy feelings he has about his situation.

While some interviewees like Jenny, Laura, and Marshall manage their feelings of insecurity in a more unconscious way, others consciously engaged in repressing their worries. This more active kind of repression work is clearly illustrated in Katie Monroe's description of how she deals with the fact that at fifty years old she has zero retirement savings. She says:

> It burns a whole in my heart when I think about it . . . I'm fifty . . . and I have nothing to fall back on. I can get up some days and I could think about that and fall into like this big depression, but I can't allow myself to do that. I'm glad every month that goes by that I was able to pay the rent; I was able to pay the bills and I still have more money in the bank than I have ever had. At this stage of the game . . . whatever is gonna happen is gonna happen. [*Sighs*] I can't drive myself nuts thinking about it. . . . The way I look at it is I'm in the best place that I've been in a long time . . . but I can't put more pressures on myself right now because there's some days where I just feel like I'm gonna snap anyway.

Through Katie's words we can see how she consciously works on her feelings. She suppresses her fears about her lack of savings for retirement and focuses instead on something more positive, her newfound ability to keep up with her bills. It is only by setting her security concerns on a shelf that Katie is able to feel like she is making it on her own. It is only by burying away her anxieties about retirement that she is able to feel she is in control.

In a society increasingly shaped by neoliberal ideology, people are faced with the following dilemma—they are supposed to bear the responsibility and the risk of attaining their own security at a historical moment when the things that would help them achieve this goal such as well-paying jobs with good benefits, affordable housing, and affordable educations are in shorter and shorter supply. To manage this contradiction, people downscale in a variety of ways. Some repackage insecurity as security and lower the bar on what it takes for them to feel secure. Others resign themselves to less and bottle up their fears. By redefining notions of security and suppressing anxiety, downscaling allows people to block out their worry, feel like they are making do, and feel like things aren't so bad. As such, it can be viewed as an adaptive response for dealing with difficult circumstances in which there are few options. Moreover, by managing their feelings in this way, downscaling reveals a desire to emotionally construct one's situation in a way that maintains a sense that they are making it on their own. Like upscaling, then, downscaling too reflects an internalization of the current cultural iteration of American individualism, the "ownership society's" ethos of self-reliance.

The View under the Magnifying Glass

> Through how it makes us see relations, define experience, and manage feeling, the culture of capitalism insinuates its way into the very core of our being. (Hochschild 1998, 11)

Through the emotional processes of upscaling and downscaling we see different groups of people in the context of macroeconomic change striving for the same goal of independence. One group accomplishes this objective by ratcheting up their needs. The other group accomplishes it by ratcheting down their needs, particularly during hard times. Consequently, we can view the need to have millions of dollars in the bank and the need to have only a few dollars in one's pocket as two sides of the same coin. They are both emotional strategies that enable people to grapple with the shift in the management of risk and to the drastic rise in income and wealth inequality.

When we examine these processes carefully, we see that these coping mechanisms reflect inequalities. For as Hochschild (2003, 116–118) points out, power doesn't work around feeling, it works through feelings, typically raising the expectations of the more powerful and lowering the expectations of the least powerful. But we also see that these coping mechanisms do more than just reflect inequality. As cultural logics, they begin to drive inequality. The feeling that one needs more and more at the top orients behavior toward accruing more capital despite already high levels of wealth. For example, a 2005 survey of 500 ultra-wealthy individuals whose net worth was at least $5 million dollars found that 34 percent sought to gain "significant" additional wealth (*Worth Magazine* 2005). In contrast, the ability of those with fewer resources to feel like one needs less and less orients behavior toward accepting less and less. The ability to make their feelings fit with their economic predicament seems to prevent them from taking a critical stance toward the predicament itself. What I found was that instead of critiquing economic hardship through a political lens, like demanding universal or affordable healthcare, people more often worked on themselves to accept or rationalize their situation. This crystallization of inequality, culturally speaking, into people's emotions becomes a legitimizing force by providing an emotional rationale for an unequal situation. It is through the upscaling and downscaling of security that we simultaneously rev up inequality and achieve an absence of the political will to stop it.

Conclusion

> It is, in the end, through the pathways of feeling that we deal with—and hopefully change—the realities of stratification far outside ourselves. (Hochschild 2003, 137)

If definitions of security were like different meals at McDonald's, those at the top would order the "Big Mac" meal, get it "super sized," and still be hungry. Those with less, who are even hungrier, would order the one dollar cheeseburger meal and after eating it tell themselves that they are very full. By exploring the emotional landscapes that lie behind the upscaling and downscaling of security, I have sought to explain why, in the context of sky-high inequality and the privatization of risk, it is "rational" for certain groups of people to develop an ability to ask for more and for others to develop an ability to ask for less. Both reactions are emotional responses at the individual level that jibe with the large-scale economic and political changes that have taken place in the United States over the past several decades. In a society where individuals are increasingly on their own, everyone is on the run to construct their own safety net and build their own security. Depending on one's location within our stratified society, some are able to accomplish the goal of independence literally, others only figuratively. Both approaches legitimize the premise of self-reliance, and in doing so become a driver for further inequality. By first charting the macroeconomic context and then exploring the micro context of people's lives, we are able to see that outside inequalities don't simply shape the social structures that surround us. Rather, systems of stratification make their way inside us, deep inside, shaping the way we feel, try to feel, and try not to feel.

NOTES

1. For a more detailed methodological description of this study, see Cooper (2008).
2. The lowest earning workers are workers at the tenth percentile of the income distribution. The highest earning workers are workers at the ninety-fifth percentile.
3. For more on this transformation in the management of risk, see Hacker (2006).
4. In this essay the term "self-provisioning" is drawn from the risk and governmentality literature, wherein the term refers, in a general sense, to the need for individuals to provide for and arrange their own welfare. This definition is distinct from that used by other scholars to refer to the labor individuals do to provide themselves with goods or services that they would otherwise purchase in the market, such as growing vegetables.
5. For more analysis of neoliberal ideology and risk, see O'Malley (2004).
6. All names and identifying characteristics of research subjects have been changed to ensure confidentiality.

REFERENCES

Autor, David H., Lawrence F. Katz, and Melissa S. Kearney. 2007. "Trends in U.S Wage Inequality: Revising the Revisionists." Working paper. http://econ-www.mit.edu/files/580.

Barclay's Wealth. 2007. "The True Value of Wealth." December 10. http://www.barclayswealth.com/files/Insights_Volume_4_The_True_Value_of_Wealth.pdf.

Bernstein, Jared. 2007a. "Updated CBO Data Reveal Unprecedented Increase in Inequality." Issue Brief #239. Economic Policy Institute. http://www.epi.org/content.cfm/ib239.

Bernstein, Jared. 2007b. "Boy, Have We Got an Inequality Problem." Economic Policy Institute. http://www.tpmcafe.com/blog/coffeehouse/2007/dec/13/boy_have_we_got_an_inequality_problem

Boushey, Heather, and Christian E. Weller. 2005. "What the Numbers Tell Us." In *Inequality Matters: The Growing Economic Divide in America and Its Poisonous Consequences*, edited by James Lardner and David A. Smith, 27–40. New York: New Press.

Burtless, Gary. 2007. "Comments on Has U.S Income Inequality Really Increased." January 11. *Brookings Institution*. http://www.brookings.edu/views/papers/burtless/20070111.pdf.

Cooper, Marianne. 2008. "The Inequality of Security: Winners and Losers in the Risk Society." *Human Relations* 61:1229–1258.

Hacker, Jacob. 2006. *The Great Risk Shift: The Assault on American Jobs, Families, and Health Care and How You Can Fight Back*. New York: Oxford University Press.

Hochschild, Arlie Russell. 1975. "The Sociology of Feeling and Emotion: Selected Possibilities." In *Another Voice: Feminist Perspectives on Social Life and Socials Science*, edited by Marcia Millman and Rosabeth Moss Kanter, 280–307. New York: Anchor Press.

———. 1998. "The Sociology of Emotions as a Way of Seeing." In *Emotions in Social Life: Critical Theories and Contemporary Issues*, edited by Gillian Bendelow and Simon J. Williams, 3–15. London: Routledge.

———. 2003. *The Commercialization of Intimate Life: Notes from Home and Work*. Berkeley: University of California Press.

Mishel, Lawrence, Jared Bernstein, and Sylvia Allegretto. 2006. *The State of Working America 2006/2007*. New York: University Presses Marketing.

O'Malley, Pat. 2004. *Risk, Uncertainty and Government*. London: GlassHouse Press.

Piketty, Thomas, and Emmanual Saez. 2003. "Income Inequality in the United States, 1913–1998." *Quarterly Journal of Economics* 118 (1): 1–39.

PNC Advisors. 2005. "Many Wealthy Americans Have Done Nothing to Protect Assets and Are Worried About Financial Security, Family Values, According to the Largest Study of Its Kind Released Today." January 10. *PR Newswire*. http://www.prnewswire.com/cgi-bin/micro_stories.pl?ACCT=701257&TICK=PNC&STORY=/www/story/01-10-2005/0002814679&EDATE=Jan+10,+2005.

Rivlin, Gary. 2007. "In Silicon Valley, Millionaires Who Don't Feel Rich." *New York Times*, August 5. http://www.nytimes.com/2007/08/05/technology/05rich.html.

Wolff, Edward N. 2007. "Recent Trends in Household Wealth in the United States: Rising Debt and the Middle-Class Squeeze." Working Paper No. 502, June. Levy Economics Institute at Bard College. http://www.levy.org/vdoc.aspx?docid=929.

Worth Magazine. 2005. "The Status of Wealth in America. A Survey of Wealth." November 1. http://www.worth.com/Editorial/Wealth-Management/Investment-Risk-Management/Survey-of-Wealth-The-Status-of-Wealth-in-America-2.asp.

PART III

Emotional Geography of Invisible Work

CHAPTER 11

The Crisis of Care

Barrie Thorne

How could any affluent country, if only out of long-term self-interest, allow so many of its children to grow up in nightmare childhoods? Ten years ago a visiting Norwegian sociologist asked me that question in an urgent and genuinely puzzled way. She had just come from a conference in San Francisco on U.S. public policy and family poverty, and she was reeling from the human import of the statistics about child poverty that she had heard. I have never forgotten her question and its stark perspective on the irrationality and injustice of U.S. policies relating to children and families.

Before turning to the larger political context, I will report from recent ethnographic research that illuminates the complex ways in which families in California are trying to cope with gaps of provisioning for the care of their children. These case studies bring lived experiences into conjunction with statistical profiles of widening and racialized social class divides. The case studies also illustrate varied and sometimes contested cultural framings of "care," "need," and "obligation." My discussion draws upon feminist theories of care, which are useful in interrogating the dramatic inequalities and the market logic that characterize the current U.S. childcare system. I will conclude by sketching an alternative vision that frames caring as a collective responsibility, and children as a social rather than privatized good.

Qualitative Case Studies of the Contemporary U.S. Childcare System

Skocpol (2000) has observed that public programs in other industrial democracies *correct* for difficulties and inequities in the private wage market. However, especially since the 1980s, U.S. public policies have tended to *exacerbate* market disparities. Althea Huston's analysis of U.S. childcare policies illustrates this point (Huston 2004). The federal welfare reform legislation of 1996 forced impoverished single mothers to take on full-time jobs, mostly at and sometimes below minimum wage. But the legislation did not provide adequate support for the care of these mothers' children. Over the past two decades the ability of low- and middle-income U.S. families to provide care has been eroded not only by cutbacks in state provisioning, but also by heightened job insecurity and the intensification of wage work (Hochschild 1997; Wallulis 1998). There is, in short, a growing crisis of care.

As Huston notes, the United States has a "market-based child care system that is highly decentralized and variable," and in the absence of adequate public subsidies, access to and the quality of paid care strongly correlate with income. The affluent have multiple market options that are flagged, like products on a supermarket shelf, by a nuanced array of labels—nannies, babysitters, housekeepers, au pairs, preschools, day care—and for school-aged children, fee-based after-school programs, lessons, and other specialized activities focused on sports, music, drama, dance, computers, and science. The result, especially among upper middle-class families in metropolitan areas, is a trend, in effect, toward gated childhoods, with children's out-of-home time organized almost entirely through markets that exclude those without the means to pay. In these privatized and relatively homogeneous enclaves, kids often have little contact with those who are less privileged in racialized hierarchies of social class.

At the other end of the class spectrum, parents from lower (and even middle) incomes lack the means to purchase quality paid care. Even if they qualify for government subsidies, they often confront long waiting lists. Low-income solo mothers and their children who are without kin or friends able to lend a daily hand lead especially pressed lives. Furthermore, low-income workers are the least likely to receive "family-friendly" benefits from employers, such as paid sick leave, vacation leave, and job flexibility, and they are much more likely to have to work evenings or nights (Heymann 2000). Deterioration in the quality of public schools and in services like public transportation, parks, and libraries compounds the problems.

The California Childhoods Project

How do employed lower-income parents provide for the care of their children? Between 1996 and 1999 Marjorie Faulstich Orellana and I worked with multilingual teams of graduate and undergraduate students to gather data about the daily lives of children, ages five through twelve, growing up in a varied social class and racial ethnic circumstances in urban California. We set out to trace the local effects of a series of large-scale trends that are reconfiguring the landscape of U.S. childhoods.

1. *High rates of immigration*, the result of economic restructuring and 1965 changes in federal immigration laws. California has received more immigrants than any other state; in 2000, 46 percent of the state's children

had at least one immigrant parent and 40 percent spoke a language other than English at home (Palmer, Song, and Lu 2002).

2. *Widening social class divides*, especially in the wake of political and economic changes of the 1980s. California's rates of child poverty have increased by more than 10 percent over the past two decades, to the current figure of 22 percent. The state also has an unusually high proportion of households with annual incomes over $200,000, while the middle class is shrinking (Palmer et al. 2002). In Oakland 25 percent of children now live below the poverty line; the median income of white households is nearly twice that of African Americans, Latinos, and Asian Americans (Gammon and Marcucci 2002). Half of the white children in Oakland now attend private rather than public schools, a figure much higher than among families of other racial ethnic backgrounds (Tucker and Katz 2002).
3. *Cuts in state provisioning for families and children*, with dramatic deterioration in the quality of public schools, parks, and recreation programs. In the 1950s and early 1960s, California had one of the best public school systems in the country, although resources diverged along lines related to race and class. In 1996, when our research began, the state ranked forty-first in per pupil school funding.
4. *The expansion of market-based infrastructures of services for families and children*, such as private schools and fee-based after-school programs, which are available only to those with the means to pay. Affluent childhoods have become more commodified and privatized; middle- and low-income families rely more on public institutions, although forces of commercialization exert a strong influence on children's lives across lines of class and culture.
5. *The speed-up of family change*, with high rates of maternal employment, a growing care deficit, and the juxtaposition of many different family forms and childrearing practices in crowded urban areas. The forces of globalization have unsettled previously dominant ideals of and assumptions about childhood (Stephens 1995).

These structural shifts are transforming childhoods in urban California as dramatically as the changes of the Progressive Era a century ago, when the passage of laws against child labor and [laws] requiring comprehensive public schooling consolidated a normative ideal of the domesticated and schooled child (Zelizer 1985). Children's lives are still organized through families and schools, but social class divides are wider than at any time in U.S. history. In urban California, these divides are increasingly institutionalized and heavily racialized.

To explore the changing contours of urban childhoods, my co-researchers and I did three years of fieldwork and interviewing in two geographic areas. I guided data-gathering in a mixed-income, ethnically diverse part of Oakland, where the children of immigrants from Mexico, Central America, China,

Vietnam, Laos, Yemen, and other countries, as well as African American and white children, converge in the public school. Orellana organized research in the Pico Union area of Los Angeles, a low-income, inner-city enclave of transmigrants from Mexico and Central America. How, our project asks, do parents and children from different economic and cultural circumstances perceive and negotiate the demographic and cultural shifts related to immigration, widening income gaps, increases in maternal employment, the decline of public responsibility for children, and the commercialization of childhoods? How do kids and "their adults" organize children's uses of time and space, the company they keep, and the process of growing older?

In mapping the daily lives of children from varied cultural and class backgrounds, we discovered an astounding array of care arrangements, some as complex and contingent as Rube Goldberg machines—and as prone to falling apart, with children often pressed to pick up the pieces (Thorne 2001). For example, we interviewed Betty Jones, a low-income solo African American mother who worked the late afternoon and evening shift as a custodian in an Oakland hospital. Her car had broken down months before and she couldn't afford repairs, so her eleven-year-old son Tyrone (all names have been changed) took responsibility for bringing himself and his six-year-old sister to school on a city bus. After school, Tyrone picked up his younger sister and they walked to a bus stop to begin an hour-long daily ride, including a transfer, from Oakland to San Leandro where their grandmother lived. The grandmother took them with her to her evening job as a custodian in an office building. After she got off work at 10 or 11 P.M., she drove the kids back to their apartment in a low-income area of Oakland.

This scheduling exhausted all of them, and Betty, the children's mother, was concerned about her own mother's willingness to continue watching after grandchildren while cleaning offices at night. Like others we interviewed with very tight budgets, Betty wanted to send her kids to the after-school program located at the public school, but she found the fees exorbitant; her income was more than used up by basics like food, rent, and utilities. Betty's swing shift job as a hospital custodian precluded the presence of her children, unlike the hospital job of another solo African American mother in our study. Deborah Payson worked regular hours in a clerical position in a different Oakland hospital, which was near the public school. Her daughter, Sheila, walked to the hospital after school and hung out until 5 P.M., when her mother got off work. While she waited, Sheila did her homework and sometimes helped with filing. Deborah was grateful that her coworkers didn't mind having Sheila around. Child-friendly worksites may become valuable resources for working parents, especially if kids can get there by themselves after school.

Dropping off and picking up kids from school has become a named chunk of daily labor in contemporary households (Thorne 2001). Many kids in Oakland live at some distance from their schools (the public school district has never had its own bus system, except for disabled students), and there is widespread anxiety about the safety of kids walking to school alone. When transportation to and from school is an issue, caregivers especially value temporal and spatial flexibility at places of employment. For example, Xiaoying Lie, a Chinese immigrant mother, was employed in a garment factory in Oakland; her husband, who worked a double shift in a restaurant an hour away from their house, was unavailable to help transport their children to and from school. Xiaoying spoke with her boss, who was also from China, and got permission to take a mid-afternoon break to pick up her fifth and sixth grade daughters from the public school and drive them home. After dropping them off, Xiaoying returned to the factory until 7 P.M. The girls took care of themselves and had dinner waiting when their mother returned for the evening.

Rhonda Franklin, an African American who drove a delivery truck, maneuvered her work schedule so that she could help out her sister, who had almost no flexibility in her daytime shift at Kmart. Rhonda planned ahead so that she could interrupt deliveries and make it to the public school by 3:30, pick up her seven-year-old niece, Jessie, and drop her off at a neighbor's house. When Rhonda couldn't get to the school and Jessie stood waiting beyond the span of time the school staff deemed acceptable, Jessie or a staff member would try to reach the aunt or mother by phone. There were also crises when the neighbor couldn't be at home. Jessie sometimes ended up staying home by herself, although she found it scary.

School schedules and work schedules often collide and can easily move out of sync.[1] For example, Pedro Ramirez, a Mexican immigrant father who worked for an Oakland delivery service, had scheduled a late lunch break to coincide with his seven-year-old daughter Rosalia's school dismissal time. Several months before, Rosalia had been switched from a late to an early morning reading group, which meant she had to be picked up at 3 P.M. instead of 4 P.M. Pedro negotiated a change in his work schedule so that he could continue to pick up Rosalia after school and drive her to the restaurant where her mother was employed as a food server. The mother had little flexibility during her work shift, which ended at 4 P.M. But her job site was a fixed and safe location, with leeway for the temporary presence of a child. Knowing that this makeshift arrangement depended on the goodwill of the restaurant owner and that her parents had few other options, the daughter sat unobtrusively on a chair near the kitchen, doing a bit of homework and watching the restaurant scene while she waited for her mother to get off work.

Compared with families with few children and with minimal ties to local relatives (a situation more typical of middle- and upper middle-class white households in Oakland), immigrant and other families who are embedded in thick networks of kin tend to have extra flexibility in organizing children's out-of-school time. Children from two large Yemeni immigrant families attended the public school that anchors our Oakland field site. In both extended families, older siblings and cousins took responsibility for walking with younger kids to and from school, and older girls did a great deal of child care and housework at home. Aunts and uncles could also be mobilized. The domestic demands of immigrant parents who are working long hours may spur other relatives to migrate in order to help with housework and child care, as in the case of grandparents who came from Hong Kong to live with their son (who had a manufacturing job) and his wife (who was employed in a garment factory). The grandmother cooked, shopped for groceries, cleaned, and did child care; the grandfather routinely took a city bus to the public school and waited for their two young grandchildren ("early bird" and "late bird" readers who got out an hour apart) and escorted them home from school.

The friendships children make in school may become conduits to the care resources of other households. For example, at the end of each school day, two close fifth-grade friends—Julie, from a white, working-class family, and Faria, from a Pakistani immigrant family—walked together to a video store owned by a friend of Faria's father, who had migrated from the same village. The store provided a safe, loosely adult-supervised way-station where the girls could wait to be picked up. Other families used the public library as a way-station, to the consternation of librarians who announced that the facility was *not* a "day care center." A third grader told us that after school let out, he walked to the nearby home of a "lady from church"; his mother, who was employed in a low-wage job, mobilized help through the Pentecostal Church they attended.

Conceptualizing Cultures of Care

My efforts to grasp the dynamics of these varied, contingent, and shifting arrangements for the out-of-school care of elementary schoolchildren have been enriched by workshops and discussions at the Berkeley Center for Working Families (CWF), which Arlie Hochschild and I co-directed between 1998 and 2002.[2] The CWF intellectual community focused on work, family, and "cultures of care"—that is, the varied resources, beliefs, and practices that shape the care that working families give, receive, and all too often might like to have but fail to acquire. We took a holistic and contextual approach, seeking to illuminate different "ecologies of care"—that is, relationships, transfers, and trajectories of care that may extend beyond households to include extended kin, paid caregivers, and an open-ended array of helping "kin," such as friends, neighbors, paid caregivers, coworkers, and acquaintances made through religious and civic organizations. Networks of care may even extend across national borders, as when immigrant parents leave their children behind or send them to relatives or friends back home in Guatemala or the Philippines (Orellana et al. 2001; Thorne et al. 2003).

Using an innovative methodological strategy, CWF researcher Karen V. Hansen (2005) developed a detailed case study of the networks that four different white working families, from across the class spectrum, organized for the care of their school-aged children. She interviewed all of the people (relatives, friends, and paid caregivers of various kinds) who were directly involved in caring for the children at the center of each network. Hansen discovered that care was variously constructed as a diffuse obligation, a favor, a gift, and a tit-for-tat exchange. Her analysis highlights the fact that care is not only a form of work; it is also deeply embedded in relationships (Ruddick 1998). Contractual arrangements, where money is involved, work through a somewhat different logic than helping relationships among kin or friends. Each logic has characteristic tensions and dynamics of reciprocity. The networks that Hansen studied, and the ones I have briefly sketched, varied in size and elasticity; some, in Hansen's terms, were more "robust and pliable," and others "thin and brittle." The contours, as Hansen argues, reflect and are shaped by particular constellations of resources (time, money, people, transportation), which are connected to but not in any simple way determined by social class.

A fuller account of the case studies I presented earlier would examine the ways in which child-care help was mobilized, sustained, and/or withdrawn in ongoing relationships between parents and relatives, friends, neighbors, coworkers, or fellow church members. Issues of reciprocity (should one offer a bit of payment or bring gifts of food to "the lady from church"?), trust (can one rely on a fellow villager of the father of one's daughter's friend?), and control (is it acceptable for the staff to discipline kids who come to the library on their own?) often emerge. One can more easily terminate relationships with a paid caregiver than, say, with a grandmother or an aunt. Differences over questions of discipline, television watching, and food (is candy allowed?) often create tensions between parents and other caregivers.

These case studies of cultures of care allude to a process that Fraser (1989) has termed "the politics of needs assessment." Conceptions of needs and how they should be met (from minimally acceptable to "good enough" to "high quality") are culturally framed and often contested. In assessing issues of childcare quality, Huston draws upon research by experts in child development. But these ideas about and measures of the needs, say, of a four-year-old or a ten-year-old (gender may also enter into the framing) are sometimes at odds with other belief systems, especially when notions of "desirable outcome" extend beyond core matters like physical safety, basic nutrition, and literacy acquisition. In our research on childhoods in Oakland, we've found that various caregiving adults, including parents and teachers, may have quite divergent ideas about issues such as the desirability of older children taking responsibility for younger siblings, the age at which a child—if a girl or a boy—should be allowed to walk to school or to stay home alone, and when and how kids should be disciplined (Thorne et al. 2003). Divergent assumptions sometimes boil up into open conflict.

Children, of course, have their own ideas about needs and rights; and in formal interviews and informal conversations they reported arguing with their parents and other caregivers about what they should eat, when they should go to bed, how much and what sort of television they could watch, and whether or not leaving elementary school means that they have also outgrown after-school programs (also see CWF research by Kaplan [2001] and Polatnick [2002]. Raising children (an adult-centered framing) and growing up (a term more in line with children's perspectives) are complex and relational processes, marked by continual negotiation and struggles over power and autonomy (Haavind 2001; Thorne 2001).

In mainstream American culture, the negotiation of increased individual autonomy and freedom (for example, making one's own choices about what to wear and how to spend free time) symbolically marks the process of growing older. But immigrants from rural areas of Asia, Mexico, Central America, and the Middle East tend to be deeply ambivalent about this emphasis on individual autonomy. Many of these families migrated to the United States in search of educational and employment opportunities unavailable in their countries of origin; they want their children to learn English, do well in school, and engage in life in this country. But immigrant parents also fear that their children will pull away from family obligations and cultural roots and succumb to the individualized excesses of "doing what you want." Non-immigrant teachers, parents, and experts in child development are sometimes troubled when they learn that immigrant kids are making significant labor contributions to their households by caring for siblings, doing housework, and working in family stores (Orellana 2001; Thorne et al. 2003). To middle-class American eyes these kids may look "adultified" and "parentified." But through the lenses of other cultural traditions, the early assumption of responsibility is a mark of growing older, and sheer necessity may press parents to rely on the labor of their children.

Our research highlights the value of linking the study of material resources with attention to cultural beliefs and practices. We have studied the experiences and practices of adult caregivers in conjunction with the perspectives and actions of children who, as I have indicated, not only receive but also may give and negotiate care.[3] We have tried to grapple with complex connections among structures of class, racial-ethnicity, gender, and age.

Social class is best understood through a relational lens, and focusing on only one stratum—such as middle-class working families or low-income single-mother families—obscures a sense of the whole. (Although research on paid work and family life has flourished over the past two decades, it is much too sliced up; for example, the literature on dual-earner middle-class families tends to be set apart from studies of working-class and impoverished families.) A relational perspective broadens research on affluent working parents, for example, to include the family lives and experiences of the nannies and housekeepers whom they employ. Many of these low-income care workers in the United States are immigrants who left children behind in Mexico, El Salvador, or the Philippines, to be cared for by relatives who may or may not be able to meet their needs. "Chains of care" (to use Arlie Hochschild's term) and transnational migration streams, as well as dramatic and interrelated patterns of global and domestic inequality should be included in any portrait of the U.S. landscape of childcare (Ehrenreich and Hochschild 2003; Glenn 1992; Hondagneu-Sotelo 2001; Parrenas 2001).

From Market Logic to an Ethic of Care

European welfare states have been far more generous than the United States in social provisioning for families and children; indeed, Scandinavians refer matter-of-factly to "the caring state," an idea that sounds like an oxymoron to contemporary U.S. ears.

Cross-national comparisons can help us grasp our own cultural assumptions, as can reflections on earlier times in U.S. history when national social provision was seen as more legitimate than it is today. For example, in the Progressive Era comprehensive public schooling was introduced in every state; in the 1930s Congress established Social Security as a general entitlement (at least for workers), and in the late 1940s the Oakland Parks and Recreation Department established free after-school programs at every elementary school in the city, a form of government provisioning that ended in the 1960s, ironically in a period when rates of maternal employment were rising. Although it was framed as a means tested rather than an entitlement tier of Social Security legislation, Aid to Families with Dependent Children was originally framed as a *child care* program rooted in a discourse of maternalism. Somehow over the ensuing decades it got reframed as a program for "free-loading" women, disparaging their needs and contributions as mothers (Mink 1998). CWF researcher Anita Garey (2002) has highlighted another discursive sign of the increased devaluing and privatization of care in the United States: current legislative moves to subsidize after-school programs carefully avoid the language of "care." Instead, advocates of state subsidies emphasize the need to promote academic achievement and to keep kids off of drugs and away from crime (as potential victims and perpetrators). On the other hand, corporations make ample use of the language of care—for example, by touting their "customer care representatives." Luxury hotels take care of "needs" (e.g., for personalized massages or for an orchid leaf presented with tissue-wrapped laundry) that guests are not even aware they have (Sherman 2002). These strange twists of discourse reflect the delegitimation of state provisioning, the power of the capitalist market, and striking inequalities in the distribution of care.

Instituting comprehensive as opposed to means-tested and stigmatized public support for children, the sick, or the elderly now feels virtually impossible in the United States. Indeed, in this mean-spirited time, the rich are getting richer with hidden transfers from the state, such as tax cuts, mortgage write-offs, and corporate bailouts—subsidies framed as entitlements and obscured by the imagery of self-sufficient families. Those with more power are able to command resources and care, under conditions favorable to them. Many of the poor, on the other hand, are getting poorer, and the public subsidies they receive are not only heavily means tested but also highly stigmatized.

How did a sense of collective responsibility for the vulnerable and dependent become so eroded? As capitalist markets have expanded, so has the fiction of the autonomous individual who acts primarily out of self-interest and whose needs are sustained by a self-sufficient, privatized family (Fineman 2000). The masculine ideal of a worker unencumbered by caregiving obligations is built into workplace structures and patterns of reward, which strongly disadvantages workers, the majority of them women, who have primary responsibilities for care (Williams 1998). Dependence and needs for care have been increasingly privatized and thus depoliticized.

An alternative vision starts not with an assumption of individual and household autonomy and the devaluing of dependency and care, but rather with a recognition of human interdependence and of *collective* rather than privatized responsibility for care. We should push for the state to exercise its redistributive powers and offer more generous programs of public assistance for families raising children. Care should be given greater recognition and value. Institutions should be redesigned so that breadwinning and caregiving are organized in more compatible and less gender unequal ways. As Nancy Fraser (1997) has written: "Women today often combined breadwinning and caregiving, albeit with great difficulty and strain. A postindustrial welfare state must ensure that men do the same, while redesigning institutions so as to eliminate the difficulty and strain. We might call this vision Universal Caregiver" (61).

Folbre (2001) has outlined a series of political strategies that would help us ameliorate the crisis in care. For example, she highlights the need for linking two social movements already under way: political mobilization by *those who need help with care* (parents, advocates for the disabled, the frail elderly, the chronically ill, and other healthcare consumers) and movements by underpaid *care-workers* who, often through unions, are organizing "living wage," "worthy wage," and "comparable worth" campaigns. Scholars can also help spur recognition that change is possible. For example, when we write about "robust" empirical trends, we should avoid the language of inevitability, as in statements like "low-wage work is here to stay." The irrationalities and injustices of poverty were made, and they can be changed by collective human action.

ACKNOWLEDGMENTS

Reprinted from *Work-Family Challenges for Low-Income Parents and Their Children*, edited by Ann C. Crouter and Alan Booth (Mahwah, NJ: Lawrence Erlbaum Associates, 2004), by permission of Taylor & Francis Group LLC.

NOTES

1. In our Pico Union research site—a densely populated, extremely low-income enclave of immigrants from Mexico and Central America—the adults (many of them undocumented) have high rates of employment but also a great deal of job instability. The men work as day laborers, janitors, or gardeners, or in restaurants. Women also work in restaurants or the garment industry, or as paid domestic workers. Marjorie Orellana surveyed all of the fourth and fifth grade students in the large year-round public elementary school that anchors the site and asked how they spent time when their school track was not in session (the three tracks rotate through two months of school and a one month break). Only 10 percent of the kids participated in a formal, off-track program such as one organized by

the YMCA. Many city programs for kids were geared toward conventional summer vacations, not to month-long breaks every two months. No programs for school-age children provided free or low-cost all-day care (Orellana and Thorne 1998). As with immigrant families in Oakland, these families relied on networks of kin, older siblings, and children's self-care; and children sometimes accompanied parents to their places of work. In a recent paper, Orellana (2001) documents the extensive labor contributions that immigrant children make to families, schools, and communities, often under the rubric of being "helpers."

2. The Berkeley Center for Working Families archival Web site, including online working papers, can be accessed at http://www.hc.edu/bc_org/avp/wfnetwork/Berkeley.

3. In my writing on contemporary childhoods I am trying to bridge a striking gap between research on adult caregivers and research on children as social actors, including their contributions as givers of care. Theoretical and empirical research on parenting/mothering/fathering/child rearing tends to efface the perspectives and agency of children. In contrast, sociologists of childhood emphasize children's standpoints and agency, but often in ways that obscure their connections with caregiving adults. Attention to the standpoints of both children and adults, and a more relational understanding of agency, can help bridge this gap (Thorne 2000).

REFERENCES

Ehrenreich, Barbara, and Arlie Russell Hochschild, eds. 2003. *Global Woman: Nannies, Maids, and Sex Workers in the New Economy.* New York: Metropolitan Books.

Fineman, Martha Albertson 2000. "Cracking the Foundational Myths: Independence, Autonomy, and Self-Sufficiency." *American University Journal of Gender, Social Policy and Law* 8:S13–30.

Folbre, Nancy. 2001. *The Invisible Heart: Economics and Family Values.* New York: New Press.

Fraser, Nancy. 1989. *Unruly Practices.* Minneapolis: University of Minnesota Press.

———. 1997. *Justice Interruptus: Critical Reflections on the "Postsocialist" Condition.* New York: Routledge.

Gammon, Robert, and Michele R. Marcucci. 2002. "Census: Racial Income Disparities Bound." *Oakland Tribune,* August 27.

Garey, Anita Ilta. 2002. "Concepts of Care in After-School Programs: Protection, Instruction, and Containment." Berkeley Center for Working Families Working Paper No. 48. http://www.bc.edu/bc/org/avp/wfnetwork/Berkeley/.

Glenn, Evelyn Nakano. 1992. "From Servitude to Service Work: Historical Continuities in the Racial Division of Paid Reproductive Labor." *Signs* 18:1–43.

———. 2000. "Creating a Caring Society." *Contemporary Sociology* 29:84–94.

Haavind, Hanne. 2001. "Contesting and Recognizing Historical Changes and Selves in Development: Methodological Changes." Paper presented at the Conference on Mixed Methods in the Study of Childhood and Family Life, Los Angeles, January 25–27.

Hansen, Karen. V. 2005. *Not-So-Nuclear Families: Class, Gender and Networks of Care.* New Brunswick, NJ: Rutgers University Press.

Heymann, Jody. 2000. *The Widening Gap: Why American Working Families Are in Jeopardy and What Can Be Done About It.* New York: Basic Books.

Hochschild, Arlie Russell. 1997. *The Time Bind: When Work Becomes Home and Home Becomes Work.* New York: Metropolitan Books.

Hondagneu-Sotelo, Pierette. 2001. *Domestica: Immigrant Workers Cleaning and Caring in the Shadows of Affluence.* Berkeley: University of California Press.

Huston, Aletha. 2004. "Childcare for Low-Income Families: Problems and Promises." *Work-family Challenges for Low-Income Parents and Their Children,* edited by A. C. Crouter and A. Booth. Mahwah, NJ: Lawrence Erlbaum Associates.

Kaplan, Elaine. B. 2001. "Using Food as a Metaphor for Care: Middle-School Kids Talk About Family, School, and Class Relationship." *Journal of Contemporary Ethnography* 29:474–509.

Mink, Gwendolyn. 1998. *Welfare's End.* Ithaca, NY: Cornell University Press.

Orellana, Marjorie Faulstich. 2001. "The Work Kids Do: Mexican and Central American Immigrant Children's Contributions to Households and Schools in California." *Harvard Educational Review* 71:366–389.

Orellana, Marjorie Faulstich, and Barrie Thorne. 1998. Year-Round Schools and the Politics of Time. *Anthropology and Education Quarterly* 29:446–472.

Orellana, Marjorie Faulstich, Barrie Thorne, Anna Chee, and Wan Shun Eva Lam. 2001. "Transnational Childhoods: The Participation of Children in Processes of Family Migration." *Social Problems* 48:572–591.

Palmer, Julian. S., Younghwan Song, and Hsein-Hen Lu. 2002. *The Changing Face of Child Poverty in California: State Child Poverty Update.* New York: National Center for Children in Poverty, Millman School of Public Health, Columbia University

Parrenas, Rhacel. 2001. *Servants of Globalization: Women, Migration, and Domestic Work.* Stanford, CA: Stanford University Press.

Polatnick, Margaret. R. 2002. Too Old for Child Care? Too Young for Self-Care? Negotiating After-School Arrangements for Middle School. *Journal of Family Issues* 23:728–747.

Ruddick, Sara. 1998. "Care as Labor and Relationship." In *Norms and Values*, edited by J. C. Haber and M. S. Halfon, 3–25. Totowa, NJ: Rowman and Littlefield.

Sherman, Rachel 2002. "'Better Than Your Mother': Caring Labor in Luxury Hotels." Berkeley Center for Working Families Working Paper No. 53. http://www.bc.edu/bc/org/avp/wfnetwork/Berkeley/.

Skocpol, Theda. 2000. *The Missing Middle: Working Families and the Future of American Social Policy.* New York: W. W. Norton.

Stephens, Sharon, ed. 1995. *Children and the Politics of Culture.* Princeton, NJ: Princeton University Press.

Thorne, Barrie. 2000. "Children's Agency and Theories of Care." Paper presented at the annual meetings of the American Sociological Association, August, Washington, DC.

________. 2001. "Pick-up Time at Oakdale Elementary School: Work and Family from the Vantage Points of Children." In *Working Families*, edited by Rosanna. Hertz and Nancy. Marshall, 354–376. Berkeley: University of California Press.

Thorne, Barrie, M. F. Orellana, W.S.E. Lan, and A. Chee. 2003. "Raising Children, and Growing up, across National Borders: Comparative Perspectives on Age, Gender, and Migration." In *Gender and U.S. Immigration*, edited by P. Hondagneu-Sotelo, 241–262. Berkeley: University of California Press.

Tronto, Joan C 1994 *Moral Boundaries: A Political Argument or an Ethic of Care.* New York: Routledge.

Tucker, J., and A. Katz. 2002. "Whites Shun Public Schools: Census Shows Nearly 50% of Caucasians Don't Use City Education System." *Oakland Tribune*, August 27.

Wallulis, Jerald. 1998. *The New Insecurity.* Albany, NY: State University of New York Press.

Williams, Joan. 1998. *Unbending Gender: Why Family and Work Conflict and What to Do About It.* New York: Oxford Press.

Zelizer, Viviana A. 1985. *Pricing the Priceless Child.* New York: Basic Books.

CHAPTER 12

The Family Work of Parenting in Public

Marjorie L. DeVault

As I move toward the zoo exit, I see a woman and baby I'd noticed earlier, then part of a larger group inside the primate building. She's now sitting by herself on a stone fence and there are two strollers next to her (one empty, I think). As I approach, she's trying to adjust one of the strollers and having trouble; suddenly it sort of collapses and the baby who's in it begins to howl. She picks up the infant and cuddles it in her arms, but it continues to wail as I walk by. She looks rather distressed, and I'm wondering if I should offer to help, but it doesn't seem that the baby is hurt, and I don't really know what kind of help I could offer.

"Parenting in public" might mean any of several quite different experiences. The note above, drawn from my observations of family groups at the community zoo, illustrates at least two aspects of the topic—the mother's care for her infant in public and my passing observation of that care. The research I discuss here has been concerned with the family outing, and my discussion will consider the emotion work involved in such an activity. The label, of course, is my analyst's term. The people engaged in these activities would refer to them more casually with phrases like "doing something." As opposed to more institutionalized activities for children and parents—classes, scouting, sports, and so on—these are ostensibly unstructured activities, usually conducted as a family, during free time outside of work and school.

I have been especially interested in this kind of activity because it seems to place parents and children in a terrain where they may be "performing" family, and where they are vulnerable to readings of those performances—it allows us to consider family life in the public realm (Lofland 1998). I draw in part on a rich strand of sociological scholarship on behavior in public places, stemming from the work of Erving Goffman, who has written about the presentation of self (1959) and about activity within a "glimpsed world" (1979). Here, I will suggest that those perspectives may be fruitfully combined with Arlie Russell Hochschild's conceptualization of "emotion work" (1983) in everyday life.

My analysis of the family outing relies on a feminist, or what Dorothy Smith (1987) calls a "generous," concept of work. This understanding of work extends well beyond activity in paid jobs to include unpaid household and caring work, as well as voluntary activity, the efforts of activists, and so on. It provides a way of thinking about work that encompasses a number of "sensitizing concepts" (Blumer 1969, 148), such as invisible work (Daniels 1987), kin work (DiLeonardo 1987), and, of course, Hochschild's generative concept of emotion work (1983). Because the modern (and postmodern) family is so strongly defined in terms of emotional ties, emotion work provides an especially useful way of thinking about the production of family life and sociability. Just how far to extend the generous concept of work is one of the interesting, and sometimes vexing, questions that comes with scholarship in this terrain, and will be one of the questions I raise later in this chapter.

My discussion draws on data collected through naturalistic observation (Adler and Adler 1994) at zoos in two northeastern U.S. cities, Syracuse, New York, and Boston, Massachusetts. Both are relatively modest community zoos; they are professionally managed and accredited, but neither is the kind of zoo that serves as a major, nationally renowned tourist attraction. (In addition to observation, I have conducted some informal interviewing on site, conducted interviews with some zoo education staff, and at one of the zoos helped out with a small evaluation project.)

In the discussion that follows, I discuss the emotion work of parenting in public at the zoo. I consider three aspects of the zoo outing that bring somewhat different kinds of emotion work to the fore: managing difficult behaviors, confronting the commercial aspects of the setting, and some of the concrete practices of moving through public space "as a family."

Troubles at the Zoo

One Sunday morning I entered the zoo and, taking stock of the groups around me, recorded these observations:

> The most noticeable group is a couple with a child in a stroller who is screaming unremittingly as they walk along. The man pushes the stroller one-handed, and they're staring straight ahead, looking uncomfortable with the noise, but resigned to it.
>
> We all pass a large building that I hadn't noticed before, which seems to be a horse barn . . . There are corrals with a couple of ponies running around, and

> the couple with the screaming kid stop, take him out of the stroller, and set him down next to the fence—I guess in hopes that the ponies will attract his interest and stop his crying. It doesn't work; he continues to scream and they load him back into the stroller and continue on their way.
>
> I follow this family into the Children's Zoo, and toward the barn and its outer stalls, where there's already another mom and young girl (about three) standing by the railing. One of the parents is holding the screaming child (who screams on with impressive persistence); they lift him up and say, "Look at that!" but to no avail.
>
> Now that they're in close proximity to others, these parents seem more embarrassed about the commotion. They look over toward the other mother and the woman says, with a slight grimace, "Having a bad day." The other woman is ready to be sympathetic and says, "I know what that's like. I've had plenty of those myself." They don't hear, apparently, and she repeats, "Bad days—I've had plenty of those myself." Mom gives some kind of brief explanation (I can't hear the details), which ends with, "And that's how it got started." And she shrugs as if to convey helplessness.

This excerpt illustrates several aspects of these experiences that I wish to analyze. It vividly displays, first of all, the sometimes quite challenging work of conducting the outing. It also reveals the sense of performativity that is sometimes present in people's conduct—first, in the parents' stoical staring straight ahead as they attempt to carry on, and, later, in their apologetic exchange that acknowledges things are not going well. In addition, this episode gives a sense of the zoo as context for this sort of activity, of how the space and its organization impose on parents—or at least guide them toward—a particular kind of parenting. Even as the child screams, the group moves from one exhibit to the next, and the parents exhort the child to, "Look at that!" The sequence of exhibits at the zoo keeps these parents oriented to a project we might call "developing the child" (Griffith and Smith 2005; Smith 1987), even when that project seems to be coming apart.

My interest in the zoo as context is an interest in the many spaces and places where parenting is undertaken outside the home, and in the ways that the work of parenting is shaped by those spaces and places. Just as Hochschild in *The Managed Heart* situates emotional labor in particular occupations and shows how the work evokes particular emotional performances, I am interested in the ways that structured spaces such as the zoo evoke family emotional performances. The zoo is certainly widely, if not exclusively, understood as a family space. That understanding carries with it a sense that it's all right if children scream at the zoo; others typically display sympathy for that sort of problem (as they might not in an upscale restaurant or on public transportation). In addition, it is a space that's relatively accessible. In her discussion of the class-based travels and experiences of parents and children, Annette Lareau identifies it as a space that serves as an "equalizer" (2003, 15).

In fact, any family outing calls on resources—time, access to transportation, the energy to pull it together, and some expense for even modest activities—that are simply not available to all families. (And both of the zoos I studied charge an admission fee for entrance, unlike some urban zoos.) Still, my observations are consistent with the idea that the zoo is a relatively accessible space. The core activity of viewing the animals seems to be entertaining for adults as well as for children, and the space is familiar enough in cultural lore that it attracts visitors across a socioeconomic spectrum. It seems to combine didactic potential with an amusement park ambiance, without the high culture demands of potential outing sites like the art museum. In addition, the widespread idea that the zoo is a quintessentially appropriate place for family fun seems related to the type of parenting work it calls forth. The ritualized observation and naming of animals we can see in virtually every group ("Look at that!" in the example above) suggests to me a stripped-down version of the parenting style that Lareau calls "concerted cultivation" (2003), a style that she sees as characteristic especially of middle-class parents but also consistent with dominant styles of interaction in the institutional world children and adults must engage as they enter more public spaces.

The extended excerpt presented earlier provides one of the most dramatic examples of tension and trouble I recorded. I saw relatively few instances of such sustained difficulty at the zoo. And we don't know how the participants experienced these episodes; they may well have been taken not as "trouble" (my characterization), but as minor bumps in the road of everyday family life.[1] Still, one task of parenting in a public place is to monitor children's behavior and guard against eruptions of misbehavior—especially misbehavior that may attract the attention of strangers. My notes provide numerous instances of parents admonishing children, urging them to manage their emotions, mediating conflicts and cutting off arguments, and generally articulating and explaining small "rules" applicable to zoo-visiting and more general ones such as those for turn-taking. In some cases, it's clear that parents are aware of other visitors as onlookers, and that they are, to some extent, performing "good parenting."

In their explicit talk ("you can only run so far ahead") and in their moment-to-moment interactions, parents define standards of behavior for the zoo—standards that vary from one group to another but fall within a broadly shared adult sense of what is appropriate. One purpose is certainly to protect children from injury. But in addition to monitoring for safety, parents teach children, as they move through the zoo, how to conduct themselves as competent and responsible actors in a public space. In guiding children's viewing activities, they show them how to assert themselves and how to respect the space and activities of other groups; how to take turns; how to persist in the activity and when to move on—in short, how to read intended uses of the space and act accordingly. They teach and encourage children to have fun, and they also enact a discipline that defines limits to the fun to be had in the particular setting.

Given the very different ways that people engage in parenting, the particulars of these teachings are specific to each family. But, just as children learn the limits of good behavior at the zoo, parents too show an awareness of their public responsibilities to control and monitor the children in their charge. By the glances and the comments they exchange with other adults, they display an acknowledgment of their vulnerability to public judgment.

Money at the Zoo

When parents and children leave their homes, they travel through a commercial landscape, encountering a variety of differentially accessible public spaces. At both of the zoos I studied, there are admission fees. It's less expensive to go to the zoo than to a major league baseball game (for example), but the price of admission surely is an obstacle for some families. Both of the zoos I studied are surrounded by relatively low-income neighborhoods, and I often felt a visceral awareness of entering a fenced-in area, with an idealized version of family fun enacted inside, and various other things happening just outside the gate.

Even within the zoo there are many moments that call for spending. Both zoos have food concessions and gift shops. At the Syracuse zoo there is a corral where children can pay to ride a pony; in Boston there was a horse-drawn wagon ride around the grounds when I began the study, which has since been replaced by a train ride through the area. The Boston zoo has introduced a seasonal butterfly exhibit, for which there is an additional admission fee, and more recently a carousel ride. These kinds of extra attractions may make the zoo more exciting for visitors, and it's easy to see that they could be prohibitively expensive to offer without additional funds. The nominal fees involved may seem inconsequential, given the kinds of commercialization that have become the taken-for-granted backdrop for contemporary, middle-class childhoods (Schor 2004). Still, they give the zoo visit a "tiered" character, so that the full experience carries expenses beyond the admission fee.

In both zoos I have seen an intensification of this kind of mundane commercialization over the decade or so that I've been collecting data. When I began the study, the Boston zoo's gift shop was a relatively simple enterprise, an alcove in one of the exhibit buildings that offered small souvenirs; the new shop there offers a wider and more expensive array of merchandise. Throughout the study, the gift shop in Syracuse stocked substantial toys, and in a recent remodeling of the front entrance area it was considerably expanded. The zoo exit there now leads past a floor-to-ceiling glass wall with shelves packed with enticing plush stuffed animals of many kinds.

Some parents and children seem to view a purchase at the shop as a routine part of the outing to the zoo, even if this view seems a rather jaundiced one, as in this instance: "The store was rather full. As I left, there was a man kind of blocking my way, and as I sidled by . . . he boomed out to a child, 'Hey, you want something to dust? I'll buy you something.'" The statement, "I'll buy you something," overheard in a public setting, can only hint at the complex interpersonal relations and histories of family life, no doubt often fraught with intense feeling. Some parents may make such purchases routinely; others never. Some may strategize to avoid the shop and therefore the question; others may have developed explicit rules about buying things or may use such opportunities for teaching children about saving and spending. The gift shop at the zoo makes these consumerist aspects of family life—however they are negotiated and experienced in a particular family—part of the leisure-time outing in this setting.

The zoo typically provides space for many activities other than just looking at animals, and many of them are free—using playground equipment, admiring gardens and sculptures, picnicking, strolling, and running about (which of course includes climbing, wrestling, and so on). In Syracuse one of the most popular activities for young children in the past was an area where the youngsters could "milk" wooden cows (the installation of hand-washing stations around the time this feature disappeared suggests that it was removed due to sanitary concerns); and there is a peek-through mural set up for making funny pictures (the giggles are free, at least, even if preserving the joke on film requires a camera). In Boston, children enjoy beating on a musical sculpture whose large slabs of metal serve as hanging chimes. Still those areas in the zoo that call for spending even small amounts of money may provoke conflict or distress, especially for those families whose resources are quite limited. Once, after I'd given a talk about my research, I received a note from a colleague who told me about her family's visit to a rural zoo in an area where many families are quite poor. She noticed that many zoo visitors "looked poor," and she heard a lack of education in their speech. She wrote to me:

> The zoo has little coin operated machines that dispense corn to feed to the animals for 25 cents . . . Poor kids would whine for a quarter and parents would shuffle off or say no or say we ain't got one or whatever, while our yuppie child and others cheerfully stuffed the chubby little antelopes, bunnies, camels, whatever. The poor kids would stand and watch for awhile and maybe whine some more or maybe pick a fight with a sibling or shuffle off. . . . The yuppie kids were seemingly oblivious although some of the parents looked uncomfortable and like they didn't know if they should just give the poor kids a quarter or ignore them or make their kids share some of the corn or what. The boundaries between families were momentarily blurred but not bent or transgressed because no one did end up giving the kids anything.

It was rather sad, she noted, and "kind of profound"—though it also seemed to me that her concluding note that boundaries were "blurred but not transgressed" hints at the way such a moment in everyday life passes by and melts away in a stream of other activities (though perhaps washing away easily for those in the more privileged position and leaving more durable stains for those with limited resources). Scenes involving money were less stark at the zoos I studied, but I could see these kinds of dynamics. Even families who avoided the train and pony rides, food stands, and gift shops encountered wishing ponds and coin-operated viewing scopes as they traveled past the exhibits. Some parents handed out coins without much comment—to such an extent that one sign in the Boston zoo had to warn, "Please do not toss coins into the wetland. They could harm the animals." Others resisted even such small expenditures or at least set limits. "A quarter?" one mother replied to a request for a coin, making clear that her daughter's request was out of line; and she then gave the girl some smaller change, which she deposited into the pond matter-of-factly.

My point here is that such quasi-commercial aspects of the setting are likely experienced quite differently by parents and children who bring different class outlooks and material resources to the zoo. Such brief moments in public likely bring to consciousness difficulties that permeate the daily lives of poorer families, even as they engage in an ostensibly simple form of family fun. Because of the public character of the zoo—its character as a "glimpsed world"—these moments also bring out socioeconomic differences that are not visible in appearances alone, placing families side by side and opening their performance in such transactions to public view. Many kinds of public and quasi-public interactions likely have such consequences, evoking the (momentary and also longer-term) emotion work of managing insights into external views of one's family and oneself. For example, Mary Romero (2001) interviewed children of domestic workers, and she recounts how they learned about their parents' subservience by watching them interact with employers, and how they found ways of interpreting what they saw. Hochschild (2003), too, suggests that children's "eavesdropping" about arrangements for care may be an important way that they learn about the "web of relationships" that constructs their everyday worlds. In a similar fashion, as children watch their parents engage in brief commercial transactions at the zoo, they likely learn how they are positioned in relation to others, what they have and can get, and perhaps a sense of what they are entitled to have.

Love and Connection at the Zoo

I have also been looking closely at how people move around the zoo in small groupings, and there is an element of emotion in that phenomenon as well. Moving about "as a family" creates a small arena of quasi-private space, even in a public setting like the zoo. It also constitutes the group, making clear that these individuals belong together, and providing "tie-signs" (Goffman 1971) that may also be read as expressions of feeling. The following example is one that we might use to raise questions about the concept of emotion work and its boundaries: "A younger child is hanging on the placard, running his hands randomly over its lower flat surface. But eventually, the man focuses his attention on another part of the placard, and he seems to point and say something about it. The woman and older child then turn away again, and the father sort of runs his hand around the younger boy's face, caressing him and also moving him away from the placard and into the hallway so they can move along." As I reflected on how to describe this moment, I added to my notes, "Watching, this gesture seems very expressive—a little effusion of care for the boy, useful in directing him, but mostly a love-touch." Now, as I read my notes, I wonder: Is this father "performing family"? Was he consciously communicating affection for his son? Was he aware of being observed? Should one analyze his gesture as a kind of family work?

When I find myself reaching this kind of conceptual boundary—and I often do, given the projects I've taken up, where family work is so often understood as "love" (DeVault 1991)—it seems to me useful to consider the kind of analytic work a sensitizing concept can do. In my own writing, the concept of emotion work has been useful for two major reasons. First, it allows us to underline the constructed character of family life. Family relations do not just happen, and they do not spring from the heart in a spontaneous upwelling of feeling (though at times we may experience them that way). Instead, people make family life happen, through their joint activities. In addition, thinking about the work of family lives provides a way of discussing some of the many subtle inequalities that are woven through family experiences (and that tend to disappear in more ideological portrayals of families, in the media or in scholarship). Varying family backgrounds—of class, race, or ethnicity—produce distinctive vulnerabilities to public scrutiny, as do visible disabilities. Varying family circumstances—the spaces and resources of different neighborhoods, for example—produce different working conditions, and these different constellations of resources may make it easier or more difficult to produce performances of family life that align comfortably with social institutions and ideologies. In addition, the responses of outsiders to families who appear "different" in some way (especially those who are visibly different in the kinds of public spaces I've been studying) may demand particular kinds of emotion work from some families more than from others—decisions that gay or lesbian parents might make about whether to "pass" or "come out," for example, or defensive maneuvers designed to shield children from the slights of public prejudice (DeVault 1999). Recognizing these layers of family emotion work can help to reveal the contours of inequality in family lives.

Conclusion

Parenting in public—and performing family—can be quite pleasurable, offering opportunities to perform, experience, and display to others the rituals of family time. It also brings distinctive vulnerabilities. Children in public places may be vulnerable to getting lost or even abducted, to injury in an unfamiliar environment, to confusion and embarrassment, or to slights directed at them or those they are with. But it is not only children who are vulnerable; parents are also acting within a space where they may feel alone and unsupported, and they are potentially always subject to the surveilling gaze and judgments of others. For most parents, most of the time, I think these are back-burner concerns, not absent but typically in the background of awareness until something happens to ignite concern. Those subject to overt displays of discrimination, I believe, often develop a kind of defensive denial, shrugging off the potential for problems. A lesbian mother, for example, told me simply, "I don't let it bother me." This seemed, for her, a useful way of asserting her family's right to be present and "out" in public space. However, we might consider the emotion work behind that simple assertion, and its personal costs.

For all parents, I would suggest, spending time in public brings concerns about what others might see and the kinds of judgments they might make. Such concerns likely recede, most of the time, in a wave of other concerns and distractions, or in experiences of pleasure and presence in the moment at hand. Still, parenting in public is inevitably, to some extent, a performance, visible to others and vulnerable to their readings. It is a kind of work that weaves care and emotion into mundane experience, and I would suggest that close analysis of its contours will teach us a great deal about the textures of family lives and the relations of families in the public realm.

NOTE

1. Indeed, when I began to write about the screaming child, I recalled a moment from my own childhood: Soon after moving to a new city, we took a family sightseeing drive. My infant brother—no doubt fed up with car travel after a long trip to our new home—cried unremittingly through the outing. I'm sure it wasn't pleasant for any of us, but in the intervening years it has become the stuff of family storytelling, remembered as an amusing anecdote.

REFERENCES

Adler, Patricia A., and Peter Adler. 1994. "Observational Techniques." In *Handbook of Qualitative Research*, edited by Norman K. Denzin and Yvonna S. Lincoln, 377–392. Thousand Oaks, CA: Sage Publications.

Blumer, Herbert. 1969. *Symbolic Interactionism: Perspective and Method.* Englewood Cliffs, NJ: Prentice-Hall.

Daniels, Arlene Kaplan. 1987. "Invisible Work." *Social Problems* 34:403–415.

DeVault, Marjorie L. 1991. *Feeding the Family: The Social Organization of Caring as Gendered Work.* Chicago: University of Chicago Press.

———. 1999. "Comfort and Struggle: Emotion Work in Family Life." *Annals of the American Academy of Political and Social Science* 561:52–63.

DiLeonardo, Micaela. 1987. "The Female World of Cards and Holidays: Women, Families, and the Work of Kinship." *Signs* 12:440–453.

Goffman, Erving. 1959. *The Presentation of Self in Everyday Life.* Garden City, NY: Doubleday.

———. 1971. *Relations in Public: Microstudies of the Public Order.* New York: Basic Books.

———. 1979. *Gender Advertisements.* New York: Harper and Row.

Griffith, Alison I., and Dorothy E. Smith. 2005. *Mothering for Schooling.* New York: Routledge Falmer.

Hochschild, Arlie Russell. 1983. *The Managed Heart: Commercialization of Human Feeling.* Berkeley: University of California Press.

———. 2003. *The Commercialization of Intimate Life: Notes from Home and Work.* Berkeley: University of California Press.

Lareau, Annette. 2003. *Unequal Childhoods: Class, Race, and Family Life.* Berkeley: University of California Press.

Lofland, Lyn H. 1998. *The Public Realm: Exploring the City's Quintessential Social Territory.* Hawthorne, NY: Aldine de Gruyter.

Romero, Mary. 2001. "Unraveling Privilege: Workers' Children and the Hidden Costs of Paid Child Care." *Chicago-Kent Law Review* 76:101–121.

Schor, Juliet. 2004. *Born to Buy: The Commercialized Child and the New Consumer Culture.* New York: Scribner.

Smith, Dorothy E. 1987. *The Everyday World as Problematic: A Feminist Sociology.* Boston: Northeastern University Press.

CHAPTER 13

Maternally Yours

THE EMOTION WORK OF "MATERNAL VISIBILITY"

Anita Ilta Garey

Sharon Baker was poised and articulate as I interviewed her about her experience of being a "working mother," and, after telling me about her work, her future plans, her husband, and her children, she summed up by saying:

> Those are the things I feel good about. All of them. It's like I want to give 100 percent to every aspect. I want to be 100 percent nurse, 100 percent community health nurse, 100 percent neighbor, community person, 100 percent wife, 100 percent mother—and that's hard. But that's what I want to do. And I feel like I do bits and pieces of it, enough to make a difference. I naturally feel like I make a difference in my kids' life. I hope my husband enjoys marriage as much as I do [*laughs*]. And I like having a job, having a family and having my husband. They're all interactive. I mean it's a triangle.[1]

Sharon, a thirty-four-year-old African American registered nurse with a full-time job, a husband, and three children, ages one, four, and seven years, thus presents herself as successfully balancing all the parts of her many roles: professional, citizen, wife, and mother. I'll call this "version 1" of Sharon's presentation of herself as a working mother.

When we came to the end of the interview, I asked Sharon if there was anything she wanted to add. At that point, she presented version 2:

> No, sounds like you hit all the points, all the major points anyway. [*Long pause.*] I don't know. I was just thinking as I'm talking about everything, I don't know how it sounds when it sounds like everything is just going along. But I go crazy half of the time, and I try not to. There are some times when I have to sit down and tell myself: "It's gonna be okay. It's gonna be okay."

> Almost as if my brain is slipping out of my head and I'm trying to tell myself and talk to myself: "It's gonna be fine." Paying the bills is added into all that. There's just all these little things, folding the clothes and five people in the house, there's a lot of clothes. Going grocery shopping and the weekends and the beeper. . . . It's not just the money to pay the bills, but actually physically sitting down and siphoning through and which one, juggling and—I don't know. It feels crazy sometimes.

In version 1, Sharon portrays her life as organized, efficient, well run, and happy; and she presents herself as a competent, in-control, and contented working mother. This was not an invalid image, but it was not a complete image either. In version 2, Sharon added something she had suppressed, or even misrepresented, in her first version: *how she feels* as she juggles the demands, tasks, and people in her life.

It should not be surprising that, until the end of the interview, Sharon's story did not include her feeling of "going crazy" trying to do everything. In the case of women with children, to suggest that something is not going right is to question their performance *as mothers*, and the feeling of "going crazy" is not in line with social expectations about what mothers are supposed to feel. In this chapter, I explore how employed women manage emotion in presenting themselves as mothers.

Maternal Visibility

Women use various strategies to indicate to others that they are "good" mothers—that is, that they are doing what mothers are supposed to do. They perform certain mother-appropriate actions; they attach to those actions meanings that validate themselves as mothers; and they tell other people about their actions (Garey 1999). Mothers who are employed feel particularly vulnerable to criticism of their performance as mothers because, in the United States, employment and motherhood are portrayed as detracting one from the other (Garey 1999).

One of the ways that mothers deal with this implicit criticism is by what I define as "maternal visibility." Maternal visibility is the attempt to call attention to or emphasize one's performance of motherhood (Garey 1999, 29). It can be accomplished in a variety of ways: by the public performance of certain activities, such as being the "field-trip mom," or by verbally expressing to others the things one does for one's child. Mothers who are employed practice maternal visibility as a way of dealing with the attitude of others that employment interferes with a woman's ability to parent, a sentiment that is captured by the often-used phrase "full-time mothers" to refer to mothers who are not employed. The implication is that working mothers are *less than* full-time mothers—are being only "part-time mothers." It is therefore understandable that they work hard to make their performance of motherhood visible, particularly in contexts that directly involve their children.[2]

Their children's schools are a particularly salient arena of interaction in which mothers engage in maternal visibility. Doris Chavez, a Mexican American nurse who works a full-time night-shift schedule (11:00 P.M. to 7:00 A.M.), emphasized that she is home during the daytime when her children are in school: "I'm usually home by 9:00 [A.M.], and I have been called before [by the school] and they know I'm sleeping. I get that straight with the teacher [*laughs*] right off the bat! You know, 'I work nights, I'm home.'" What Doris is getting straight is that she is as reachable as any non-employed mother, and getting it "straight with the teacher" is an act of maternal visibility. Whether the activity is organizing their children's birthday parties, helping them with their homework, reading to them at bedtime, making cookies for the class party, being the field-trip mom, or driving them to soccer practice, mothers who are employed emphasize—make visible—the mother-appropriate activities in which they are engaged.

The performance of motherhood is done in relation to dominant social and cultural expectations about what women who are mothers are expected *as mothers* to do. To say that motherhood is performed is not to say that the content of the performance is necessarily false or disingenuous. Rather, the performance of motherhood is to "do motherhood," in the same manner that that people "do gender" (West and Zimmerman 1987) or "do family." "Doing" gender refers to the way that a person performs activities *as a man* or *as a woman*, and to how the performance of these activities is judged by others as being either inside or outside the bounds of appropriate behavior for a man performing a particular activity or appropriate behavior for a woman performing that activity. West and Zimmerman note that "to 'do' gender is not always to live up to normative conceptions of femininity or masculinity; it is to engage in behavior *at the risk of gender assessment*" (1987, 136; emphasis in original). If, for example, actions and demeanor are within the bounds of cultural standards regarding appropriate gendered behavior, then the assessment and the approval of the behavior are not likely to be noticed by the actor or the observer. The fact that a person's actions are being judged is made explicit when those actions are seen as falling outside the limits of acceptable gendered behavior. In either case, however, our behavior is at risk of being judged.

These expectations for mothers vary over time and across cultures, but people within a shared dominant culture recognize and understand these expectations, even if their own beliefs, traditions, or community culture differ from them. From varying social locations and with varying access to resources, people respond to social expectations by adopting, modifying, reinterpreting, or rejecting them. Regardless of their response, they have no trouble identifying and locating themselves in relation to these expectations. The cultural expectation for mothers is not only that they will do particular things with and for their children, but also that they will do these things as natural expressions of being mothers. Therefore, in addition to the instrumental work of mothering (such as seeing that children are fed, chauffeuring them to various activities, being the field trip mom, and the like) is appearing as if this work were effortless. Social and cultural expectations for mothers are, therefore, not only about what mothers are expected to do, but also about what mothers, *as mothers*, are expected to think and feel. Women use maternal visibility to highlight their mothering activities, but the emotional effort it takes to maintain the performance is often invisible.

Sharon Baker recognized that there was a discrepancy between "how it sounds when it sounds like everything is just going along," and how she actually feels ("but I go crazy half of the time"). And she makes efforts to change that feeling ("and I try not to") by bringing her feelings into line with what she knows other people think she should feel—and what she herself wants to feel. Sharon consciously, and eloquently, draws attention to the emotion work in her presentation of self as a working mother. In version 1 Sharon is upbeat and optimistic, in line with the narrative that all parts of her work and family life are meshing smoothly. In version 2 she focuses on the toll it takes on her, something that her emotion work, when successful, keeps hidden.

Performing Emotion Work

Social expectations about appropriate feelings, based on role and situation, are referred to as "feeling rules" (Hochschild 1979). In her path-breaking essay on the subject, Arlie Hochschild points out that when "the individual is conscious of a moment of 'pinch,' or discrepancy, between what one does feel and what one wants to feel . . . the individual may try to eliminate the pinch by working on feeling" (Hochschild 1979, 562). When we try to manage our feelings in this way, to bring them into line with what we think are the appropriate emotions for a particular situation, we are engaged in "emotion work" (Hochschild 1979). Emotion work is not simply displaying the appropriate emotional demeanor; it is, in Hochschild's framework, "deep acting," the attempt, not necessarily successful, to conjure up the appropriate feelings (Hochschild 1979).

There are often multiple layers of emotion work in being maternally visible, as is illustrated by the following example from my interviews. Jane Bradley is a thirty-one-year-old white registered nurse with two children under the age of five. She works two days a week on the surgical ward of a general hospital. During an interview about her work and family life, Jane related the following story about her interaction with a friend:

> The other day . . . I said something like, "Well, I'm glad I'm going to go to work today, I'm feeling a little bored this week." And [my friend] looked at me, and she always seemed so upbeat and she just had her third baby and is going around doing all this stuff with the kids, and she said, "Usually I'm so bored, I could die." And just like a flash her whole face changed for a second, and then it came back and she got all the kids in the car and said, *said cheerily*,

> "See you later!" and drove off. And I just thought, "Oh! I had no idea she felt that way." Later, we talked about it; she said, "I would just love to have something I could go to a couple days a week."

In her telling of this story, Jane portrays her friend's presentation of self as a mother completely and happily ("cheerily") immersed in her children and their activities. In other words, her friend appears to be doing what mothers are expected to do ("going around doing all this stuff with the kids") and feeling what mothers are supposed to feel ("she always seemed so upbeat"). But when her friend briefly reveals the effort it takes for her to appear "upbeat" all the time, Jane gets a glimpse of the effort involved in her friend's presentation of self. This surprises Jane because she had accepted her friend's performance of motherhood, including her demeanor and expressed feelings, as authentic, natural expressions of real feelings.

The interaction Jane recounts is exactly the kind of situation in which we become aware of emotion work. Hochschild points out that "it is when this tripartite consistency among situation, conventional frame, and feeling is somehow ruptured . . . that the more normal flow of deep convention—the more normal fusion of situation, frame, and feeling—seem like an enormous accomplishment" (1979, 563). Once Jane understands that her friend feels "so bored [she] could die," then doing things with three little children all day and every day looks like very hard work. And when Jane's friend puts her cheery face back on, it looks like very hard emotion work. Her friend's revelation, however, validates Jane's own mix of motherhood and employment. Being a stay-at-home mom was not without its problems.

In Jane's narrative, her friend's behavior is presented as a slip in performance, a slip that allows us to see the emotion work behind the presentation. But there is another interpretation to consider, one that takes closer account of the specific situation in which the interaction took place and allows Jane's friend a bit more agency. Her friend's behavior may not have been a "slip" at all, but may have been part of an intended presentation of self *to Jane.* There are, after all, two mothers in this story.

There is always an audience that must be taken into consideration when interpreting the actions or presentations of others. With Jane, a working mother, as the audience, her non-employed friend may have wanted to demonstrate to Jane that staying home with children all day every day was not an easy, natural thing to do. It took effort—not just physical energy, but psychic energy as well. In Goffman's terms, Jane's friend was giving "a dramatization of one's work" (Goffman 1959, 31). In this case, the work being dramatized is the emotion work she performs in doing motherhood.

In telling me about her friend, Jane is also giving her own presentation of self as mother, which she conveys to me, the listener, by the implied comparison between herself and her friend. Jane is both a worker (an employed nurse) and a mother. As a working mother she is faced with the problem of making it clear that she is successfully meeting the expectations for mothers even though she is employed. Jane makes the case—to me and to herself and to anyone else to whom she tells this story—that her work/family arrangement makes her more successful at motherhood than many women who are not employed at all. During her interview, Jane often talked about the situations of mothers who were not employed, and each story she told recounted what she saw as the problems of mothers whose time was spent exclusively with children, such as self-righteousness regarding working mothers or the way in which mothers' overinvolvement with their children stifles children's initiative. Her examples and opinions seemed intended to counter the common assumptions that being a good mother means being constantly available to one's children. At the same time, she was not challenging the specific expectations associated with motherhood, and she was quite sympathetic to the work involved in being home with one's children:

> Well, it's not always easy to be at home, and we're doing all these other things to kind of maintain—particularly now in the public school system, where they really need, you know, the PTA, . . . they really like to have a parent monitor in each class, and it's usually all the moms and people who stay at home. They're able to do it. So you hear a lot of discussion—particularly the group of women I know, because they're like the president, vice president, treasurer, all of the PTA, the local PTA. . . . So they do take it seriously, and they do put in a lot of time and effort.

Jane acknowledged the work of being a mother and also talked about the need for mothers to be available to their children more than would be allowed by a forty-hour-a-week job. She rejected the notion that quality time made up for the amount of time spent with children and thought that mothers should be available for the unanticipated needs of their children or for the "teachable moment." Working at the hospital only two days a week, Jane's examples all support the case that her arrangement—part-time employment—is the optimal environment for being a successful mother.

Examining Jane's narratives of maternal visibility reveals the possibility of a third layer of emotion work. Her narrative expresses what she is feeling (that is, *glad* to be going to work; *feeling bored* after days at home with the children), but I think that she is also attempting to produce particular feelings in the listener. And this, too, is emotion work. Emotion work is not only practiced upon the self, but also "by the self upon others, and by others upon oneself" (Hochschild 1979, 562). The audience to whom Jane declares her boredom with being at home is a friend who "just had her third baby and is going around doing all this stuff with the kids." What are the emotions her friend might feel in response to Jane's remark and to Jane's implied criticism, whether intentional or not, of being a "stay-at-home" mom? Jane tells me that her friend responded by briefly revealing a slip of her mask of the happy mother and later admitting that "I would just love to have something I could go to a couple days a week." In the situation Jane describes, the emotion elicited from her friend is admiration, or perhaps envy, for Jane's work-family arrangement. In comparison, Jane presents herself as a mother who is authentic with and about her children because she admits her feeling that being with children all day every day is boring and because she has arranged her own life in a way that incorporates both her children's needs and her own. When Jane relates this incident to me and others, she is doing emotion work in an attempt to elicit from others feelings of respect and admiration for her way of being a working mother.

Conclusion

Perceiving and acknowledging the emotion work entailed in maternal visibility bring two things to our attention: the effort required to fit experience to expectation, and the places of disjuncture between felt emotion and feeling rules. In studies of work and family, it is important to recognize both. Women with children know the conventional feeling rules for mothers, and they try to bring their own feelings into line with those rules—to feel happy rather than bored, as Jane's friend tried to do; to feel calm and in control rather than "as if my brain is slipping out of my head," as Sharon attempted. Mothers who are employed also talk about how they like, sometimes love, their jobs and about how they wouldn't want to stay at home all the time, but they do so while also performing emotion work that attempts to bring those feelings into line with the feeling rules for mothers and to make others feel that they are feeling as mothers should, as Jane attempted to do. Maternal visibility *is* emotion work and represents one response to the potential criticism that their employment prevents mothers from properly "doing motherhood."

Emotion work is not simply the display of situation-appropriate feelings; it is the attempt to experience the desired or expected emotion or to create a desired or expected emotion in others. It is a strategy for smooth social and individual functioning. Although emotion work is used to resolve cases of dissonance between expected and experienced feeling, it can also set off warning bells for the self-reflexive person. Why am I trying to change my feelings? Why aren't my feelings okay? What am I afraid of? In other words, for some people, feeling the pinch between what we feel and the cultural expectations for what we should feel can be an occasion for examining the dissonance rather than, or perhaps in addition to, smoothing it over. Sharon, with whom I began this chapter, is being self-reflexive when she says, "I was just thinking as I'm talking about everything" and points to the dissonance between her presentation of self and what she feels when she tells me, "I don't know how it sounds when it sounds like everything is just going along. But I go crazy half of the time, and I try not to."

Mothers often respond to my talks and writings on maternal visibility by telling me that the process is familiar and that they perform maternal visibility in their own lives. "Oh yes," one mother said, "I always bake homemade cookies for my daughter's classroom on holidays and special occasions. That way, no one can say I'm not doing my part as a mother." Another woman confided that she did not seek employment because she did not want anyone to blame any future problems her children might have on the fact that she was a working mother. Their responses indicate their acceptance of doing maternal visibility as just another part of the job of being a mother; there is, they explain, a rational reason for the practice.

Many social scientists would be tempted to treat a finding of maternal visibility as a variable, probably as a variable that could serve as an indicator of some other underlying process—for instance, as an indication of mothers' insecurity about their ability to be adequate mothers or as a measurement of insincerity or ambivalence in individual women's feelings about motherhood. I argue for a very different approach to mothers' reports and researchers' direct observation of maternal visibility. I do not see them as steps toward constructing explanatory or predictive variables. Rather, I have treated reports and observations as signs of profound contradictions in the cultural value system within which mothers act, are judged, and judge themselves. The researcher's observation of emotion work is the recognition that a contradiction exists, a contradiction that might otherwise have gone unnoticed. This recognition becomes a tool of analysis for the researcher, pushing her to ask, "What is it that needs to be reconciled?" and "Why?" From this research perspective, I see the emotion work involved in the performance of maternal visibility as the attempt by mothers to reconcile a contradiction between what they feel and what they think they should feel and between their actual socioeconomic position and the idealized maternal situation.

Contradiction is at the root of emotion work. The emotion work of maternal visibility is a sign of two contradictions confronted by mothers, especially working mothers, in the United States. One, in the face of a cultural vision of mothers as absorbed by, and wholly content with, caring for their children, real mothers want to do things and have lives that are not entirely defined by having children. Two, in an economic system in which families' desirable standard of living, or even the acceptable minimum standard, requires women's employment and income, and in which jobs are structured without consideration of the schedules and needs of parents and children, women want and need to work outside the home and also to be seen as good and loving mothers. In contemporary society, the practice of motherhood requires finessing these contradictions.

NOTES

1. All names are pseudonyms in this chapter, which is based on my study of how employed women with children construct identities as working mothers (Garey 1999).

2. The use of maternal visibility is context-specific. At work, women often downplay their mothering activities in order to present themselves as committed to their jobs and professions.

REFERENCES

Garey, Anita. 1999. *Weaving Work and Family.* Philadelphia: Temple University Press.

Goffman, Erving. 1959. *The Presentation of Self in Everyday Life.* Garden City, NY: Doubleday.

Hochschild, Arlie Russell. 1979. "Emotion Work, Feeling Rules, and Social Structure." *American Journal of Sociology* 85:551–575.

West, Candace, and Don H. Zimmerman. 1987. "Doing Gender." *Gender & Society* 1:125–151.

CHAPTER 14

Invisible Care and the Illusion of Independence

Lynn May Rivas

Twenty minutes into the interview, Bill coughs. I notice that his voice is beginning to deteriorate. Earlier, he told me that he had a problem "dehydrating when he talks a lot." We are in his bedroom. On a table next to him is a glass of water with a plastic top and a straw. Since he is unable to use his hands, I offer, "Um, do you want, would you like some water?" Bill raises his voice and calls, "Joe!" Then he explains, "I have an attendant." "Okay," I reply. I'm disappointed, because I'm asking questions about his relationship with his attendant, and I was hoping to have privacy during the interview. Bill again calls, "Joe!" Then, addressing me, he says, "I'm okay." He makes still another cry of "Joe" and again tells me, "I'll be okay."

Joe does not come. Bill's voice is loud enough to be heard in the rest of the apartment, but just barely. I think I should volunteer to look for Joe or to call for him with my louder voice. But Bill's insistence that he'll be okay, coupled with his earlier refusal of my offer to hold the water glass, leaves me uncertain what to do. I do nothing. We continue the interview for another fifteen minutes until Bill again calls out, "Joe! Joe! Hey, Joe-hey, Joe-hey, Joe, Joe."

Bill's roommate pokes his head into the room and says, "I think Joe's outside." Bill says, "Oh, okay." Then he continues answering my questions. Thirty seconds later, his roommate reappears and says, "Actually, I don't think he's in the house. I don't know where he's at." His roommate leaves and Bill says, "Joe is really wonderful, he probably just cut out for a few minutes."

We continue the interview, but I am uncomfortably aware of the fact that talking without water is causing Bill to dehydrate. Furthermore, his voice is deteriorating and he is getting harder to understand—so much so that when I review the tape for transcription, many of his responses are lost. Nevertheless, I say nothing. Ten more minutes pass before he again calls, "Joe-hey, Joe-Joe, are you around?" By this point, I feel frantic. I can't imagine why he won't let me give him water. "Do you want me to go outside and see if I can find him?" I ask in desperation, not sure what I should do. Bill responds, "Would you?"

I find Joe sitting in the sun directly outside the apartment. I tell him that Bill wants him, and he explains that he was waiting for me to leave. I wonder what Joe will think when he gets to Bill's room. Will he think that I am unwilling to hold the glass of water? I want to tell Joe that I offered to give Bill the water, that I appreciate his giving us privacy, and that I am sorry to interrupt his break. I resist the impulse, however, saying nothing. I follow Joe back to Bill's room, and during the last twenty minutes of our interview he stands next to Bill, offering him a sip of water every few minutes, seamlessly.

Individualism and Independence

American individualism stresses personal independence and autonomy in all of its aspects. The archetypal account of self-reliance is Henry David Thoreau's *Walden* (1904). But although Thoreau appeared to have a completely independent day-to-day existence, he came to Walden with a history and with resources. He neither built his home without a hammer nor learned to fish by himself. The nurturing he received as a child allowed him to achieve the robust physical condition he called upon in his time of isolation. Indeed, when we think of all the objects, beliefs, and interactions that make our lives possible, it is difficult to sustain the notion that anyone is self-made.

Nevertheless, the idea of the self-reliant man occupies the center of the American imagination. Its persistence as one of our dominant cultural ideals lends it the power to obscure the actual interdependent state of our lives. We do not grow our own food or sew our own clothes. Most of us don't even cook our own meals. Yet we share a fantasy of being self-made individuals, independent and autonomous. Why do we continue to uphold a false reality as a dominant ideal? In American society, in order to be deserving of valued cultural goods one has to portray oneself as someone who is independent. In other words, one has to represent oneself as something one is not.

Denying dependence can only be accomplished by ignoring the contribution of others. We are trained from childhood to disregard the role of people involved in our care; by the time we are adults this erasure is second nature. Think of all the times you were praised for your independence; haven't we all heard a parent exclaim something like, "Oh, look how independent he or she is" . . . at the age of two! To tell a child that they are doing things by themselves, when they in fact are not, is to teach the child how to not notice the contributions of others.

Most of the activities of children, like those of all of us, are nested in the activities of many other people. Children, who put their clothes on without assistance in the moment, have received much assistance in being clothed in general. To assert that the child is independent is to overlook the contributions of countless people, from the efforts of the seamstress who made the dress to the mother who bought the dress. The fact that children do not take note of the efforts of the seamstress can be understood perhaps by the fact that the garment was not sewn in front of them. What is remarkable, however, is that the efforts of mothers are so invisible. Ironically, our mothers will teach us to deny their own contribution. Mothers may assemble all the ingredients and cooking utensils; they may give directions or even participate in the actual mixing. Nevertheless, in the end, the children made the cookies by themselves and the efforts of their mothers magically disappear. Under these conditions, the fantasy that many Americans share of being self-made individuals, independent and autonomous, is not so surprising.

Rights, respect, and status depend on one's ability to present oneself as independent. Individuals with severe disabilities, like all of us, need to assert independence in order to gain the privileges of independence. For disabled individuals this often means minimizing the visibility of the paid care that facilitates a disabled person's daily life. Joan Tronto points out that it is not only individuals with disabilities, but all of us, who "prefer to ignore routine forms of care" because they threaten our autonomy (1993).

Invisible Work

For all that, however, personal attendant work consists of literal, physical acts—things one can see and touch. How can that labor be transformed into something unseen? In fact, what is made invisible is not the labor itself, but the workers. When workers are invisible, consumers of personal attendant services can feel that they have accomplished their daily activities by themselves. The best care workers, according to some disabled individuals and attendants, are those whose presence is barely felt. Benjie, an immigrant care worker, describes what he considers quality care.

> It's being able to put yourself in a situation where you are almost not seen . . . where the recipient of care is so able to do what he wants . . . it almost feels like, "I'm doing this," and you're not even in the picture in his mind . . . when he's so in tune with what he's doing, what he wants to do and feels really good, and you're almost nonexistent and yet you're there . . . [It's] like you're there, but you're not there . . . [when they can do something] without even realizing that they're doing it because you're there, that's quality work right there.

Personal attendants work in individual homes, are generally poorly paid, and rarely receive health benefits, vacation pay, or sick leave. They can be fired at will, without notice. Given the striking lack of opportunity this job provides, it is not surprising that the demand for personal attendant services is met largely by one of the most vulnerable populations of workers: immigrant women. The low status and social invisibility of these women allows them more easily to achieve the invisibility required for the job. This social invisibility is necessary because personal attendants are essential to the home-care consumers' identities as "independent" individuals.

Independence, after all, is not simply a passive status: it is something people "do" (West and Fenstermaker 1995; West and Zimmerman 1991).[1] Personal attendants, beyond performing caregiving tasks, participate in creating an illusion of independence for the disabled individuals they serve. Together with the consumers of their services, personal attendants accomplish this by transferring the authorship of many caregiving tasks from the worker to the consumer. This is a collaborative process, through which not one but two identities are constructed: care receivers are constructed as independent, and caregivers are constructed as invisible.

Women and members of certain ethnic groups are often thought to be "natural" caregivers (Glenn 1991). Not surprisingly, some consumers claim that workers who were mothers or who came from foreign countries (bearing, as Ron asserts, "old-world values") make the best caregivers. One consumer, Janet, offers that "foreign people stick around longer, and unfortunately, they take better care." Another, Sue, avers that immigrants "just care a lot more and have much more of a helping attitude than, let's say, an American." George, a self-described consumer advocate, agrees, noting that "some feel the best workers are illegal immigrants."

Immigrant women are easily cast into roles that require invisibility, because they already belong to a category that is socially invisible. Furthermore, when care activities are naturalized and essentialized, the work they entail is effectively erased. Immigrant women are the caregivers par excellence because both they and their work are often rendered invisible. What's more, caregivers often actively participate in this erasure. D'avian, a woman of color who works as an attendant, says it is important for personal attendants "to do it [the work] like they really want to." When the effort of care turns into something the worker wants to do, the labor vanishes (Hochschild 1983).

Nonetheless, care workers and their work are made invisible by a range of factors, including the work itself, the workers' social characteristics and roles, and the degree to which the work does or does not conflict with these roles or characteristics. Care work is considered women's work, and as a general rule it is undervalued. As one personal attendant observed, "You can make more washing a dog than you can washing a human being." Associated with bodily functions, care work can also be considered humiliating or degrading. Part of the worker's job is to exhibit an absence of disgust (Isaksen 2000). Receivers of care, too, may find the arrangement humiliating. Needing help with bodily functions can be particularly shame-provoking for adults (Scheff and Retzinger 2000). One consumer told me, "If they're moms, it's easy, because they are used to diapers. That's the worst part for people, is dealing with the bowel movement. Because I need help with that, too. What I usually say is, 'Pretend you're changing a diaper,' and um, yeah, they usually cope pretty well." I asked this consumer how it felt to know that the workers had to cope. The consumer replied, "In the beginning, it was one of the hardest things in the world. But now it's part of living."

The attendant's job, therefore, is to reduce the amount of shame the consumer feels, first of all by not showing disgust. In a study that compared the care provided by paid caregivers to the care provided by family members, Lise Isaksen found that care related to stressful emotions, such as tasks involving bodily functions, requires "distance" (2000). Paid strangers are able to deliver care in a way that is less shaming for the receiver. Women workers are further enabled to do this kind of work invisibly because it is similar to work like changing diapers, which is considered part of the female gender role. And what makes this uncomfortable intimacy of the attendant's job comfortable is the attendant's invisibility. After all, a disabled receiver of care cannot retreat to another room for privacy, as an employer of a domestic worker might. Rather, his or her body is central to the attendant's work. "I'm like an extension of his body," said Julie, an attendant. For the consumer, this results in a loss of privacy; for the home-care worker, it produces another kind of burden, as he or she must constantly manage his or her emotions. One consumer responding to my question about the lack of privacy said, "Sometimes you just have to say, 'I really need to take a nap. Don't talk to me for a half hour,' or something." When I spoke with attendants, the obligation to manage their emotions emerged as an oppressive aspect of the job. Ironically, this emotional labor is not recognized as work. Rather, it is invisible.

Invisibility, and the transfer of authorship of one's efforts to another person, requires the desire, or at the very least the consent, of the caregiver not to be seen. Caregivers hand over authorship of their caring work. This is not to say that care receivers share no responsibility for this situation. Rebecca, for example, expressed a desire for the care she receives to be done without effort, or, in other words, to be done invisibly: "Quality care is when that attendant has left, I feel good, I feel refreshed, clean, sitting in my chair correctly. I have everything I need for the day, and I have an attendant who has come in and done it effortlessly."

One consumer, who has an attendant assist him at work, uses language to take authorship of his attendant's activities. "I'm running around the office, sending out faxes, photocopying, laser-beaming, you know that kind of stuff," he recounts, although he is not physically able to carry out any of these activities. Disabled individuals are not the only ones who use language to transfer authorship. Indeed, the transfer of authorship is pervasive throughout society. For example, can't we easily imagine an able-bodied executive offering, "Can I get you a cup of coffee?" when in fact it is his secretary that will be doing the getting?

The degree to which care workers participate in their own invisibility varies. Only one attendant in my sample explicitly envisioned quality care as requiring invisibility. Others tended to define quality care as involving a kind of intense focus on the care receiver. Elisa, an immigrant worker, is proud of the fact that she knows what her employer's needs are even before those needs are articulated. "When they were looking toward something or even moving their lips, I knew what they needed. Immediately I provided them with water, tea, food."

There is, however, no reciprocal gaze on the caregiver. It can be argued that the disabled employer's bodily needs are so great that this focus is justified. But one must not underestimate the needs of the caregiver, which are not as obviously embodied, but may nevertheless be great. Personal attendants are often new immigrants, unfamiliar with the customs, norms, laws, and language of their adopted country. Some face additional struggles because they are undocumented. Working in a largely unregulated occupation, personal attendants are especially vulnerable to racism, sexism, sexual harassment, and taxing working conditions. Poor to begin with, these workers tend to be badly compensated. And when they're women, their care workload generally extends beyond their clients to their families. Often they have no one to take over their care responsibilities or to help them when they need care themselves.

These workers are also vulnerable in that they must constantly struggle for respect. Every time a worker was present in the course of my interviews, sometimes coming within a few feet of me for a brief interaction with the consumer, the consumer failed to introduce us. This was particularly striking given that the subject of the interview was the relationship between caregivers and care receivers. None of the caregivers I observed at consumers' homes introduced themselves, and it was difficult to make eye contact with them in order to introduce myself. By failing to make eye contact, the attendants reinforced and helped produce the invisibility that caused the consumers not to introduce them in the first place.

If we accept the view that the invisibility of personal attendants is particularly demeaning and oppressive, how do we make sense of the idea that personal attendants consent to their invisibility? First of all, not all workers who consent to being invisible desire it. When someone implied that an attendant did not need to be introduced at a meeting because he was "just the caregiver," the attendant commented, "It does hurt, you know." Some attendants do desire invisibility. Since their job is to confer independence, it makes sense that workers who want to do a good job will participate in making themselves invisible. They will be further motivated if they care about their employers. Ironically, handing over the authorship of caring labor may itself be the most caring part of care.

Are workers who articulate a desire to be invisible oppressed by being made so? Must one feel oppressed to be oppressed? I believe that the transfer of authorship is a negative phenomenon even for those who consciously work to make it happen. To be made invisible is the first step toward being considered nonhuman, which is why making another person invisible often precedes treating them inhumanely. To use Marxist terms, invisibility is the most extreme form of alienation—the ultimate manifestation of self-estrangement.

Alienation of Carework

In the traditional capitalist-worker transaction, what is appropriated is surplus value. Here, however, what is produced is the activity of carework, and so it is the authorship of this activity that may be appropriated. The personal attendants I spoke with recognized and resented the fact that they were unseen and undervalued. Karen observed: "We should be respected as hardworking people, as doing a hard job. [But] how much respect have we gotten in history books?" These personal attendants want it both ways. They want to be valued and recognized as important people, yet they also want to help the consumer feel independent, which means that they must transfer the authorship of their actions and make themselves invisible. Interestingly, the attendants do not connect their invisibility in relation to the consumer to their invisibility in relation to the larger society.

That many personal attendants fail to see their participation in the transfer of authorship as problematic is not surprising. In a culture like ours, few individuals embrace dependence or interdependence. The attendant may want to do care work in a visible, self-affirming way that neither negates his or her own contribution nor conceals the dependence of the person being cared for. But he or she is often faced with a recipient who experiences being cared for as a painful reminder of dependence. Under these circumstances, workers may feel compelled to hide the true nature of care. Once the worker makes this choice, the necessary result is that he or she will be undervalued for the work. How could something unseen be completely valued? Some will argue that individuals whose job it is to be invisible are valued for their very invisibility. But the jobs of invisible people are the lowest paid, and this low pay reflects the value such workers possess in the eyes not only of society but also of the people for whom they are caring.

One consumer of attendant services, George, questioned my use of the term "caregiver." He said, "Caregiver? That's a controversial term . . . say 'personal attendant' instead." George was referring to a controversy within the disabled community regarding the role of personal attendants and their relationships with consumers of care. Informing this debate is the disability community's history with "care" that imprisoned them in institutions and made them the victims of "caregiving" professionals, or left them at the mercy of abusive or controlling familial relationships (DeJong 1983). Consumers who reject the word "care" see it as implying too much passivity on the part of the care receiver. Others embrace an idea of caregiving in which receivers recognize their dependence on their personal attendants and understand that personal attendants can also fulfill emotional needs (Zola 1983).

Most of the consumers I interviewed considered businesslike relationships with their personal attendants to be ideal. Interestingly, however, this expectation directly conflicts with what the attendants felt was the most essential quality for their jobs. Maria explains:

> Of course they need to have their basics. The house needs to be cleaned, they need to eat, they need to shower, that kind of thing. But I think it goes beyond

> that, you have to show that you care . . . because they're not objects and it's not just a job, you know; you get attached. . . . You're working with human beings, and that's where the difference lies—working with people and working with things. . . . They also need to feel like they're still humans who deserve respect, love, and care.

Jacob, another attendant agrees:

> I enjoy the atmosphere and conversation I create with whoever it is that I'm with, and there really isn't much that happens besides that. [All the physical tasks] are incidental . . . I think the most important thing in the relationship is that the attendant like the consumer. . . . The absence of a businesslike relationship creates an opportunity for the attendant to like the employer more.

The attendants I interviewed described their work almost as a religious calling. Mohamed, who acted as a translator in my interview with his wife, told me, "She is doing these things for the satisfaction of our conscience, of our spirituality." Working as a personal attendant is a labor of love. Money changes hands, but this is not commodified care. The immigrant women and women of color I interviewed unanimously said that good care required that they love the receiver. Patting her chest, D'avian told me, "It has to come from here . . . You just got to have that love." Nothing brought attendants more satisfaction than when care receivers loved them back. In other words, the ideal employment situation was not one where they were thinking only about the consumer, but one in which the consumer also thought about them. These were relationships that seemed more familial than businesslike. Cecilia asserted, "I like to work as a home health-care worker better [than in a nursing home] because when you go to their house it is as if you are going to care for a relative, a family member." Maria, reflecting on the elderly woman, now deceased, for whom she used to care, said, "We became really good friends. . . . I loved her like a grandmother."

The consumers I interviewed, however, including those who were close to their attendants, expressed a desire for a different kind of relationship. Rebecca echoed many of their sentiments when she said, "I tend to like to put up a wall with my attendants." That care receivers are not particularly open to more personal relationships with their caregivers is not surprising, since these jobs pay so poorly that few caregivers tend to stay in them for long. Given the expectation of high turnover, consumers I interviewed expected their attendants to do little more than accomplish discrete tasks.

In the past, family members supplied the intimate bodily care that is now performed by personal attendants. The care provided by personal attendants is public care; it is paid and performed by non-kin, albeit in the domestic spheres. Deborah Stone cautions, "When we stop doing care and instead hire someone else to do it, the care becomes commodified and . . . we look at other people as means not ends" (1991). When care is commodified, the care receiver becomes an independent purchaser of services to which he or she feels entitled. The care receiver does not experience the caregiver as generously expressing affection and concern through his or her work; rather the worker is simply doing a paid job. When I asked him what his caregiver had done that was above and beyond the call of duty, Ron replied, "I can't think of a good answer to that. I don't know of anything that I ask of them that isn't what I consider to be part of that attendant's job." Several of the consumers I interviewed responded similarly. At first I thought these answers reflected on the care workers in question. But upon further questioning, I realized that this was not a personal assessment of their attendant so much as a structural assessment. The consumer felt that they had fully purchased the time of their personal attendant; therefore, there was nothing the attendant did within his or her work time that the consumer did not consider part of the job. When the job expands to include everything the attendant does, it becomes impossible for the caregiver to express real caring, because nothing he or she does is understood as a gift.

On the other hand, it's no wonder that disabled consumers want to distance their bodily needs from their personal relationships. Some of the disabled individuals I interviewed involved their friends in their personal care, but most are very careful to draw a line. One consumer explained, "I really try to keep that to a minimum, because that really does cut into the friendships." Those who do rely on friends to provide care often see their friendships suffer as a result. One interviewee told of a friendship that ruptured under the strain of her care needs. She lost not only a friend but also the person who was meeting her important needs.

What would it be like to live in a society where the need for care and the work of care were supported materially and symbolically? Maybe in such a society we wouldn't mind when our friends cared for us, and our friends wouldn't find caring for us a burden. The state would enfranchise disabled consumers to choose the "best person for the job." Dependence would not be stigmatized. Under these conditions, consumers and personal attendants could meet each other as equals, forging a mutually respectful relationship that would transcend commodification.

Conclusion

As a Latina woman, I would under many circumstances have no difficulty being invisible enough to provide good care. However, as the anecdote at the beginning of this essay illustrates, in my role as a researcher from the University of California I was not a preferred provider of a certain type of care. Bill could not tolerate my assistance with the glass of water because I was not sufficiently invisible to perform such intimate care. Had I helped Bill drink, he would not have been able to maintain an image of himself as independent. But when his paid caregiver raised the cup to his lips, the act was invisible. In other words, the very same work is either visible or invisible, depending upon who does it.

Furthermore, not all care work requires the same level of invisibility. Physically intimate types of care work, for example, require the most invisibility on the part of the caregiver. Bill allowed me to get his attendant, because this fell within the range of activities not likely to stigmatize the beneficiary as dependent. On the other hand, the fact that he was not comfortable asking me to get his attendant, and that I had to offer, could mean that even this gesture threatened his sense of autonomy.

We are all dependent on others to varying degrees. A language that denies this fact fuels a system that obscures the ways in which other people care for us. Words such as independence, self-reliance, and self-made help create, and are created by, a dynamic within which people are ignored and devalued. Joan Tronto reminds us that by "not noticing how pervasive and central care is to human life, those who are in positions of power and privilege can continue to ignore and degrade the activities of care and those who give care" (1993).

Independence is perhaps the most fundamental of our cultural myths; it supports the organization of our society and justifies the distribution of goods, real and ideal. The labels independent and dependent, rather than reflecting empirical reality, are myths used to justify inequality. The transfer of authorship of tasks is ubiquitous in American society. It occurs between executives and secretaries, between children and mothers, between disabled individuals and their caregivers. Nevertheless, two things are true: no one is invisible and no one is independent. If we recognize our dependence on others, we must acknowledge that we fall short of the cultural ideal of independence. We must further acknowledge our debt to those upon who we depend.

When individuals with care needs have to worry about whether or not their caregiver will come the next morning, perhaps it is simply too frightening for them to face the extent of their dependency. Rejecting "care" because of its connection to dependence, and embracing a businesslike, commodified relationship (in which the receiver becomes a "consumer"), disabled people can nurture the illusion of choice and control. However, without resources to pay competitive wages, most of these care receivers have few options regarding who will care for them or how much care they will receive. Furthermore, in a strictly commodified relationship, caregivers and care receivers become means instead of ends, a dynamic that denies the full subjectivity of both.

Consumers of personal attendant services deserve good care delivered by people they can rely on. Personal attendants deserve reasonable wages, decent working conditions, and to have their efforts recognized. Both parties deserve arrangements that hold out the possibility for mutual respect and love, for relationship and community. The fact that some people need more assistance than others should affect the larger polity more than it does. Rather, the workers and their efforts are not the only invisible parties; the disabled population and its needs are invisible as well. All of us need to take responsibility for the caring needs of our society. We need to reject claims of independence when they legitimate the unequal distribution of rights and resources. We need to recognize that independence is a fantasy not just for disabled individuals but for everyone.

ACKNOWLEDGMENTS

A version of this essay titled "Invisible Labors: Caring for the Independent Person," © Lynn May Rivas, was published in *Global Woman: Nannies, Maids, and Sex Workers in the New Economy*, edited by Barbara Ehrenreich and Arlie Russell Hochschild, 70–84 (New York: Metropolitan Books, 2003).

NOTE

1. The "doing" of identity in Candace West and Donald Zimmerman (1991) as well as Candace West and Sarah Fenstermaker (1995) is conceived as something people accomplish through interaction. One does not do identity alone; the real or imagined presence of another is necessary. However, while their conception involves interaction, it does not involve collaboration.

REFERENCES

DeJong, Gerben. 1983. "Defining and Implementing the Independent Living Concept." In *Independent Living for Physically Disabled People: Developing, Implementing, and Evaluating Self-Help Rehabilitation Programs*, edited by Nancy M. Crew and Irving K. Zola, 4–27. San Francisco: Jossey-Bass.

Glenn, Evelyn Nakano. 1991. "From Servitude to Service Work: Historical Continuities in the Racial Division of Paid Reproductive Labor." *Signs* 18 (1): 1–43.

Hochschild, Arlie Russell. 1983. *The Managed Heart: Commercialization of Human Feeling.* Berkeley: University of California Press.

Isaksen, Lise. 2000. "Toward a Sociology of Gendered Disgust: Perceptions of the Organic Body and the Organization of Care." Working Papers Series. Berkeley: University of California, Center for Working Families.

Scheff, Thomas, and Suzanne Retzinger. 2000. "Shame as the Master Emotion of Everyday Life." *Journal of Mundane Behavior* 1 (3): 303–324.

Stone, Deborah. 1991. "Caring Work in a Liberal Polity." *Journal of Health Politics Policy and Law* 16 (3): 547–552.

Thoreau, Henry David. 1904. *Walden.* New York: E. P. Dutton & Co.

Tronto, Joan. 1993. *Moral Boundaries: A Political Argument for an Ethic of Care.* New York: Routledge.

West, Candace, and Sarah Fenstermaker. 1995. "Doing Difference." *Gender & Society* 9 (1): 8–37.

West, Candace, and Donald Zimmerman. 1991. "Doing Gender." In *The Social Construction of Gender*, edited by Judith Lorber and Susan Farrell, 13–37. Newbury Park, CA: Sage Publications.

Zola, Irving K. 1983. "Developing Self-Images and Interdependence." In *Independent Living for Physically Disabled People: Developing, Implementing, and Evaluating Self-Help Rehabilitation Programs*, edited by Nancy M. Crew and Irving K. Zola, 49–59. San Francisco: Jossey-Bass.

PART IV

Commodifying Intimate Life

CHAPTER 15

Remaking Family through Subcontracting Care

ELDER CARE IN TAIWANESE AND HONG KONG IMMIGRANT FAMILIES

Pei-Chia Lan

"I told her that I hire you to help me achieve my filial duty," Paul Wang, a sixty-year-old Taiwanese immigrant owning a software company in Silicon Valley, California, said as he recounted to me his conversation with the in-home careworker he employed for his mother suffering from Alzheimer's disease. The cultural norm of filial piety has traditionally governed intergenerational relationships in ethnic Chinese (Han) families. Yet many middle-class immigrant households from Taiwan and Hong Kong, like their American class peers of other ethnic origins, now seek services provided by nonfamily workers to care for their aging parents.[1] The commercial transfer of elder care offers a lens for us to examine the transformation of kin relations and cultural practices among immigrant families, as well as the variegated consequences of the "commercialization of intimate life" (Hochschild 2003) in the context of immigration.

The commodification of elder care may indicate the weakening of intergenerational ties, but it may also facilitate the maintenance or reinforcement of family bonds. The changes in elder care arrangements demonstrate how immigrant families negotiate kin relations in response to different care regimes and cultural norms when traveling across borders. I use the phrase "subcontracting filial piety" to describe the process whereby immigrant adult children transfer the filial duty of caring for their aging parents to nonfamily employees. Using various kinds of financial sources—private money, public funds, or a combination of both—the adult children incorporate careworkers into their domestic lives as their filial agents and fictive kin, thus maintaining the cultural ideal of filial piety and remaking the Chinese family on foreign soil.

Commodification of Filial Care

Arlie Hochschild has written: "Less and less do we produce care. More and more we consume it. Indeed, increasingly we 'do' care by buying the right service or thing" (2003, 3). The interchange between love and gold nevertheless raises concerns about possible corruption and disruption of informal relations, such as the commodification of care and the marketization of intimacy (Ungerson 2000).

Viviana Zelizer (2005) identifies a common way of thinking as "separate spheres" or "hostile worlds," which views economic activities and intimate relations as distinct arenas, and as such their mixing results in inevitable disorder. Instead, she calls for an alternative approach of "connected lives," in which moral obligations in the intimate sphere can be confirmed and assured by market compensation.

I would like to further argue that the dichotomous thinking about market and intimacy, or money and love, is rooted in Western cultural scripts of domestic intimacy based on the ideal of the European bourgeois family.[2] In line with the cannon of separate spheres, the home was defined, first, as a haven from the uncertainties and calculation of commercial life and, second, as "the locus of social and personal morality" (Laslett and Brenner 1989, 387). This view also presumes the nuclear family as the fundamental form of domestic organization, despite the reality that the nuclear household is a relatively recent development among white Protestants in northwest Europe and the United States (Dalley 1988).

The ideas and practices of domesticity differ in other parts of the world. In Taiwan, intergenerational cohabitation is traditionally privileged. Filial duty as an act of reciprocation results from the fact that intergenerational relationships serve as channels for the exchanges of resources and power (Pyke 1999). The parent-child bond is governed by an implicit moral contract: child rearing is viewed as a social investment with an expectation of delayed repayment—in the Chinese term, *bao-da* (payback); children, especially sons, are thus obligated to return the debts through filial care for their aging parents.

However, the domestic collectivity as an intimate sphere is not immune from power inequalities, especially along the lines of gender, age, and generation. In Han-Chinese societies, taking care of aging parents is traditionally considered the duty of sons, although the actual work of caregiving is mostly burdened on the sons' wives. Similar to the formation of "global care chains" (Hochschild 2000; Parrenas 2000), there are "filial care chains" composed by a series of personal links across power divides based on the paid or unpaid work of caring. It consists of two linkages: first, *gender transfer* of the filial duty from the son to the daughter-in-law and, second, *market transfer* of carework from the daughter-in-law to nonfamily employees, who are still predominantly women. Market transfer becomes a strategy of patriarchal bargaining for daughters-in-law to avert subordination to the patrilineal family authority (Lan 2006).

Moreover, we should situate the formation of filial care chains in the institutional context of "care regime," which embodies values, norms, and rules that provide a regulative framework to shape behaviors and policies toward care (Sainsbury 1999). The changing arrangements in elder care among immigrant families demonstrate how carework is embedded in particular institutional regimes that organize the public and private in distinct patterns.

Methods and Data

Through snowballing personal referrals, I conducted in-depth interviews with sixteen immigrants from Taiwan and Hong Kong in eight households residing in the San Francisco Bay Area. These households share a similar immigration pattern: adult children settled in the United States first, and their overseas parents came later as dependents. Eight informants were elderly parents between sixty-eight and eighty-eight years old, including three widows, one widower, and two married couples. I also interviewed eight adult children, including one man, three women, and two married couples. In three of the households, both parents and children were interviewed; I failed to do so in the other four households due to the death of the parents or unavailability of the adult children. I also interviewed eleven female home careworkers (ten from mainland China and one from Taiwan) and spent some time observing interactions between elderly clients and home careworkers.[3]

Transplanting Families on Foreign Soil

Immigrant seniors, like other elderly people, need care not only for their physical frailty and emotional loneliness, but also to achieve independence and autonomy. When relocating overseas, power dynamics between adult children and their aging parents are subject to change. As Jessica Chao, a sixty-year-old Taiwanese, described, "The minute you arrive here [in the United States], you switch the roles . . . They [parents] don't speak English; they don't know how to drive; it's as if they become children again." The linguistic and cultural barriers render elderly immigrants dependent on their children or sometimes grand children to assist in all sorts of daily affairs.

Separate residence has gradually become the dominant intergenerational residential pattern among middle-class Taiwanese immigrants in the United States. In three households in this research aging parents and adult children share the same residence. One of these is the household of John Chen, a fifty-five-year-old Taiwanese business owner residing with his parents. When I asked him if he ever thought of alternative residential arrangements, he lowered his voice even though his parents lived in the other annexed building. He said, "We dare not think about it. . . . People might say you're not filial, right? Why taint yourself with that stigma? But, on the other hand, the filial norm is rooted in Taiwan. When people are in the U.S., who cares? Your neighbors here don't know you. Who minds what you did?"

Although following the traditional custom, John keenly recognized the decline of social control by the norm of filial piety when residing in the United States. Many immigrant adult children during interviews referred to American norms to justify their residential separation and financial independence from their parents. Kevin Li, a sixty-three-year-old retired manager, offered comments on this subject, "You know American laws are like this: children grow up and leave their parents, so they are not obligated to take care of their parents. But our civil law [in Taiwan] is different. In Taiwan, if you don't support your parents, you are guilty of abandoning them. This is a crime. The government can force you to take care of your parents! But it's different in the States."

Taiwan's family law symbolically announces that children should respect parents filially and specifies children's legal obligation to support their needy parents and cohabitating parents-in-law.[4] Attached to the potential criminal charge of abandonment, the law honors and enforces the moral contract between parents and children. Delegating elder care to the private sphere, Taiwan's government did not introduce any social security or welfare programs for senior citizens until the mid-1990s.[5] The web of social security is even thinner in Hong Kong, where a compulsory retirement pension scheme was absent until the implementation of MPF (Mandatory Provident Fund Schemes) in 2000 (Yu 2007).

Relocated to a new land and new care regime, Taiwanese and Hong Kong elderly immigrants found themselves an "American filial son"—a term they called the U.S. government—who sends them monthly allowances on time without bargaining or complaints. Although the U.S. welfare regime is a liberal model that favors means-tested programs to universal entitlements, the government still provides institutional resources that empower immigrant elders to avoid overdepending on children. Medicare, a universal entitlement, is the most important federal health insurance program for people older than age sixty-five. In addition, because most elderly immigrants own few assets and earn little income in the United States, they are eligible for low-income elderly benefits, including Medicaid (or Medi-Cal in California), cash grants of supplemental security income (SSI), rental assistance,[6] food stamps, and in-home care service.

The state of California also provides the elderly with in-home care services through the program of In-Home Supportive Services (IHSS). This program currently employs more than 300,000 independent providers, mostly immigrant and minority women, who offer nonprofessional, custodial care in the homes of low-income elderly and disabled individuals (Boris et al. 2004). For home careworkers in the IHSS program, the California government is the "employer" who pays for their services, and care recipients are "clients" or "consumers" who hold the decision to subsume or terminate contracts.[7] Third-party payment also assists alliances between individual careworkers and their elderly clients. Some home careworkers reported that government-funded care recipients tend to be more benevolent and flexible on working hours and sick leaves than clients who purchase services out of their own pockets.

IHSS not only subsidizes care services provided by nonfamily workers but also compensates previously unpaid caring labor offered by family members. Family caregivers may become waged employees of IHSS. Adult children who accommodate their low-income parents can also apply for food and housing subsidies. By placing monetary value on caring labor between family members, this policy frames care as a public interest rather than a private matter. This idea contrasts with the privatized notion of elder care in the Chinese cultural context. John Chen, who was one of the primary caregivers for his ill father, commented, "I never heard that the government would pay you for taking care of your own parents. In Taiwan, taking care of your own family is your own business." Other informants criticized these measures as "ridiculous" or "not right" because they consider care for parents a family obligation and moral duty rather than a paid job.

Patterns of Subcontracting Elder Care

By introducing three immigrant families who develop different arrangements for subcontracting elder care, I illustrate the range of financial resources and opinions toward receiving public benefits for the elderly. Their arrangements and practices of elder care—where care takes place, who gives care, who pays for care, whom they hire, and how they divide the labor of care—indicate how they reconstitute the meanings and boundaries of the family, as well as how they negotiate ethnic difference and reproduce class distinction in the fabric of everyday life.

Purchasing Quality Care

Paul Wang came to the United States to pursue a master's degree in the mid-1960s and, after graduation, started working in Silicon Valley. He later established his own software company with the assistance of his wife. Three of his siblings followed a similar immigration path and are now all employed as professionals in California. In the early 1980s they proudly moved their parents from Taiwan to enjoy the pleasant climate in California, as well as to witness the success of their children. The parents lived with Paul, the eldest son, in an affluent South Bay suburb. Paul explained why they chose to reproduce the traditional pattern of three-generational cohabitation in the United States: "Living together is a must be in our culture. I like [it] that way, too. To place parents in a strange place, and in a strange culture like the U.S., it's a crime in my perspective."

Paul's mother was diagnosed with Alzheimer's disease a few years ago. Paul firmly objected when one of his siblings suggested that their mother be placed in a nursing home, and he insisted on hiring full-time home careworkers at whatever cost. Since then, they have been hiring home careworkers for three shifts to accompany his mother day and night.

When I asked Paul if his mother is eligible for SSI or IHSS home care service, he answered, "I know many people do that. I didn't. I can afford without doing that. It looks kind of bad to receive checks from Social Security." Paul considers receiving elderly benefits as a social stigma and holds doubts about the quality of free public care. Because the employment cost is divided among four siblings who are all professionals, hiring live-in home careworkers out of their pockets does not pose a serious financial burden but rather becomes a status marker that underscores their filial concern for their mother. In Paul's own words: "I dare say that I am a filial son. How many people can do something like we do? There is always someone to be her [Paul's mother's] company. And it's very easy for us children. We only need to pay."

Although praising himself as a filial son, Paul admitted to me that the difficulty involved in personal care is another reason why he decided to outsource care for his mother, "Honestly, taking care of the elderly, like helping them with a bowel movement . . . that is really hard and dirty. Once I had no choice and I had to help my mom do it. I had to close my eyes during the whole time."

Paul defines his duty instead as a supervisor who makes frequent visits to check on the workers and ensures that his mother is in good hands. In this case, Paul Wang considers his filial responsibility as taking care of his mother, a duty achieved by his generous financial contribution in paying caregivers and his efforts to supervise the quality of care. In contrast, the daily chores of caregiving, especially the emotionally stressful hands-on care tasks, are transferred to home careworkers who are usually low-income immigrant women.

Paul prefers hiring a Taiwanese careworker who charges a much higher rate than recent immigrants from mainland China. Lily Yu, a forty-year-old single Taiwanese woman, has been caring for Paul's mother for more than three years. When I asked Lily if she faced job competition from low-cost Chinese immigrants, she expressed total confidence in her "quality" service: "No, no, because we [Taiwanese] were educated in different ways [from Chinese]. We learn Confucianism. We know how to respect the elderly. We have better ethics and manners. Mainlanders—they have got rid of all these during the Cultural Revolution, right?"

Scholars who study the employment of child careworkers have found that most parents are willing to pay a higher salary to caregivers of similar ethnic backgrounds, whom they consider more trustworthy (Uttal 1997; Wrigley 1995). A similar rationale explains why Taiwanese employers prefer Taiwanese home careworkers to Chinese workers. They consider workers of similar cultural, social, and educational backgrounds to be more reliable filial agents and more qualified to become fictive kin.

Paul's mother has suffered from deteriorating memory and sometimes thinks that she is in Taiwan rather than in the United States. Lily helps her with almost everything, including cooking, housecleaning, bathing, dressing, and, most important, emotional attendance. Lily explained to me the principle of her caregiving, "One of my major jobs is to listen to her. She's losing it day by day. She sometimes called me the name of her daughter. The other worker would correct her and told her to do this and that, and she would be mad. I don't. I see her as my mother. So I know what I shouldn't say to my mom and what made my mom mad. I don't correct her; I just follow her thoughts and finish what she said."

When adult children transfer the duty of filial care to careworkers, they expect that the workers serve as their extension to play the role of surrogate children. Lily also uses care for her mother as an analogy to describe the ideal care she provides for her client. As an evidence of her intimate care, she proudly mentioned that Paul's mother sometimes mixed up the names of her biological children and surrogate children. However, Lily also told me that Mrs. Wang often insists that her daughter, when coming to visit, should bathe her, a task usually performed by the careworkers. Without explicitly stating it, the mother clearly expresses her desire for a kind of filial care that involves interactions on the basis of personal intimacy instead of merely monetary contributions from her children.

Seeking Publically Funded Help

Carol Yang and her husband were born in Canton in the 1960s, fled to Hong Kong during the Cultural Revolution, and immigrated to the United States in the early 1980s. Both high school graduates, they work full time as laboratory testers and struggle to make ends meet—particularly to pay the mortgage on their house in a lower middle-class suburb near Oakland. Financial tightness is not the only challenge in their lives; they also face a serious "time bind" (Hochschild 1997). In addition to running between jobs and taking care of her three children, Carol has to make frequent visits to her mother and mother-in-law, both of whom live alone in Oakland.

Before hiring a careworker for her mother, Carol went over to her mother's house to cook every morning before work so Mrs. Yang could microwave her meals during the day. After work, Carol went over again to clean up and help her mother take a bath. She described her hectic schedule in the past: "My life was like standing on a fire wheel!" Six years ago, Mrs. Yang fell down at home and became dependent on a wheelchair. Carol considered sending her to a nursing home, but the mother strongly objected. In extreme despair, Carol found out about the IHSS program, which granted her 120 hours of home care service per month. The public funds allow Mrs. Yang to hire a home careworker who provides service five days a week, five hours a day.

Mei-Lan Wu is a fifty-six-year-old junior college graduate and a former supervisor in a local government in Canton. She has been caring for seniors or children of immigrant families since she moved to the United States in 1993. When I met her, she had cared for Mrs. Yang for more than two years. The first time I accompanied Mei-Lan to work, I could see from far away that Mrs. Yang was sitting by a window eagerly waiting for her arrival. Because Mrs. Yang speaks only Cantonese, I relied on Mei-Lan to translate her words into Mandarin. During the interview, Mrs. Yang reminded Mei-Lan a few times not to tell me something. As I asked Mei-Lan what she did not want to tell me, Mei-Lan said, "She said [she has] only me. She doesn't want to talk about the others [the children], not in front of you."

Mei-Lan spent more time with Mrs. Yang than any of Mrs. Yang's adult children did. From Monday to Saturday, she arrived by noon and prepared lunch; Mrs. Yang had to finish dinner so Mei-Lan could clean up before she left at 5 P.M. The late lunch and early dinner schedule was due to the time constraint of the IHSS subsidy, which, in this case, paid for five hours of carework per day. Debra Stone (2000, 104), who interviewed home careworkers in New England, found that "not having enough time to do what you think the client needs is a source of stress and guilt for caregivers." Although restrained by bureaucratic schedules, Mei-Lan developed a personal relationship with Mrs. Yang and provided customized care, such as learning her preferences in food, always preparing chewable and warm dishes, and bringing her favorite pastries from Chinatown from time to time. The most considerate services provided by Mei-Lan included putting red lipstick and nail polish on Mrs. Yang and purchasing colorful undergarments for her, both acts that are supposed to bring good fortune for the ill and elderly, according to the Chinese custom.

After Mei-Lan acquired U.S. citizenship, she decided to take a long vacation to visit her son in Canton. After Mei-Lan quit, Mrs. Yang called her almost every day and cried on the phone, complaining about the replacement worker. When Mei-Lan went back to visit Mrs. Yang, the new worker questioned her: "How could you work for her *mong-cha-cha* [Cantonese, literally translated as "blurry sight," meaning being muddleheaded due to a lack of information]?" The new worker referred to the situations such as Mei-Lan staying late without overtime pay or performing duties not specified in the contract, such as offering massages. The new worker followed the contract rules negotiated by the union. Mrs. Yang cried and said to Mei-Lan, "The union is helping her [the new worker] exploit me!"

Both Mrs. Yang and her daughter have adopted Mei-Lan as their "fictive kin" (Stack 1974) whose role is beyond an employee. For employers, "the family-type tasks provided by the stranger-caretaker can be reconstructed as *appropriate* and the realm of privacy and intimacy can be maintained" (Karner 1998, 72). Yet, a fictive kinship relationship is a double-edged sword for home careworkers. On one hand, home careworkers create meaning for this undervalued job through building emotional bonds with care recipients. On the other hand, they face tensions over reconciling a family-like relationship, characterized by love, patience, and specialness, with an employment relationship that features rational calculation of rights, bureaucratic schedule, and fairness (Stone 2000).

Public Funds that Divide and Unite the Family

Julia Lin is a forty-eight-year-old software engineer in San Jose. She and her husband both came to the United States for graduate education and started their careers in the fast-growing high-tech industry. The couple spends long hours at work, and they frequently stay in the office during evenings and weekends. Julia's parents relocated from Taiwan to San Jose in the mid-1980s, and they assisted Julia and her husband with child care, cooking, and other household chores. After the grandchildren went to high school, Julia's parents moved to a rental property owned by Julia and her husband. Julia's seventy-five-year-old father, Mr. Lin, explained to me why they moved out from their daughter's: "There's more freedom [living apart]. Everybody can keep his or her own territory. They [the daughter and son-in-law] are rearing their children. They have their own parenting style. We would become dislikable if we intervene. But we would intervene more or less if we lived there, right?"

In fact, Mr. and Mrs. Lin "rent" the house from their daughter. I was surprised when Julia first told me of this practice, which significantly violates the filial norm—care for aging parents should be the children's moral (read: *unpaid*) duty. I carefully phrased my question: "They pay rent to you? Your parents are quite courteous, aren't they?" Julia answered me in a taken-for-granted tone: "I have to pay mortgage, too. Plus, I charge them only half the market price." The rent Julia charged her parents, $500 per month for a moderate-sized house in San Jose, was indeed far below the market value. While I was wondering if Julia had become so assimilated to the individualist culture in the United States that she felt at ease marketizing relationships with her parents, Julia added more comments that helped solve my puzzle: "You probably know that if they [the parents] live in their own house, there is no government subsidy. If they rent one, the government will give them some money, not much but enough to cover [the rent]."

Julia's case is not a rare one. To my knowledge, quite a number of Taiwanese and Hong Kong immigrant adult children charge rent to parents who stay in their houses. In addition to facilitating a rental subsidy from the government, paying rent becomes a means for the elderly to transfer income to their children so the parents can still maintain eligibility for low-income benefits. Although the practice of charging rent seems to indicate the marketization of parent-child relationships, it actually reveals strong family bonds without which the trading of economic resources among kin would be impossible.

Because Chinese parents are supposed to reside with and be cared for by the son's family, Mr. and Mrs. Lin moved out of their daughter's house and paid rent as a symbolic act to mark the appropriate order of the patriarchal family tree. However, to save face for their daughter in front of others, they also downplay the fact that they pay rent, because a filial daughter should still offer unpaid care for her parents.

To subcontract filial care via public funds involves multidirectional flows of money among parents, children, and the government. The act of paying rent in this case is not a simple economic transaction but, first, a family strategy of trading financial resources among kin to extract public funds and, second, a symbolic performance that honors the patrilineal kinship scheme.

Conclusion

The Chinese term *chia*, which has been said to constitute the basic unit of Chinese society, entails multiple meanings: kinship organization, residential cohabitation, and economic ties. Drawing on the tripartite dimensions of family, I analyze the ways Taiwanese and Hong Kong immigrants reconstitute the family through subcontracting elder care.

The first dimension regards where care takes place. *Tong-zhuo-kong-shi* (living together and eating together) is traditionally considered the substance of Chinese family life. Given the decline of three-generational cohabitation, contemporary families still attempt to maintain residential proximity, such as living in different flats of the same building, to facilitate frequent visits and dinner sharing. Because placing parents in a nursing home is a care arrangement considered to be a violation of filial norm, adult children manage to maintain residential cohabitation with their ill parents by hiring nonfamily workers who provide full-time care.

The second dimension—who gives care—indicates shifting interdependence among family members. Many elderly immigrants came to the United States to care for their grandchildren whose parents were struggling with careers in a foreign country without sufficient kin support. The pattern of residential cohabitation often breaks down when intensive care is no longer needed for teenaged grandchildren. Intergenerational cohabitation usually resumes when aging parents become frail or ill, shifting their role from care provider to care recipient.

The employment of home careworkers as fictive kin reconstitutes the boundary of family. Kinship analogies enable adult children to maintain a cultural sense of filial care and allow elderly recipients to place on careworkers kin expectations beyond the assigned duties in a contract relationship. Many home careworkers also understand the cultural significance of the kinship metaphor and accept the job obligation of being the surrogate children of care recipients.

The third dimension—who pays for care—goes to the core issue of the commodification of care. The subcontracting of filial care reveals a complex interchange between money and love: When different kinds of "monies" (Zelizer 1989) are involved in the purchase of care services—parents' savings, children's contributions, and government subsidies—how do they symbolize the meanings of care and relate to the formation of parent-child relationships?

For upper middle-class immigrants, spending money to purchase intensive and quality care provided by trustworthy nonfamily workers is perceived as an act of filial piety associated with the logic that the more one pays, the more one cares. In contrast, receiving public funds generally incurs social stigma, and the quality of free public care is considered to be inferior. Some adult children refuse to receive public funds or services because this care arrangement indicates a lack of concern for their parents; in other words, the more public funds one receives, the less one cares.

The interchange between money and love involves a different equation for those immigrant families who receive public care. Because most benefits for the elderly in the United States are means-tested programs, the eligibility is limited to the financially needy—which refers to elder parents receiving no financial support from their children. And the U.S. government subsidizes resources and services provided by family members, which are nevertheless supposed to be children's moral payment to parents in the Chinese cultural context. The meeting of Chinese filial norms and the U.S. care regime leads to an ironic result: the less children care, the more public funds parents receive.

Nevertheless, we cannot take the marketization of intergenerational relationships at face value. In reality some immigrant families circulate financial resources among kin to make their parents eligible for low-income benefits on paper. This becomes, in effect, a family strategy developed to extract public funds based on an individualistic assumption in the United States that parents and adult children are financially independent. As a result, the commodification of care does not weaken family bonds but actually reinforces kin connections as economic ties.

ACKNOWLEDGMENTS

Reprinted from "Subcontracting Filial Piety: Elder Care in Ethnic Chinese Immigrant Families in California," *Journal of Family Issues* 23, no. 7 (2002), by permission of Sage Publications.

NOTES

I am grateful for the comments of Barrie Thorne, Arlie Hochschild, Elizabeth Rudd, and Marta Gutman, as well as the editorial assistance of Karen V. Hansen and Anita Ilta Garey. I also thank Shirley Ouyang for transcribing the interviews. This research was funded by the Alfred P. Sloan Foundation Center for Working Families at the University of California, Berkeley.

1. Kritz, Gurak, and Chen (2000) analyzed the U.S. census data and found that elderly immigrants from Asia and Latin America, compared to natives and other immigrants, are more likely to be living with children. However, it is unclear whether this variation reflects cultural differences or disparities in economic resources (Abel 1990). To disentangle this analytic conflation, my research focuses on middle-class immigrants.

2. Yen-Ling Tsai (2008) made a similar critique on the U.S. literature on domestic workers.

3. All these workers had legally entered the United States to join their siblings or other immediate relatives. Four of the home careworkers were employed by the families in this research. All interviews were audiotaped, and each lasted from one to two hours.

All interviews were conducted in Mandarin Chinese. The interviews were translated into English by me as quoted in the article. To protect the privacy of informants, all names used in this article are pseudonyms. See Lan (2002).

4. According to the civil and criminal law in Taiwan (Republic of China), one is obligated to support his or her parents or cohabitating parents-in-law who cannot maintain a living on their own. Those who violate these obligations may commit the crime of abandonment and can be sentenced for as long as ten years.

5. A universal program of health insurance was implemented in Taiwan in 1996. Some cities and counties offer a small amount of cash for the elderly on a means-tested or universal basis.

6. Through the program of Section Eight Housing Choice Voucher, the California state government offers rental assistance for low-income seniors. The participant tenants need to pay only 30 percent of their monthly income for rent, and the rest is covered by public funds.

7. This framework of employment has facilitated the unionization of home careworkers and campaigns for wage increases and health insurance in alliance with client groups (both disabled and senior organizations).

REFERENCES

Abel, Emily K. 1990. "Family Care of the Frail Elderly." In *Circles of Care: Work and Identity in Women's Lives*, edited by Emily Abel and Margaret Nelson, 65–91. Albany, NY: State University of New York Press.

Boris, Eileen, Gawon Chung, Linda Delp, Ruth Matthias, and Carol Zabin. 2004. "CPRC Briefing Paper: Workforce Needs in California's Homecare System." *UC Berkeley Labor Center*. http://laborcenter.berkeley.edu/homecare/IHSSworkforce04.pdf.

Dalley, Gillian. 1988. *Ideologies of Caring: Rethinking Community and Collectivism*. Basingstoke, UK: Macmillan Education.

Hochschild, Arlie. 1997. *The Time Bind: When Work Becomes Home and Home Becomes Work*. New York: Metropolitan Books.

———. 2000. "The Nanny Chain." *The American Prospect* 11:32–36.

———. 2003. *The Commercialization of Intimate Life: Notes from Home and Work*. Berkeley: University of California Press.

Karner, Tracy. 1998. "Professional Caring: Homecare Workers as Fictive Kin." *Journal of Aging Studies* 12:69–82.

Kritz, Mary, Douglas T. Gurak, and Likwang Chen. 2000. "Elderly Immigrants: Their Composition and Living Arrangements." *Journal of Sociology and Social Welfare* 27:84–114.

Lan, Pei-Chia. 2002. "Subcontracting Filial Piety: Elder Care in Ethnic Chinese Immigrant Households in California." *Journal of Family Issues* 23:812–835.

———. 2006. *Global Cinderellas: Migrant Domestics and Newly Rich Employers in Taiwan*. Durham, NC: Duke University Press.

Laslett, Barbara, and Johanna Brenner. 1989. "Gender and Social Reproduction: Historical Perspectives." *Annual Review of Sociology* 15:381–404.

Parrenas, Rhacel. 2000. "Migrant Filipina Domestic Workers and the International Division of Reproductive Labor." *Gender and Society* 14:560–580.

Pyke, Karen 1999. "The Micropolitics of Care in Relationships between Aging Parents and Adult Children: Individualism, Collectivism, and Power." *Journal of Marriage and the Family* 61:661–672.

Sainsbury, Diane. 1999. "Gender and Social-Democratic Welfare States." In *Gender and Welfare State Regimes*, edited by Diane Sainsbury, 75–113. New York: Oxford University Press.

Stack, Carol. 1974. *All Our Kin*. New York: Basic Books.

Stone, Debra. 2000. "Caring by the Book." In *Care Work: Gender, Labor and the Welfare State*, edited by M. H. Meyer, 89–111. New York: Routledge.

Tsai, Yen-Ling. 2008. *Strangers Who Are Not Foreign: Intimate Exclusion and Racialized Boundaries in Urban Indonesia.* Department of Anthropology, University of California, Santa Cruz.

Ungerson, Clare. 2000. "Cash in Care." In *Care Work: Gender, Labor, and the Welfare State,* edited by M. H. Meyer, 68–88. New York: Routledge.

Uttal, Lynet. 1997. "'Trust Your Instincts': Cultural and Class-Based Preferences in Employed Mothers' Childcare Choices." *Qualitative Sociology* 20:253–274.

Wrigley, Julia. 1995. *Other People's Children: An Intimate Account of the Dilemmas Facing Middle-Class Parents and the Women They Hire to Raise Their Children.* New York: Basic Books.

Yu, Wai Kam. 2007. "Pension Reforms in Urban China and Hong Kong." *Ageing and Society* 27:249–268.

Zelizer, Viviana. 1989. "The Social Meaning of Money: 'Special Monies.'" *American Journal of Sociology* 95:342–377.

———. 2005. *The Purchase of Intimacy.* Princeton, NJ: Princeton University Press.

CHAPTER 16

The Viacom Generation

THE CONSUMER CHILD AND THE CORPORATE PARENT

Juliet B. Schor

Some months after my book *Born to Buy: The Commercialized Child and the New Consumer Culture* was published, I was giving a seminar at one of the large Boston teaching hospitals. The topic was food marketing. I'd gotten into the garage elevator with a family of four, two young parents and their infant and toddler. It was midday during the week, so I assumed that whatever brought them to the hospital was probably serious, given that both mother and father were likely taking off work to be there. I worried for them. They were a family of color, and this was an urban hospital serving a low-income population. The walk from the parking garage to the seminar room was long and wound through the main areas of the hospital. As we wended our way together I overheard the toddler asking for McDonald's. The request came again, and as we neared the main lobby, I realized why—the golden arches were on the premises. By the time we actually reached the restaurant, the boy was in full-flung tantrum mode, completely out of control and inconsolable, demanding that they stop for a meal. It was a painful, embarrassing scene. Anxious not to be late for my seminar, I left them with the conflagration in full force, so I don't know how things turned out. Did the parents given in and buy the Happy Meal? Were they late for their appointment? Was the toddler seriously ill?

The experience was profoundly disturbing to me. As a student of marketing to children, I am well aware of the ubiquity of fast-food outlets, particularly in the neighborhoods of low-income children of color. I have written about conflict between parents and children over consumer products. But having this experience in the hospital, whose mission is to care for people, while on my way to teach about the harms of food marketing, touched an emotional nerve. I'd done my field work with the advertisers and marketers, not with children themselves, so I hadn't witnessed too many of these scenes during my research.[1]

Cultures of Care: The Corporate Parent

The McDonald's incident is important because it's indicative of a major change in the way children are being raised, or "parented," in the United States. Increasingly, the corporation is the entity feeding, clothing, entertaining, socializing, moralizing, and "caring for" children. Viacom, the parent company of some of the most popular youth-oriented media brands, is defining the generation, with a trajectory from Nickelodeon to MTV. These two entities have enormous impacts not only on what kids see, like, and buy, but also on how they constitute their sense of self. Marketers consider themselves to be on 360° duty with kids, from breakfast to bedtime, weekday and weekends, home, school, and church. It's the first stage of what they call the "cradle to grave" approach. Children have been drawn ever earlier into a commercialized nexus of food, media, clothing, sport, music, and play. Corporations such as Viacom, Disney, Nike, Microsoft, and Coca-Cola are influencing children in previously unimagined ways. As family life contracts, corporate influence grows. What are the implications of corporate parenting? How did it happen? How far has it gone? What are its effects?

Arlie Hochschild's work provides a valuable framework for answering these questions. She illuminates the ways in which the practices and structures of one part of society are transported and reproduced in another. In *The Managed Heart* she addresses the commodification of human feeling—for example in a labor market context, where airline stewardesses were required to "sell" their smiles and moods to passengers. Viacom sells feelings too, but in the consumer market, to children who are hungry for the soothing, exciting, and, as kids age, seductive emotional experiences they have on offer. In *The Time Bind*, the theme was "work becoming home" and "home becoming work" through the growth of emotional community among colleagues and the application of Taylorist principles of efficiency in families where nurturing relations are in short supply. The home is becoming market-like in another way too as corporate products substitute for home production and corporate values infiltrate daily life. In the essays in *The Commercialization of Intimate Life*, Hochschild plumbs a variety of issues associated with the ways in which market practices are reshaping intimate life and, conversely, the benefits of intimacy are for sale in the market. Children's consumer culture represents a new frontier in these dynamics, which is colonization of family life, or more particularly parenting by market forces. Increasingly, the giant corporations that dominate sectors such as media, fast food, candy and soda, toys, and athletic footwear shape children's desires and values, keep them company for many hours, and teach them. This transportation of values, ways of relating, and emotional practices from the market into the family is at the center of Hochschild's analyses, and it is what I found in my research on the commodification of childhood.

And how have marketers been so successful in prying open the front door of the American home, moving into territory once occupied by parents, family members, and teachers? Hochschild's themes of longer hours of work and the time famine, outsourcing of domestic labor, and a culture of maternal guilt have been key here. Market researchers are well aware of the time pressures facing families and deliberately enlist guilt as a way of getting mothers to agree to a wide variety of commercial products and styles that not long ago would have been off-limits to children. Using ethnography, interviewing, and most of the tools of contemporary social science, marketers have moved into bedrooms, kitchens, even bathrooms, to scrutinize everyday life. To see how far they've come, it's worth returning to earlier marketing practices.

From the Gatekeeper Model to the Corporate Parent

While some products, most notably candy, have always been marketed directly to children, for many decades most products were advertised to parents in what the industry came to call the "gatekeeper" model. Mom was the gatekeeper who decided which products were appropriate and/or desirable for little Janey or Johnny. With the rise of modern advertising (Marchand 1985), mothers were targeted with messages about the benefits of their product for children's health, education, and well-being. Beginning in the 1920s and 1930s, companies such as Campbell's Soup, Ralston Purina, and even General Electric used newly popular theories of child development to "teach" mothers what the experts thought and to convince them that the route to happy, healthy children was through their products. Food ads touted the nutritional virtues of their products and assured mothers children would love them ("Children Love Wheatina!" "Wonder Bread Builds Strong Bones Twelve Ways"). If we consider the triangle of children, mothers, and marketers, the dominant model was that marketers attempted to ally with mothers to cement purchase decisions. Indeed, as Roland Marchand argues (1985, 228–232), marketers presented parents with the idea that their product could "captivate children" for their own good, enticing them to consume what mom and dad wanted, rather than having to resort to counterproductive "irritable coaxing" to steer children away from the "forbidden fruits." The advertising of this period is famous for its psychological manipulation and sometimes used guilt to convince mothers that without the product they'd fall prey to dangerous conflict with the child. The official ideology of the alliance of mother and marketer was that it operated in the best interest of the child—product quality enhanced children's physical well-being, reduced conflict between parent and child, and fostered emotional happiness.

The Demise of Parental Gatekeeping and the Growth of Marketing

The gatekeeper model remained important for decades after it developed, even as the crude appeals to guilt waned. But over time the rise of children's television provided opportunities for advertisers to speak directly to kids. In the 1950s, breakfast cereals and toys dominated the commercial messages of Saturday morning cartoons, which were the children's programming block. However, the much larger shift toward direct child targeting came in the 1980s, with the rise of cable television, a children's network (Nickelodeon), and the expansion of child-oriented programming more generally. One of the nation's leading child advertisers explained to me that the turning point from the gatekeeper model to what he calls "the unmanned tollbooth," (or "EZ-Pass") happened in the 1980s when Kraft realized they could "drive cheese to children"—that is, market it directly to kids (Schor 2004, 41). This strategy was likely responsible for the rising popularity of macaroni and cheese and led to direct marketing of a large and growing list of food products, such as ketchup, French fries, yogurt, Happy Meals, tacos, soft drinks, chips, chicken, burgers, and many others. While food represents the largest and arguably most damaging of the commodity groups, the direct targeting approach spread to a wide range of products, including toys, fashion, music, electronics, autos, and tourism.

This shift accelerated in the 1990s and the 2000s. The proliferation of media outlets for children on television, radio, film, and Internet meant that there were plenty of advertising opportunities at rates far below prime-time television. In addition, children increasingly had money to spend, as a result of parental, grandparental, and other cash transfers. Although there is no hard data on the size of children's own purchasing power, a leading industry expert estimates that annual spending among children aged four to fourteen is more than $40 billion, up from about $6 billion in 1989 (McNeal 1999, 17; pers. comm.). The largest product category is sweets, snacks, and beverages, which account for a third of total expenditures (McNeal 1998, 57).

As a consequence, marketing aimed at children increased dramatically in the 1990s and was estimated to be roughly $15 billion a year in 2004, up from about $2 billion in 1999 (Schor 2004). Trends since then are not well documented. The holy grail for advertisers, however, has been the so-called influence market, which is the sway that children hold over parental purchases. In a reversal of the gatekeeper model, the more common pathway from ad to expenditure is now via children's product requests. In 1996 Cheryl Idell produced an influential, now-infamous report known as the "nag factor study," which touted the growing influence of children on parental purchases, estimated to have reached the $700 billion range by the mid-2000s and thought to be growing at 20 percent a year (McNeal 1999; pers. comm.). Children are weighing in on everything from food to vacation destinations to consumer electronics to the choice of the family car.

The growth of children's influence did not happen automatically. A number of social trends facilitated it, and marketers have adroitly exploited them. One has been the shift from authoritarian parenting styles, in which Father and (by proxy) Mother know best, to a democratic style of parenting in which children's opinions are solicited and paid attention to. This parallels the shift in gender ideologies of marriage, from traditional to egalitarian. Second, there is a growth in domestic outsourcing (Hochschild 1989, 1997, 2003) that is more amenable to child influence, whether it's over the brand of frozen dinner to purchase, the choice of restaurant, or the family vacation. Busy-ness and time pressure have contributed to this dynamic. Marketers report that when families have less free time, they are more likely to allow children, who often have more time and inclination to research brands, to decide about categories such as consumer electronics. Mothers also have less time to return products or fight with their children about consumer choices, so that facilitates "kid-fluence" (the industry term). Marketers have also found that maternal guilt about working outside the home or other perceived shortfalls in culturally defined standards of mothering can be manipulated to get mothers to agree to children's demands. Finally, marketers often urge Mom (their term) to say yes by touting a product benefit, such as calcium enriched or nutritional. "Throw in a vitamin," advised one marketer at a national conference. Tell them Alpha-Bits are educational, another explained to me. Sophisticated ethnographic research goes into figuring out what new boundaries of parental resistance to unhealthy or questionable products can be breached. As one of my informants explained, the day she realized mothers were allowing open access to Oreos, traditionally a heavily guarded product, the light bulbs went off in her head. Eventually she started to feel guilty about her role in marketing junk food to kids and left her job.

Marketing Channels? Rethinking the Triangle of Parents, Marketers, and Children

The result of these trends is that parents have been more inclined to let marketers determine product choices through the medium of children. According to a national poll conducted by the Center for a New American Dream, 40 percent of children say they have asked their parents for an advertised product they know parents will disapprove of before even asking; 60 percent say they keep asking after being turned down; and just over half (55 percent) say they are usually successful in getting their parents to give in. The poll found that children report having to ask an average of nine times before their parents relent (http://www.newdream.org).[2]

More recently marketers are recommending a less confrontational approach. This may be because the shift to child-directed purchasing has been largely accomplished (as well as because of parental backlash to marketers' use of nagging). Instead, marketers talk about a "training" model in which parents are taught to purchase the items children prefer. Children have trained their parents to exercise more control over total purchases because most parents still limit children to a certain number of product requests.

Taken together these developments have led children to operate much more as agents of marketers within the family. Can we say they are channeling marketers? That formulation is too strong. After all, children must be theorized as independent actors, with their own desires, agendas, and strategic actions (James, Jenks, and Prout 1998). But marketers are increasingly influential in setting those desires, agendas, and actions through their involvement in defining what is cool, their insertion into social dynamics, and their relentless advertising (Schor 2004; Schor and Ford 2007). Simple manipulation (or channeling) models are wrong, but so too are accounts in which children are the driving force for purchase decisions, with marketers just bowing to preexisting preferences and desires. That formulation, in which marketers "channel" children, is what industry claims, but it wrongly minimizes the impact of marketing (Schor 2004, chap. 9; Cook 2004, chap. 1). Together, children and marketers have forged a powerful new commercial alliance that is driving expenditures, product innovation, market trends, and dynamics of family life. It's a highly Hochschildian transformation.

The Viacom Generation: Brands and the Symbolic Environment

The premise of this chapter is that corporations increasingly have been acting as parents. The direct targeting and influence marketing models have been particularly strong in food, clothing, and toys. In the media space, corporate parenting takes another form, which is that they structure the symbolic environment in which children live. As George Gerbner famously noted more than a decade ago, corporations are increasingly telling the stories of our culture, in contrast to earlier generations in which parents, grandparents, and community elders passed on tales, morals, values, and culture. Now it's Disney and Viacom who teach our kids about good and evil, love and hate, violence, sex, friendship, race relations, and duty. Partly this is because children spend so much time with electronic media, which exceeds time spent in school and interacting with parents. According to a 2005 study the average eight- to eighteen-year-old currently spends six hours and twenty-one minutes a day using media (Rideout et al. 2005, 6). Younger children also have very high levels of media use. In a 1999 study children aged two to thirteen were found to watch more than two hours of television per day, and their total media time was five and a half hours per day (Rideout et al. 1999, 29). Although preschool children tend to have lower television viewing than school-age children, 25 percent of them have televisions in their bedrooms and watch an average of two hours a day (Rideout et al. 1999, 29; Woodward 2000, 4). Children of color have much higher media use. The 2005 data found that black children watched four hours and five minutes of TV daily, compared to two hours forty-five minutes for white children, with Latino/as in-between, at three hours twenty-three minutes (Rideout et al. 2005, 16).

While there are many stories that programming provides, a number are prominent. One is a simplistic morality tale of good and evil with high levels of violence used for good. A second is the sexualization of girls, even if they exhibit the marketing creation of "girrlll power." These two, and their adverse effects on children, have been widely discussed in the literature. In my research I found that media corporations have also become adept at the construction of an adult-free utopian environment that soothes children's stresses, anxieties, and fears. Nickelodeon, a Viacom brand, has been the leader in this regard. As a Nickelodeon executive explained to me, their philosophy is that "kids rule." They do extensive research to develop mesmerizing, child-centric characters and themes and believe that today's children are under enormous, perhaps unprecedented stress and pressure. Their strategy is to try to alleviate it by creating carefree, utopian spaces in which kids are empowered and have endless amounts of fun. (While utopian themes have long been present in children's literature, they are now being mobilized for corporate gain.) In contrast to the dreary, productivist spaces of school and increasingly home, the corporate haven has no homework, no tests, no rules, and, perhaps most important, no powerful adult authority figures such as teachers or parents. When these figures do appear they may be challenged, ridiculed, overpowered, or ignored. Nickelodeon's trademark "tude" (or defiant, sassy attitude toward adults), its "sliming" campaigns (in which adults are covered with a gross green goo), and its relentless "kids rule" philosophy has been powerful in creating a precocious corporate-driven, substance-free rebelliousness among young kids. It stands in contrast to authentic teen rebellions rooted in political and social factors. The "anti-adult" bias that has been prominent in Nickelodeon's formula for success can be found throughout children's commercial culture.[3]

This symbolic positioning of adults versus children has wide ramifications. For example, it has permeated the culture of food. Advertisers have made junk food "cool" and healthy food "uncool," what parents or teachers "want you to eat." In much the same way that tobacco has been positioned to youth as an inspirational, hip, rebellious product, unhealthy food has also been symbolically coded in this way. (This should not be surprising. Some of the largest food processing companies, Kraft and Nabisco, were owned by tobacco companies Phillip Morris and RJ Reynolds as this marketing was developed.) The influence of advertising on deep symbolic structures has also been powerful in the areas of gender, sexuality, violence, material desire, and body image. The general point is that increasingly the transmission of values, norms, and culture is falling to corporate entities, and is less likely to be driven by parents, schools, religious institutions, the state, or other traditional agents of social reproduction.

Corporations as Predators? The Production of Harms

In 1996 Ralph Nader published a report on the commercialization of childhood in which he argued that corporations had become predators toward children. Nader attempted to mobilize the strong social outrage that is present for sexual predators, on the grounds that the effects of corporate marketing are similarly damaging (Nader 1996). At the time, Nader's call received little attention, but more recently the movement against corporate harms has begun to grow. Media attention, parental activist groups, a wide coalition to address childhood obesity, and other forces have intensified the debate about corporate influence on children.

The argument that marketing and commercialization are harmful has a number of dimensions to it. Most of the attention has been directed at the nature of advertised products and the role of ads in increasing consumption. Fast food and branded food, much of which is unhealthy and perhaps even habit-forming, is the most heavily advertised and widely consumed product category and has been linked to the epidemic of childhood obesity and its attendant illnesses, such as diabetes (Schor and Ford 2007). Alcohol and tobacco are also heavily marketed to children, through both ads and programming. While alcohol and tobacco companies are not allowed to directly target children, the absence of regulation preventing exposure through programming or events that are not explicitly categorized as "for children" means that kids are exposed to many ads for these products, via sporting events, magazines that cater to both adults and youth (for example, *Sports Illustrated*, *Rolling Stone*), and other advertising venues where audiences cross age lines (Center on Alcohol Marketing and Youth 2002). The intentions of the companies are difficult to prove, and opinions may vary on whether, for example, Budweiser's use of friendly animals in its ads is intended to create appeal for children. Without access to proprietary company materials it is difficult to know definitively. But outcomes are available for observation. Bud commercials are consistently favorites among nine- to fourteen-year-olds, for example. The upper end of this age range is the point at which significant numbers of kids begin using tobacco, other drugs, and alcohol, a practice that puts them at higher risk for lifelong problems with these substances (Schor 2004, chap. 7).

The interlocked corporate block selling junk food, tobacco, and alcohol has tremendous access to children in a variety of venues. Trusted children's brands (even PBS) team up with these corporations via collaborative marketing, such as PBS partnering with McDonald's and Scholastic selling Disney products or Bratz dolls through its catalogs. Schools have been heavily involved in pushing these products, including the food products owned by Phillip Morris (later Altria).[4] Big Food's approach to its critics has paralleled that of Big Tobacco (Schor 2004), and to date they have been largely successful in forestalling regulation of their activities. (There have been a few local and state bans on junk food sales and marketing in public schools, particularly for soft drinks.) Whether an effective political coalition can come together to regulate or transform these companies remains to be seen; however, it is likely that the answer to that question will depend on the larger political environment (Ruskin and Schor 2005; Schor 2006, 2009). While children remain one of the more sacralized and valued social groups, their symbolic potency is weak in comparison to the real economic and political power of these corporations.

These products hardly exhaust the harmful or potentially harmful items marketed to children. Others include the proliferation of violent products, games, and media programming; unrealistic body images and their connection to eating disorders; sexualization; and ongoing race and gender stereotyping. A 2007 American Psychological Association Task Force reported that sexualization is widespread and responsible for a variety of harms, including diminished mental capacity, depression, and lower self-esteem (APA Task Force on the Sexualization of Girls 2007).

Other aspects of commercialized childhood present different harms. The psychic colonization of processes of desire and construction of self has been linked to the rise of a range of emotional disorders (Twenge 2000). My research found that children who are more immersed in consumer culture suffer higher levels of anxiety and depression and are more likely to suffer psychosomatic symptoms such as headache, stomachache, and boredom (Schor 2004, chap. 8; 2008). This may be because the marketing message says that one needs the product to be "cool," worthy, whole, or socially acceptable. By fostering dissatisfaction with what one has, or is, psychological equilibrium is undermined. Corporate child-rearing also promotes materialism and the ideology that products yield happiness and well-being. However, a now-substantial literature has shown that materialist values do just the reverse and are a significant risk factor for developing depression, anxiety, low life vitality, poor social functioning, psychosomatic medical conditions, risky behaviors, and psychological disorders (Kasser 2002).

Finally, the literature contains a lively debate about whether advertising to children is inherently unfair and exploitative because children are developmentally unable to withstand its entreaties and seductions. Studies address whether kids can tell the difference between ads and programs, whether they understand persuasion and intent, and so forth. Proponents of this position argue that ads should be banned, irrespective of the product being sold (Kasser and Kanner 2004; Schor 2004, chap. 2). More recently, the growth of deceptive, place-based, and viral marketing has moved the debate beyond ads in general to the types of advertising now being deployed against children. When pressed the companies and their advertisers deny the vulnerability of children, claim that they are empowering them, and downplay the dangers of their products. But mostly they just avoid debate or claim that they are changing.

Conclusion: The Politics of Children and Commercialization

By assailing the impacts of increased corporate influence on children I do not intend to invoke a golden age of 1950s authoritarian parenting, a preference for highly protectionist middle-class parenting models, or an unconscious class bias against popular culture that can be found in many high cultural capital parents (for example, licensed characters are bad unless they come from European storybooks). I believe in more democratic family relations, I think children should have access to money and consumer markets, and I appreciate the ways in which kids can use third parties to gain leverage against parents to actualize their desires. I am critical of the sentimentalized middle-class notions of children that hold that kids should be extra "commercium," to use Viviana Zelizer's (1985) term, and think that economic activity such as trading, bartering, earning, and spending is appropriate for even young children. In contrast to some of the activist groups that are fighting the commercialization of childhood, I want to differentiate between commerce in general and the corporate domination of children's markets at this particular moment in time. This is a point that is too often elided, especially in the public discourse. The problem is mainly that large corporations whose motives are making money, and who have little or no regard for the real well-being of children, are far too influential in structuring children's lives. They're fast food, tobacco, fashion, alcohol, toy, and media giants with enormous political power and minimal commitment to social responsibility. These firms increasingly talk a language of caring, but mainly they are pushing a panoply of harmful products through dubious means (Schor 2004). They are not held accountable for the negative impacts of their actions, from obesity to emotional distress to environmental hazards to violence, and they are working hard to keep things that way. This is what was so upsetting about the McDonald's incident—that an inner-city hospital, of all places, was promoting McDonald's; that the parents had been reduced to such a powerless position; and that when I got to the seminar, I learned that the public health advocates and researchers in nutrition were taking money from the big food corporations who were at the heart of the problem.

I am somewhat less dismayed today. In recent years the institution called the corporation is coming to be seen as deeply pathological, as the success of the film and book *The Corporation* attests. Fast-food outlets are being uninvited from hospitals and schools. Turning big corporations into the family nanny may be an idea whose time has come and gone.

NOTES

Arlie Hochschild's work and friendship has been an inspiration to me for more than two decades.

1. For a discussion of methods and sources for this research, see Schor (2004).
2. Poll commissioned by the Center for a New American Dream and conducted in May 2002 by Widmeyer Communications. This information is based on a nationally representative telephone study of 750 American youth ages twelve to seventeen. The margin of error for the poll is +/− 3.5 percent.
3. For an earlier formulation, see Kanner (2002). This point has also been made by Mark Crispin Miller.
4. In 2007 Altria spun off its Kraft Foods unit.

REFERENCES

American Psychological Association Task Force on the Sexualization of Girls. 2007. *Report of the APA Task Force on the Sexualization of Girls*. Washington, DC: American Psychological Association. http://www.apa.org/pi/wto/sexualization.html.

Bakan, Joel. 2004. *The Corporation: The Pathological Pursuit of Profit and Power.* New York: Free Press.

Center on Alcohol Marketing and Youth. 2002. *Television: Alcohol's Vast Adland.* Washington, DC: Center on Alcohol Marketing and Youth.

Cook, Daniel Thomas. 2004. *The Commodification of Childhood: Personhood, the Children's Wear Industry and the Rise of the Child-Consumer, 1917–1962.* Durham, NC: Duke University Press.

Hochschild, Arlie Russell, with Anne Machung. 1989. *The Second Shift: Working Parents and the Revolution at Home.* New York: Viking.

———. 1997. *The Time Bind: When Work Becomes Home and Home Becomes Work.* New York: Metropolitan Books.

———. 2003. *The Commercialization of Intimate Life: Notes from Home and Work.* Berkeley: University of California Press.

James, Allison, Chris Jenks, and Alan Prout. 1998. *Theorizing Childhood.* New York: Teachers College Press.

Kanner, Bennice. 2002. "From Father Knows Best to The Simpsons—On TV, Parenting Has Lost Its Halo." In *Taking Parenting Public,* edited by Sylvia Ann Hewlett, Nance Rankin, and Cornel West, 45–56. Lanham, MD: Rowman & Littlefield.

Kasser, Tim. 2002. *The High Price of Materialism.* Cambridge, MA: MIT Press.

Kasser, Tim, and Allen D. Kanner. 2004. *Psychology and Consumer Culture: The Struggle for a Good Life in a Materialistic World.* Washington, DC: American Psychological Association.

Marchand, Roland. 1985. *Advertising the American Dream: Making Way for Modernity, 1920–1940.* Berkeley: University of California Press.

McNeal, James. 1999. *The Kids Market: Myths and Realties.* Ithaca, NY: Paramount Publishing.

Nader, Ralph. 1996. *Children First! A Parent's Guide to Fighting Corporate Predators.* Washington, DC: Corporate Accountability Research Group.

New American Dream. "Kids and Commercialism—Polling Data." http://www.newdream.org/kids/poll.php.

Roberts, Donald F., Ulla G. Foehr, and Victoria Rideout. 2005. *Generation M: Media in the Lives of 8–18 Year Olds.* Menlo Park, CA: Kaiser Family Foundation.

Roberts, Donald F., Ulla G. Foehr, Victoria J. Rideout, and Mollyann Brodie. 1999. *Kids and Media @ the New Millennium: A Comprehensive National Analysis of Children's Media Use.* Menlo Park, CA: Kaiser Family Foundation.

Ruskin, Gary, and Juliet Schor. 2005. "Fast Food Nation: Who's to Blame for Childhood Obesity?" *The Nation,* August 29.

Schor, Juliet B. 1992. *The Overworked American: The Unexpected Decline of Leisure.* New York: Basic.

———. 2004. *Born to Buy: The Commercialized Child and the New Consumer Culture.* New York: Scribner.

———. 2006. "When Childhood Gets Commercialized, Can Children Be Protected?" In *Regulation, Awareness, Empowerment: Young People and Harmful Media Content in the Digital Age,* edited by Ulla Carlsson, 101–122. Göteborg, Sweden: International Clearinghouse on Children, Youth and Media.

———. 2007. "In Defense of Consumer Critique: Re-visiting the Consumption Debates of the 20th Century." *The Annals of the American Academy of Political and Social Science* 611:16–30.

———. 2008. "Mental Health and Children's Consumer Culture." *Journal of the American Academy of Child and Adolescent Psychiatry* 47:486–490.

Schor, Julie, and Margaret Ford. 2007. "From Tastes Great to Cool: Children's Food Marketing and the Rise of the Symbolic." *Journal of Medicine, Law and Ethics* 35:10–21.

Twenge, Jean M. 2000. "The Age of Anxiety? Birth Cohort Change in Anxiety and Neuroticism, 1952–1993." *Journal of Personality and Social Psychology* 79:1007–1021.

Woodward, E. H. 2000. *Media in the Home.* Philadelphia: Annenberg Public Policy Center at the University of Pennsylvania.

Zelizer, Viviana. 1985. *Pricing the Priceless Child.* New York: Basic Books.

CHAPTER 17

Consumption as Care and Belonging

ECONOMIES OF DIGNITY IN CHILDREN'S DAILY LIVES

Allison J. Pugh

When I asked Judy Berger, a quiet, reflective, white middle-class mother, if she regretted buying anything for her eight-year-old son, Max, it would not have been surprising had she named the GameBoy. She had just finished telling me in great detail about the extent of her son's obsession with the electronic handheld toy and the deep misgivings she had about it. After all that, I almost felt silly asking the question—but her answer startled me. It is not that she rued buying the GameBoy for Max, she insisted. "I guess I felt almost like it wasn't really [. . .] like I couldn't have not bought it, because now we are there in our life," she said, her words tripping over each other uncharacteristically. While she wanted Max to be happy, for two years that desire had not been enough to overcome her intense dislike of the gaming systems, which she regarded as addictive, violent, and sedentary. The turning point was when she came to realize that GameBoys had so saturated the social lives of eight-year-old boys they knew that she did not think she could relegate Max to the kind of social pathos of the outsider. It was not the thought of Max's happiness that led her to buy the gaming system, but rather the prospect of his social exclusion that made her reevaluate her opposition. But her distaste for the GameBoy remained. "It is kind of sad that it feels like it is a given that you will have one," she finally conceded. "It is too bad that that is where we are."[1]

The commodification of childhood is advancing, with children in the United States spending some $30 billion themselves and influencing another $670 billion spent on their behalf (Schor 2004). The daily lives of children are permeated now with moments of buying, from symbolic rituals to transportation to lunches.

As Arlie Hochschild (2003, 36) observed, increasingly "companies . . . expand the number of market niches for goods and services covering activities that, in yesteryear, formed part of unpaid 'family life.'"

As the market seeps into childhood, scholars debate whether or not we should be worried. Are children the victims of an ever more sophisticated onslaught by powerful corporate interests (Schor 2004; this volume)? Or are they "wise consumers," savvy social actors who can innovate, using advertising content for their own strategic ends (Buckingham 2000)? Is the commercialization of childhood a new and alarming trend, or is it the outgrowth of longstanding historical practices of intermingling economic exchange and personal lives (Kline 1993; Linn 2004; Zelizer 2004)? Should we shield children from the more sexual, violent, exploitative, or materialistic corners of adult culture, or is it impossible to separate childhood from the features of the wider culture in which it is embedded (Cook 2004; Williams 2005)?

The reader might be forgiven for thinking that the answer to all of these questions, however contradictory, is "yes." I argue that these debates, while important, miss a central point about spending on children: the impact of commercialization on the emotional experience of childhood—specifically, on children's relationships with parents and with friends. Just like the rise of a "divorce culture" generated by the prevalence of divorced couples changed widespread cultural assumptions about the expectations of trust and obligation in marriage (Hackstaff 1999), the rise of children's consumer culture has so permeated children's daily lives as to establish a new cultural environment in which to grow up. By its sheer domination of childhood today, commodification has reframed expectations about what parents should provide, what children should have, and what having or not having signifies. In this chapter, I consider these developments from the perspective of three years of ethnographic research on children's consumer culture and families in California. I found that Judy Berger's dilemma exemplifies that of many parents: she did not regret her decision to buy the GameBoy, but she regretted the cultural imperative that necessitated its buying—an imperative stemming from Max's relationships with others.

Consumption, Care, and Belonging

For thousands of years we have understood consumption as a means of distinguishing those like ourselves from others who are not, most often from others below. In a particularly influential argument, Pierre Bourdieu (1984) contended that parents and schools socialize children into having tastes that ultimately stratify them through at times unconscious cultural practices inculcating a certain approach to particular cultural goods, such as classical music. While his focus was on inequality, Bourdieu's argument presaged a dual sense of consumption as a means of forging group bonds, or a sense of belonging, and as a component of childrearing, or care.

Some scholars have focused on the latter sense, arguing that consumption can be a form of care located at the intersections of the market and intimacy, forging "connected lives," as Viviana Zelizer (2004) observed. These researchers suggest that consumption acts as a symbolic language through which buyers make connections to others, a devotional rite involving what British anthropologist Daniel Miller called "the material culture of love" (1998). In this vein, parents buy for children to strengthen emotional bonds, bonds under some strain from such stressors as increasing work hours (Hochschild 1997; Thompson 1996), divorce (Pugh 2002), or poverty (Edin and Lein 1997; Power 2003). As Sharon Zukin observed, "the things we need to buy are framed by our love for the significant others we buy for" (2004, 30). These studies portray consumption as a form of care.

Other researchers look at buying not as caring but as having (as in having a particular good or experience) or as belonging. A British study of youth and advertising found that many teenagers agonized over moments of being unable to participate when their friends recalled commercials or sang jingles, which the authors considered the rites of group membership (Ritson and Eliot 1999; see also Chee 2000). Teenagers told the researchers about their experience of being "left out," "talked around," or "blanked'" when they could not take part in the conversation. At stake was a form of social invisibility, an exclusion from social participation or citizenship.

Corporate advertisers work with all of these hypotheses—attaching to commodities meanings of distinction, care, and belonging. With more than $17 billion spent per year targeting children, corporate marketing is increasingly sophisticated and unfettered. Children are particularly vulnerable to their tactics; consumer researchers have found that children are unaware of the advertisers' persuasive intent until about the age of seven (Horovitz 2006; for a review, see John 1999). Some important recent scholarship has documented the onslaught of campaigns to tap into children's desires, brought on in part by the deregulation of children's television in the 1980s and the development of powerful market tactics to lure buyers (Cook 2004; Cross 1997, 2000; Schor 2004). While it is clear, then, that childhood is a media-rich environment, we know less about what this environment means for the children and parents who live in it. Eva Illouz counsels against knee-jerk assumptions about the pernicious effects of commodification, but nonetheless points us in the direction of relationships: "We need not presume that the realm of commodities debases the realm of sentiment," she wrote, but "the vocabulary of emotions is now more exclusively dictated by the market" (2007, 91).

From this scholarship, we can understand that consumption for children permeates their relationships, sometimes as an arbiter of belonging, sometimes as a conduit for care. How do parents and children view these dual roles for commodified goods and experiences? How do these twin tasks reveal themselves in children's daily lives? How does commercial culture thread its way through children's emotional connections, with peers and with parents?

Methods

I investigated these questions by conducting an ethnography of childhood consumer culture in Oakland, California. For three years I observed children aged five to nine at a low-income after-school setting and for six months each at two other more affluent school sites, one private and one public. I helped children while they did their homework, pushed them on the swings, sat on the sidelines while they climbed in play structures, and held their hands while we went on field trips. I listened to their jokes and stories, went to birthday parties, took them to the library or to free concerts, ate with them, and watched them receive awards or go on parades. I also listened to parents from fifty-four families, in interviews generally lasting for two to four hours, sometimes over several visits. Through these efforts, I immersed myself in everyday childhoods of divergent class and racial backgrounds and in the worlds of parents struggling with the practices and meanings of consuming for children. In my book *Longing and Belonging: Parents, Children and Consumer Culture* (2009), I trace how children navigate the world of commodified goods and experiences, particularly when they lack specific items that seem to matter socially. I also explore parents' motivations and fears, including the prospect and meaning of their children's experiences of being different at school. Through the twin prongs of belonging and care, I delve into how consumer culture permeates children's emotional connections to others and look at the implications this development has for contemporary childhood and parenthood.

The Economy of Dignity

On a cold afternoon at the private school Arrowhead Academy some children sought refuge from the damp chill in a one-room portable building they called "the addition," where the school's after-school program hosted the knitting club and other activities. Some children sat or lay down on the carpet turning yarn into "puffballs," small balls of yarn sold around the school for a penny each. Two first-grade boys built with Legos in the corner, and another group of four played a board game, while two staff members helped knitters begin or end projects. One child made a purple scarf for her mother, proudly announcing that "knitting is better than buying."

There were several low conversations taking place among the children, and one group of second-grade girls began to talk about birthday parties. Tamsin was excited about her upcoming party, during which her mother planned to repeat a favorite ritual. Every year, Tamsin explained, her mother would devise a treasure hunt in which all the guests would search throughout her house, spurred on by little rhyming clues and small presents. The girls in the small group around Tamsin are curious, interested. It is clear that they will be invited, although others nearby—including some boys and other children in other grades—will not. Tamsin describes the trinkets her mother has given in preceding years while the surrounding girls exclaim or ask questions.

While the rest of us listen, Claire, a first grader sitting near the couch and some distance away from Tamsin, chimes in. Claire bends over her puffballs and remarks that she herself had a birthday party a few weeks ago at the "Bladium," an indoor sports palace where birthday parties start at $300. Claire, who had turned seven at this party, was younger than some of the other children in the addition, but she nonetheless cheerily described her party—how many guests there were, the soccer they played. "I was the worst goalie," she said, smiling ruefully. Tamsin and the other girls listen, as do the rest of the knitters, and no one scoffs, rolls her eyes, or patently ignores Claire; indeed, she secures the momentary dignity of their attention, and the fleeting connection to others, made slightly unusual by the fact that she is younger.

In some ways, this vignette—mundane and without undue drama—captures important features about contemporary childhood. The ambiance is not wholly permeated with rank materialism—witness the pronouncement "knitting is better than buying"—and neither is every object branded. It is not that a child's every moment is spent acquiring, selling, or thinking about consumer goods. Yet market culture is often present in the children's conversations, an important arbiter of who gets to pipe up and who stays silent, a passport for their participation in their social world. As Randall Collins (2004, 297) suggests, talk is a kind of ritual, serving to "mark boundaries of inclusion and exclusion." In order to join in the birthday party conversation, the norms of children's talk rituals meant that only children with celebrations somehow equal in stature—in elaborate preparations, in rarity, in superior fun, in commodified "enchantment"—could leap in to share, while children who celebrated their birthday in the park with pizza and a cake could not speak up, silenced by their lack of relevant possession or experience (Ritzer 1999).

Such conversations form the crux of what I have termed the "economy of dignity," the system by which children make themselves audible and therefore relevant to their peers. Similar to Arlie Hochschild's (1989) "economy of gratitude," in which married couples exchange recognition of gifts of time, work, or feeling, the economy of dignity refers to an emotional market of recognition, in this case of children's claims to belong in their social world. In their daily, ordinary talk, children negotiate what sort of commodities or experiences count for belonging, enabling them to participate. I call this an emotional market because children's participation creates both their visibility and their connection to others, and the processes that engender children's talk evoke intense feelings among the children, which then create their own ramifications in school and in their homes.

I use dignity to capture the sense of this participation as a fundamental psychological and social need, what Amartya Sen (1999, 361–362) called an "absolute capability . . . to take part in the life of the community." With dignity, children are visible to their peers and granted the aural space, the very right to speak, in their own community's conversation. While dignity specifically does not refer to the competitive status-seeking behavior widely assumed to underlie consumer desire, I do not mean to suggest that I never saw children seeking to induce the jealousy of others. Rather, in view of Veblen's (1994 [1899], 21) observation that buyers buy to "gain the esteem and envy of one's fellow-men," children seemed to spend as much or more time and energy searching for esteem than for envy, seeking to join the circle rather than better it.

Sometimes children argued about what was valuable, as in one noteworthy exchange at the low-income afterschool center I call Sojourner Truth, in which the children who attended were supposed to make posters listing what they were thankful for. One girl urged her classmate to write "thankful for what you have," to which Marco, a recent Mexican immigrant, retorted, "I am thankful for my ancestors." But it was rare for children's interactions to feature such a direct conversation about what might count as tokens worthy of dignity. More commonly, children seemed to avoid comparison and instead would mention their own experiences or possessions without weighing the advantages or disadvantages of theirs versus those of another. Would they not have made observations of this sort more directly if they had sought a triumphant domination over others based on superiority, instead of a connection to others based on similarity? Claire might have argued that the Bladium was an improvement over any home birthday, no matter how many trinkets were involved, while Tamsin might have disparaged the Bladium for its impersonality. By adding their own experience alongside that of their peers, rather than forcing a win-or-lose challenge, these young children seem to be less striving to conquer than forging connections based on the scrip of the moment, which, for Claire, was "those of us with fun birthday parties."

What Scrip Signifies: The Claim to Care

Children in all three sites experienced economies of dignity that they then had to navigate with the resources at their disposal. While the schools in this study differed vastly by income and by school climate, meaning their explicit attention to how children treat each other, what counted as scrip in these economies varied more in degree than kind and at each field site was a fluid and dynamic set. Children found they could achieve visibility through claims to particular skills or knowledge or other prized characteristics, but they often made the most symbolic value out of claiming access to popular culture—from actually owning or using to merely knowing about many objects or experiences that were advertised in their worlds, such as sneakers, movies, or collectible cards and toys. The prominence of popular culture both reflected and shaped the power of corporate marketers to at least establish the menu from which children would select what mattered at the moment.

Children used these forms of scrip to enter their conversations, and along the way to symbolize sought-after qualities, such as relative autonomy, talent, wealth, skill, or long family pedigrees. But children's tokens of value also established the bona fides of another claim: that of the child as cared for. Care scholars have documented the ways in which care is both "labor and relationship," involving at once the interactive tasks and feelings of caring for another (Ruddick 1998). In my research I saw children add another dimension to care: the social uses to which they put the caring consumption they received from parents acted as a form of scrip in their economies of dignity. This action, which we might call "care-displaying," is one that struck at the core of children's identity as worthwhile, that traversed income inequality, and that linked the dual uses of consumption as both belonging and care.

Under this logic, then, possessions signaled to children that they were cared for. Poignant examples abounded at Sojourner Truth. On numerous occasions, the children seemed to equate care with provisioning, as was visible in the Mother's Day cards they created. One read, "My mom is special to me because she keeps me warm, she buys me clothes, she buys me toys and food, walks with me, reads to me, pays for the house. That's why I think my mother is special," read one card. One small boy declared that his mother refused to let him accept candy from other students, adding in the same breath that she was taking him to McDonald's that weekend. Rather than seeing the boy's statements as contradictory, we might surmise that both served as evidence of care: his mother cares about him enough to shield him from the implied danger in others' candy *and* to indulge him in commercialized pleasure.

Ultimately, part of the deeper appeal of possessions, destinations, and other mediated claims—in which the child used particular objects or events to represent good qualities about themselves—was in their ability to symbolize the child's membership in a larger community of care. We can read these symbolic efforts like the "negative space" of a painting to gather a sense of children's anxieties about what they actually lacked—such as autonomy, age, wealth, or the claim to someone's loving attention. These pointed demonstrations (and their underlying anxiety) were not limited to low-income children. Children in more affluent locales seemed also to work hard to convey that they were cared for, and they often seemed to be intentionally portraying themselves as somebody's focal point. The difference was that affluent children used a wider variety of tactics to do so: Tamsin used the elaborate preparation her mother undertook to represent her own centrality as the object of somebody's extensive caring, and other children talked about their extracurricular lessons in the same way, as if the "concerted cultivation" (Lareau 2003) of their individual talents and skills was, similarly, evidence of care. Annette Lareau observed that through such middle-class cultivation, "children learn they are special" (39). Data from my fieldwork suggest they also learned to equate parental scrutiny, especially that accompanied by parental spending, with what it meant to be cared for.

The Equation of Belonging and Care

There is evidence that parents made the same equation of care with the consuming they did to ensure children's belonging. Like Judy Berger, children's belonging needs could vanquish the affluent parent's abiding distaste for particular commodities. Katerina, from the affluent public school Oceanview, was second-guessing her television restrictions because "sometimes I worry. I don't know if that's the thing to do, because in the school they talk, and other children have seen so many shows." Birthdays were an important moment, Deborah Lamont observed. "Birthday parties are a lot of pressure," she said. "You have to come up with these ideas that are fun and the children want to go to. And that are novel, and . . . In addition to being expensive. It's really common to spend $500 on a birthday party." Yet she didn't question the necessity of the practice nor the influence it wielded in the children's economy of dignity at Oceanview. "Party bags are an important thing," she noted. "You have to have cool things for the guests."

For low-income parents, the pressure was acute and could trump other budgetary priorities. Askia Jenkins, who lived in subsidized housing with her three kids, lamented the stress she felt because of the things her children wanted. "The thing that I hate about society is that they put so much emphasis that things have to have a certain name brand," Askia said. "You know, it has to be . . . with our kids—Sean John, Rocawear, Air Force One, Jordans. You know, these are the styles that my kids like to wear and that they see other kids wearing." While Askia complained that those styles were name brands, she did not question the fact that her children cared about what other people wore. She understood the source of her children's consumer desire as the social meaning generated by their economy of dignity.

Sandra Perkins, a nursing aide with three children, railed against buying Michael Jordan–branded sneakers for her son, who thought he was going to be "some big record producer." Yet other purchases were unavoidable, despite her disinclination: "Well, I do Halloween. I buy Rasheed and Lexine costumes. I really don't like to because I really think it's a waste of money, really. To spend all that money on a costume and they're only going to wear it one time. But I do it because they have the parades and stuff at school." Sandra knew that the "parades and stuff at school" meant that having a costume would be an essential component of dignity, and that the children's peers would notice if they did not participate. For Sandra, as for other low-income mothers, the symbolic import of Halloween costumes meant that the children had to have them and elevated their desires to the level of needs, even as others might discount these needs as *only* psychological.

Angela Lincoln, a janitor, reported struggling to make the food last for herself and her three children before the end of her monthly paycheck. Yet when she talked about getting her son a Playstation, she was matter-of-fact. "You have to manage your money," she said, dolefully. "You can't neglect the kids, though." Shirley, a mother of three, described how she managed to buy her son the electronic games he wants. "What I do is I just sacrifice something. I'll work extra hours somewhere just so this can be the Christmas." Thus children's consumption desires, transformed into needs by the economy of dignity, were a top priority for low-income parents, sometimes even pegged ahead of other basics like clothes, food, or even rent, and worth extraordinary efforts to procure.

Discussion and Conclusion

The emotional impact of the commercialization of childhood reverberates in two directions, in the ratcheting up of what it takes to belong and in the equation of parent spending with care. These effects are relational, they transform the webs of connection that children inhabit, and they are felt in affluent and low-income communities alike. In other work (Pugh 2009), I explore how children's lives, and those of American families generally, have changed to help produce the conditions in which these reverberations are so powerfully felt. For our purposes here, however, my research demonstrates that the economy of dignity reaches across class lines to shape children's relationships everywhere.

The implications are vast, but three are particularly important. First, because children hitch so many of their bids for connection to others to their demonstrated knowledge of popular culture, corporate marketing has a direct conduit to their hearts. Children are thus subject to the planned obsolescence, the fleeting nature of popular fads generated by the market cycle. This is not to say that all intimacy should be devoid of "pollution" by market exchange, in some variation of the "hostile worlds" argument Zelizer (2004) rejected. But the harnessing of children's social bonds to profit-seeking forces is more than just the neutral commingling of cultural symbols; any reckoning of the economy of dignity must incorporate the powerful targeted marketing efforts as that which largely establishes the framework of options from which children draw their meaningful tokens of belonging.

Second, like "divorce culture," the commodification of childhood changes the environment for all children, affecting even those children whose parents have attempted to curtail their exposure to corporate marketing. Thus the economy of dignity demonstrates that individual parents—however much they say "no" in their own homes, however much they restrict or prohibit screen time or otherwise follow expert counsel—are limited in their ability to protect their children from consumer culture. Children are immersed in this environment, in part defined by the media exposure of some sort of critical mass, and thus any successful attempt to control or change childhood culture can only be a collective one—at the school, neighborhood, or media level.

This inescapability has its most pernicious effects on low-income parents, who struggle to meet the basic needs of their children and whose struggles are increased when those basic needs expand. While parents and children can engage in protracted negotiations in which they contest just how necessary a given item is, ultimately low-income parents viscerally recognize the importance of their children's tokens of dignity. As the standards of a good-enough childhood increase, however, parents face new tokens again and again, posing particular challenges for low-income families who stand between the rock of their children's psychological needs and the wall of their limited means to meet them.

Perhaps the most poignant of implications of the economies of dignity is the contrast between what children reach for, in yearning, and what they manage to obtain. The commodified object or experience through which children seek to link to others mediates human connection through the market, often serving as much to distance people as to bring them together. If what children want is to belong to their communities, or to experience care from loving adults, then surely buying the GameBoy is like treating not the cause of their longing but the "referred pain" of their consumer desires (Hochschild 2003). The shifting sands of children's consumer culture are the foundation on which children find themselves daily having to build their relationships.

NOTES

I would like to thank Anita Garey and Karen V. Hansen for their comments on earlier drafts. This chapter is based on research I conducted for my book *Longing and Belonging: Parents, Children and Consumer Culture* (2009), which was written with the help of a grant from the Alfred P. Sloan Foundation's Workplace, Work Force and Working Families program. In addition, the research was supported by the National Science Foundation under Grant No. 0221499, as well as by the Center for Working Families and the Institute for the Study of Social Change, both at the University of California, Berkeley.

1. All names of people and institutions, and some of their identifying characteristics, have been changed to preserve their confidentiality.

REFERENCES

Bourdieu, Pierre. 1984. *Distinction: A Social Critique of the Judgment of Taste.* Translated by Richard Nice. Cambridge, MA: Harvard University Press.

Buckingham, David. 2000. *After the Death of Childhood.* Cambridge, MA: Polity Press.

Chee, Bernadine. 2000. "Eating Snacks, Biting Pressure: Only Children in Beijing." In *Feeding China's Little Emperors: Food, Children and Social Change,* edited by Jun Jing, 48–70. Stanford, CA: Stanford University Press.

Collins, Randall. 2004. *Interaction Ritual Chains.* Princeton, NJ: Princeton University Press.

Cook, Dan. 2004. *The Commodification of Childhood: The Children's Clothing Industry and the Rise of the Child Consumer.* Durham, NC: Duke University Press.

Cross, Gary. 1997. *Kids' Stuff: Toys and the Changing World of American Childhood.* Cambridge, MA: Harvard University Press.

———. 2000. *An All-Consuming Century: Why Commercialism Won in Modern America.* New York: Columbia University Press.

Edin, Kathryn, and Laura Lein. 1997. *Making Ends Meet.* New York: Russell Sage Foundation.

Hackstaff, Karla. 1999. *Marriage in a Divorce Culture.* Philadelphia: Temple University Press.

Hochschild, Arlie, with Anne Machung. 1989. *The Second Shift: Working Parents and the Revolution at Home.* New York: Viking.

———. 1997. *The Time Bind: When Work Becomes Home and Home Becomes Work.* New York: Metropolitan Books.

———. 2003. *The Commercialization of Intimate Life: Notes from Home and Work.* Berkeley: University of California Press.

Horovitz, Bruce. 2006. "Six Strategies Marketers Use to Make Kids Want Things Bad." *USA Today,* November 22, as cited by The Campaign for a Commercial Free Childhood,

"Marketing to Children Overview," *http://www.commercialexploitation.org/factsheets/overview.pdf*.

Illouz, Eva. 2007. *Cold Intimacies: The Making of Emotional Capitalism.* Cambridge, MA: Polity Press.

John, Deborah Roedder. 1999. "Consumer Socialization of Children: A Retrospective Look at Twenty-Five Years of Research." *Journal of Consumer Research* 26:183–213.

Kline, Stephen. 1993. *Out of the Garden: Toys, TV and Children's Culture in the Age of Marketing.* New York: Verso.

Lareau, Annette. 2003. *Unequal Childhoods: Class, Race, and Family Life.* Berkeley: University of California Press.

Linn, Susan. 2004. *Consuming Kids: The Hostile Takeover of Childhood.* New York: New Press.

Miller, Daniel. 1998. *A Theory of Shopping.* Ithaca, NY: Cornell University Press.

Power, Elaine. 2003. "Freedom and Belonging through Consumption: The Disciplining of Desire in Single Mothers on Welfare." Paper presented at the annual meeting of the British Sociological Association, University of York, UK, April 11–13.

Pugh, Allison. 2002. "From Compensation to Childhood Wonder: Why Parents Buy." Working Paper No. 39, Center for Working Families, University of California, Berkeley.

———. 2009. *Longing and Belonging: Parents, Children and Consumer Culture.* Berkeley: University of California Press.

Ritson, Mark, and Richard Elliott. 1999. "The Social Uses of Advertising: An Ethnographic Study of Adolescent Advertising Audiences." *Journal of Consumer Research* 26:260–277.

Ritzer, George. 1999. *Enchanting a Disenchanted World: Revolutionizing the Means of Consumption.* Thousand Oaks, CA: Pine Forge Press.

Ruddick, Sara. 1998. "Care as Labor and Relationship." In *Norms and Values: Essays on the Work of Virginia Held*, edited by J. G. Haber & M. S. Halfon, 3–25. Lanham, MD: Rowman & Littlefield.

Schor, Juliet. 2004. *Born to Buy: The Commercialized Child and the New Consumer Culture.* New York: Scribner.

Sen, Amartya. 1999. "The Possibility of Social Choice." *American Economic Review* 89 (3): 349–378.

Thompson, Craig. 1996. "Caring Consumers: Gendered Consumption Meanings and the Juggling Lifestyle." *Journal of Consumer Research* 22 (4): 388–407.

Veblen, Thorstein. 1994 [1899]. *The Theory of the Leisure Class.* New York: Dover Publications.

Williams, Christine. 2005. *Inside Toyland: Working, Shopping and Social Inequality.* Berkeley: University of California Press.

Zelizer, Viviana. 2004. *The Purchase of Intimacy.* Princeton, NJ: Princeton University Press.

Zukin, Sharon. 2004. *Point of Purchase: How Shopping Changed American Culture.* New York: Routledge.

CHAPTER 18

Interracial Intimacy on the Commodity Frontier

Kimberly McClain DaCosta

Good advertising does not just circulate information. It penetrates the public mind with desires and belief.

—Leo Burnett

A couple of years ago, as my daughter and I were watching television, an ad for the telecommunications company Verizon appeared featuring the Elliot Family. In its depiction of family life, the ad was not at all unusual—a teenage girl chatted on the phone with her friend while a young boy helped his father navigate the Internet. In its depiction of the family itself, however, the ad was not at all typical. While the father appeared to be a white man, his darker-skinned, curly-haired children did not. Upon seeing the ad, my daughter remarked, "Well you don't see *that* everyday!" Raised in an interracial extended family, my daughter in fact does see *that* everyday. What she meant was seldom does she see such families depicted in mainstream commercial space.

The Elliots ad, however, is part of a discernible trend in which interracial families—and interracial intimacy more broadly—are becoming part of the commercial landscape. Browse in any store, real or virtual, watch any television channel, and flip through the pages of a magazine, and chances are good that you will find at least one advertisement, product, or show depicting interracial intimacy in some form. In the contemporary commercial landscape, you can purchase shampoo for mixed race women and girls, T-shirts displaying your mixed ethnic pride, and biracial dolls. You can buy children's stories and coloring books with interracial families and "multicultural markers" to color them with. Interracial couples can buy wedding cake toppers for their big day and watch television shows about interracial families like the one they may soon create. Increasingly, cereal, makeup, laundry detergent, pain reliever, furniture, and even phone service is pitched to you by mixed race models and interracial families (both real and fictitious). And with an Internet connection, you can purchase interracial intimacy itself by joining interracial dating Web sites and buying or viewing interracial pornography.[1]

Each of these products, services, or media offerings represents the various ways in which interracial intimacy is being commercialized. By "interracial intimacy," I mean explicit depictions of racially different bodies in romantic, family, or caring contexts; but also depictions of mixed race people, the proof as it were, of that intimacy. Since the advent of the new race question in the 2000 Census that allowed respondents to mark one or more racial categories, the commercialization of interracial intimacy has accelerated as marketers and entrepreneurs have set about attempting to understand the putative needs of this new category of consumer while developing products designed to meet those "needs." At the same time, images of interracial families and mixed race people are increasingly being used in advertisements.

As someone who teaches about family life and how concepts of race change over time, the commercialization of interracial intimacy is especially interesting to me. For most of U.S. history, interracial intimacy in the form of sex, marriage, and domesticity has been a taboo practice, largely hidden from view, highly stigmatized, or made invisible by the unwillingness of public authorities to recognize or legitimize it. Today interracial intimacy is increasingly practiced, tolerated, and acknowledged. The ascendancy of Barack Obama to the presidency of the United States is a good indicator of such a shift (and the public discussion of his biography is a catalyst for its continuation). So, too, is the increasing visibility of images of interracial intimacy on the consumer culture landscape.

I am interested in what the commercialization of interracial intimacy can tell us about the cultural understandings of race in America. Admittedly, I am not writing about work in the usual sense (as paid and unpaid labor), nor about how families cope with the changing nature of such work. Rather, I am writing about *cultural* work; specifically, the work that the commercialization of a specific kind of family relationship (interracial intimacy) does to express and contain racial change. In this chapter I examine interracial intimacy in the context of the "commodity frontier." According to Arlie Hochschild, the commodity frontier describes both a market condition and a cultural condition (2003). In market terms, on the commodity frontier, time-starved and stressed families increasingly purchase the care that family members need, be it meals, childcare, or emotional support. In cultural terms, the commodity frontier defines our present condition in which the purchase of goods and services promises to aid in self-creation and liberate us from the constraints of everyday life, much like the myth of the American geographic frontier once did.

Hochschild's notion of the commodity frontier is meant to capture an aspect of the market's encroachment into the territory of family life. In the context of a sped up capitalism in which both men and women are in the paid labor force, families have needed to speed up as well, and have become structurally weakened and emotionally depleted in the process. Increasingly, the market has stepped in to do what this weakened family can no longer. In Hochschild's formulation, the commodity frontier is two-sided. On one side, the family is a frontier for *companies* looking to "expand the number of market niches for goods and services [that once] formed part of the unpaid labor of 'family life'" (2003, 36). On its other side, the market is a frontier for *families*, new territory upon which to hunt for those goods and services that promise to help families meet the daily wants and needs of their members.

Hochschild develops her concept of the commodity frontier to explain a particular relationship between the market and families; specifically, how market logics encroach upon the logics governing family care. Hochschild's concept of the commodity frontier has been quite generative, inspiring analyses of what it means when other aspects of care (emotional or material) are commercialized (for example, the greeting card industry or weddings) (Blakely 2008; West 2007). I am trying to do something slightly different here: to understand why a particular form of intimacy is so well suited to serve as a commercial symbol in the present moment.

I argue that interracial intimacy on the commodity frontier promises to allow consumers to symbolically cross geographic frontiers as they consume the images of globalized, hybrid, immigrant bodies and the products to which they are attached. At the same time, this consumption shapes and seeks to manage anxieties about sexual and geographic racial boundary crossings. My intention, therefore, is to apply and extend Hochschild's commodity frontier concept beyond its empirical and conceptual origins.

In my analysis of the cultural work that the commercialization of interracial intimacy performs, I focus most closely on advertising (and less on the products and services catering to multiracials or the buying and selling of interracial intimacy itself). Interracial pornography and dating sites cater to a niche audience rather than a broad consumer base, making them less than ideal for my purposes. Unlike marketing to multiracials or those interested in experiencing interracial intimacy, the motivation underlying the depiction of interracial intimacy in advertisements has relatively little to do with appealing to a niche market. For example, Benetton, the Italian clothing company, pioneered the use of interracial intimacy in their ads in the 1980s, long before attempts to count and understand this population. Since the late 1990s, mainstream companies such as Verizon, Pepsi-Cola, Quaker Oats, and the Gap have also begun to use racially ambiguous people and interracially intimate scenes in their ads with some regularity. These companies are using images of interracial intimacy and mixed race bodies to appeal not only or even primarily to mixed race consumers, *but to a broad, ethnically nonspecific audience.* In other words, these companies are using interracialism as a branding tool. By "branding tool" I mean the ways that advertisers attempt to imbue essentially similar goods with seemingly unique meanings so that consumers will buy them. A common way they do that is by presenting commodities as sources of pleasure with "the ability to create identity, freedom, enchantment, beauty and style" (Schor and Holt 2000, xi). As such, the use of interracial intimacy in advertisements is a useful barometer of changing cultural norms about race.

Advertisements are mass media texts that, as Eva Illouz points out, "condense and codify meanings, languages, and outlooks otherwise existing in a diluted, diffuse, and scrambled form by lay actors . . . [They] are purged of all irrelevant meanings and thus tap directly into the pool of cultural symbols" (1997, 18). Advertising not only condenses and codifies extant cultural meanings, it *provides* symbols and cultural scenarios through which to communicate. As such, advertising, like other media forms, has the power to legitimate certain expressions just by showing they are part of the cultural lexicon. As part of an economy of symbols in which image is closely tied with market value, the willingness (or lack thereof) of companies to use images of interracial intimacy in their advertisements—which ones and for what purpose—tells us something about the cultural and social position of racialized groups and the meaning of racial difference in our time. And while I am aware of debates in the field as to whether or not advertising influences or merely reflects dominant ideas,[2] resolving such disputes is not necessary for my purposes. That an institution with such scope, reach, and influence is beginning to depict what has long been one of the most taboo social relationships in American life is reason enough to investigate the trend.

Multiracials and interracial intimacy are increasingly in style. But what does it mean to be "in style"? Why are companies using these images as branding tools for their products? And what kind of cultural work does this imagery do?

Multiracials as Branding Tool

Interracial intimate relations and the multiracial body have long served as a thermometer of America's racial temperature. At times the racially mixed have been lightning rods, vilified as evidence of their parents' racial disloyalty and deviant sexuality, and feared as harbingers of the degeneration, if not demise, of "pure" races. More recently, they've been celebrated as bridges of racial harmony and unity, a maverick new people inherently disposed against prejudice. Not surprisingly, contemporary ads depicting interracialism nearly always employ this more ostensibly positive symbolism, seeking as they do to appeal to a mass audience that includes a near majority non-white population. But even more important, these depictions of interracialism and their increasing visibility on the consumer cultural landscape have to do with convergences between the changing cultural and social position of multiracials and trends in advertising generally.

Multiracial demographics and the symbolism of racial mixedness fit very nicely into an advertising model that has dominated the industry since the 1970s. "Hip consumerism," as cultural critic Thomas Frank dubs it, is defined by advertising that draws from the symbols of the sixties counterculture and "offer[s] to help consumers overcome their alienation, to facilitate their nonconformity and . . . celebrate rule breaking and insurrection" (1997, 28). Much of the content of this hip consumerism draws from and seeks to appeal to youth to capture this large demographic and appeal to the desires of older people to feel young.

While hip consumerism as a stylistic convention has reigned in the industry for a generation, during that time the advertising environment has changed considerably. The expansion of media outlets, the selling of ad space in zones where it was once excluded (like schools), and the attempt to brand nearly everything (for example, selling the "naming rights" of public facilities) have created a saturated ad environment in which advertisers seek new ways to capture the attention of consumers who are less responsive to ads and actively try to avoid them. One method advertisers use to capture the short and wandering attentions of viewers is to "shock" them into paying attention—to present them with an idea or image that challenges prevailing social norms and/or which they are unaccustomed to seeing (Nava 1997).

At the same time, companies are increasingly interested in capturing ethnic consumer dollars, an interest that has fueled an expansion in ethnic target marketing. For an industry interested in creating "hip" messages, targeting ethnic audiences, while appealing to the young with a message they are not used to seeing, interracial intimacy is a tailor-made marketing vehicle.

The majority of ads depicting interracialism follow in some way the contours of hip consumerism. One of the most recognizable (and most controversial) is Benetton's 1989 ad featuring the torso and arms of a bare-chested black woman nursing a white baby. This ad was part of one of the earliest ad campaigns employing interracialism to craft a brand image. From one perspective the image depicts cross-racial nurturance, caring, and bonding. The sharing of bodily fluid (breast milk) for the sustenance of an infant undermines notions of biological racial difference. Indeed, this is the message Benetton claims the ad was meant to convey—a reminder of our "common humanity" despite superficial differences in skin color. From another perspective, however, the ad recalls black women's use as wet nurses to white children under slavery. Rather than communicating our common humanity, the ad communicates the *in*humanity of slavery and racial domination. Indeed, according to Benetton, the most vocal critics of the ad were African Americans citing this historical legacy.

While Benetton may indeed have intended to underscore the common humanity of people across racial boundaries, they were also quite aware of the shock value of the ad. In an analysis of their evolution as a brand known as "a subverter of stereotypes," Benetton describes the phase of advertising that included the breastfeeding images as their "cycle of difference," in which "happy" images of racially integrated groups of kids were replaced "by couples representing an all-new interpretation of difference. In this cycle, the word 'different' became a close cousin of 'controversial.'"[3]

Creating controversial ads, however, was a deliberate choice made at the *inception* of the ad campaign, not the *ex post facto* assessment of the public's response that this quotation suggests. The intention of the ads in the series, used from roughly 1986 to 1991, was to present images capable of *eliciting* controversy. According to Benetton's Web site, "All of these conflicts were based on taboos, on the impossibility of co-existence, on a difference that separates rather than unites. By acknowledging these differences and prohibitions, the brand appeared more involved. It took sides, rather than presenting a simple 'objective' portrayal of the world; it made a commitment to foster the cohabitation of opposites, to break down barriers and ensure dialogue. Benetton had a plan: to integrate opposites, to unite differences under a single flag, the flag of its own logo."

While controversial at the time, it is also the most awarded image in the company's history. It remains the most memorable, in part because the story of the ad is continuously revived. Indeed, it has been and continues to be analyzed in the marketing literature as both cautionary tale and effective advertising how-to-guide. The polarizing quality of the ad was, of course, its strength. Within a few years of the onset of the "cycle of difference" campaign, Benetton, a small Italian clothing company, became a multinational company with international brand recognition to match.

A decade after Benetton's "cycle of difference" campaign, another clothing company looked to interracialism to bolster flagging sales. Levi's described its campaign as intended to convey an "unconventional, streetwise attitude" and used images of mixed race bodies ("a virtual melting pot of cultures and races") to symbolize this attitude (Kane 1998a). One ad features a woman of African descent with a golden afro, sporting bell bottom jeans. She is holding a sign that reads, "I can't be prejudice [*sic*], I'm mulatto." According to the ad manager on the project, the campaign sought to create images that were "familiar yet utterly surprising" (Kane 1998b). The familiar in this ad is found in her dress and hair style (think Angela Davis circa 1970). The "utterly surprising," one assumes, is the character's declaration of her "mulatto" identity, though perhaps not for the reasons its creators intended. Though Levi's relies on contemporary tropes of racial hybridity (like the one that says mixed race people cannot "be prejudice") to convey a streetwise authenticity, the character's use of an outdated and offensive term belies such assertions. Unlike Benetton's use of interracial intimacy as a branding tool, Levi's campaign was not particularly successful in reviving flagging sales or remaking Levi's as a hip brand (Liedtke 2008).

The Benetton and Levi's examples show the versatility (and volatility) of images of interracial intimacy in ads. Sometimes interracialism is used to convey hip authenticity or rebellion, at other times to provoke a reaction or suggest racial harmony. Whatever the intended message, the creators of these ads chose these images because of their power to symbolize something new. Over time, of course, that which is new inevitably gets old. Other symbols are then sought to convey the impression that the company is forward-looking, vibrant, and relevant.

While the approach pioneered by Benetton in the 1980s (a mosaic of racially different people in intimate contexts) remains a part of the ad landscape, increasingly ads employing images of interracial intimacy emphasize the mixed race body. One metric of this trend is the growth of the careers of mixed race models. In the last decade, for example, nearly every major cosmetics brand has had a mixed race woman as their "face" of the moment.[4] The fact such models have been hired is not all that surprising when one considers that in an effort to capture ethnic consumer dollars most cosmetics companies have several spokesmodels at any given time, increasingly of different races. What is more remarkable are the reasons companies and casting agents offer for *why* mixed race models are used. Mixed race models are consciously chosen for their particular racial difference. They symbolize in two ways the "unexpected" that marketers are after in the age of hip consumerism and saturated ad space. Some of these models are sought because the elements of their racial mixedness seem clearly visible, in which differently racialized physical features cohere in one body. This look has been particularly sought after in an age of technological change and globalization. Says one casting agent, "The mix of Asian facial features and kinky hair . . . conjures up an immediate sense of both globalization and technology. Of Devon Aoki, an American model of Japanese and European ancestry and the face of Lancôme cosmetics in 2004, the company enthused, "Aoki embodies a new generation that's enthusiastic and passionate, a generation that seeks modernity, creativity and expertise." Others models are sought because they look *racially ambiguous.* Of Ujjwala Raut, a top model from India and "face" of Yves St. Laurent, the director of her management company (IMG Models) said, "Ujjwala is a woman of colour, but look at her and begin to play a guessing game: is she Mexican, Spanish, Russian? The fact you can't be sure is part of her seductiveness" (TheAge.com 2004).

We might expect the "seductiveness" of racial indeterminacy to be employed in a cosmetics campaign or on the runway, products and contexts that emphasize the cultivation of beauty and desire, but to sell phone service? "America, Meet the Elliots," reads the March 2004 press release from Verizon announcing the launch of their new ad campaign. "They're a multicultural family from Anywhere USA," it continues, "poised to show the country how Verizon's products and services make their lives easier and more rewarding." The press release goes on to detail the members of the family ("Father, Tom; Mother, Marta," even the dog, Hambone) and features descriptions of each of their four children (for example, "Raphael, 12, a techno-centric son whose favorite activity is surfing the Web").

While the press release is straightforward in announcing the mixed or "multicultural" composition of the family, the ads themselves are more coy. The first ads in the series of seven featured the children and father only, like the one my daughter and I watched in which white Dad looks on while his darker and curlier-haired son tutors him in the basics of email. The deployment of racial difference is subtle and deliberately so, designed to seduce the viewer into paying attention, drawn first into wondering just who, or rather what *race*, Mom is.

The Elliots series of ads are part of a wider Verizon campaign that also targets ethnic consumers. Ads featuring the Davis family are meant to attract black customers, while the Sandovals are targeting Latino consumers. Each of the families, Verizon tells us, "are likeable and not quite traditional." What is notable here is that the Elliots are intended as the mass market vehicle of the campaign—the family designed for its likely appeal to a broad audience.

The Elliots features that rarity in ads: an interracial family in a domestic family context. While the Benetton ads of two decades ago suggested domestic intimacy through their depiction of activities usually associated with family caregiving—breastfeeding, couples with babies—these were decontextualized images set against a white background, the emphasis on the figures as symbols of something else. And while the intended tone of these Verizon ads are markedly different from those of Benetton (subtle versus confrontational) and use interracialism in different ways (emphasizing racial sameness versus racial difference), each rely for their impact on interracial intimacy's ability to signal something new. According to a vice president for brand management at Verizon, as an interracial family the Elliots draw the viewers' attention because of their novelty ("You're less likely to tune these ads out, or say, 'I've seen this before'") (Stevenson 2004). For Verizon, the Elliots's interracialism makes them not quite traditional enough to draw viewers in without marking them as an ethnic family.

Interracial Intimacy on the Commodity Frontier

If, as Eva Illouz (1997, 18) asserts, media texts like ads "make up an abbreviated lexicon of the main concerns, anxieties and dreams of our culture," what cultural sense can we make of the appearance of interracial intimacy in ads? Why are companies seeking to use images of interracial intimacy when a short time ago they were nowhere to be found? And why are these companies using them to reach white and non-white consumers alike? When I first began analyzing this growing trend in advertising, I was inclined to accept the market-driven explanations that marketers themselves give for their choice of images: that is, interracialism in ads is "new" and so helps products, companies, and even advertising firms create a distinctive brand image. But these answers are not completely satisfactory, for they do not address why the chosen symbol of newness is a racial representation as opposed to, say, a new style of film editing, a new slogan, or a new logo. If we frame the commercialization of interracial intimacy as an outpost on the "commodity frontier," rather than just a savvy marketing tactic, interesting analytical possibilities emerge as to why this particular kind of racial representation is being employed.

The commodity frontier, Hochschild tells us, does much of the emotional and ideological work that the myth of American geographic frontier once did.

The geographic frontier promised liberation from the constraints of everyday life and supported American optimism and the myth that every man could create one's life and self. "For the geographic frontier," Hochschild writes, "the point of focus is a person's location on land. For the commodity frontier the point of focus is a location in a world of goods and services. Instead of 'going somewhere,' the individual 'buys something.' And buying something becomes a way of going somewhere" (2003, 40–41).

The commercialization of interracial intimacy brings together the commodity frontier Hochschild describes with the geographic frontier for which she suggests it is a symbolic and cultural replacement. Indeed, the geographic frontier was always already racially coded, as the freedom and self-realization sought on the American geographic frontier often came at the expense (and geographic displacement) of Native peoples. Racial difference marks geographic distance in so far as race is commonly understood to represent ancestral origins in populations located in different regions of the world. Interracial intimacy represents a kind of bridging of that distance, as well as the cultural differences to which racial division has given rise. Interracialism on the commodity frontier promises to allow consumers to cross geographic frontiers (if only symbolically), as we consume the images of these hybrid/ immigrant/globalized bodies and the products attached to them.

In Hochschild's formulation, the geographic frontier is a cultural precursor and analogue to the commodity frontier, each a vehicle for expressing and perhaps satisfying a particularly American quest for freedom and self-realization. The commodity frontier, though certainly not new, has become more dominant in the contemporary period than it has ever been, while the geographic frontier has disappeared as a real entity and so too as a myth capable of animating American desires.[5]

Perhaps, however, it is more accurate to say that the symbolic terrain of the geographic frontier has shifted in the contemporary period from the Western lands of North America that enchanted the nineteenth-century imaginary, to lands beyond the continental/U.S. border—particularly to India and China—as the center of economic power under global capitalism moves eastward. Interracial imagery in ads symbolizes the U.S. look eastward, particularly in its emphasis on Asian/white couples and multiracials of Asian ancestry.

If the commercialization of interracial intimacy is an outpost on the commodity frontier in which people (including the makers of these ads themselves) seek "to go somewhere" by buying things branded with interracial imagery, we are led to ask, "Where are they going?" and "What fantasies of liberation are they entertaining?" Hochschild suggests that on the commodity frontier, the objects of our fantasies are less the objects themselves (the perfect car or house) and more about subjective identity (the perfect self or relationship that consuming these products and services promises). The hidden appeal in so much of modern commodification, Hochschild tells us, is its promise to deliver us from a state of ambivalence in the context of rapid social change. "Thus, the prevailing myth of the frontier, commodification, and the subjective realm have fused into one—a commodity frontier that is moving into the world of our private desires" (2003, 41).

Perhaps, then, the depiction of interracial intimacy in ads is a compelling symbol today because it promises to free us from our ambivalence over changing racial demographics and dynamics—in particular, racial boundary crossings borne of intermarriage and migration in an increasingly globalized and sped up economy. The use of interracial intimacy as a branding tool emerges at a time when two contradictory forces are active in American social and political life with respect to race. Americans are at once ambivalent about the economic dislocations brought about under global capitalism, concerned about the ascendancy of the economies of China and India, and fearful about immigration and terrorism (both of which are imagined as perpetrated by racial others). At the same time, Americans are demonstrating an unprecedented acceptance of racial difference and interracialism, most notably in the election of Barack Obama. In the context of these contradictory forces, established racial hierarchies are in flux and interracial intimacy takes on a heightened symbolism fueled by both desire and fear.

Much of the marketing of interracial intimacy presents a decidedly unambivalent and optimistic ideal of racial harmony through which racial division is transcended via racial blending and cultural hybridity. Benetton sought "to unite differences under a single flag," while Levi's suggested that through racial mixing racial divisions are ameliorated. Interracial families in the Verizon ads symbolically bridge the geographic distance between peoples that phone lines do in a more tangible way. Rather than the fears of takeover and inundation that public discourse around immigration too often reflects, the Verizon commercials reflect a notion of assimilation, a blending into American mainstream middle-class family life and culture. These representations express a kind of fantasy—an unambivalent ideal—and as Hochschild reminds us, those ideals often express the very ambivalence they seek to transcend.

Always a potent symbol of the racial dynamics of a given period, advertisers present an updated vision of the mulatto for our times. Ads emphasizing the mixed race model's body echo older images of the mulatto but include only those elements that are putatively positive in the age of hip consumerism. She is a bridge between racial groups, one who goes against social convention and signals the future. The "quintessential colonized body," as Mia Bagneris (2008) provocatively describes renderings of the mulatto in eighteenth-century art, has become the *quintessential globalized body* in contemporary advertising. Most of these renderings of interracial intimacy depend on a reiteration of notions of geographic distance and cultural and racial difference for their hip, border-crossing, transgressive message to remain readable and evocative.

Whereas renderings of interracial intimacy often present a decontextualized and exotic mixed race body or couple, the more novel representations contextualize interracialism, depicting interracial *families* in family settings. The domestication of interracialism that the Elliots represent serves to make interracial intimacy appear normative. Racial mixedness is employed self-consciously by their creators, but also subtly. There is a radical blandness to these ads wherein interracial intimacy is presented as so acceptable as to be unremarkable.

In one sense, this is a welcome counter to most representations of interracial intimacy—a move away from the exoticization of mixed race bodies and a subtle recognition of changing demographics and social norms about race. But there is something unsettling about them as well, particularly when one looks at the larger ad environment in which they appear. Many companies are reluctant to use such images, and some explicitly reject them, concerned that they are inconsistent with their brand's image or that they will offend their customer base. Perhaps this is why in ads depicting interracial families there is a noticeable absence of interracial families that include a black partner.[6] From this perspective, such ads appear less progressive and more conformist, their makers followers of social norms of acceptable interracialism rather than trailblazers of cultural change.

"Every myth," Hochschild points out, "has an element of both reality and unreality" (2003, 40). As modern mythmakers, advertisers capture both what is real about interracial intimacy in America (that it exists and that real families live this way) and also what is unreal (that racial harmony, understanding of cultural difference, and freedom from ambivalence about racial change can be had through either the consumption of interracial bodies or goods branded with interracial imagery). The ideals and fantasies expressed in contemporary commercial representations of interracial intimacy are variable and sometimes contradictory. Marketers trade on culturally resonant meanings of interracial intimacy as both taboo and exotic while also creating novel representations of interracial intimacy as both normative and nonthreatening.

Hochschild argues that the cultural fallout from the expansion of the commodity frontier is a heavier symbolic weight placed on the family, especially the wife and mother role. Partly a response to the outsourcing of caregiving, partly a response to a destabilized economy, "the more shaky things outside the family system, the more we seem to need to believe in an unshakable family and, failing that, an unshakable figure of mother-wife" (2003, 39). The symbol of mother, Hochschild argues, is "efficient"—capable of holding within the figure of one person all the meanings associated with the larger institutions (family and community) destabilized by prevailing economic and cultural shifts.

Much like the mother is hypersymbolized in response to destabilizing forces in the economy and family system, the multiracial body and the interracial family of which it is a part are hypersymbolized in response to a destabilized global economic system, racial hierarchies, and changing family demographics. Perhaps, then, the "shakier" the established economic and racial order seem, the more we need to believe that interracial intimacy can return us to more solid ground. In this sense, the multiracial body and interracial family are efficient symbols of the dreams and anxieties concerning race in the contemporary period.

Hochschild is ambivalent about the encroachment of the market side of the commodity frontier into family life, concerned about the ways that the market "changes our benchmarks" for the expectations we have of how families and intimate relationships ought to be (2003, 43). Of the commercialization of interracial intimacy, I am ambivalent as well. In so far as it repeats racial stereotypes and substitutes images of racial harmony for a politics of racial justice, it offers little to help make sense of the larger questions about race and power that make interracial intimacy and families knowable as such. Nevertheless, the representation of interracial intimacy in ads changes our benchmarks in positive ways in so far it expands the terrain of what is considered normal for families. As my teenage daughter commented upon seeing the Elliots ads, "That's cool." When I asked her why, she said, "It's nice that pop culture is telling us it's okay to date outside your race. It's like they're saying, 'We're okay with it. Go ahead.' 'Cuz if enough people see ads like that, they'll think interracial dating is okay too." Already aware of the relative rarity of interracial families like hers, and the infrequency of interracial dating in her school, my daughter looks to popular culture to normalize what she takes for granted, but which she knows most of her peers do not. And though a portrayal of interracial intimacy is neither intimacy itself nor the racial equality that it is often used to symbolize, the chance that representation in the culture allows for the historically unseen or misrepresented to feel normal is no small thing in a child's (or anyone's) life. Perhaps this particular aspect of the commercialization of intimate life is something we need not feel so ambivalent about.

NOTES

1. Shampoo (Mixed Chicks, Curls, Curly Qs); T-shirts (LikeMinded People, LovingDay); dolls (RealKidz biracial dolls, Woodkins paper dolls); children's books (*Brendan Buckley's Universe and Everything in It*; *Black, Brown and Tan: My Two Grandmas*); markers (Crayola Multicultural Washable Markers); wedding cake toppers (Melting Pot Gifts); television (*Jon and Kate Plus Eight* on TLC network); cereal (Life's The Oh Family; Kashi); makeup (Revlon, Lancôme, Maybelline); laundry detergent (Tide with Bleach); Pain reliever (Tylenol); furniture (IKEA); phone service (Verizon); interracial online dating (EbonyIvoryLove, Interracial Romance).

2. While there are more subtleties to their arguments than I have space to discuss, writers like Susan Linn (2004) and Juliet Schor (2004) put the accent on advertising's power to influence consumers. Schudson (1984) I regard as representative of scholars who accent advertising's role as a magnifier of existing social trends, consumer behavior, and desires.

3. The campaign also included ads depicting a nude white woman and black woman holding an Asian baby, all three wrapped in a blanket. Another included a white man playfully smooching a black woman.

4. For example, L'Oreal (Noemie Lenoir), Revlon (Halle Berry), Maybelline (Adriana Lima), Lancôme (Devon Aoki).

5. Hochschild distinguishes between "newer and older" expressions of the commodity frontier according to the degree to which distinctions were made between service and server. Contemporary domestic commodification is centered on purchasing services—a person's

labor or a commodity. Under slavery that distinction was largely collapsed where families seeking domestic labor bought not just a person's labor but also the person herself.

6. Although most of the ads I have found include only Asian/white or Latino/white pairings, there has been a noticeable increase in ads featuring black/white couples. In June 2008, for example, a new ad for Coleman sporting goods began running on the HGTV network depicting a black woman and white man holding hands and kissing. More recently, eHarmony, the dating service, has begun to feature black/white couples in their testimonials.

REFERENCES

Bagneris, Mia. 2008. "Coloring the Caribbean: Agostino Brunias and the Painting of Race in the British West Indies, c. 1765–1800." Ph.D. diss., Harvard University.

Benetton. http://press.benettongroup.com/ben_en/about/campaigns.

Blakely, Kristin. 2008. "Busy Brides and the Business of Family Life: The Wedding-Planning Industry and the Commodity Frontier." *Journal of Family Issues* 29:639–662.

Burnett, Leo. 1995. *100 LEO's.* New York: McGraw Hill.

Frank, Thomas. 1997. *The Conquest of Cool: Business Culture, Counterculture and the Rise of Hip Consumerism.* Chicago: University of Chicago Press.

Hochschild, Arlie. 2003. "The Commodity Frontier." In *The Commercialization of Intimate Life,* edited by Arlie Russell Hochschild, 30–44. Berkeley: University of California Press.

Illouz, Eva. 1997. *Consuming the Romantic Utopia: Love and the Cultural Contradictions of Capitalism.* Berkeley: University of California Press.

Kane, C. 1998a. "TBWA/Chiat Day Brings 'Street Culture' to a Campaign for Levi Strauss Silver Tab Clothing." *New York Times,* August 14.

———. 1998b. "Levi Strauss Is Trying to Regain Market Share for Its Jeans, Especially among Young Consumers." *New York Times,* May 5.

Liedtke, Michael. 2008. "Levi's Has Best Year in Decade: Tax Accounting Changes Help Boost S.F. Firm's Figures." *Associated Press,* February 13.

Linn, Susan. 2004. *Consuming Kids: The Hostile Takeover of Childhood.* New York: New Press.

Nava, Mica. 1997. "Framing Advertising: Cultural Analysis and the Incrimination of Visual Texts." In *Buy This Book: Studies in Advertising and Consumption,* 34–50. New York: Routledge.

Schor, Juliet B. 2004. *Born to Buy: The Commercialized Child and the New Consumer Culture.* New York: Scribner.

Schor, Juliet B., and Douglas B. Holt, eds. 2000. *The Consumer Society Reader.* New York: New Press.

Schudson, Michael. 1984. *Advertising, The Uneasy Persuasion: Its Dubious Impact on American Society.* New York: Basic Books.

Stevenson, Seth. 2004. "Customers Like Me: Verizon Uses Race to Make You Look." *Slate.com.* http://www.slate.com/id/2099476/.

TheAge.com. 2004. "They've Got the Look." http://www.theage.com.au/articles/2004/04/19/1082357106748.html.

West, Emily. 2007. "When You Care Enough to Defend the Very Best: How the Greeting Card Industry Manages Cultural Criticism." *Media, Culture and Society* 29:241–261.

PART V

Global Care Chains

CHAPTER 19

The Globalization-Family Nexus

FAMILIES AS MEDIATING STRUCTURES OF GLOBALIZATION

Nazli Kibria

The idea of globalization is a central paradigm of our time, informing the work of a wide range of groups and interests, from scholars to economic development workers to human rights activists. Globalization refers in general terms to a trend of worldwide connectedness: "the intensification of worldwide social relations which link distant localities in such a way that local happenings are shaped by events occurring many miles away and vice-versa" (Giddens 1990, 64). Whether through the expansion of the global economy or the development of an intensified consciousness of the world as a whole, globalization is broadly about the global movement and absorption of goods, ideas, and other aspects of the social world. The precise character and consequences of these trends have been assessed differently and indeed often excite debate and controversy.

In *Global Families*, Meg Karraker notes that scholarship on the family has yet to engage with globalization theory. She writes: "the vernacular of globalization theory has not yet permeated family sociology or family studies" (Karraker and Ferguson 2008, 11). In a similar vein, but with respect to theories of globalization, I have been struck by the quite limited conceptual role that has been assigned to the family in the discourse of globalization. What seems to be prevalent in theories of globalization is an understanding, usually implicit, of the family as a recipient of globalization—a sphere that is "acted on" by globalizing forces. To put it in positivist terms, globalization in this scheme is the independent variable and the family is the dependent variable. With few exceptions, the family, if it does appear in these discussions, is used to illustrate the effects of globalization, with little concern for how globalization itself may be shaped by the family. Globalization and family are thus viewed as separate and distinct rather than as deeply intertwined features of the social world. As a result, what remains invisible are the dialectical features of the relationship and the manner in which families are not simply shaped by globalization but also work to constitute it.

So how can we make the family more visible, pulling it out of the margins and into the center of globalization discourse? And perhaps more to the point, how can we usefully organize a dialogue between the fields of globalization and family studies? Arlie Hochschild, through her deeply influential writings, has given us a keen understanding of and appreciation for the complex intersections of family and economy. In *The Time Bind*, for example, she offers us a window into how women and men in the postindustrial United States come to feel, understand, and respond to the unrelenting demands of the corporate workplace, in ways that are powerfully mediated by the obligations and relationships of family life (Hochschild 1997). She describes how, for many workers under these conditions, experiences and expectations of family and labor market converge in a trend that holds important long-term implications for the structure and character of both family and labor market.

Inspired by Hochschild's insights, I suggest that we turn our attention to the notion of the family as a critical mediating structure of globalization. This framework, I believe, offers a useful approach, a place from which to at least begin the task of unpacking the globalization-family nexus. Thus I anchor my analysis here in a notion of family as a crucial intermediary between individuals and globalization processes; it is a sphere of influence that channels these dynamics, thereby shaping the character of globalization itself. "The family," as I use it throughout the chapter, is intended to convey a dynamic, contested, and variable social institution that is broadly concerned with the organization of kinship and the care of children, as well as intimacy and sexuality.

Drawing on an emerging body of innovative research in family studies that looks at the impact and significance of globalization processes for family life around the world, I suggest three specific ways in which we can begin to think about the family as a critical mediating structure of globalization: as a shock absorber of globalization, as an engine of globalization, and as a cultural interpreter of globalization.

Family as Shock Absorber of Globalization

My first point acknowledges what has clearly been the most prevalent conception of the family in relationship to globalization processes. It is of the family as "shock absorber"—a collectivity that is engaged in attempts to cope with the blows and disruptions generated by globalization for its members. For example, in *Forgotten Families*, Jody Heymann highlights the devastating impacts of the contemporary post-1990s global economy on working parents with children (2006). She describes how such families struggle to survive, attempting to absorb the shocks of an environment of heightened economic pressures coupled with declining state supports. This is not to say that the family is always effective as a shock absorber, or that there are not conflicts and costs associated with the family's efforts to cope, often borne disproportionately by some members of the family rather than others. But quite apart from their success or equity, the survival strategies of families play a critical role in the enabling of globalization. That is, in their capacity as shock absorbers, families serve to facilitate globalization processes.

For families in the developing world today, survival strategies may likely include the international labor migration of one or more members to the more prosperous segments of the world. Among the notable features of the contemporary migration era is its "feminization," with women constituting a growing proportion of those who migrate abroad for jobs with the goal of remitting money for the economic survival and well-being of their families. A rich body of scholarship, from studies of Sri Lankan women workers in the Middle East to Filipina migrants in Western Europe and North America (Gamburd 2000; Parrenas 2001), documents the intense challenges faced by these women. These include the task of managing and giving meaning to family ties and roles, especially those of mothering, given physical distance from children. Thus the struggles of these women is at least one of the ways in which the phenomenon of "deterritorialization" or the "the compression of time and space" that is widely viewed to be at the heart of globalization, assumes social form. That is, migrant women may strive to cope with physical separation from family and community through frequent phone calls and e-mail exchanges. As they do so, both the gaps and the compressions of time and space that are part of globalization take on specific social meanings and significance.

In her discussion of the international domestic labor regime, Hochschild has noted the presence of "global care chains" that are composed of "personal links between people across the globe based on the paid or unpaid work of caring" (2000, 32). Global care chains are the cumulative products of the efforts of families to manage or to absorb the shocks generated by the pressures and demands of the global economy. In the prosperous societies of the North, families hire domestic labor in an effort to overcome a caregiving deficit that has become acute as women have entered the labor force in growing numbers. In the developing world, economic scarcities create intense challenges for families, spurring mothers and daughters to seek jobs abroad, creating a ready supply of domestic workers for the North. But even as we acknowledge the strategic character of global care chains, it is important not to lose sight of their constitutive significance. Once in place, global care chains, with their complex networks and relations, organize globalization itself. For example, as Bashi (2007) describes in her study of Caribbean migration to New York, global care chains are often at the hub of larger international migration networks. That is, global care chains may be a center for the development of networks that organize larger migration streams.

Family as Engine of Globalization

The notion of family as engine of globalization pays heed to how the family serves to integrate women, men, and children into the global market. Indeed, a growing body of scholarship draws our attention to how the family as a social and symbolic site is involved in generating consumption, thereby driving the global market. Jeffrey Dennis, for example, argues that idealized notions of the nuclear family are involved in the ongoing creation of consumer needs and desires (2002). That is, with its compact, bounded, and well-defined structure, the idealized nuclear family evokes a "McDonaldized" family experience of predictable, calculable needs that are fulfilled through the consumption of market goods and services. As highlighted by Hochschild's notion of the "commodity frontier," these needs also reflect the continued expansion of market goods and services for activities that were previously unpaid and performed in the family (2003). The family thus evokes, and, indeed, at times demands, the integration of its members, as worker-consumers, into the global market.

In her work on the new middle class of contemporary India, Fernandes affirms the role of the nuclear family imaginary in societies that are experiencing rapid integration into the global economy (2006). She notes the prominence of nuclear family images in Indian advertising that is geared to selling to the middle class. Idyllic images of prosperous and modern-looking nuclear families, with mother, father, and one or two children, serve as mirrors of aspiration in which desires for market goods and services merge with desires for a happy family life. What results, according to Fernandes, is a middle class composed of "citizen consumers," defined by an ethos of consumerism that accounts, among other things, for their political support of India's policies of liberalization or the opening up of the Indian economy to the global market.

The consumerism of the new Indian middle class is also expressed in their reported propensity for lavish weddings that are marked by extravagant displays of globalized consumerism: "Spanish flamenco dancers, fresh orchids from Thailand, ice sculptures . . . a veritable flotilla of flaunted wealth" (Das 2005). Noting the lavish wedding to be a worldwide trend, Cele Otnes and Elizabeth Pleck argue that its rise reflects the powerful worldwide fusion of consumerism with the myths of the nuclear family, especially that of romantic love and marriage (2003). At the same time, weddings may also be occasions for the display of social status, not only for the couple and immediate family but also for the larger kin group that is involved. That is, as a conspicuous demonstration of its financial capacity to consume well, the lavish wedding may serve to express, affirm, and, indeed, elevate the social position of the family.

The troubling issue of dowry in South Asia offers further evidence of how the family, as part of the social organization of caste, class, and gender inequality, has a close and interactive relationship to the production of consumerism and the global economy. Analysts have noted the rising significance and presence of dowry—the transfer of resources from bride to bridegroom's family—within marriage transactions in contemporary South Asia. Sharada Srinivasan argues that the expansion of dowry in South Asia has generally reflected the integration of agrarian, nonindustrial communities into the market economy (2005). These changes result in newly articulated aspirations for social mobility that are then reflected in dowry inflation. That is, drawing on available structures of gender inequality, men and their families seize the opportunity presented by marriage transactions in a market context to bargain for goods and resources that might elevate their social status. Dowry inflation further feeds globalization processes by encouraging the international labor migration of women in South Asia. That is, the forces that propel growing numbers of women in South Asia to seek employment abroad include the goal of accumulating for a good dowry, one that will ensure a good marriage, either for themselves or for their daughters. Dowry is thus a formative element of the global care chains that link South Asian migrant labor women and their families with those of the prosperous societies of the North.

Family as Cultural Interpreter of Globalization

The notion of family as cultural interpreter of globalization draws our attention to the family as a site of negotiation for the cultural currents that are a part of globalization. The idea of globalization loses some of its abstraction when we consider how it is often in the family that globalization takes on significance and form. That is, it is in the mundane, often messy relations and realities of family life, such as the struggle to feed children well or to fulfill obligations to parents, that globalization becomes a meaningful part of people's lives.

The family is often viewed as a site of resistance to change, as a repository of tradition that is stubbornly defiant in its rejection of modernizing social change. This dynamic of resistance is at least one way in which the family shapes and enters into the complex cultural mosaic of globalization. Globalization is increasingly associated not with the cultural homogeneity and convergence that is suggested by global media and advertising, but rather with varied and fluid cultural developments. Jan Pieterse is among those who have argued that the global landscape is one of growing cultural diversity (2004). That is, globalization creates opportunities for the unique meshing together or creolization of local and global cultures into hybrid forms. Globalization also promotes cultural diversity through the dynamics of "localization" by which globalization offers enhanced opportunities for the cultivation and resurgence of local solidarities and cultures.

Family relations and activities are clearly an important site for the negotiation and expression of the cultural diversities of globalization. Take, for example, love and food, two important areas of human experience. Among middle-class Indians today, the expectations and rituals that surround marriage decisions are often marked by intense negotiation across generational lines. A culturally hybrid system of "arranged meetings" has apparently emerged whereby families assert traditional values and loyalties by arranging meetings for their adult unmarried children with potential partners whom they deem suitable (Raj 2003). The young men and women, for whom a globalized ethos of romantic love is meaningful, are then encouraged to date and perhaps to fall in love and get married. And as far as food, the development of a transnational Indian packaged food industry that has invigorated local cuisines has apparently enhanced the ability of Indian families, especially mothers, to use family meals as occasions for the symbolic affirmation of highly localized ethnicities. Tulasi Srinivas argues that, in locales ranging from Bangalore to Boston, the globalization of the Indian food industry has enabled Indian middle-class families, to consume family meals of the foods that connect them to their specific region of origin (2006).

Conclusion

In conclusion, this chapter has been motivated by a desire to bring the family out of the periphery and into the center of current globalization debates. As I have emphasized throughout this chapter, I see the family—or more precisely, family relations, expectations and experiences—as deeply contested and varied, not stable or monolithic, matters. In fact, among the particular values of looking at the family as a fluid social form is that it brings our attention to the role of human agency, or the ability of people to actively make globalization processes. An understanding of the family as a critical mediating structure of globalization offers us, I believe, a powerful window into the human dimensions and challenges of globalization.

REFERENCES

Bashi, Vilna F. 2007. *Survival of the Knitted: Immigrant Social Networks in a Stratified World.* Stanford, CA: Stanford University Press.

Das, Anupreeta. 2005. "Middle-Class India Plows New Wealth into Big Weddings." *Christian Science Monitor,* September 29 . http://www.csmonitor.com/2005/0929/p01s04-wosc.html.

Dennis, Jeffrey. 2002. "McDonaldization of the Family." In *McDonaldization: The Reader,* edited by George Ritzer, 107–116. Newbury Park, CA: Sage Publications.

Fernandes, Leela. 2006. *India's New Middle Class: Democratic Politics in an Era of Economic Reform.* Minneapolis: University of Minnesota Press.

Gamburd, Michele R. 2000. *The Kitchen Spoon's Handle: Transnationalism and Sri Lanka's Migrant Housemaids.* Ithaca, NY: Cornell University Press.

Giddens, Anthony. 1990. *The Consequences of Modernity.* Stanford, CA: Stanford University Press.

Heymann, Jody. 2006. *Forgotten Families: Ending the Growing Crisis Confronting Children and Working Parents in the Global Economy.* New York: Oxford University Press.

Hochschild, Arlie. 1997. *The Time Bind: When Work Becomes Home and Home Becomes Work.* New York: Metropolitan Books.

———. 2000. "The Nanny Chain." *American Prospect* (January 3): 32–36.

———. 2003. "The Commodity Frontier." In *The Commercialization of Intimate Life: Notes from Home and Work,* 30–45. Berkeley: University of California Press.

Karraker, Meg, and Susan J. Ferguson. 2008. *Global Families*. Boston: Allyn & Bacon.
Otnes, Cele C., and Elizabeth H. Pleck. 2003. *Cinderella Dreams: The Allure of the Lavish Wedding*. Berkeley: University of California Press.
Parrenas, Rhacel. 2001. *Servants of Globalization: Women, Migration and Domestic Work*. Stanford, CA: Stanford University Press.
Pieterse, Jan Nederveen. 2004. *Globalization and Culture: Global Mélange*. Lanham, MD: Rowman & Littlefield.
Raj, Dhooleka. 2003. *Where Are You From? Middle-Class Migrants in the Modern World*. Berkeley: University of California Press.
Srinivas, Tulasi. 2006. "'As Mother Made It': The Cosmopolitan Indian Family, Authentic Food and the Construction of Cultural Utopia." *International Journal of Sociology of the Family* 32:191–222.
Srinivasan, Sharada. 2005. "Daughters or Dowries? The Changing Nature of Dowry Practices in South India." *World Development* 33:593–615.

CHAPTER 20

Homeland Visits

TRANSNATIONAL MAGNIFIED MOMENTS AMONG LOW-WAGE IMMIGRANT MEN

Hung Cam Thai

This chapter examines the complex transnational dimensions and trajectories of Vietnamese low-wage immigrant men and reflects on the ways in which return visits to their homeland alter or highlight these men's sense of masculinity and social class. Homeland return visits—the occasional or recurring sojourns made by members of migrant communities to their homeland—offer an important window into understanding how immigrant men make sense of their family and work as they organize transnational lives, forming relationships linking together their country of origin and their country of settlement, a process that has been given much attention among scholars of migration since the early 1990s (Brettell 2006; Guarnizo, Portes, and Haller 2003; Guarnizo and Smith 1998a; Schiller, Basch, and Blanc-Szanton 1992; Vertovec 2004). Although a lively body of research in recent years has paid significant attention to the emergence of transnational cultures, there is currently little attention given to the role of masculinity within this body of research. A central point I make in this chapter is that the related categories of social class and masculinity need to be expanded globally. This is because much of what we know about both concepts in the West are still nation-specific, despite the enormous increase in transnational flows of capital and people in recent years (Connell 1995; Wright 1997).

Globally expanding research on the related concepts of social class and masculinity is particularly relevant to the lives of immigrants whose low wages take on different social and economic meanings when they make visits to their homeland in developing countries. For some immigrants, as Mary Waters succinctly points out, "their sense of self is tied to the status system in the home country"

(1999, 102). That status system is often reworked in complex ways as immigrants take on transnational lives. Moreover, the relationship between return visits and men's sense of masculinity and social class provides a basis for understanding how immigrant men understand their gender ideologies and practices across international borders—for example, their desirability as a husband and as a family man. This focus is particularly important because immigrants continue to work in the lowest sectors of the U.S. formal and informal labor markets (Chiswick 1982). Vietnamese American men, for instance, earn on average 30 percent less than their white counterparts, and they are one of the lowest income-earning ethnic groups in the United States (Yamane 2001). The issue of work, gender, and marriageability among low-wage Vietnamese immigrant men is also worthy of exploration, because, unlike the general population, research has shown that among Asian American immigrants in the low-wage labor market, especially in California, women tend to get jobs more easily, work longer hours, and earn more money than men (Espiritu 1999).

My analysis of homeland return visits as a social practice among immigrant Vietnamese men is inspired by Arlie Russell Hochschild's concept of "magnified moments." As Hochschild defines them, magnified moments are "episodes of heightened importance, either epiphanies, moments of intense glee or unusual insight, or moments in which things go intensely but meaningfully wrong. In either case, the moment stands out; it is metaphorically rich, unusually elaborate and often echoes" (1994, 4). The notion of "return" has been conceptualized in the scholarly literature primarily as "return migration," which refers to "the movement of emigrants back to their homelands to resettle" (Gmelch 1980, 136). *Return visits*, distinct from return migration, allow migrants to "maintain multiple, yet socially meaningful, identities in both their current place of residence and their external homeland" (Duval 2004, 51). Return visits are what Hochschild might call "magnified moments" in the transnational activities of immigrants. Much of Hochschild's empirical work centers on magnified moments of social life. In a study of overworked parents, for example, we learn about the moment when parents drop their children off at day care centers (Hochschild 1997). These moments magnify the social organization of time and the unequal relations between children and adults within and between the care center and the outside world. It is a moment that tells us about an entire way of viewing a culture of care (Hochschild 1995).

Magnifying Moments in the Vietnamese Diaspora

In this chapter, I tell the stories of two men whom I met in the course of conducting a larger study on the emergence of a transnational marriage market linking women in Vietnam and Vietnamese men living and working in Vietnamese immigrant communities in the United States (Thai 2008). During fourteen months of fieldwork done in distinct intervals in Vietnam and in the United

States from 1997 to 2001, I got to know a total of sixty-nine transpacific marriages in the Vietnamese diaspora. In this distinct and emergent global marriage market, the immigrant Vietnamese men typically go to Vietnam to marry through arrangement, subsequently returning to their places of residence in the Vietnamese diaspora (most are from the United States, Canada, France, and Australia) to initiate paperwork to sponsor their wives. During this waiting period, I came to know them by first entering the lives of the brides in Vietnam and later the U.S.-based grooms (Thai 2008). In the process of these marital arrangements, most of the grooms had returned to Vietnam for the first time since their emigration from Vietnam. That is, the first time they met their wives was also the first time that many of them returned to their home country after some years of being away.

Return migration in order to resettle in their homeland is rare for the overseas Vietnamese population, making the return visit an important social practice. Compared to the situations of other Asian immigrants, it is relatively difficult for immigrants in the postwar Vietnamese diaspora to reintegrate and resettle back to Vietnam. Most postwar Vietnamese immigrants left Vietnam as political refugees during the last quarter of the twentieth century (Long 2004). For these return migrants, it is complicated to buy land and property, as well as to obtain paperwork for long-term residence. In fact, return visits have only recently been made possible due to changes in national policies by the Vietnamese government and recent international diplomatic relations among nation-states, particularly between the United States and Vietnam.[1] In 1986, after having no contact with most of the outside world for over a decade, the government of Vietnam adopted a new socioeconomic policy called *Doi Moi* (renovation), which did not end state ownership or central planning, but moved the country from complete state-sponsored socialism to partial free-market capitalism (Ebashi 1997; Morley and Nishihara 1997). The normalization of economic and social ties by 1995, the year when U.S. President Bill Clinton established full diplomatic relations with the country (Morley and Nishihara 1997), gradually increased the number of individuals from the Vietnamese diaspora who returned to Vietnam to visit family members or to vacation. Return visits, therefore, are an important social practice that enables migrants to sustain transnational family ties. It is a crucial magnified moment for Vietnamese emigrants who begin to take on transnational identities. The Vietnamese government estimates that there are currently more than one million overseas Vietnamese who return to visit annually, a dramatic increase from 87,000 in 1992 and 8,000 in 1988 (Thomas 1997).

The analysis in this chapter is based on the *first* return visit to Vietnam that the men took to meet their future wives as well as subsequent trips they took while their wives waited in Vietnam for paper clearance to migrate. Indeed, these are not just moments of meeting their wives-to-be, but are also extraordinary moments of a transnational journey. Some of them had only returned to

Vietnam for the first time for the sole purpose of marriage, while for others the first return visit may have prompted a desire for a transpacific marriage. These visits are not just based on nostalgic notions such as "home" and "roots." They are embedded in complicated emotional desires, to be sure, but these visits also have powerful implications for destabilizing and altering myriad social relations in the community of origin. They produce new social hierarchies along class and gender lines as well as restore traditions that have been seemingly abolished over time. I have discussed these implications and analyzed specific marriages elsewhere; in this chapter I take the opportunity to analyze return visits as an analytical category in the larger discussion on contemporary transnational cultures, particularly as return visits raise important questions about the meanings of work, marriage, and family among immigrants who are just beginning to form and organize transnational lives (Thai 2003a,2003b, 2008).

A fundamental concern here is the question of how transnational mobilities can simultaneously challenge as well as reinforce patriarchy. "Instead of being a social equalizer that empowers all migrants alike," Luis Guarnizo argues, "transnational migration tends to reproduce and even exacerbate class, gender, and regional inequalities" (1997, 281). In her study of Filipino transnational communities, Yen Le Espiritu notes that the idealization of the home "becomes problematic when it elicits a nostalgia for a glorious past that never was, a nostalgia that elides exclusion, power relations, and difference or when it elicits a desire to replicate these inequities as a means to buttress lost status and identities in the adopted country" (2003, 15). The fact that men in my study returned to Vietnam for a spouse is a telling story about gender relations in their transnational journey from Vietnam to the West and back to their homeland. In my interviews with informants about their transnational networks and in my more than twenty-five trips to Vietnam to do fieldwork since 1997, I always heard people telling me that return visits were made generally first by men, followed by women and children in later return visits. But, in general, single men are some of the first groups of people who return to Vietnam, some for the sole purpose of finding a wife. For many men in this study, return visits to Vietnam elicited enormous emotions and shifts in their identities that help to remake class and masculinity in powerful ways.

Masculinity

At the most basic level of cultural ideology, masculinity is a "personal and collective project" that often assumes an association between breadwinning and manhood (Donaldson 1993, 645). In the mid-1980s, a "new sociology of masculinity" was proposed in order to critically examine power relations among men and between men and women (Carrigan, Connell, and Lee 1985). Since that framework was introduced, much of the scholarly work on the topic invokes the plural *masculinities* to account for the diverse range of men's experiences.

Although most scholars agree that masculinity does not constitute a singular ideology or practice, it is clustered around what Connell calls "hegemonic masculinity," which "asserts the naturalness of male domination, based on solidarities between men as well as on the subordination of women" (Connell 1995; Jackson 1991, 201). While the notion of hegemonic masculinity is directly linked to the institution of male dominance, few men actually embody it, although most men "benefit from the patriarchal dividend of dominance over women" (Kendall 2000). And although hegemonic masculinity operates across the spectrum, most scholars agree that it often marginalizes working-class men while excluding men of color and gay men. As Donaldson has pointed out, the salient analysis in studies of contemporary manhood is the relationship between social class and masculinity; for some men, for example, class privilege may minimize other kinds of marginality (such as racial marginality) (1993).

Studying low-wage immigrant men beginning to build and sustain transnational ties to their homeland helps to shed light on the effects of global and transnational forces on gender relations in immigrant communities and the homeland. This task is a particularly important one because immigrants are more and more frequently turning to their home countries for social, economic, and political activities. Furthermore, as Robert Courtney Smith explains, immigrant men "are seen to want to return home or to imagine themselves returning, whereas women want to settle or imagine themselves settling, because men lose status and power in the United States and women gain them" (2006, 13). The narratives of the men in this study reveal how low-wage immigrant men construct their masculinity given that their lives are placed "at the intersection and interstices of vast systems of power: patriarchy, racism, colonialism, and capitalism, to name a few" (Chen 1999, 589).

In what follows, I consider intersecting aspects of these Vietnamese low-wage immigrant men's lives that precede and follow their return visits to their communities of origin. For analytical clarity, I supply narratives of two men, Chanh and Loc, to illustrate two different patterns by which men take on, redefine, or challenge meanings of masculinity as they move from the categories of refugees to immigrants to transmigrants through return visits to their homeland.[2] The stories of these two men offer an exploratory look at how some men "achieve" and others "restore" masculinity across transnational social fields. Examining the interview data revealed these distinct patterns among Vietnamese immigrant men just beginning to develop transnational identities.[3]

Achieving Masculinity

Among men who *achieve* masculinity through their return visits, most migrated as children and generally did not have experiences with the labor market prior to their emigration from Vietnam. These men had a mixture of socioeconomic backgrounds as children, but for the most part, they were low-wage working adults. Except for a few men who worked in ethnic enterprises such as nail salons, where average hourly wages ranged from eight dollars to twelve dollars per hour, the Vietnamese American low-wage men in this study generally earned on average from six dollars to eight dollars per hour. These men usually worked in hourly wage, secondary labor-market jobs that offered them little stability (Sakamoto and Chen 1991). For the most part, they worked long hours for low pay. Their yearly salaries ranged between $8,000 and $24,000, and many of them fell below the U.S. poverty level at the time I conducted fieldwork (Dalaker 2001). For many of these men, low-wage status frequently translated into low marriageability, which is directly related to their sense of masculinity (Thai 2003). Many of the men in this study pointed out that lack of financial resources in Vietnamese migrant communities made them less desirable marriage partners. Moreover, many of them also talked about their low-wage jobs as unrespectable, which they felt was connected to their sense of being a man. This link between work status and masculinity makes sense in light of other studies that have found that men are more likely than women to view their work lives as the most central aspect of their self-identity (Lamont 1992, 2000; Rubin 1976). Both temporarily and in the long run, return visits to their homeland frequently offered these men an opportunity to achieve masculinity by being able to transform their low-wage income and U.S. residency to greater disposable income and higher social status in Vietnam. Many spoke of how this wage convertibility offered them a sense of emotional belonging.

The story of Chanh Tran, a thirty-two-year-old jewelry repairman who lived near Seattle when I met him, illustrates how return visits allow some men to remake social class in order to achieve masculinity as they take up transnational identities. When I asked Chanh, for instance, how he felt the first time he made a return visit to Vietnam, he quickly explained to me, "As soon as the plane touched the airport, I knew there was something there for me. I definitely had the feeling that I was home." One of the ways in which class identity becomes so poignantly evident for the men in this study is the way in which they talk about the affordability of consumption in Vietnam, an indicator of how their low economic status took on different meanings as they returned to Vietnam. As a case in point, when I asked Chanh why he felt there was "something there" for him when the plane touched the airport, he explained, "Before I decided to come to Vietnam, I wanted to know what to expect, and so I talked to some of my friends who had gone, and to my cousin who made visits to Vietnam. Most of the men told me how everything in Saigon is catered to men, that everywhere you go, it's really cheap and you can have a good time without having much money, and everyone treats you very nicely."

Chanh's family migrated to the United States when he was seven, being part of the first large group of Vietnamese refugees evacuated directly out of Vietnam a few days before the fall of Saigon on April 30, 1975.[4] Chanh came of age in a suburban town two hours outside of Seattle in a family of four. His father worked on the assembly line at a factory when they arrived in the United States, eventually becoming a manager of the plant, while his mother took on nursing as an occupation. Chanh said he was an ambitious student in high school, excelling in math and sports. He "confessed," as he framed it, that he was enamored early in his life by the idea of having money because one of his uncles owned a lucrative jewelry store near where they lived. "I wanted to earn as much money as I could, to help my parents, and to provide for my future family," he explained. Many of the immigrant men I spoke to in this study made strong links between making money and providing for their families, including their wives and parents, as crucial to their identity as men. For this reason, and although he graduated in the top tenth of his high school class, Chanh decided not to attend college immediately after high school, but instead took on an apprenticeship with his prosperous uncle. Chanh earned more than his friends after high school, but over time his income stagnated as his friends who went on to college eventually earned more than he did. When I met him, Chanh had not been able to open up his own jewelry store as he had hoped, and he was still earning by the hour working for his uncle. Reflecting on his choice of work, Chanh told me he had strong regrets for not having gone to college. He said he felt extremely marginal in his circle of friends, especially in the Vietnamese communities and networks in which he and his family were embedded. "I definitely think that there is a stigma for not having a college degree, and most people in the Vietnamese community I know who came to the United States the same time I did went to college. I regret not having gone to college because it definitely gave me less status in the community. At the time that I decided on not going [to college], I thought that I would eventually open a jewelry store like my uncle and would make a lot of money."

Some scholars have argued that the homeland "is not only a physical place that immigrants return to for temporary and intermittent visits, but also a concept and a desire—a place that immigrants visit through the imagination" (Espiritu 2003, 10). I contend that it is precisely the magnified moment of the return visit that allows some immigrants to realize their social status and to take on their economic privilege relative to the people in their homeland. In short, crossing physical boundaries also results in the crossing of social boundaries and a change of social contexts. For instance, when I asked Chanh to elaborate on the moment his plane landed during his first visit in 1998, he explained, "When we landed, the moment we stepped outside the airport and got a taxi to drive to my uncle's house, everything was cheap. I could afford to pay for taxis and other things that I couldn't pay in the U.S. The rest of the trip was awesome because I was able to pay for many of the times we went out."

Restoring Masculinity

Among the men in this study, only 30 percent (n = 21/69) migrated when they were under the age of eighteen. The vast majority—70 percent—of the men in this study were adult migrants, having come of age in their homeland. It is these men for whom, through return visits, *restoring* masculinity was made possible by developing transnational ties to their homeland. Thus, I use the term "restore" to capture an experience of social class directly linked to masculinity that was lost due to migration and, perhaps, regained upon making return visits. Men who restored masculinity differed from men who achieved masculinity primarily because the former group had reached adulthood in their homeland before emigration and had either entered or finished secondary education before they arrived on Western soil; many of them had already entered the labor market prior to migrating abroad. Moreover, most of them were unable to translate or transfer their skills or social status once they migrated to the West. In other words, these men, if they had done so at all, had achieved masculinity in their homeland before they migrated, but they experienced tremendous downward mobility and a resulting diminution of their sense of masculinity as a result of migration. The visits to their homeland served to restore their masculinity.

The story of forty-four-year-old Loc Phan highlights how migration can bring substantial loss to one's sense of status, especially when the homeland is drawn upon as the reference point for understanding one's position in the global status hierarchy. As part of the urban middle class in Saigon, Loc aspired to become a physician after he graduated from high school in 1974, but his parents told him that he could not attend college because they wanted to start making preparations to leave Vietnam when the war ended. His father had connections in the Mekong Delta with someone who organized boat trips for potential refugees to go to another Southeast Asian country so they could be "processed" by various Western countries as political asylees. Eventually, Loc's family became boat refugees and arrived in a suburb of Orange County where his parents had family ties. At the time that I met him, Loc was working for minimum wage in the produce department at a large ethnic supermarket near the ethnic enclave of Little Saigon in Orange County. He had been working there for nearly fifteen years, after a number of odd jobs in various ethnic enterprises, and had been living with his parents in government subsidized housing since 1979, when they arrived in the United States after spending a few years in the refugee camp in Malaysia. Loc had hoped that, over time, he could start his own business. But working in low-wage work meant that he could not save enough capital to start any kind of business.

In talking about the pre-migration years, Loc revealed that his childhood was one of privilege by any global measure—he grew up in a household with successful parents who owned a factory that produced office furniture for the domestic market. As an adolescent, Loc had luxuries he never encountered as a young adult: domestic servants, chauffeurs, and the best education available in his context. It was this affluence that shaped how Loc understood his social standing as a young man coming of age in the cultural context in Vietnam. As a high school graduate in 1974, nearing the end of the war in Vietnam, Loc had already formed a romantic relationship with a classmate, to whom he had promised marriage prior to his family's migration. When I asked him what happened to that first romantic relationship, Loc explained, "Well, of course, I told her that I would return in a few years and marry her. But that didn't happen. The bad part of it is that I couldn't afford to go back there until two years ago, and of course I don't expect her to wait for me for that long. I thought I would be sad, but when I came back to Vietnam for the first time, there were so many people I met, so many old friends. So I wanted to make new relationships, meet new people, maybe find a wife on that trip."

For these men, restoring masculinity was possible most often because they were able to develop a triangular relationship based on identifiable historical and geographical places that connect them to the community to which they migrated and to the community from which they originated (Guarnizo and Smith 1998b, 13). In other words, the men in my study were able to restore masculinity only because they had built a transnational status system through their migration that linked their community of origin and community of destination. The effect is that such men are able to restore masculinity upon their return to the homeland precisely because of the economic divide between their homeland and their immigrant communities that offered them the opportunity to "convert" their low wages from the West to high status on their return visits to Vietnam (Thai 2005). Partly because of the lack of knowledge about life in the United States, Loc's relatives and friends in Vietnam frequently thought of migration as desirable, which enhanced his status when he returned home. As Loc explained, "I saw many people of my youth, some of them became very successful in Saigon, but they did not judge me for what I do in the United States. Some really wanted to find ways to go to the United States. I don't know why they want to. I think they have much better lives in Saigon. But they always think the United States is a land of opportunity. They don't know that it's hard to make money unless you have a lot of money."

Yet it is precisely this perception of the United States among locals in Vietnam and Loc's ability to convert low wages to high status in Vietnam that offered him the opportunity to remake notions of social class in the context of a transnational status system. When I asked Loc to recount how he felt during the first visit back, he described his feelings in this way:

> When I returned to Vietnam for the first time, I didn't know for sure if I was going to tell people that I worked at the supermarket all these years. But when I went there, I remember not feeling as poor as I do in America! So even for many people I knew in Saigon, my job at the supermarket was a dream job. I remember this very clearly because the first time I went back in 1998, they opened up one of the first Western-style supermarkets in Saigon and I took some of my friends there and I told them with this feeling of shame that I work at one of those places in the United States. And some of them told me they thought it was a great job! [*Laughs*] I didn't feel like I was this poor man like I do in the United States working in a job that no one cares about.

Remaking Class and Masculinity through Return Visits and Transnational Ties

I have suggested that Hochschild's notion of magnified moments sheds light on the linkage between masculinity and social class through a focus on homeland return visits. Return visits are powerful moments for low-wage immigrant men in the Vietnamese diaspora, potentially transforming how the social construction of gender and class can be reworked in transnational contexts. Such visits to Vietnam have the potential of eliciting enormous emotions and a strong sense of belonging to the homeland among Vietnamese immigrant men. I suggest that return visits produce and fashion such emotions in ways that remake class and masculinity in the context of transnational ties. Among immigrants, social class and gender relations are particularly enmeshed as men take on new identities across international borders, especially among men who potentially have more to benefit from returning to their homeland. A number of prominent scholars have made it clear that migration powerfully reshapes gender relations in post-migrant communities (Espiritu 1997; Hondagneu-Sotelo 1994; Hondagneu-Sotelo 2003; Kibria 1993). But few have studied how return visits to the homeland can alter or amplify gender relations during the post-migration years, especially how men take on new gender ideologies and meanings of social class after making return visits to the homeland.

NOTES

This chapter is based on a paper presented at the 2008 Annual Meetings of the American Sociological Association in Boston and an invited lecture at Loyola Marymount University in Los Angeles. I would like to express gratitude to Anita Garey and Karen Hansen for generous feedback on the chapter.

1. When one speaks of postwar Vietnamese returnees to their homeland, it should be understood in the context of the origin of mass refugee migration when the Vietnamese represented the core group of refugees who fled Southeast Asia shortly after the withdrawal of American troops from Vietnam and the fall of Saigon on April 30, 1975.
2. To protect the privacy of informants, all names have been changed. As well, I have changed the names of villages in Vietnam and small towns in the United States. I have kept the real names of all metropolitan areas. And while full Vietnamese names are usually indicated in the order of last, middle, and first names, I will use "American" standards of referencing names, since I used this format when I got to know informants.
3. These patterns should be viewed as Weberian ideal types. Some men undergo multiple, sometimes overlapping, patterns of change.
4. Although Saigon's name was changed to Ho Chi Minh City when the South surrendered to Northern Vietnamese military troops in 1975, most people I met in contemporary Vietnam still refer to the city as "Saigon," or simply "Thanh Pho" [The City]. I echo their frames of reference by using the name "Saigon," and "Saigonese" to refer to the locals there.

REFERENCES

Brettell, Caroline B. 2006. "Global Spaces/Local Spaces: Transnationalism, Diaspora, and the Meaning of Home." *Identities* 13:327–334.

Carrigan, Tim, Bob Connell, and John Lee. 1985. "Toward a New Sociology of Masculinity." *Theory and Society* 14:551–604.

Chen, Anthony S. 1999. "Lives at the Center of the Periphery, Lives at the Periphery of the Center." *Gender & Society* 13:584–607.

Chiswick, Barry R. 1982. "Immigrants in the U.S. Labor Market." *Annals of the American Academy of Political and Social Science* (March): 64–72.

Connell, Raewyn W. 1995. *Masculinities.* Berkeley: University of California Press.

Dalaker, Joseph. 2001. "U.S. Census Bureau, Current Population Reports, Series P60–214, Poverty in the United States: 2000." Washington, DC: U.S. Government Printing Office.

Donaldson, Michael. 1993. "What Is Hegemonic Masculinity?" *Theory and Society* 22:643–657.

Duval, David Timothy. 2004. "Linking Return Visits and Return Migration among Commonwealth Eastern Caribbean Migrants in Toronto." *Global Networks* 4:51–67.

Ebashi, Masahiko. 1997. "The Economic Take-Off." In *Vietnam Joins the World,* edited by James Morley and Masashi Nishihara, 37–65. Armonk, NY: M. E. Press.

Espiritu, Yen Le. 1997. *Asian American Women and Men: Labor, Laws and Love.* Thousand Oaks, CA: Sage Publications.

———. 1999. "Gender and Labor in Asian Immigrant Families." *American Behavioral Scientist* 42:628–647.

———. 2003. *Home Bound: Filipino American Lives across Cultures, Communities, and Countries.* Berkeley: University of California Press.

Gmelch, George. 1980. "Return Migration." *Annual Review of Anthropology* 9:135–159.

Guarnizo, Luis E. 1997. "The Emergence of a Transnational Social Formation and the Mirage of Return Migration among Dominican Transmigrants." *Identities: Global Studies in Culture and Power* 4:281–322.

Guarnizo, Luis E., Alejandro Portes, and William Haller. 2003. "Assimilation and Transnationalism: Determinants of Transnational Political Action among Contemporary Migrants." *American Journal of Sociology* 108:1211–1248.

Guarnizo, Luis E., and Michael P. Smith. 1998a. *Transnationalism from Below.* New Brunswick, NJ: Transaction.

———. 1998b. "The Location of Transnationalism." In *Transnationalism from Below,* edited by Michael P. Smith and Luis Guarnizo, 3–34. New Brunswick, NJ: Transaction.

Hochschild, Arlie Russell. 1994. "The Commercial Spirit of Intimate Life and the Abduction of Feminism: Signs from Women's Advice Books." *Theory, Culture, and Society* 11:1–24.

———. 1995. "The Culture of Politics: Traditional, Postmodern, Cold-Modern, and Warm-Modern Ideals of Care." *Social Politics* 2:331–346.

———. 1997. *The Time Bind: When Work Becomes Home and Home Becomes Work.* New York: Metropolitan Books.

———, with Anne Machung. 2003. *The Second Shift: Working Parents and the Revolution at Home.* New York: Penguin.

Hondagneu-Sotelo, Pierrette. 1994. *Gendered Transitions: Mexican Experiences of Immigration.* Berkeley: University of California Press.

———. 2003. *Gender and U.S. Immigration: Contemporary Trends.* Berkeley: University of California Press.

Jackson, Peter. 1991. "The Cultural Politics of Masculinity: Towards a Social Geography." *Transactions of the Institute of British Geographers* 16:199–213.

Kendall, Lori. 2000. "'Oh No! I'm a Nerd!' Hegemonic Masculinity on an Online Forum" *Gender & Society* 14:256–274.

Kibria, Nazli. 1993. *Family Tightrope: The Changing Lives of Vietnamese Americans.* Princeton, NJ: Princeton University Press.

Lamont, Michèle. 1992. *Money, Morals, and Manners: The Culture of the French and the American Upper-Middle Class.* Chicago: University of Chicago Press.

———. 2000. *The Dignity of Working Men: Morality and the Boundaries of Race, Class, and Immigration.* New York: Russell Sage Foundation.

Long, Lynellyn D. 2004. "Viet Kieu on a Fast Track Back." In *Coming Home? Refugees, Migrants, and Those Who Stayed Behind,* edited by Ellen Oxfeld and Lynellyn D. Long, 65–89. Philadelphia: University of Pennsylvania Press.

Morley, James W., and Masashi Nishihara. 1997. "Vietnam Joins the World." In *Vietnam Joins the World*, edited by James W. Morley and Masashi Nishihara, 3–14. Armonk NY: M. E. Press.

Rubin, Lillian Breslow. 1976. *Worlds of Pain: Life in the Working-Class Family*. New York: Basic Books.

Sakamoto, Arthur, and Meichu D. Chen. 1991. "Inequality and Attainment in a Dual Labor Market." *American Sociological Review* 56:295–308.

Schiller, Nina Glick, Linda Basch, and Cristina Blanc-Szanton. 1992. "Transnationalism: A New Analytic Framework for Understanding Migration." In *Towards a Transnational Perspective on Migration*, edited by N. G. Schiller, L. Basch, and C. Blanc-Szanton, 1–24. New York: New York Academy of Sciences.

Smith, Robert Courtney. 2006. *Mexican New York: Transnational Lives of New Immigrants*. Berkeley: University of California Press.

Thai, Hung Cam. 2003a. "Clashing Dreams: Highly Educated Overseas Brides and Low-Wage U.S. Husbands." In *Global Woman: Nannies, Maids and Sex Workers in the New Economy*, edited by B. Ehrenreich and A. R. Hochschild, 230–253. New York: Metropolitan Books.

———. 2003b. "The Vietnamese Double Gender Revolt: Globalizing Marriage Options in the Twenty-first Century." *Amerasia Journal* 29:51–74.

———. 2005. "Globalization as a Gender Strategy: Respectability, Masculinity, and Convertibility across the Vietnamese Diaspora." In *Critical Globalization Studies*, edited by R. P. Appelbaum and W. I. Robinson, 76–92. New York: Routledge.

———. 2008. *For Better or for Worse: Vietnamese International Marriages in the New Global Economy*. New Brunswick, NJ: Rutgers University Press.

Thomas, Mandy. 1997. "Crossing Over: The Relationship between Overseas Vietnamese and Their Homeland." *Journal of Intercultural Studies* 18:153–176.

Vertovec, Steven. 2004. "Migrant Transnationalism and Modes of Transformation." *International Migration Review* 38:970–1001.

Waters, Mary. 1999. "West Indians and African Americans at Work: Structural Differences and Cultural Stereotypes." In *Immigration and Opportunity: Race, Ethnicity and Employment in the United States*, edited by Frank Bean and Stephanie Bell Rose, 194–227. New York: Russell Sage Press.

Wright, Eric Olin. 1997. *Class Counts: Comparative Studies in Class Analysis*. New York: Cambridge University Press.

Yamane, Linus. 2001. "The Labor Market Status of Foreign Born Vietnamese Americans." Claremont Colleges Working Papers, 2001–15. Claremont, CA.

CHAPTER 21

Childbirth at the Global Crossroads

Arlie Russell Hochschild

The auto-rickshaw driver honks his way through the dusty chaos of Anand, Gujarat, India, swerving around motorbikes, grunting trucks, and ancient large-wheeled bullock-carts packed with bags of fodder. Both sides of the street are lined with plastic trash and small piles of garbage on which untethered cows feed. The driver turns off the pavement onto a narrow, pitted dirt road, slows to circumvent a pair of black and white spotted goats, and stops outside a dusty courtyard. To one side stands a modest white building with a sign that reads, in English and Gujarati, "Akanksha Clinic."

Two dozen dainty Indian women's sandals, toes pointed forward, are lined along the front porch. For it is with bare feet that one enters a clinic housing what may be the world's largest group of gestational surrogates—women who rent their wombs to incubate the fertilized eggs from clients from around the globe. Since India declared commercial surrogacy legal in 2002, some three hundred and fifty assisted reproductive technology (ART) clinics have opened their doors. Surrogacy is now a burgeoning part of India's medical tourism industry, which is slated to add $2 billion to the nation's gross domestic product by 2012. Advertisements describe India as a "global doctor" offering First World skill at Third World prices, short waits, privacy, and—important in the case of surrogacy—absence of red tape. To encourage this lucrative trend, the Indian government gives tax breaks to private hospitals treating overseas patients and lowers import duties on medical supplies.

In his 2007 book, *Supercapitalism*, Robert B. Reich argues that while industrial and clerical jobs could be outsourced to cheaper labor pools abroad, service jobs would stay in America. But Reich didn't count on First World clients flying to the global South to find low-cost retirement care or reproductive services. The Akanksha clinic is just one point on an ever-widening two-lane global highway that connects poor nations in the Southern Hemisphere to rich nations in the Northern Hemisphere, and poorer countries of Eastern Europe to richer ones in the West. A Filipina nanny heads north to care for an American child. A Sri Lankan maid cleans a house in Singapore. A Ukrainian nurse's aide carries lunch trays in a Swedish hospital. Marx's iconic male, stationary industrial worker has been replaced by a new icon: the female, mobile service worker.

We have grown used to the idea of a migrant worker caring for our children and even to the idea of hopping an overseas flight for surgery. As global service work grows increasingly personal, surrogacy is the latest expression of this trend. Nowadays, a wealthy person can purchase it all—the egg, the sperm, and time in the womb. "A childless couple gains a child. A poor woman earns money. What could be the problem?" asks Dr. Nayna Patel, Akanksha's founder and director.

But despite Patel's view of commercial surrogacy as a straightforward equation, it's far more complicated for both the surrogates and the genetic parents. Like nannies or nurses, surrogates perform "emotional labor" to suppress feelings that could interfere with doing their job. Parents must decide how close they are willing (or able) to get to the woman who will give birth to their child.

As science and global capitalism gallop forward, they kick up difficult questions about emotional attachment. What, if anything, is too sacred to sell? I follow a kindly embryologist, Harsha Bhadarka, to an upstairs office of the clinic to talk with two surrogates whom I will call Geeta and Saroj. (Aditya Ghosh, a journalist with the *Hindustan Times*, has kindly offered to join me.) The room is small, and the two surrogate mothers enter nodding shyly. Both live on the second floor of the clinic, but most of its twenty-four residents live in one of two hostels for the duration of their pregnancy. The women are brought nutritious food on tin trays, injected with iron (a common deficiency), and supervised away from prying in-laws, curious older children, and lonely husbands with whom they are allowed no visits home or sex.

Geeta, a twenty-two-year-old light-skinned, green-eyed beauty, is the mother of three daughters, one of whom is sitting quietly and wide-eyed on her lap. To be accepted as a surrogate, Akanksha requires a woman to be a healthy, married mother. As one doctor explains, "If she has children of her own, she'll be less tempted to attach herself to the baby."

"How did you decide to become a surrogate?" I ask.

"It was my husband's idea," Geeta replies. "He makes *pav bhaji* [a vegetable dish] during the day and serves food in the evening [at a street-side fast-food shop]. He heard about surrogacy from a customer at his shop, a Muslim like us. The man told my husband, 'It's a good thing to do,' and then I came to madam [Dr. Patel] and offered to try. We can't live on my husband's earnings, and we had no hope of educating our daughters."

Geeta says she has only briefly met the parents whose genes her baby carries. "They're from far away. I don't know where," she says. "They're Caucasian, so the baby will come out white." The money she has been promised, including a monthly stipend to cover vitamins and medications, is wired to a bank account that Patel has opened in Geeta's name. "I keep myself from getting too attached," she says. "Whenever I start to think about the baby inside me, I turn my attention to my own daughter. Here she is." She bounces the child on her lap. "That way, I manage."

Seated next to Geeta is Saroj, a heavy-set, dark woman with intense, curious eyes, and, after a while, an easy smile. Like other Hindu surrogates at Akanksha, she wears *sindoor* (a red powder applied to the part in her hair) and *mangalsutra* (a necklace with a gold pendant), both symbols of marriage. She is, she tells us, the mother of three children and the wife of a vegetable street vendor. She gave birth to a surrogate child a year and three months ago and is waiting to see if a second implantation has taken. The genetic parents are from Bangalore, India. (It is estimated that half the clients seeking surrogacy from Indian ART clinics are Indian and the other half, foreign. Of the foreign clients, roughly half are American.) Saroj, too, knows almost nothing about her clients. "They came, saw me, and left," she says.

Given her husband's wages, 1,260 rupees (or $25) a month, Saroj turned to surrogacy so she could move to a rain-proof house and feed her family well. Yet she faced the dilemma of all rural surrogates: being suspected of adultery—a cause for shunning or worse. I ask the women whether the money they earn has improved their social standing. For the first time the two women laugh out loud and talk to each other excitedly. "My father-in-law is dead, and my mother-in-law lives separately from us, and at first I hid it from her," Saroj says. "But when she found out, she said she felt blessed to have a daughter-in-law like me because I've given more money to the family than her son could. But some friends ask me why I am putting myself through all this. I tell them, 'It's my own choice.'"

Since Dr. Patel began offering surrogacy services in 2004, 232 surrogates have given birth at Akanksha. A 2007 study of forty-two Akanksha surrogates found that nearly half described themselves as housewives and the rest were a mix of domestic, service, and manual laborers. Hindu, Muslim, and Christian, most had seventh to twelfth grade educations, six were illiterate, and one—who turned to surrogacy to pay for a small son's heart surgery—had a bachelor's degree. Each surrogate negotiates a different sum: one surrogate carrying twins for an Indian couple discovered she was being paid less (about $3,600) than a surrogate in the next bed who was carrying one baby for an American couple for about $5,600.

Observers fear that a lack of regulation could spark a price war for surrogacy—Thailand underselling India, Cambodia underselling Thailand, and so on—with countries slowly undercutting fees and legal protections for surrogates along the way. It could happen. Right now international surrogacy is a highly complex legal patchwork. Surrogacy is banned in China and much of Europe. It is legal but regulated in New Zealand and Great Britain. Only seventeen of the United States have laws on the books; it is legal in Florida and banned in New York.

In India, commercial surrogacy is legal but unregulated, although a 135-page regulatory law, long in the works, will be sent to Parliament later this year. Even if the law is passed, however, some argue it would do little to improve life for women such as Geeta and Saroj. For example, it specifies that the doctor, not the surrogate, has the right to decide on any "fetal reduction" (an abortion). Moreover, most Indian federal laws are considered "advisory" to powerful state governments, and courts—where a failure to enforce such laws might be challenged—are backlogged for years, often decades. Dr. B. N. Chakravarty, the Calcutta-based chair of the surrogacy law drafting committee, says that the growth of the industry is "inevitable," but it needs regulating. Even if the law were written to protect surrogates and then actually enforced, it would do nothing to address the crushing poverty that often presses Indian women to "choose" surrogacy in the first place.

For N. B. Sarojini, director of the Delhi-based Sama Resource Group for Women and Health, a nonprofit feminist research institute, the problem is one of distorted priorities. "The ART clinics are posing themselves as the answer to an illusory 'crisis' of infertility," she says. "Two decades back, a couple might consider themselves 'infertile' after trying for five years to conceive. Then it moved to four years. Now couples rush to ARTs after one or two. Why not put the cultural spotlight on *alternatives*? Why not urge childless women to adopt orphans? And what, after all, is wrong with remaining childless?"

But Dr. Patel, a striking woman in an emerald green sari and with black hair flowing down her back, sees for-profit surrogacy as a "win-win" for the clinic, the surrogate, and the genetic parents. She also sees no problem with running the clinic like a business, seeking to increase inventory, safeguard quality, and improve efficiency. That means producing more babies, monitoring surrogates' diet and sexual contact, and assuring a smooth, emotion-free exchange of baby for money. (For every dollar that goes to the surrogates, observers estimate, three go to the clinic.) In Akanksha's hostel, women sleep on cots, nine to a room, for nine months. Their young children sleep with them; older children do not stay in the hostel. The women exercise inside the hostel, rarely leaving it and then only with permission. Patel also advises surrogates to limit contact with clients. Staying detached from the genetic parents, she says, helps surrogate mothers give up their babies and get on with their lives—and maybe with the next surrogacy. This ideal of the depersonalized pregnancy is eerily reminiscent of Aldous Huxley's 1932 dystopian novel *Brave New World*, in which babies are emotionlessly mass produced in the Central London Hatchery.

Patel's business may seem coldly efficient, but it also has a touch of Mother Teresa. Akanksha residents are offered daily English classes and weekly lessons in computer use. Patel arranges for film screenings and gives out school backpacks and pencil boxes to surrogates' children. She hopes to attract donations from grateful clients to help pay children's school fees as well. "For me, this is a mission," Patel says.

In light of appalling government neglect of a population totally untouched by India's recent economic boom, this charity sounds wonderful. But is it wonderful enough to cancel out concerns about the factory?

After leaving Anand, I head to Dr. Nandita Palshetkar's office in Mumbai. With Alifiya Khan, another journalist from the *Hindustan Times*, I meet with Leela, a lively twenty-eight-year-old who gave birth to a baby for Indian clients about six months ago. Like Geeta and Saroj, Leela had been desperate for money, but her experience of pregnancy was utterly different. On the day I meet her, she is dressed in a pink sari, hair drawn back from her olive-skinned face into a long black braid. She leans forward, smiling broadly, eager to talk about her baby, his genetic parents, and her feelings about being a surrogate mother.

At age twenty, Leela married a fellow worker at a Mumbai-based company canteen. "I didn't know he was alcoholic until after we married," she says. "My husband ran up a $7,000 debt with the moneylender who sent agents to pressure him to repay it. . . . We couldn't stop the moneylender from hounding us. I decided to act. I heard from my sister-in-law that I could get money for donating my eggs, and I did that twice. When I came back to do it a third time, madam [Dr. Palshetkar] told me I could earn more as a surrogate."

Was she able to pay off the debt? Leela lowers her head: "Half of it."

She ate better food during her paid pregnancy than during her other pregnancies and delivered the baby in a better hospital than the one where she delivered her own children. Unlike others I spoke with, Leela openly bonded with her baby. "I am the baby's *real* mother," she says. "I carried him. I felt him kick. I prayed for him. At seven months I held a celebration for him. I saw his legs and hands on the sonogram. I suffered the pain of birth."

The baby's genetic parents, Indians from a nearby affluent suburb, kindly reached out to Leela. The genetic mother "sees me as her little sister, and I see her as my big sister," Leela says. "They check in with me every month, even now, and call me the baby's 'auntie.' They asked if I wanted to see the baby. I said 'yes' and they brought him to my house, but I was disappointed to see he was long and fair, not like me. Still, to this day, I feel I have three children." A friendship of sorts arose between the two mothers, although Leela's doctor, like Patel, discouraged it. "I deleted their phone number from my list because madam told me it's not a good thing to keep contact for long," she says.

In a November 2008 *New York Times Magazine* article titled "Her Body, My Baby," American journalist Alex Kuczynski describes searching through profiles of available surrogates. "None were living in poverty," she writes. Cathy, the woman she eventually chose to carry her son, was a college-educated substitute teacher, a gifted pianist, and fellow fan of Barack Obama. They shared a land, a language, a level of education, a political bent—coming together to create a baby didn't seem like such a giant leap. But when the surrogate and genetic mother come from different corners of the globe—when one is an Indian woman who bails monsoon rains from her mud-floor hut and the other is an American woman who drives an SUV and vacations at ski resorts—the gap is more like a chasm. And as one childless American friend (rendered infertile through a defective Dalkon Shield intrauterine device) told me, "If I had hired a surrogate, I'm not sure how close I'd want to be to her. How open can you keep your heart when it's broken? Sometimes it's better not to touch unhealed wounds." A code of detachment seems almost necessary to circumvent the divide.

But detachment isn't so easy in practice. Even if you can separate the genetic parents from the surrogate, you cannot separate the surrogate from her womb. One surrogate mother told the sociologist Amrita Pande, "It's my blood, even if it's their genes." Psychologists tell us that a baby in utero recognizes the sound of its mother's voice. Surrogates I spoke with seemed to be struggling to detach. One said, "I try to think of my womb as a carrier." Another said, "I try not to think about it." Is the bond between mother and child fixed by nature or is it a culturally inspired fantasy we yearn to be true?

I asked Dr. Chakravarty if he thought that some children born of surrogacy would one day fly to India in search of their "womb mothers." (The proposed regulation requires parents to reveal to an inquiring child the fact of surrogacy, though not the identity of the surrogate.) "Yes," he said. But chances are such an eighteen-year-old would not find her womb mother. Instead, she might come to realize she had been made a whole person by uniting parts drawn from tragically unequal worlds.

In a larger sense, so are we all. Person to person, family to family, the First World is linked to the Third World through the food we eat, the clothes we wear, and the care we receive. That Filipina nanny who cares for an American child leaves her own children in the care of her mother and another nanny. In turn, that nanny leaves her younger children in the care of an eldest daughter. First World genetic parents pay a Third World woman to carry their embryo. The surrogate's husband cares for their older children. The worlds of rich and poor are invisibly bound through chains of care.

Before we leave the Akanksha clinic in Anand, the gentle embryologist, Bhadarka, remains across the table from Aditya and me after Geeta and Saroj have left the room. I ask Bhadarka if the clinic offers psychological counseling to the surrogates. "We explain the scientific process," she answers, "and they already know what they're getting into." Then she moves her hands across the table and adds softly, "In the end, a mother is a mother, isn't that true? In the birthing room there is the surrogate, the doctor, the nurse, the nurse's aide, and often the genetic mother. Sometimes we all cry."

ACKNOWLEDGMENTS

Reprinted from "Childbirth at the Global Crossroads," *The American Prospect* 20, no. 8 (October 5, 2009), by permission of The American Prospect, 1710 Rhode Island Avenue NW, Floor 12, Washington, DC 20036, www.prospect.org.

Special thanks to Aditya Ghosh and Alifiya Khan.

REFERENCES

Reich, Robert B. 2007. *Supercapitalism: The Transformation of Business, Democracy, and Everyday Life.* New York: Knopf Doubleday Publishing Group.

Huxley, Aldous. 1998 [1932]. *Brave New World.* New York: Harper Collins Publishers.

Kuczynski, Alex. 2008. "Her Body, My Baby." *New York Times,* November 28, 2008. http://www.nytimes.com/2008/11/30/magazine/30Surrogate-t.html.

Afterword

Arlie Russell Hochschild

Farmer Zuckerman, as this book's editors playfully remind us, was astonished to read the words "some pig" on a spiderweb in the barn on his farm. So in E. B. White's classic children's story, *Charlotte's Web*, farmer Zuckerman thought his pig must be a miracle and decided not to kill him for market. His wiser wife, Edith Zuckerman, recognizing skill and care when she saw them, replied, "Some *spider.*" In this extraordinary volume, the editors and authors apply a keen Edith Zuckerman–like eye to family and work life in America and beyond.

Over the years, in my office at the University of California at Berkeley, at the Center for Working Families, at conferences, over dinners, on hikes, over email, I've learned about many of these books' cutting-edge ideas from the amazing vantage point of a teacher. Let me just say a word about that. Many of these former students have shared arresting stories from their research all over the globe, alerted me to "must-read" books, proposed new ideas, and altogether enlarged my mind and soul. If Charlotte were weaving a message in her web about teachers, it would say "Learn." And if she were weaving a message in her web about students, it would say "Teach."

It has often been easier for me to discover a solution to problems in student research projects than to untie the tiresome knots in my own. But teaching isn't about correcting mistakes. For me, teaching has been far more like a collaborative treasure hunt. Virtually without exception the students I've worked with have come to me with brilliant core ideas. My job was to find and point. Sometimes the treasure was abbreviated in a breathless last paragraph. Sidelined in a footnote. Frozen in overly abstract language. Abducted by another thesis entirely. Sometimes it was front and central to begin with. Maybe the wisest teaching words I've said have been "*There* it is!" or "No, you *aren't* crazy." Or simply, "Great! Go into detail." So, to me, teaching is not about getting rid of the bad stuff but discovering the buried gems. Ideas, I believe, are formed early in life—not by our genes certainly, but by early family experiences—and whatever race, class, gender, sexuality, or national issues are embedded in them. Early family life shapes empathy, and empathy turns out to be the real jewel in the life of any researcher. There again, the main job of a teacher—certainly the initial job—is to recognize what a thinker has feelings about, and to follow them to their own unique contribution. So we have to rethink the usual view that "teachers teach" and "students learn." To these editors, these authors, and my other students, my deepest thanks for all you have taught me.

In a recent conversation, Anita Garey and Karen Hansen spoke with me about their project to "bring the family back in." The field of the sociology of the family has, they believe, been chipped away—part of it going to migration studies, other parts to the fields of class, race, sexuality, and gender, and still others to consumption studies—leaving the field of the family in a state of theoretical incoherence. It's almost as if the field had outsourced parts of its tasks to other specialties and hadn't asked itself what it now was. In the tradition of George Homans's classic piece, "Bringing the Men Back In"—itself a critique of hyperstructuralists—Karen and Anita argue for a central place for studies of families.

This is a powerful idea, and the essays here offer important leads in developing it. But if we are to bring the family back in, as the editors urge, it can't be the "same" family of theoretical yesteryear—not the family as passive reflector of economic waves (*à la* Marx), nor the family as a system of hierarchical roles (*à la* Parsons), nor the family of postmodernism (a different theory for each family.)

To bring the family back in, we need to invent a whole new vocabulary to describe exactly what, these days, we see. The family is a shock absorber of many trends originating outside itself—volatile capitalism, a widening class gap, shrinking government aid, immigration and globalization, to mention a few. As each set of trends is absorbed, new tensions emerge—between immigrants and settlers, rich and poor, white and non-white, right wing and left. In responding to each new pattern, the family acts as an emotional workshop.

We need to develop a conceptual tool kit and vocabulary to plumb these emergent tensions. Families are the original workshops for emotion. As Paul Russell, my late brother, a psychoanalyst, once remarked, reversing Descartes, "I *feel*, therefore I am," or "We *are* what we *feel*." It is through the family that we are *enabled* to feel as we do. It is through the family that we learn to expand or contract the circle within which we feel empathy. It is through the family that we uphold certain feelings and ride over others. The family introduces us to cultural prototypes of feeling—which, like differently tuned keys on a piano, allow us to hear different inner notes. Apart from telling us what a feeling *is*, families give us ideas about what in one situation or another feeling *should* be. Parents might tell a child, "You love your Uncle Fred" or "Christmas is fun." Or families simply imply. School is scary. Trust kin. Distrust marriage. Hate the government. Given our respective families' structures of feeling rules, we learn to manage our feelings, evoking optimism here, suppressing sadness there. It is through how we see, define, and appraise feelings that we, in turn, develop structures of feeling rules—the underside of ideologies—and develop the emotional toolkits with which to navigate life. Family is our first training camp.

All this does not mean we abandon a macroanalytic perspective; it means we understand macro trends in emotional terms. For example: we all know that other people direct—and sometimes inappropriately project—feelings on us. One day in an undergraduate Sociology 1 class, I asked students to describe a time when they felt that someone had seen them in a way that had to do more with the category—racial, gendered, etc.—they were part of than who they really were as an individual. A young Asian woman said she often felt that others assumed she was a math whiz and uninterested in art, when she actually struggled with math and excelled in art. A black male student said he felt that others assumed he must resent whites when, in truth, he took people one by one. A tall broad-shouldered white male felt that others saw him as privileged and prejudiced, while actually he was neither. Some, I came to think, were the objects of desirable projections (the projectively rich) and others the objects of undesirable projections (the projectively poor). It is at home that we learn both to project feelings onto others and to respond to projections others place upon us—refracted as these projected images are through society's prevailing ideological prisms.

Indeed, it is at home that we learn the basic ideological prisms themselves. Individualism, the dominant American ideology, leads each person to take personal credit for success and personal blame for failure. So in much of America, the rich feel pride and the poor feel shame. The homeless are ashamed of being homeless, the poor ashamed of being poor, the ill-educated ashamed of being ill-educated. So we are faced with two problems instead of one—the macro problem of scarce housing, poverty, poor schools, and the micro problem of feeling shame for being hurt by these problems. But it is in the family that the child learns a family's position in the national or international system of assigning pride and shame.

Families these days may be outsourcing some aspects of care, mate selection, and entertainment, but—now more than ever—families form the emotional center of life. They are where we learn to feel. If, as C. Wright Mills said, the job of sociology is to trace links between private troubles and public issues, then the sociology of emotion lies at the very heart of sociology—and of the family that Anita and Karen are "bringing back in." This book draws together key tools for doing so. So, in the spirit of Edith Zuckerman, and with gratitude and awe, let me say, these are *some* editors and authors.

Notes on Contributors

PATRICIA BERHAU completed a Ph.D. in the Department of Sociology at Temple University. Her dissertation, "Class and the Experiences of Consumers: A Study of the Practices of Acquisition," addressed her interests in the sociology of consumption and social stratification. After spending the last few years being the primary MESH coordinator for her own family, she recently accepted a position with a consumer counseling and education organization in New Jersey.

MARIANNE COOPER received her Ph.D. in sociology from the University of California at Berkeley. Arlie Russell Hochschild was her advisor and remains her personal and professional mentor. She feels deeply indebted to Arlie for everything she has taught her about the power and the practice of sociology, for giving her a model to aspire to of how to do sociology with creativity and brilliance, and for showing her how to be a sociologist with compassion and heart. Her research focuses on the intersections of family life, gender, work, emotions, and inequality. Her essay in this book is drawn from her forthcoming book, *Doing Security in Insecure Times.*

KIMBERLY MCCLAIN DACOSTA is associate professor and assistant dean of students in the Gallatin School at New York University. Her research explores intersections of cultural ideas about race, the family, and most recently consumption. She is the author of *Making Multiracials: State, Family and Market in the Redrawing of the Color Line* and is currently working on an ethnographic study of African American advertising firms. She had the good fortune to have Arlie as a teacher and advisor while in graduate school at Berkeley. Arlie is everything one could hope for in a mentor—smart, creative, and compassionate. Her work is a continual source of inspiration, a reminder of the promise of sociology for understanding the complexity of our world.

Marjorie L. DeVault is professor of sociology in the Maxwell School of Citizenship and Public Affairs at Syracuse University. Her research focuses on gender and work, including unpaid household and family work, and she has written extensively on qualitative and feminist research methodologies. She is the author of *Feeding the Family: The Social Organization of Caring as Gendered Work and Liberating Method: Feminism and Social Research*, and the editor of *People at Work: Life, Power, and Social Inclusion in the New Economy*. She is currently writing about family time outside the home.

Barbara Ehrenreich is the author of thirteen books, including the *New York Times* best seller *Nickel and Dimed*. A frequent contributor to the *New York Times*, *Harpers*, and the *Progressive*, she is a contributing writer to *Time* magazine. She lives in Virginia.

Rebecca J. Erickson is a professor of sociology at the University of Akron. Her earliest and most recent investigations target how the emotional demands facing human service workers influence individual and organizational outcomes. First introduced to the concept of emotion management as a graduate student, she has spent the past twenty years attempting to further social scientific understanding of Hochschild's original insights. To pay tribute to the far-reaching influence of *The Managed Heart*, she organized a special session at the annual meetings of the American Sociology Association in 2003 to commemorate the twentieth anniversary of the book's publication.

Anita Ilta Garey is associate professor of human development and family studies and sociology at the University of Connecticut. Her research and teaching focus on families and family members, particularly mothers, in relation to social institutions and within specific social and cultural contexts. Her book *Weaving Work and Motherhood* received the 2000 William J. Goode Book Award from the Family Section of the American Sociological Association. She coedited *Families in the U.S.: Kinship and Domestic Politics* (with Karen V. Hansen) and *Who's Watching: Daily Practices of Surveillance among Contemporary Families* (with Margaret K. Nelson). She feels extremely fortunate to have been mentored during graduate school and beyond by Arlie Hochschild, whose creative and generative practice brings out the best in her students. She is also immensely grateful to Karen V. Hansen for her unwavering support, friendship, intellectual camaraderie, and determination to get *At the Heart of Work and Family* out the door and into the hands of its readers.

Karen V. Hansen is professor of sociology and women's and gender studies at Brandeis University. She is the author of *Not-So-Nuclear Families: Class, Gender, and Networks of Care*, which received the William J. Goode Book Award, Honorable Mention, and *A Very Social Time: Crafting Community in Antebellum New England*. She feels exceedingly lucky to have taken that sociology of gender class from Arlie Hochschild in 1985, because in it she met Anita Garey, with whom she later edited *Families in the U.S.* and became lifelong friends. She also began to work with Arlie, a mentor who consistently inspires and emboldens her. A former Guggenheim fellow, she is now writing *Encounter on the Great Plains* about the unlikely coexistence of Dakota Indians and Scandinavian settlers.

ROSANNA HERTZ is the Luella LaMer Professor of Sociology and Women's Studies at Wellesley College, where she has taught since 1983. Her books include *Single by Chance, Mothers by Choice: How Women Are Choosing Parenthood without Marriage and Creating the New American Family* and *More Equal Than Others: Women and Men in Dual-Career Marriages.* She is the eightieth president of the Eastern Sociological Society. She enjoys browsing family blogs and mom Web sites.

ARLIE RUSSELL HOCHSCHILD is Professor Emerita at the University of California, Berkeley. Her books include *The Managed Heart, The Second Shift, The Time Bind, The Commercialization of Intimate Life,* and the coedited *Global Woman: Nannies, Maids and Sex Workers in the New Economy.* Her numerous awards for her work and achievement include the American Sociological Association's (ASA) Jessie Bernard Award in 2008, the ASA Public Understanding of Sociology Award in 2000, and Lifetime Achievement Awards from both the ASA Sociology of Emotions Section and the Anthropology of Work Section of the American Anthropological Association. Three of her books have been selected as "notable books of the year" by the *New York Times Book Review* and plays have been based on two. Her work has been translated into fourteen languages. She is currently finishing a book on emotional capitalism.

NAZLI KIBRIA is associate professor of sociology and director of graduate programs in sociology at Boston University, where she teaches courses on international migration, contemporary South Asia, and the sociology of childhood. She is also a member of the Executive Board of the Center for the Study of Asia at Boston University. Her publications include *Family Tightrope: The Changing Lives of Vietnamese Americans* and *Becoming Asian American.* She is currently working on a book about family and identity formations in the Bangladeshi diaspora.

PEI-CHIA LAN is associate professor of sociology at National Taiwan University. She was a postdoctoral fellow at the Center for Working Families at University of California, Berkeley, in 2000–2001 under the supervision of Arlie Hochschild and Barrie Thorne. Her fields of specialty include gender, work, and migration. She is the author of *Global Cinderellas: Migrant Domestics and Newly Rich Employers in Taiwan,* which won the 2007 Distinguished Book Award from the Sex and Gender Section of the American Sociological Association and the 2007 ICAS Book Prize: Best Study in Social Science from the International Convention of Asian Scholars.

ANNETTE LAREAU is the Stanley I. Sheerr Professor in the Social Sciences at the University of Pennsylvania. She teaches in the Department of Sociology. She is the author of *Unequal Childhoods: Class, Race, and Family Life*, which won the American Sociological Association (ASA) Culture Section's Best Book Award, the ASA Section on Childhood and Youth Distinguished Scholarship Award, and the ASA's William J. Goode Best Book in Sociology of the Family Award. She is also the author *Home Advantage: Social Class and Parental Involvement in Elementary Education*. With Dalton Conley she edited *Social Class: How Does It Work*.

MARGARET K. NELSON is the A. Barton Hepburn Professor of Sociology at Middlebury College. Her two most recent books are *Who's Watching: Daily Practices of Surveillance among Contemporary Families* (coedited with Anita Ilta Garey) and *Parenting Out of Control: Anxious Families in Uncertain Times*. She is currently working on a project she calls "making and unmaking kin," which explores how people determine who does—and who does not—have membership in their families.

STEVEN M. ORTIZ is associate professor of sociology at Oregon State University. His research on sport marriages explores the intersection of work, family, gender, and emotions. His articles have appeared in the *Journal of Contemporary Ethnography, Qualitative Inquiry, Sociological Perspectives, Symbolic Interaction*, and *The American Sociologist*, and he has authored chapters in *Research in Community Sociology—The Community of the Streets and Studies in Symbolic Interaction*. Arlie Hochschild was a guiding influence during his graduate studies at the University of California at Berkeley, including chairing his dissertation committee and inspiring him to combine family sociology with sport sociology from a symbolic interactionist perspective. She has continued to impact his teaching and research through her insightful scholarship.

JULIE E. PRESS was formerly assistant professor of sociology at Temple University. Her research interests include the sociology of gender, work and family, and race, urban poverty, and social inequality. Her Philadelphia Survey of Child Care and Work examined the relationship between child care problems and mothers' employment outcomes. Dr. Press's work is published in the *Journal of Marriage and Family, Gender and Society*, the *Journal of Family Issues*, the *Journal of Family and Economic Issues*, the *Journal of Women, Politics, and Policy*, and the Russell Sage Foundation volumes *Prismatic Metropolis* and *Urban Inequality*. She is currently managing her children's extracurricular activities full time.

ALLISON J. PUGH is assistant professor of sociology at the University of Virginia. As her advisor at Berkeley, Arlie Hochschild encouraged her to find the heart, the empathic center, of her research. This lesson had deep ramifications for more than just her research; it felt as profound as learning how to see all over again. Pugh's work focuses on how inequality shapes childrearing, intimacy, and care, with particularly close attention to the relationships between families and the market. She is the author of *Longing and Belonging: Parents, Children and Consumer Culture.* Current research includes an investigation of the social construction of postindustrial families, an exploration of the impact of childhood research on general social theory, and a look at the effects of care on caregivers (with Jennifer Silva). She is a recipient of a Sloan Foundation's Work-Family Career Development Grant.

Lynn May Rivas is the executive director of the Consumer Directed Services Network, a workforce development organization that encourages labor/management collaboration in the nonprofit caring services sector. She received her Ph.D. in 2007 from the Department of Sociology at the University of California, Berkeley, where she brought a Hochschild inspired "care" perspective to her studies of Union/Community Coalitions. A longtime labor activist, she has worked with various unions, accumulating experiences that have given her an enduring interest in the dynamics of caring labor.

Juliet B. Schor is professor of sociology at Boston College. She met Arlie Hochschild through common sociological and economic interests. Her work and friendship have been an inspiration for more than two decades. She is the author of *Plenitude: The New Economics of True Wealth, Born to Buy, The Overworked American, The Overspent American,* and *The Consumer Society Reader* (with Douglas Holt). Schor is a former Guggenheim Fellow and the recipient of the 2006 Leontief Award for Advancing the Frontiers of Economic Knowledge. She is a cofounder of the Center for a New American Dream (http://www.newdream.org), an organization devoted to ecological and social sustainability.

Jeremy Schulz has had the pleasure of working with Arlie Hochschild on his Ph.D. thesis, which examines the influence of national and societal environments on the ways in which French, Norwegian, and American business professionals organize their work lives and their private lives. The dissertation research has received support from the Labor and Employment Research Fund of the University of California, the American-Scandinavian Foundation, and the Foreign Language and Area Studies Program. Jeremy's previous research touches on diverse topics such as consumerism, elite distinction, and the sociology of ideology.

Vicki Smith is professor and chair of sociology at University of California, Davis. She studies work and employment and is the coauthor, with Esther B. Neuwirth, of *The Good Temp.* Vicki has never held a forty-hour, Monday–Friday, 8–5 job in her life, not even once, although she has had some temp jobs and some permanent jobs that turned out to be temporary or transitional. She has extensive experience with the micropolitics of second- and third-shift management. While a graduate student at the University of California at Berkeley in the early 1980s, she took Arlie Hochschild's graduate seminar on gender and recalls reading materials for that class (probably interview transcripts) from Arlie's yet-to-be published book *The Second Shift.* Arlie was a member of Vicki's dissertation committee as well.

Hung Cam Thai is associate professor of sociology and Asian American Studies at Pomona College and the Claremont University Consortium, where he is also vice president of the Pacific Basin Institute. He was deeply influenced by Arlie's graduate seminar on the sociology of the family and her mentorship in graduate school and beyond.

Barrie Thorne, Professor of Sociology and Gender and Women's Studies at UC Berkeley, is an ethnographer who teaches and writes about gender, childhoods, families, and schools. She is the author of *Gender Play: Girls and Boys in School,* and co-editor of *Feminist Sociology: Life Histories of a Movement* and *Rethinking the Family: Some Feminist Questions.* In the late 1990s she and Arlie Hochschild created and taught a graduate seminar, "Cultures of Care," and they co-directed the Berkeley Center for Working Families. Their essay, "Feeling at Home at Work: Life in Academic Departments" (*Qualitative Sociology*) grew out of many conversations about the odd emotional and relational cultures of academia.

Lightning Source UK Ltd.
Milton Keynes UK
UKOW02f2003010914

237904UK00001B/15/P